From Just War to Modern Peace Ethics

I0022395

Arbeiten zur Kirchengeschichte

Begründet von
Karl Holl† und Hans Lietzmann†

herausgegeben von
Christian Albrecht und Christoph Markschies

Band 120

De Gruyter

From Just War to Modern Peace Ethics

Edited by

Heinz-Gerhard Justenhoven and William A. Barbieri, Jr.

De Gruyter

FSC MIX Papier aus verantwor-tungsvollen Quellen FSC® C016439 www.fsc.org

ISBN 978-3-11-048848-7
e-ISBN 978-3-11-029192-6
ISSN 1861-5996

Library of Congress Cataloging-in-Publication Data

A CIP catalog record for this book has been applied for at the Library of Congress.

Bibliographic information published by the Deutsche Nationalbibliothek

The Deutsche Nationalbibliothek lists this publication in the Deutsche Nationalbibliografie; detailed bibliographic data are available in the Internet at http://dnb.dnb.de.

© 2012 Walter de Gruyter GmbH & Co. KG, Berlin/Boston

Printing: Hubert & Co. GmbH & Co. KG, Göttingen
∞ Printed on acid-free paper

Printed in Germany

www.degruyter.com

Contents

From Just War to Modern Peace Ethics:
An Introduction

For two millennia, Christian thought has grappled with the question of how to reconcile gospel teachings on love and justice, violence and peace with the realities of an obdurate and often violent world. At various points in that history, the sources of scripture and tradition have been invoked in support of suffering nonresistance and holy wars, of revolutionary insurgency and nonviolent direct action, of limitations on "just" wars and persecution of heretics. At the core of these various religious responses to conflict has been an ongoing effort to develop principled responses that somehow negotiate the tension between Jesus's demanding ethic of charity and the need to uphold order amidst the finitude and fallenness of human society. This effort has persisted through seismic historic shifts including the fall of the Roman Empire and the onset of the Dark Ages, the emergence of the medieval synthesis of classical and Christian culture, the early modern conquest of the New World, and the upwelling of secular political forms and scientific progress during the Enlightenment. In the last century, this undertaking has been shaped by two catastrophic world wars, the nuclear brinksmanship of the Cold War, the largely nonviolent collapse of autocratic and totalitarian regimes around the world in the late 1980s, and various recent genocides and "asymmetric wars." Because ethical teachings are necessarily shaped in part by the social and intellectual conditions within which they are articulated, this chiaroscuro history has unsurprisingly produced a diversity of interpretations of Christian norms regarding war and peace. At the same time, these accounts – having been enacted within a common horizon marking the Christian encounter with mundane existence – exhibit the unity of a recognizable tradition of thought.

Like any tradition, the ongoing Christian reflection on violence has encompassed different strands of thought. How to plot out the narrative of this reflection is a complex, and contested, theological, philosophical, and historiographical task, and it is this task that provides the context for this book. How the tradition is narrated is important because it helps define the terms of debate and application of Christian ideas, and can thus be used to establish, or at least privilege, some viewpoints at the expense of others. Roland Bainton's well-known 1960 study *Christian Attitudes Toward War and Peace*, which described successive historical phases of Christian pacifism, just war theory, and crusade, implicitly made a case for the authenticity of Christian rejections of violence.[1] Some years later, an ecumenical colloquy of ethicists developed an interpretation of the tradition emphasizing its time-honored, if implicit, presumption against harm (or principle of nonmaleficence);[2] this narrative carried with it the practical consequence of establishing a common ground of sorts between pacifism and just war theory. By contrast, a recent attempt has been made to delineate a "classic" just war theory that stands over against both pacifism and "contemporary" just war theory.[3] The distinctive features of the "classic" theory – its conception of justified violence as punitive or corrective in nature and its comparatively permissive stance regarding preventive war – lent themselves to arguments on behalf of a vigorous policy of humanitarian intervention, an aggressive response to the terrorism of 9/11, and decisive action in the U.S.-led attacks on Iraq of the last two decades. As these episodes evince, there is a politics of classification and periodization accompanying characterizations of the tradition.

More generally, it is not uncommon to speak of "just war" and "pacifism" as relatively fixed and cohesive stances on the proper Christian response to conflict and violence. It is frequently assumed, for example, that there is a coherent Christian "just war theory," made up of distinct criteria regarding when it is licit to go to war (*jus ad bellum*) and what it is licit to do in war (*jus in bello*); that this theory was first articulated by Augustine, and received successive expositions and revisions from Aquinas, Vitoria, Suarez, Grotius, and other jurists and theorists of natural law; and that it is currently endorsed in much the same form by the Catholic church, by most mainline Protestant denominations, and by various secular thinkers and legal institutions. It is sometimes assumed, as well, that "pacifism" is a monolithic category associated, alternatively, with a retiring nonresistance and withdrawal from social responsibilities, or an energetic commitment to nonviolent direct action. On occasion, too, "holy war" can be invoked in a manner that ignores subtle but im-

---

1   Roland H. Bainton, *Christian Attitudes toward War and Peace: A Historical Survey and Critical Re-Evaluation* (New York: Abingdon Press, 1960).

2   Notably James Gustafson, James Childress, Bryan Hehir, and Richard B. Miller.

3   Proponents include James Turner Johnson, George Weigel, Michael Novak, Jean Bethke Elshtain, and J. Daryl Charles.

portant distinctions between, for example, the genres of crusade and *jihad*. Rarely are some of the fundamental questions attending this discourse raised: Can holy wars really be distinguished from just wars, or must they by definition be considered just as well? Can one word – pacifism – usefully bundle together the diversity of Christian endorsements of peace and rejections of war and violence? And is there really a historically constant just war theory?

All too often, these terms are deployed without an adequate sense of the at times deep differences in context that have informed the respective positions of Christian thinkers – and their classical and secular counterparts – on war and peace. A central theme of this book is that narratives regarding the history of Christian arguments about war and peace are best served by paying close attention to the historical record. Doing justice to the specificity of the discussions of the ethics of war in different thinkers requires carefully considering the historical events to which they responded, the social and political structures they took for granted, the shape and technology of war in their day, the theological currents that shaped them, and the philosophical assumptions that informed their thought. Moreover, a fresh appreciation of the history of Christian reflection on this topic must hold open certain critical questions: Do different thinkers mean the same thing with "peace" and "war"? Is there a consistent presumption against war or harm in the Christian moral tradition? How is "violence" understood in scripture and tradition, and what is its moral weight? How have assumptions about the difference between the "divine" and the "human" or "secular" shaped views on the justice of war? What degree of continuity characterizes the thinking of Christian writers at different points in the tradition?

These are the methodological markers that guide the essays collected in this volume. From the studies presented here, a complex and variegated picture emerges, one that challenges some prevailing assumptions and popular narratives regarding just war theory, in at least three respects. First, as our authors show, apart from the broad parameters set by the practice of Christian meditation on the morality of social conflict, it is hard to support the notion that there has been a single fixed just-war framework illuminated throughout the centuries. Even where there has been a common invocation of just-war criteria by different thinkers, this has been done in the context of different theological and philosophical problematics. In addition and secondly, there are pertinent ways in which writers at different points in the tradition have presented theological vistas – on both peace and war – at odds with those produced by both their predecessors and their successors. Third, though, as recent treatments of the topic in particular show, the just-war idea need not be contrasted with nonviolent or pacifist ideals, but may be developed within a broader system defined in terms of peace. This book, in sum, undertakes to provide a basis for a reassessment of the character and legacy of Christian thinking on just war and the ethics of peace.

It does so through a tour of critical points in the tradition under the guidance of an assemblage of international scholars, each of whom brings to bear his or her expertise on a particular figure or question. The tour begins with Cicero, who was the first to use the expression "just war" and served as an important source for the Christian thought of Augustine. As Andrea Keller shows, Cicero's political philosophy shaped an ethic of war that limited its rationale to occasions of punishment or defense. War could be justified only in response to specific sorts of wrongs; however, the duty of justice extended to shielding not just one's own but also others from wrongs. Hence Rome acted licitly in waging war only in order to punish those who harmed Rome and to defend itself and its allies against aggression. If Augustine may rightly be seen as an important initiator of theological reflection on just and unjust wars in the Christian tradition, Keller concludes, he must also be seen as a Roman thinker in the tradition of Ciceronian philosophy.

Did Augustine at all intend to develop just war criteria? Johannes Brachtendorf credits him with having developed a theology of peace within which the state is accorded a relative, but not absolute, value in guaranteeing a worldly peace for the church to preach the gospel. While Brachtendorf acknowledges that Augustine can be thought to have developed some just war criteria *in nuce*, Roland Kany presents a strongly contrasting view. According to him, Augustine simply responded in an *ad hoc* manner to the various questions about war and peace which arose during his lifetime, but did not see himself as promulgating a distinctive Christian theory of war. Just war criteria were quoted by Augustine simply as the usual opinion of his time. Kany concludes that the beginnings of specifically Christian just war thinking are not yet to be found in Augustine's works, and goes on to note that Thomas Aquinas, in his later articulation of just war ideas, invoked teachings attributed to Augustine in the *Decretum Gratiani*, but was not himself able directly to consult Augustine's writings.

According to Gerhard Beestermöller, one of Thomas Aquinas's chief objectives was to provide an answer regarding the legitimacy of the Crusades. For Thomas, a war against a Muslim ruler could not be justified on the grounds that he was an unbeliever, but only if he did not fulfill his duty as a ruler in protecting his subjects, Christians as well as Muslims. Non-Christian rulers failed to fulfil their duty not because they did not believe in Christ themselves, but because Christians were tempted to turn away from their belief in Christ through their offices. In Thomas's understanding, this circumstance constituted a disturbance of the political peace, since for him, political and spiritual peace formed one unit. This point illustrates the centrality of the notion of *auctoritas legitima* in Thomas's just war thinking.

During the early modern period of exploration and discovery, Francisco de Vitoria's lecture "On the Indians" reflected the struggles within the church regarding the Spanish conquest of America. James Muldoon demonstrates how before he could discuss the legitimacy of conquest, Vitoria had to consider evidence of the rights of the American Indians and to address the foundations of international law as a common structure encompassing the Old and the New World. These foundations are traced by Heinz-Gerhard Justenhoven, who shows that for Vitoria, military force can be justified only as a response to the breaking of international law. Due to technical developments in warfare, such as the invention of firearms and cannons, Vitoria had to deal with new ethical issues in limiting the violence of warfare.

Martin Luther did not take up the scholastic debates on just war. The starting points of his reflections about war and peace, according to Volker Stümke, were rather his biographical background and the Bible. Within that context he endorsed a reduced doctrine of just war, permitting only defensive wars. For the legitimacy of the latter he formulated three conditions. Firstly, the causes and aims of the war must be secular. Secondly, negotiations must be conducted before any resort to force. Thirdly, the rule of law must be fulfilled and applied in a manner consonant with avoiding, where possible, any further escalation of war.

As Markus Kremer's discussion emphasizes, Francisco Suárez's reflections on just war are part of his conception of virtue and deal in particular with the virtues of justice and charity. Justice in war is related to the suitability of punishments meted out in war, moderations of the conduct of war and the proper treatment of prisoners-of-war; while the virtue of charity is demonstrated in the offer of reconciliation, in weighing up the possible consequences of the war and in prohibiting capital punishment. With his account of virtue, Kremer insists, Suárez did not want to replace natural right, but instead wanted to complement it. His central aim was to point out that the Christian nations were obliged to observe the laws of war particularly strictly because of their love of God.

Suarez followed in Aquinas's footsteps in wrestling with the question of whether the just war idea was articulated more compellingly through an analogy with the notion of capital punishment (public killing) or with lethal self-defense (private killing). James Bernard Murphy analyzes the use of these analogies in both thinkers, pointing out along the way problems they pose both for the Scholastics and for contemporary thinkers. He concludes by making a case for shifting our understanding of the grounds of *ad bellum* considerations from a conception of punishment to one emphasizing defense.

With Hugo Grotius, theological just war thinking is further integrated into the foundation of international law. Christoph Stumpf traces how, for Grotius, war could be legitimate with regard to both natural law and arbitrary divine law. In countering portrayals of Grotius as a secularizing thinker and proponent of individual rights, Stumpf carefully elucidates the theological grounding of Grotius's thought, the resultant doctrine of human obligations (as opposed to human rights), and his further account of distinctively Christian obligations in regard to war. Christians should relinquish their rights, if necessary to avoid harm for innocent people.

Under the conditions of modernity it becomes possible to discern the gradual emergence from traditional just war thinking of what could be called modern peace ethics. As Philip J. Rossi, S.J. spells out, Immanuel Kant contributed to the development of this trend by integrating the Enlightenment idea of political peace as an achievable goal with the traditional attempt to limit the use of military force. In describing peace as the highest political good, Kant defined the achievement of peace as the regulative principle for "the right of states," i.e. for international order. This political peace can be achieved in history. Kant's notion of perpetual peace was consonant, moreover, with just-war provisions regarding *ad bellum, in bello,* and what have come to be called *post bellum* requirements. Thomas Mertens completes this discussion by showing how in the Doctrine of Right in his "Metaphysics of Morals," Kant explained that certain rights existed with regard to war only until an international order enforcing peace was established. Counter to some interpretations of him as a just war thinker, it follows, Kant should be read as privileging a pacifist perspective.

The closing section of this book details the manner in which Catholic tradition has appropriated and developed a modern peace ethic. First,

Robert Araujo, S.J. traces the political activities of the Holy See up through the papacy of Benedict XVI, emphasizing the scope of Catholic support for an international order actively promoting peace. In this respect the Catholic Church has invested itself in the same sort of program for pursuing peace outlined by Kant. Gerard Powers adds to this perspective his account of how the emergence in recent Catholic thought of the paradigm of "peacebuilding" has expanded the focus of the ethics of peace beyond considerations of just war. Peacebuilding encompasses, in addition to *post bellum* concerns such as compensatory justice and reconciliation, measures aimed at conflict prevention, conflict mediation, and conflict transformation. In light of this shift, the articulation of a new theology of peace has become a pressing concern. Heinz-Gerhard Justenhoven concludes the volume by elucidating the rudiments for such a theology through a careful examination of the comprehensive peace agenda developed by John Paul II during his long pontificate. Human rights, especially to freedom of religion and conscience, constitute the linchpin of the modern Catholic peace ethic.

Do the studies brought together in this book add up to a new narrative regarding the development of Western Christian thought with respect to the ethics of war and peace? In the broadest sense, this volume helps trace the history of attempts to bring the theological and philosophical resources of the Christian tradition to bear on the problem of violence in a post-lapsarian world. That history, the authors show, has not unfolded smoothly or in a linear fashion. Rather, it has been deeply marked by the vicissitudes of social, cultural, and political affairs, and as a result has been characterized by occasional discontinuities, gaps, diversifications and fragmentations even as it has attempted to retain its overall identity as a tradition of thought. At the same time, the essays in this volume reflect an overarching directionality to the tradition, leading from an older, medieval focus on a just-war framework to the broader perspective of peace ethics opened up by the conditions of modernity. A more thoroughgoing elaboration of this complicated story, one that does justice to the complex history of Christian ethical reflection on conflict and reconciliation, will require more applications of the sort of hermeneutical care informing the approach of this book. In that regard, this collection is an invitation to further research.

William A. Barbieri   Heinz-Gerhard Justenhoven

Cicero: Just War in Classical Antiquity

Andrea Keller

The Roman philosopher Cicero (106–43 B.C.) was the first to use the expression "*bellum iustum*" (just war).[1] His thoughts on war and justice influenced the Christian theory of just war, from Augustine to Thomas Aquinas. Amongst others, these two theologians used Cicero's texts in order to answer their own questions concerning the justice of war.[2] Therefore, studying Cicero can also contribute to a better understanding of the theological doctrine of the Just War Theory.

As an advocate, politician and philosopher, Cicero was a member of the upper class and was educated in rhetoric and Greek philosophy. According to how Cicero viewed himself, he wanted to serve the Roman people both as a politician and as a philosopher who communicated the most important issues of Greek philosophy to his contemporaries in their own language of Latin (off.2,2–6).[3] That is why he is called a political Platonist[4], ethical politician and political ethician[5]. He left us

---

1 See Sigrid Albert, *Bellum iustum. Die Theorie des "gerechten Krieges" und ihre praktische Bedeutung für die auswärtigen Auseinandersetzungen Roms in republikanischer Zeit.* Frankfurter Althistorische Studien, vol. 10 (Kallmünz: 1980). 20; Silvia Clavadetscher-Thürlemann, *Polemos dikaios und bellum iustum. Versuch einer Ideengeschichte* (Zurich: 1985), 177; Jörg Rüpke, *Gerechte Kriege – gerächte Kriege. Die Funktion der Götter in Caesars Darstellung des Helvetierfeldzuges*, in: Der Altsprachliche Unterricht, vol. 33, Book 5, 5–13 (1990), 8; Klaus M. Girardet, "Gerechter Krieg". Von Ciceros Konzept des *bellum iustum* bis zur UNO-Charta, in: Gymnasium, Vol. 114, Book 1, 1–35 (2007), 191.

2 The passage in Cicero, rep.3,35 (see below) is quoted or paraphrased e.g. by Augustine (Aug.quaest.hept.6,10), Isidore of Seville (Isid.etym. 18, 1, 2–3) and Thomas Aquinas (S.th. II-II, q.40, a.1; S.th. II-II, q.188, a.3, arg. 4).

3 See Günter Gawlick and Woldemar Görler, "Cicero", in: *Grundriss der Geschichte der Philosophie. Begründet von Friedrich Ueberweg*, ed. Hellmut Flashar, vol. 4/2, *Die Hellenistische Philosophie* (Basle: 1994): 991–1168, 1018; Jonathan G. F. Powell, "Introduction: Cicero's Philosophical Works and their Background." In *Cicero the Philosopher. Twelve Papers,* ed. Jonathan G. F. Powell (Oxford: 1995), 1–35, 30 f.

4 "Vor allem sah er [Cicero] sich als ein politischer Platoniker" (Wilfried Stroh, *Cicero. Redner – Staatsmann – Philosoph,* Beck'sche Reihe, Wissen, vol. 2440 (Munich: 2008), 9).

a great opus of letters, political and forensic speeches as well as philosophical and oratorical works.

In various works, Cicero thought about war and justice, however he did not develop a theory of just war as Thomas Aquinas did later.[6] Instead, he contemplated different questions concerning war and justice in different works and contexts. Nevertheless it is possible to figure out some main thoughts. Cicero's initial point is that war is unjust, although there are a few conditions under which a war is not unjust which one can identify in various passages within his opus. This article will not analyze these passages in their entirety, however there will be comments on the three main texts.

The most elaborated passage about the justification of war is found in Cicero's last work "De officiis" (On Duties) from 44 B.C. In this work, his reflections on war were embedded in his theory of justice. Therefore, this passage will be examined first. In his earlier essay "De re publica" (The Republic) from 51 B.C., there is also fragment on unjust war, as well. This fragment is cited by the later Christian theologians as they ask the question, is it legitimate to wage war under certain circumstances.[7] Hence, the passage in "De re publica" will be compared to the passage in "De officiis". Finally, Cicero's remarks on just war in his essay "De legibus" (The Laws), which was presumably written in the fifties B.C,[8] will be analyzed.

---

5   Peetz describes Cicero from two different points of view: as ethical politician ("ethischen Politiker") and as political ethician ("politischen Ethiker") (Siegbert Peetz, "Philosophie als Alternative? Ciceros Politische Ethik." In *Christian Meier zur Diskussion. Autorenkolloquium am Zentrum für Interdisziplinäre Forschung der Universität Bielefeld (Alte Geschichte),* ed. Monika Bernett, Wilfried Nippel and Aloys Winterling (Stuttgart: 2008), 181–199, 199). He comes to the conclusion that Cicero as a political ethician is wiser than Cicero as an ethical politician (ibid.).

6   Thomas, S.th. II-II, q.40, a.

7   See above.

8   Gawlick/Görler (1994), 1035; Andrew R. Dyck, *A Commentary on Cicero.* In *De legibus* (Ann Arbor: 2004), 7; Klaus M. Girardet, *Die Ordnung der Welt. Ein Beitrag zur philosophischen und politischen Interpretation von Ciceros Schrift De legibus,* Historia Einzelschriften, vol. 42, (Wiesbaden: 1983), 1; Jonathan G. F. Powell, "Were Cicero's *Laws* the Laws of Cicero's *Republic?*" In *Cicero's Republic,* eds. Jonanthan G. F. Powell and John A. North, *Bulletin of the Institute of Classical Studies, Supplement 76* (London: 2001), 17–39, 18; Manfred Fuhrmann, *Cicero und die römische Republik. Eine Biographie* (Düsseldorf: 2006), 164.

Cicero also reflects upon just war in the oratorical work "De inventione" and several letters and speeches. As the theory behind Cicero's concept of just war can be best identified in the philosophical works "De officiis", "De re publica" and "De legibus", this article will focus on these three works.

1 War in "De officiis"

1.1 The Principles of Justice in "De officiis"

The title of Cicero's ethical essay "De officiis" is a translation of the Greek title "*Peri tou kathēkontos*", a book that was written by the Stoic philosopher Panaetius (c. 185–109 B.C.). The Greek term "*kathēkon*" is translated with "duty", however, "*kathēkon*" has a broader meaning than "duty". The term "duty" stands for an ethically required act. In contrast, the term didn't necessarily have an ethical meaning for the Stoics. They used the term "*kathēkon*" to describe an appropriate act of human beings, animals or plants.[9] This is an act that corresponds to reason, respectively to nature, therefore, it is rationally, however not necessarily ethically justifiable.[10] By the rendering of "*kathēkon*" as "*officium*" Cicero translated the Stoic meaning into the Latin expression.[11] For Cicero "*officium*" or "duty" is "that for which a persuasive reason can be given as to why it has been done"[12] (off.1,8; cf. fin.3,58). Unlike the early Stoics, who differentiated between two types of duties, the *officia perfecta*, which are morally good, and the *officia media*, which are morally indifferent, Cicero considers all types of duties as morally good (off.3,13–17).

For Cicero, reason correspondingly, nature, is a guide for moral honorableness (*honestum*) and the duties that can be derived from honorableness (off.1, 11–14; 3,21–28). Nonetheless, he did not commit a natu-

---

9 See Andrew R. Dyck, *A Commentary on Cicero. In De officiis* (Ann Arbor: 1998), 8.

10 See Wolfgang Kersting, "Pflicht." In *Historisches Wörterbuch der Philosophie,* ed. Joachim Ritter, Karlfried Gründer and Gottfried Gabriel, vol. 7 (Basle: 1989), 405–433, 406. For an elaborated explanation see Maximilian Forschner, *Die stoische Ethik. Über den Zusammenhang von Natur-, Sprach- und Moralphilosophie im altstoischen System* (Darmstadt: 1995).

11 Dyck (1998), 7.

12 For this and the following translations of "De officiis" see: Cicero, "On duties." ed. M. T. Griffin and E. M. Atkins, *Cambridge texts in the history of political thought* (Cambridge: 1991).

ralistic fallacy because reason is not only human reason, but reason which becomes manifested in nature.[13] Cicero did not deduce from nature what should be done. In Cicero's opinion, nature itself drives human beings as well as the other creatures to do what is right, even if they do not perceive it.

"De officiis" consists of three books, each dealing with a different question. In the first book, the question is answered of how to decide whether an action is honorable (*honestum*) or not, and if there are two honorable actions, which of is the two is more honorable. In this context, Cicero described the four cardinal virtues. The second book deals with the question of whether something is advantageous[14] (*utile*) or not, and again, if there are two advantageous actions, which of the two is more advantageous. The third book shows how to deliberate if "something apparently beneficial [utile] appears to conflict with what is honourable" (off.1,9). Based on these questions, Cicero rendered advice (*praecepta*) for all areas of life (off.1,7).

One of the four cardinal virtues described in the first book of "De officiis" is justice (off.1, 20–41). The aim of justice is to preserve the fellowship among men (off.1, 15). Hence, Cicero deduced two principles of justice:

> "Sed iustitiae primum munus[15] est, ut ne cui quis noceat, nisi lacessitus iniuria, deinde ut communibus pro communibus utatur, privatis ut suis" (off.1,20).

> "Of justice, the first office is that no man should harm another unless he has been provoked by injustice; the next that one should treat common goods as common and private ones as one's own" (off.1,20).

---

13 See Friedo Ricken, *Philosophie der Antike,* Urban-Taschenbücher, vol. 350, Grundkurs Philosophie, vol.6 (Stuttgart: 2007), 219; Troels Engberg-Pedersen, "Discovering the good: *oikeiōsis* and *kathēkonta* in Stoic ethics." In *The Norms of Nature. Studies in Hellenistic ethics,* eds. Malcolm Schofield and Gisela Striker (Cambridge, New York, New Rochelle: 1986), 145–183, 172; Malcolm Schofield, "Two Stoic approaches to justice." In *Justice and Generosity. Studies in Hellenistic Social and Political Philosophy. Proceedings of the Sixth Symposium Hellenisticum,* eds. André Laks and Malcolm Schofield (Cambridge: 1995), 191–212, 192.

14 According to the Oxford Latin Dictionary in Stoic philosophy the term "utile" as the opposite of "honestus" has the meaning of "advantageous" (*Oxford Latin Dictionary* 1968–82, vol. 2, 2117).

15 According to Dyck the expression "*munus*" is used here as a variation for "*officium*" (Dyck (1998), 109).

For our purpose, the first of these two duties is important. Later Cicero added, that it is also unjust not to defend someone or not to obstruct the injustice when one is able to (off.1,23). That means it is a duty of justice not to harm anyone and to deflect injury inflicted upon others. There is only one exception from this duty: when one has suffered injustice. Cicero returned to this exception in off.1, 34. He emphasized that even when we are wronged, we must fulfill certain duties:

> "Sunt autem quaedam officia etiam adversus eos servanda a quibus iniuriam acceperis. Est enim ulciscendi et puniendi modus [...]".

> "Moreover, certain duties must be observed even towards those at whose hands you may have received unjust treatment. There is a limit to revenge and to punishment."

Hence, the duties consist of restraining revenge and punishment[16], probably to the point where the man who did harm repents his injustice. The purpose of punishment should be that neither the transgressor nor others act unjustly in the future.

1.2 The Limitations of War

These duties to limit punishment must be observed in public affairs as well, namely in reference to the laws of war (*iura belli*) (off.1,34).[17] This means that Cicero considered war as punishment. In the following (off.1,34–40), he described the duties of which a politician must be aware of in regard to warfare. He developed ethical rules for correct behavior at the beginning, during and after wars. This paper focuses on the question, under which conditions is it justified to wage war.

If war is equated with punishment, it follows that a war can only be just if undertaken as a consequence of an unjust act. Thus, war of aggres-

---

16 Most likely "revenge and punishment" here is a hendiadys, because in the Roman Republic both expressions had the same meaning. "Revenge" as well as "punishment" signified a penalty imposed by court because of a violation of law (see Nikolaus Forgó, "Poena." In *Der neue Pauly*, eds. Hubert Cancik and Helmuth Schneider, vol. 9 (Stuttgart, Weimar: 2000), 1187 f; Hans-Joachim Gehrke, "Rache." In *Der neue Pauly*, eds. Hubert Cacik and Helmuth Schneider, vol. 10 (Stuttgart, Weimar: 2001), 745–747, 747; Detlef Liebs, *Römisches Recht. Ein Studienbuch*, UTB für Wissenschaft, Uni Taschenbücher, vol. 465 (Göttingen: 1993), 190.

17 "Atque in republica maxime conservanda sunt iura belli." – "Something else that must very much be preserved in public affairs is the justice of warfare" (off.1,34).

sion is always unjust. However, even in the case that one has suffered an injustice, war is not always legitimate. Cicero differentiated between two types of conflict: "the one proceeds by debate, the other by force" (off.1,34). One should only resort to the latter, if the former is not possible, as debate is the proper concern of men, and force only appropriate for animals. That means that one must intend to resolve the conflict by debate and only if that is impossible is one allowed to wage war.[18] The next condition follows immediately: "Wars, then, ought to be undertaken for this purpose that we may live in peace[19], without injustice [...]" (off.1,35). As it was for Plato and Aristotle, for Cicero war was thus, a means to an end, i.e. peace without injustice.[20] This means war is only permitted in order to restore a state of justice after an unjust act.

In limiting the occasions for war[21] Cicero did not agree with his contemporaries who regarded war as an opportunity of gaining honor, glory and power.[22] Cicero did not deny that it is possible to win honor and glory (off.2,45), however, this cannot be the purpose of a war. According to Cicero, one can only gain honor and glory through just acts (off.1,62; 2,43). That is why it is impossible to receive glory in an unjust war. In his opinion, you may only gain glory if the war was just and led to peace.

In his philosophical thoughts on war, Cicero pointed out stricter limitations than did his predecessors Plato and Aristotle. The two Greek philosophers only limited war between Grecian cities, however not the conflicts between the Greeks and the barbarians, as the latter were considered slaves by nature (Plat.Rep.470b-d; Arist.Pol. I 8, 1256b23–26). However, in Cicero's opinion, all human beings constitute a community as all

---

18 See Helga Botermann, *Ciceros Gedanken zum "gerechten Krieg".* In *De officiis* 1,34–40, Archiv für Kulturgeschichte, vol. 69 (1987), 1–29, 10.

19 The Latin expression *"pax"* (peace) originates from *"paciscor"* which means "to conclude a contract". *Pax* designates a state of non-violence after a war which is achieved by a conquest or a contract (see Johannes Scherf and Peter Kehne, "Pax." In *Der neue Pauly,* eds. Hubert Cancik and Helmuth Schneider, vol. 9 (Stuttgart, Weimar: 2000), 454–456, 454; Karl-Heinz Ziegler, *Friedensverträge im römischen Altertum.* In *Archiv des Völkerrechts,* vol. 27 (1989), 45–62, 46.

20 Cf. Plat.Leg.628c-e and Leg.803d-e; Arist. EN X 7, 1177b4–12 and Pol. VII 14, 1334a2–10.

21 See also Girardet (2007), 5.

22 Beard and Crawford ascertain that the consequential military expansion rooted in the system of Roman office-holding itself, "since Roman magistrates, in their role as generals, traditionally had only one year to win the glory of a successful military campaign" (Mary Beard and Michael Crawford, *Rome in the Late Republic. Problems and interpretations* (London: 1985) 74.

men possess reasoning and the ability to speak. This enables and drives them to congregate, unite and protect each other (off.1,11–12). If some-one violates the principles of justice, this person infringes upon the rules of nature because he abolishes the human community (off.3, 21). So no one should harm another, be he of the same family, the same nation or a foreigner (off.3,27–28). The principles of justice are valid for everyone. That is why one must observe the rules of justice and in turn, the rules of war against any enemy. Moreover, the possession of reason and language enables men to resolve their conflicts by debate, contrary to animals only capable of resolving them with physical force. This obliges men to use reason and language and only if that is not possible, are they allowed to fall back on force (off.1,34). According to Cicero, in this manner, one can recognize in nature and justify with persuasive reasoning, that one should not wage war against another unless one was harmed and is incapable of establishing peace without injustice by other means, except by war.

1.3 The Fetial Law

After explaining the ethical duties in reference to waging war, Cicero ar-gued that there also were Roman laws which were both ethically and re-ligiously justified. He referred to the fetial law (*ius fetiale*). In literature, a broad debate exists concerning the question of what the fetial law or fetial ritual was. The difficulty consists in the fact that the earliest testimonies of fetial law originated from Cicero and his contemporary Varro[23] (116–27 B.C.) both who were not familiar with the ritual as it was no longer performed.[24] They only could have referred to sources. Furthermore, they provided very sparse information. Livius (59 B.C.–17 AD) later described the fetial law in detail,[25] but it is presumed that he combined different sources that did not belong together.[26] Because it is difficult to figure

---

23 See Varro ling.5,86.
24 See Thomas Wiedemann, "The *Fetiales:* A Reconsideration." *The Classical Quar-terly, New series,* vol. 36, (1986), 478–490, 481; William V. Harris, *War and Im-perialism in Republican Rome 327–70 B.C.* (Oxford: 1979), 166 f.
25 Liv.1,32,5–14.
26 See Andreas Zack, *Studien zum "Römischen Völkerrecht". Kriegserklärung, Kriegsbeschluß, Beeidigung und Ratifikation zwischenstaatlicher Verträge, interna-tionale Freundschaft und Feindschaft während der römischen Republik bis zum Be-ginn des Prinzipats.* Göttinger Forum für Altertumswissenschaft, Beihefte, vol. 5 (Göttingen: 2001), 31; Christiane Saulnier, "Le rôle des prêtres fétiaux et l'appli-

out the character of the original ritual,[27] this text will only refer to Cicero. In "De officiis" Cicero stated the following about fetial law:

> "Ac belli quidem aequitas sanctissime fetiali populi Romani iure perscripta est, ex quo intellegi potest nullum bellum esse iustum nisi quod aut rebus repetitis geratur aut denuntiatum ante sit et indictum." (off.1,36)

> "Indeed, a fair code of warfare has been drawn up, in full accordance with religious scruple, in the fetial laws of the Roman people. From this we can grasp that no war is just unless it is waged after a formal demand for restoration, or unless it has been formally announced and declared before-hand" (off.1,36).

The question is whether Cicero is pointing out new duties or affirming the ethical duties he had already mentioned. It must also be examined which significance he ascribed to the fetial law in this context. The debate about these questions in literature is controversial. Some authors only focus on the fetial law, so that they reach the conclusion that Cicero's reflections about "*bellum iustum*" were only of legal nature.[28] The majority of the authors discover a connection between fetial law and ethical limitation that a war cannot be just unless it is punishment for an unjust action of the adversary.[29] Beyond that, Botermann discovers a parallel between the claim for debate (*disceptatio*) in off.1, 34 and the "demand for restoration" (*res repetere*) in off.1, 36.[30] In the following, reasons which are in favor of this opinion will be given.

---

cation du "ius fetiale" à Rome." *Revue historique de droit français et étranger*, vol. 58, No. 4 (1980): 171–199, 184–186.

27 Walter Moskalew, *Fetial Rituals and the Rhetoric of the Just War*, vol. 67, No. 4, *The Classical Outlook*, (1990), 105–110, 106; John Rich, *Declaring War in the Roman Republic in the Period of Transmarine Expansion*, Collection Latomus, vol. 149 (Brussels: 1976), 58.

28 See Luigi Loreto, *Il bellum iustum e i suoi equivoci. Cicerone ed una componente della rappresentazione romana del Völkerrecht antico*, Storia politica costituzionale e militare del mondo antico, vol. 1 (Naples: 2001), 15–18, 28; Antonello Calore, *Forme giuridiche del 'bellum iustum'*. Corso di Diritto romano (Brescia: 2003–2004, Milan: 2003), 170–191.

29 Botermann (1987), 16 f.; Albert (1980), 25; Maximilian Forschner, *Naturrechtliche und christliche Grundlegung der Theorie des gerechten Krieges in der Antike (bei Cicero und Augustinus)*, vol. 111, *Gymnasium*, Book 6 (2004), 557–572, 558 f.; Herbert Hausmaninger, "'Bellum iustu1961 m' und 'iusta causa belli' im älteren römischen Recht", *Österreichische Zeitschrift für öffentliches Recht*, vol. 11 (1961), 335–345, 340–345; Michaela Kostial, *Kriegerisches Rom? Zur Frage von Unvermeidbarkeit und Normalität militärischer Konflikte in der römischen Republik*, Palingenesia, vol. 55 (Stuttgart: 1995), 52–55.

30 Botermann (1987), 16 f.

According to the fetial law as described by Cicero, a war is unjust unless "it is waged after a formal demand for restoration, or[31] unless it has been formally announced and declared beforehand" (off.1,36). The focus of this analysis will be on the first condition, as the objective is to demonstrate the connection between demand for restoration and claim for debate. *Res repetere* ("demand for restoration") means that one reclaims something someone else has taken away, or something one has lent to someone (Cic.off.1,36; 3,95; see also rep.3,35). In civil law as well as in litigations between peoples, one party could stake a legal claim for a property which would then be examined by the court. An example of a demand for restoration by a foreign people was the case of the Sicilians who brought their former *praetor* Verres to trial for plundering the province. Cicero was the prosecutor on behalf of the Sicilians in this trial. Thus, in Ancient Rome there was the possibility of resolving legal rights problems by debate instead of war. Presumably, this is what Cicero had in mind when he demanded only to wage war, if debate is not possible (off.1,34). It is likely that in Cicero's opinion, the demand for restoration in the fetial law corresponded to his claim not to begin a war, if one could resolve a conflict by debate. It is possible that the fetial law had other functions in earlier times. Harris is probably correct, when he points out:

> "The *rerum repetitiones* were in a precise sense non-negotiable demands, and they were usually set at an unacceptable level. In fact it must normally have been expected that the demands would be refused."[32]

However, Cicero seemed to interpret the demand for restoration as an example of the tradition of the Romans, having suffered injustice, to de-

---

31 Dyck supposes that the construction "aut ...aut" in off.1,36 is negligence and refers to a similar passage in rep.3,35 (see below) (Dyck (1998), 142). This negligence is probably ascribable to the fact that "De officiis" was written in hurry and was not revised by Cicero (Dyck (1998), 8 f., 53; Gawlick/Görler (1994), 1047; Patrick G. Walsh, *Introduction.* In: Cicero: On obligations (*De officiis*), trans. with an Introduction and Explanatory Notes by P. G. Walsh (Oxford: 2000), ix-xlvii, ix). In the following I therefore assume that in off.1,36 it must rather mean that a war is unjust unless it is waged after a formal demand for restoration and unless it has been formally announced and declared beforehand (see Botermann (1987), 16; Jonathan Barnes, "Cicéron et la guerre juste." *Bulletin de la Société française de Philosophie* vol. 80, No. 2 (1986), 37–80, 48). Thus, there are two conditions that have at least to be fulfilled: first the formal demand for restoration and secondly the announcement, respectively declaration, of war (cf. rep.3,35).

32 Harris (1979), 167 f.

mand restoration and to attempt to resolve the conflict by debate. That fits to his ethical claim in off.1,34. Should this is correct, for Cicero, the adversary had the opportunity to avert war as the Romans stuck to the fetial law.[33]

Thus, it is presumed that Cicero referred to the fetial law in off.1,36 to give an example of the duty exposed in off.1,34. A war is unjust, if there was no demand for restoration, which means that after the injury, no effort was made to resolve the conflict by peaceful means.

Some authors argue that Cicero wanted to legitimate Roman wars of the past by affirming that the Romans have always followed his ethical demand, respectively the fetial law.[34] Others doubt that this was Cicero's intention.[35] As proven, Cicero argued that in the Roman tradition there was the fetial law, but it did not serve as legitimation for the past. His aim was rather to strengthen the ethical demand by demonstrating that it was also a Roman tradition to attempt to resolve conflicts by peaceful means first.[36] A common method used by Cicero and his contemporaries was to refer to examples (*exempla*). Those examples not only illustrated discourse, but also had a normative function. This normative power derived from the wisdom, the achievements and the reputation ascribed to the forefathers (*maiores*) and the continuity of the tradition.[37]

Against this background, it can be assumed that Cicero's keynote concerning the question, of when it is legitimate to wage war, can be found in off.1, 34–35 and that the fetial law mentioned in off.1,36 serves as an example of normative power for the ethical rule developed beforehand in off.1,34. That means that Cicero's thoughts concerning war are mainly ethical in this context. In summary, the party who has suffered an injury is obliged to attempt to resolve the conflict by debate, and only if this is not possible, is it permitted to wage war. This is a duty of nature as well as

---

33 Girardet, Kostial and Calore agree that this was the case (Girardet (2007), 8 f.; Kostial (1995), 48, 57–59; Calore (2003), 174).

34 See for example Forschner (2004), 558.

35 See Albert (1980), 24 and Botermann (1987), 25, 29.

36 Cf. Albert (1980), 24.

37 See Frank Bücher, *Verargumentierte Geschichte. Exempla Romana im politischen Diskurs der späten römischen Republik*, vol. 96, *Hermes, Einzelschriften* (Stuttgart: 2006), 163 f., 171; Michael Stemmler, "Auctoritas exempli. Zur Wechselwirkung von kanonisierten Vergangenheitsbildern und gesellschaftlicher Gegenwart in der spätrepublikanischen Rhetorik." In *Mos maiorum. Untersuchungen zu den Formen der Identitätsstiftung und Stabilisierung in der römischen Republik*, eds. Bernhard Linke and Michael Stemmler, Historia Einzelschriften, vol. 141 (Stuttgart: 2000), 141–205.

a Roman tradition. Furthermore, the purpose of the war must be the installation of peace without injustice. If these requirements are not fulfilled, a war is unjust.

1.4 Further Duties in War

In "De officiis" Cicero mentioned further duties concerning warfare and behavior after wars (off.1, 35–40). He demanded, e.g. after a victory, to spare those "who were not cruel or savage in warfare" (off.1, 35). It was also important to Cicero to be trustworthy towards the enemy (off.1, 39–40; off.3, 107–108). As mentioned above, for Cicero, even the enemy belongs to the human community, and must not be injured. There is only one exception: a pirate does not count as an enemy, but as a common foe of all. Therefore "there ought to be no faith with him" (off.3, 107).[38]

Furthermore, Cicero pointed out that in warfare, not all means are justified to win a war. The Romans for example, were not permitted, to collaborate with a deserter from King Pyrrhus who had promised to kill the king by giving him poison. According to Cicero, they returned him to the king as they did not want to win the war through a criminal act; not even a war against an enemy who had waged war without provocation (off.1,40). A further limitation of war is discussed in off.1, 38. Cicero differentiated between two goals of a war: existence on the one hand, and glory and rule on the other. In reference to the latter, he demanded that the war was waged less bitterly.[39] The individual examples reveal Cicero's aims. First of all, the duties of justice must be fulfilled, even if this involves disadvantages in war. Secondly, the enemy should be treated as mildly as possible (off.1,37).

---

38 According to the general Roman opinion there can be no valid contract with pirates, because they were not included in international law (see Karl-Heinz Ziegler, "Pirata communis hostis omnium." In *De iustitia et iure. Festgabe für Ulrich von Lübtow zum 80. Geburtstag,* eds. Manfred Harder and Georg Thielmann (Berlin: 1980), 93–103, 98).

39 In this article Botermann's view, that Cicero realized that the goals of the Roman wars of his time were rather glory and rule than existence, will be supported. Hence the same rules should be valid and furthermore the enemies should be treated with more mildness (Botermann (1987), 25; see also Girardet (2007), 5).

1.5 War as Defense of the Allies

According to Cicero there are two forms of injustice:

> "unum eorum, qui inferunt, alterum eorum, qui ab is, quibus infertur, si possunt, non propulsant iniuriam" (off.1,23).

> "Men may inflict injury; or else, when it is being inflicted upon others, they may fail to deflect it, even though they could" (off.1,23).

Correspondingly, there are two types of justice; not to inflict harm upon anyone and to deflect injury inflicted upon others. The first type has already been scrutinized and thus, the second type will be analyzed.

If it is a duty to deflect injury inflicted upon others, you also have to defend other countries when they are attacked and you are capable of helping them. Cicero did not mention that at this point, however, he did in off.2, 26–29. In that passage, he explained why fear is not an appropriate means to establish rule in the long run (off.2, 25). He referred to the Roman Empire as an example. Initially, he described how rule should be based on an idealistic picture of the past (off.2,26). He then added contrasts to this picture of the present situation, which he characterized as a disaster (off.2,27–29). He argued that the Roman Republic failed, because it preferred being feared of instead of being esteemed (off.2,29).

To being with, I will focus on rule, as it should be. Cicero described it as follows:

> "Verum tamen quam diu imperium populi Romani beneficiis tenebatur, non iniuriis, bella aut pro sociis aut de imperio gerebantur, exitus erant bellorum aut mites aut necessarii, regum, populorum, nationum portus erat et refugium senatus, nostri autem magistratus imperatoresque ex hac una re maximam laudem capere studebant, si provincias, si socios aequitate et fide defendissent." (off.2,26)

> "But as long as the empire of the Roman people was maintained through acts of kind service and not through injustice, wars were waged either on behalf of allies or about imperial rule; wars were ended with mercy or through necessity; the senate was a haven and refuge for kings, for peoples and for nations; moreover, our magistrates and generals yearned to acquire the greatest praise from one thing alone, the fair and faithful defence of our provinces and of our allies." (off.2,26)

According to Cicero, this type of rule was more a patronage (*patrocinium*) than a dominion[40] (*imperium*) (off.2,27). A patronage was characterized

---

40   See *Oxford Latin Dictionary* 1968–82, vol. 1, 843 f.

by the fact that the Roman magistrates and generals only waged wars to defend Rome's provinces and allies. Cicero was of the opinion, that in the past, the "magistrates and generals yearned to acquire the greatest praise from one thing alone, the fair and faithful defence of our [Rome's] provinces and of our allies" (off.2,26). This means that the Roman politicians treated the conquered peoples as clients.[41] On the one hand, the defeated peoples lost their right to fight on their own behalf, and had to supply the Romans with their troops. On the other hand, the Romans were obliged to defend them against foreign troops.[42] This obligation was not a legal institution,[43] which led Cicero to reminding his contemporaries of their duties towards the provinces[44]. That showed that from Cicero's point of view, Rome had a particular duty to defend its provinces and allies. According to off.1, 23 you must obstruct injustice inflicted upon anyone, if you are capable of doing so. Consequently, the Romans had to help anyone, but especially their provinces and allies.

Cicero deemed the victory of Sulla as the turning point from just patronage to an unjust dominion (off.2, 27).[45] After reporting on the cruelties of Sulla towards the Roman citizens, Cicero referred to Caesar without naming him. He accused him of having waged war against Massilia who was Rome's ally (off.2, 28).[46] Caesar had captured the city of Massilia in 49 B.C. in a civil war, because it had sided with Pompey, Caesar's

---

41 Clients are "the dependent states that, for reasons of historical development and the categories of Roman political thinking, stood to Rome in the relation of a client to his patron, owing the Roman People *officia* in return for *beneficia* received" (Ernst Badian, *Foreign Clientelae*, 264–70 B.C., (Oxford: 1958), 154). See also Dieter Nörr, *Aspekte des römischen Völkerrechts. Die Bronzetafel von Alcántara*, Bayerische Akademie der Wissenschaften, Philosophisch-Historische Klasse, Abhandlungen, Neue Folge, Book 101 (Munich: 1989); Dieter Nörr, *Die Fides im römischen Völkerrecht*, Juristische Studiengesellschaft Karlsruhe, Book 191 (Heidelberg: 1991), 13–22.

42 See Jochen Bleicken, *Lex publica. Gesetz und Recht in der römischen Republik* (Berlin, New York: 1975), 36 f.; Jochen Bleicken, *Die Verfassung der Römischen Republik. Grundlagen und Entwicklung*, UTB für Wissenschaft, Uni-Taschenbücher, vol. 460 (Paderborn, Munich, Vienna, Zurich: 1995), 264; Gabriele Thome, *Zentrale Wertvorstellungen der Römer II.* Texte – Bilder – Interpretationen (Bamberg: Auxilia, 2000), 68 f.

43 See Badian (1958), 159; Bleicken (1995), 264.

44 Cf. div. in Caec.11; ad Q.fr.1,1,27.

45 According to Dyck Cicero was not the only one who identified Sulla's victory and his despotically governance as a turning point in Roman history (Dyck (1998), 402 f.). See e.g. Sallust (Sall.Catil.11,4–8).

46 See Dyck (1998), 404 f. Cf. Phil.8,18 f.; 2,94.

enemy.[47] This is an example of an unjust war that was waged based on a
politician's individual interest. From Cicero's viewpoint, acts of this nature led to the disaster of the Roman Republic (off.2,29).

It follows that according to Cicero's principles of justice, there are two
exceptions as to when war is legitimate: firstly, when one has suffered injustice and cannot resolve the conflict by debate and secondly, when one
is capable of defending someone from injustice. These two exceptions
were already mentioned in the earlier work "De re publica", as it will
be proven now.

2 War in "De re publica"

The work "De re publica" deals with political philosophy. The main topic
is the question of how an ideal state should be structured. The line of
thought is developed based on a fictitious dialogue between several statesmen taking place in the past. The essay is subdivided into six books. The
first book is about different forms of government: monarchy, aristocracy
and democracy. It is stated that the best form is a combined constitution,
which is the constitution of the Roman state. The second book illustrates
the genesis of the Roman state, as an example of the development of the
best constitution. The relationship between rule and justice is discussed in
the third book. The fourth book includes thoughts about education. The
fifth book deals with the justice of the statesmen. The sixth book contains
a dream of the Roman statesman Scipio, in which he learns about his destiny that is fulfilled at the time of the composition of "De re publica".
The first two books are well-preserved, whereas the other books are rather
fragmentary.

Cicero referred to just war in the second and third book. In the second book, he described the enactment of the fetial law by King Tullus
Hostilius as an achievement of the Roman state (rep.2,31). Due to the
fact that the description of fetial law is very similar to the descriptions
found in off.1,36 and rep.3,35 respectively,[48] I will not go into further
detail.

The fragment about just war, which will now be analyzed, can be
found in the third book. In this book, Philus and Laelius, participate

---

47 Iris Samotta, *Das Vorbild der Vergangenheit. Geschichtsbild und Reformvorschläge
    bei Cicero und Sallust,* Historia Einzelschriften, vol. 204 (Stuttgart: 2009), 146.
48 See below.

in a dialogue, discussing whether the thesis is correct that a state can not be governed without injustice (rep.2,70; 3,0 (=Aug.civ.2,21)). Philus' opinion was that rule is unjust in itself. On the contrary, Laelius asserted that rule can be practiced in a just or unjust manner (rep.3, 36 f.). According to Laelius (and to Cicero, whose opinion was most likely found in the speech of Laelius,[49]) rule should be just. Laelius argued that a state that is not governed with justice will be extinguished, which should not happen (rep.3,34). This is the broader context of the following fragments:

> "Illa iniusta bella sunt quae sunt sine causa suscepta. Nam extra ulciscendi aut propulsandorum hostium causam bellum geri iustum nullum potest. [...] Nullum bellum iustum habetur nisi denuntiatum, nisi (in)dictum, nisi de repetitis rebus." (rep.3,35)

> "Those wars are unjust which are undertaken without provocation. For only a war waged for revenge or defence can actually be just. [...] No war is considered just unless it has been proclaimed and declared, or unless reparation has first been demanded." (rep.3,35)[50]

Unfortunately the exact context in "De re publica" cannot be reconstructed. The available fragments originate from the work "Etymologiarum sive originum" (Etymologies) of Isidore of Seville (560–636 AD).[51] Based on

---

49 In his dialogues Cicero often used the method of the so-called "disputatio in utramque partem" (the arguing of an issue from both sides) to deliberate the arguments in favor and against a thesis in order to approximate the truth (Gawlick/ Görler (1994), 1023–1025). He usually argued in favor of the weaker thesis first (Gawlick/Görler (1994), 1025). In this dialogue Philus speaks first and Laelius afterwards. This supports the assertion that Cicero's opinion is reflected in Laelius' speech (see Zetzel, James E. G., *Natural Law and poetic Justice. A Carneadean Debate in Cicero and Virgil.* vol. 91, *Classical Philology,* 297–319, 298, 301; Olof Gigon, "Studien zu Ciceros De republica." In *Die antike Philosophie als Maßstab und Realität* (Zum 65. Geburtstag von Olof Gigon (28. Januar 1977), ed. Olof Gigon. Pub. by Leila Straume-Zimmermann, *Die Bibliothek der alten Welt, Reihe Forschung und Deutung* (Zurich, Munich: 1977a), 208–355, 264). Another reason for that is the fact that Philus first resists speaking against justice and only does so after revealing that his speech does not correspond to his own opinion (rep.3,8) while after the speech of Laelius everybody agrees (rep.3,42). Finally Scipio, who speaks after Philus and Laelius and pursues the thought of the dialogue, also agrees with Laelius (rep.3,43; see Gigon (1977a), 267 f.).

50 For the translations of "De re publica" see: Cicero: *De re publica. De legibus.* With an English translation by Clinton Walker Keyes, *Loeb Classical Library* (Cambridge (MA), London: 2000).

51 Isid.etym. 18, 1, 2–3.

these quotations from Cicero, the theological author explained the difference between just and unjust wars.

When Cicero had Laelius speak about justice of wars, in a passage about just rule referring to the Roman Empire, it seemed likely that as in off.2,26–29, Cicero wanted to remind the Romans that they are patrons and therefore, not allowed to wage unjust wars. First, he asserted that wars without reason are unjust. As reasons he identified punishment (*ulcisci*) and defense (*propulsare hostes*).

At this point, Cicero did not explain why these reasons are just. Perhaps he did so in the lost text. We can only presume that he had the same principles of justice in mind as he did in "De officiis". There are several clues that Laelius held a Stoic view[52], which is an argument in favor of this opinion. Another argument is that in both texts, off.1, 34–36 and rep.3,35 respectively, Cicero made reference to the fetial law. If this Roman tradition was an example of the duty of justice in off.1,34–36; first to attempt to resolve a conflict by debate, then it probably had the same function in rep.3,35. Granted that the same is meant in "De re publica" as in "De officiis", Cicero explained that just rule implies not to wage war, unless it is waged for punishment or defense. This could be part of Laelius' reply of to the reproach of Philus, that it was unjust of the Romans to conquer the entire world (*orbis* <*terrarum*>) (rep.3,20). Laelius could have proven that a rule over a people conquered in a war of punishment or defense is just (cf. off.2,26). What is certain, is that Laelius in rep.3,35 established a duty for rulers as he did, for example in rep.3,41. In this passage he indirectly claimed to respect the rights of, and the treaties with, the allies by complaining about the fact that, if all Roman politicians violated those rights as Tiberius Gracchus did in Asia, the stability of the Roman state would be in danger. If a ruler or ruling state does not govern with justice, which means not to wage war unless it is waged for punishment or defense (rep.3,35), the state will be extinguished in the long run, which is comparable to the dissolution of the entire universe (rep.3,34). That means Cicero demanded from his contemporaries to maintain what their forefathers achieved through just rule.

---

52 First of all, the "real" Laelius was a Stoic (see Karl Büchner, *M. Tullius Cicero: De re publica*. Kommentar, Wissenschaftliche Kommentare zu griechischen und lateinischen Schriftstellern (Heidelberg: 1984), 35). Secondly, the passages rep.3,33 and rep.3,39 seem to be Stoic. According to Zetzel the speech of Laelius is "either (depending on your view of Hellenistic philosophy) strongly Platonic or heavily Stoic" (Zetzel (1996), 301).

3 War in "De legibus"

The essay "De legibus" dealing with the philosophy of law, was not completed by Cicero, however, it was published posthumously.[53] Today, only its first three books remain. The first book as well as the beginning of the second book (till leg.2, 17) contain general thoughts about the philosophy of law. The last half of the second book deals with Roman sacral law. The third book is about the Roman Constitution.

In the second book, Cicero mentions the fetial priests and assigns them the function of ensuring faith (*fides*) and law (*ius*) in reference to the undertaking, carrying on and ending of war are observed (leg.2,21; 2,34). Cicero lists the different administrative offices in the Roman Republic in the third book. Relating to the officials in the provinces he states:

> "Imperia potestates legationes, cum senatus creverit populusve iusserit, ex urbe exeunto, duella[54] iusta iuste gerunto, sociis parcunto,[55] se et suos continento, populi [sui] gloriam augento, domum cum laude redeunto." (leg.3,9)

> "Officials with and without imperium and ambassadors shall leave the city when the Senate shall so decree or the people so command; they shall wage just wars justly; they shall spare the allies; they shall hold themselves

---

53 Olof Gigon, "Literarische Form und philosophischer Gehalt von Ciceros De legibus." In *Die antike Philosophie als Maßstab und Realität* (Zum 65. Geburtstag von Olof Gigon (28. Januar 1977), ed. Olof Gigon. Pub. by Leila Straume-Zimmermann, *Die Bibliothek der alten Welt, Reihe Forschung und Deutung* (Zurich, Munich: 1977b), 356–377, 356; Girardet (1983), 2; Fuhrmann (2006), 164; Gawlick/Görler (1994), 1035; Peter L. Schmidt, *Die Abfassungszeit von Ciceros Schrift über die Gesetze,* Collana di studi Ciceroniani, vol. 4 (Rome: 1969), 292.

54 The term "*duellum*" is an archaic expression of "*bellum*" ("war") (cf. Cic.orat.153. See also Dyck (2004), 306; 310; Karl L. Noethlichs, "Krieg." In *Reallexikon für Antike und Christentum. Sachwörterbuch zur Auseinandersetzung des Christentums mit der antiken Welt,* eds. Georg Schöllgen, Heinzgerd Brakmann and Sible de Blaauw, e.a. , vol. 22 (Stuttgart: 2008), 1–75, 4; Jonathan G. F. Powell, "Cicero's Adaptation of Legal Latin in the *De legibus.*" In Aspects of the Language of Latin Prose, eds. Tobias Reinhardt, Michael Lapidge and James N. Adams, Proceedings of the British Academy, vol. 129 (Oxford: 2005), 117–150, 135 f.; *Oxford Latin Dictionary* 1968–82, vol. 1, 228).

55 Cf. Virgil (70–19 B.C.): "[…] tu regere imperio populos, Romanae, memento – haec tibi erunt artes – pacique imponere morem parcere subiectis et debellare superbos" (Verg.Aen.VI 851–853).

and their subordinates in check; they shall increase the national renown; they shall return home with honour."[56]

As in the second book, Cicero listed the offices in the third book first and then explained them in the same order. Unfortunately, the explanation of the office in leg.3,9 is lost;[57] left is only the explanation of what Cicero meant by "they shall return home with honour" (leg.3,18):

> "nihil enim praeter laudem bonis atque innocentibus neque ex hostibus neque a sociis reportandum".

> "For nothing but honour from enemy or ally should be brought home by good and upright officials."

This is at least a hint concerning the general intention of leg.3,9. Provided that honor can only be achieved by just actions, and taking into consideration that Cicero spoke of "good and upright officials", the demand in leg.3,9 is about the officials' correct behavior in the provinces. It seems that Cicero not only mentioned legal, but ethical aspects as well. This will be worked out in the following.

First of all, it must be explained whom Cicero meant with "*imperia potestates legationes*". According to Dyck, these abstract terms designate office-holding magistrates. "*Imperium*" in this context means the military power of higher magistrates,[58] "*potestas*" the subordinated magistrates[59] and "*legatio*" the ambassadors. These magistrates should "leave the city when the Senate shall so decree or the people so command" (leg.3,9). It was common practice In the Roman Republic that a provincial command followed an urban magistracy. Dyck points out that Cicero wanted to break this automatic sequence by "placing foreign missions firmly under the control of the sovereign bodies, the senate and the people".[60] With the help of this measure Cicero weakened the power of the magistrates in favor of the senate.

Waging wars was the task of the magistrates in the provinces, as they had to defend the provinces, i.e. the Roman Empire, against foreign attacks. As the explanation of leg.3,9 is lost, we can only assume that, as in "De officiis" or "De re publica", Cicero restricted the wars to wars of

---

56   For the translations of "De legibus" see: Cicero: *De re publica. De legibus.* With an English translation by Clinton Walker Keyes, Loeb Classical Library (Cambridge (MA), London: 2000).
57   See Girardet (2007), 18; Dyck (2004), 489.
58   Dyck (2004), 464.
59   Girardet (1983), 136.
60   Dyck (2004), 464.

punishment or defense, when he demanded that the magistrates should "wage just wars justly". An argument in favor of this assumption is that the entire fragment of leg.3,9 resulted in restricting the power of the magistrates.[61] This was already proven in the demand that the senate and the people should determine the provincial commands; however it also applied to the following demands. "The magistrates should spare the allies" probably meant that the allies should be defended against enemies (cf. off.2, 26–29) and that the magistrates should "hold themselves and their subordinates in check" meant that they should not exploit the provinces. Cicero worked out the details of these demands in his letters to his brother Quintus, who was the magistrate in the province of Asia at that time (ad Q.fr.1,1,7–34). The provincial command was an opportunity for the Roman magistrates to enrich themselves, as their power there was unlimited.[62] According to Dyck "the problem of the mistreatment of Rome's allies weighed upon Cicero".[63] Due to the fact that there no law existed, Cicero tried to solve this problem by demanding ethically correct behavior.[64] Bleicken observes that this procedure was a common reaction of the citizens in the late Roman Republic. In the moment of the crisis of the customs (*mores*), the customs were progressively confirmed and almost became laws.[65] It seems that this was also the case when Cicero mentioned, in his book of law "De legibus", the ethical duty of only waging just wars

Though it is not possible to derive the meaning of "just war" from the context of "De legibus" alone, there are no contradictions when one assumes that in leg.3,9 the same principles of justice, as found in "De officiis", are taken as a basis. Even if one leaves the exact meaning of "just war" in leg.3,9 open, the context itself suggests that Cicero wanted to limit wars.

---

61 See also Samotta (2009), 345 f. According to Girardet in this passage as well as in the whole text of "De legibus" a new sense of responsibility for the Roman provinces is expressed (Girardet (1983), 14, 16. See also Bleicken (1995), 263–265).

62 Bleicken (1995), 263.

63 Dyck (2004), 556.

64 See Catherine E. W. Steel, *Cicero, Rhetoric, and Empire,* (Oxford: Oxford Classical Monographs, 2001), 190–197.

65 Bleicken (1975), 373–377.

4 Conclusion

It was revealed that, at least in "De officiis" and "De legibus", Cicero's
objective was to limit wars, as inferred from the context of thoughts
on war and justice. He did that based on justice, which becomes obvious
in "De officiis". In this late ethical work, Cicero contemplates the ethical
duties derived from the four cardinal virtues. From the duty of justice,
amongst other things, he derived two principles; the duty of not harming
anyone unless provoked by injustice (off.1,20) as well as the duty to defend someone or to obstruct injustice when one is capable of doing so
(off.1,23). The first duty is complemented in off.1,34. Even in the
event that one has suffered injustice, war is not always legitimate. If
one has suffered injury, one is obliged to try to resolve the conflict by debate, and only if this is not possible, is one allowed to wage war. Furthermore, the purpose of war must be the installation of peace without injustice. In off.1, 36, Cicero referred to the Roman tradition, the fetial law, as
an example of this duty. The second duty of justice is not explicitly connected with war, however one can trace back Cicero's explanations to this
duty in off.2,26–29. Therefore, you must defend other people from injustice when you are capable of doing so.

Cicero's remarks on unjust war in "De re publica" (rep.3,35) can be
understood in the same sense. In this work, the focus is on the rulers' just
behavior. Due to the fact that the Roman politicians not only ruled over
the Roman people, but also over Rome's provinces and allies; Cicero had
to decide what to do when the latter were attacked.

In the third book of "De legibus", the focus lies on the magistrates'
just behavior within the provinces. The context suggests that Cicero
wanted to restrict the power of the magistrates in the provinces and to
remind them to do what is ethically correct, as there were few laws preventing the magistrates from using their power of office in order to enrich
themselves and gain personal power at the expense of the provinces and
allies.

Abbreviations

Cicero

(according to Thesaurus Linguae Latinae, Index, Leipzig [5]1990, 52–57)
div. in Caec = Divinatio in Q. Caecilium

fin.	= De finibus bonorum et malorum
leg.	= De legibus
off.	= De officiis
orat.	= Orator (ad M. Brutum)
Phil.	= In M. Antonium orationes Phillippicae
ad Q.fr.	= Epistulae ad Quintum fratrem
rep.	= De re publica

Other abbreviations

Arist. EN	= Aristotle: Nichomachean Ethics
Arist.Pol.	= Aristotle: Politics
Aug.civ.	= Augustine: De civitate Dei (The City of God)
Aug.quaest.hept.	= Augustine: Quaestionum in Heptateuchum
Isid.etym.	= Isidore of Seville: Etymologiarum sive originum (Etymologies)
Liv.	= Livy: Ab urbe condita
Plat.Leg.	= Plato: Nomoi (Laws)
Plat.Rep.	= Plato: Politeia (Republic)
Sall.Catil.	= Sallust: De coniuratione Catilinae
S.th.	= Thomas Aquinas: Summa Theologica
Varro ling.	= Varro: De lingua latina
Verg.Aen.	= Virgil: Aeneis (Aeneid)

Augustine's Theology of Peace and the Beginning of Christian Just War Theory

Roland Kany

1 The Art of Quotation

At the beginning of the First World War Michael von Faulhaber, at that time Bishop of Speyer, seized the opportunity to demonstrate to Germany in forceful language that even Catholics can be ardent patriots. This was by no means to be assumed; in the preceding decades there had been serious Protestant and Prussian doubts as to whether Catholics in Germany were really oriented toward Berlin and Potsdam and not only toward Rome. Now Bishop von Faulhaber proclaimed: "The German army has moved out with flashing shields of steel. I am utterly convinced that in terms of the ethics of war this military campaign will constitute a classic example of a just war for us."[1] On August 9, 1914, when conferring blessing on the young men being sent off to war during a church service at the cathedral in Speyer, von Faulhaber conjured Biblical and post-Biblical paradigms: Samuel's battle against the Philistines; the heroic death of Christ, which is renewed in every holy sacrifice of the Mass; and the holy war, more specifically, the Second Crusade, which Bernard of Clairvaux, too, had once advocated from the chancel in Speyer.[2] Now, for Bishop von Faulhaber, it is a matter of "going through Hell and high water for the illustrious Crown", a matter of "singing Hallelujahs of praise for this war."[3] Today we know how this ended. Von Faulhaber

---

1   Michael von Faulhaber, *Waffen des Lichtes. Gesammelte Kriegsreden,* Freiburg 1915, 132: "Das deutsche Heer ist mit stahlblanken Schilden ausgezogen. Nach meiner Überzeugung wird dieser Feldzug in der Kriegsethik für uns das Schulbeispiel eines gerechten Krieges werden."
2   Ibid, 2–4.
3   Ibid, 178: "Eine Edelfrucht auf dem Blutacker ist auch jene nationale Begeisterung, die für den erlauchten Träger der Krone durchs Feuer geht und in diesem Krieg ein Alleluja singt."

also reconsidered and tempered his enthusiasm before the end of the war, experiencing a personal crisis.[4]

It would be bitterly unfair for a historian, given his or her knowledge of the course of history, to superciliously pass judgment on the dead. Few human beings actually exist without biases and blind spots typical of their times. Historiography is generally more concerned with understanding the factors that have promoted or allowed such biases and blind spots. In the case of Bishop von Faulhaber, a biographically rooted preference for the military and the wish for a widespread acceptance of Catholics in the German Empire (the Second Reich) were conceivably among the determinants of his religiously charged militarism in 1914. He apparently found the justification for his position in the theological-political theory of the just war. Augustine is generally considered the father and the leading proponent of this theory.[5] In my lecture I will explore whether this assumption is correct as well as how Augustine's theology of peace is related to the development of a Christian theory of just war. I will limit my reflections to the discussion of several quotations, which have had decisive historical consequences.

Doubtlessly, Bishop von Faulhaber did not have direct recourse to Augustine's works for the theory of the just war. For insight into the theory and theology of the just war familiar to the Catholic theologians of his generation, it seems expedient to consult one of the essentially interchangeable Neo-Scholastic textbooks of moral theology around 1900. I have selected a classic of casuistry, the *Compendium theologiae moralis* by Jean-Pierre Gury (1801–1866). Initially published in 1850, Gury's

---

4   Johann Klier, *Von der Kriegspredigt zum Friedensappell. Erzbischof Michael von Faulhaber und der Erste Weltkrieg* (Munich 1991), 237.

5   Robert Hubert Willem Regout, *La doctrine de la guerre juste de Saint Augustin à nos jours, d'après les théologiens et les canonistes atholiques* (Paris 1935); Frederick H. Russell, *The Just War in the Middle Ages* (Cambridge 1975); Jonathan Barnes, "The Just War". In *The Cambridge History of Later Medieval Philosophy. From the Rediscovery of Aristotle to the Disintegration of Scholasticism 1100–1600*, ed. Norman Kretzmann and Anthony Kenny and Jan Pinborg (Cambridge 1982), 771–784; Lisa Sowle Cahill, *Love Your Enemies: Discipleship, Pacifism, and Just War Theory* (Minneapolis 1994), 55–80; Richard Sorabji, "Just War from Ancient Origins to the Conquistadors Debate and its Modern Relevance." In *The Ethics of War: Shared Problems in Different Traditions*, ed. Id./David Rodin (Aldershot 2006), 13–29, 15–17; more subtly differentiated are: Timo J. Weissenberg, *Die Friedenslehre des Augustinus. Theologische Grundlegung und ethische Entfaltung* (Stuttgart 2005) 122–171; John Mark Mattox, *Saint Augustine and the Theory of Just War* (London/New York, 2006), 44–82.

work became a standard textbook in moral theology during the second half of the nineteenth century.[6] Following a brief definition of war and the differentiation between a war of aggression and a war of self-defense, Gury states that war is allowed *per se*, either to avert an injustice or to secure the rights of the state. Then Gury names three classic conditions or criteria, which must be fulfilled for a war to be considered just and permissible. The first of these three criteria is *Auctoritas legitima*, the lawfully legitimated authority, that is, no higher authority exists which or who could decide and settle the dispute: what this signifies is that only the sovereign (of the state) can declare a just war; "private" wars, that is, wars declared by private persons, are not permissible. The second criterion for a just war is the *causa iusta et gravis*, a just and serious cause, which must be far more important than the damages which would arise from the war. Among the examples which Gury gives are the reconquering of a realm or province as well as the averting of a serious injustice being perpetrated against the state. The third criterion for a just war is the *debitus bellandi modus*, the proportionality of means, that is, the fitting means of conducting war, which Gury understands simply as the demand for reparation to be directed to the opposing state before beginning a war; if this demand is met, then the plans for war must be abandoned.

Behind this Neo-Scholastic casuistry is, immediately recognizable and additionally emphasized through an express reference, the *Quaestio de bello* of the *Summa theologiae* of Thomas Aquinas. There the crucial first article addresses the question whether any war is permissible.[7] Thomas Aquinas initially introduces four arguments against the permissibility of war, for example, from Jesus' Sermon on the Mount: "offer the wicked man no resistance."[8] The counterargument (*sed contra*) then follows, which Thomas Aquinas quotes from a text by Augustine. In the body of the article Thomas Aquinas subsequently develops his own doctrine of the just war, presenting the three requirements for a just war within the context of his answer to the opening question. These are the same three criteria for a just war still found, in a revised form, in works by Gury and the other moral theologians of modernity. Thomas Aquinas defends each of these three criteria with a quotation from Augustine, and

---

6   Johannes Petrus Gury, *Compendium theologiae moralis. Editio in Germania prima,* (Regensburg, 1853), 115 f.
7   Thomas Aquinas, *Summa Theologiae II-II,* 40, 1.
8   Matthew 5:39. *S. th.* II-II, 40, 1, trans. T. Heath (*Summa Theologiae,* vol. 35: Consequences of Charity, New York 1972), 81.

generally uses quotations from Augustine to justify his refutations of the
four arguments originally invoked in support of pacifism. It can thus be
argued that Thomas Aquinas' doctrine of the just war appears to be completely based on Augustine.

Corresponding to the accepted method of his time,[9] Thomas Aquinas
did not actually compile the quotations from Augustine directly from the
works of the Church Father. The same quotations, with a more extensively quoted context, are also found in *Causa* XXIII of the *Decretum Gratiani*, which was compiled around 1140 and is usually regarded as the work
signalizing the advent of classic canon law.[10] The *Decretum Gratiani* already utilizes the scholastic method and, for example, in *Causa* XXIII,
takes up the issue of the just war, presenting a fictional case and following
authoritative sources to reach a solution. On the question of the just war,
the *Decretum Gratiani* primarily cites texts attributed to Augustine; some
of these texts, however, are no longer considered authentic today. Like
Thomas Aquinas, the compiler or compilers of the *Decretum Gratiani*
did not primarily excerpt the original sources themselves, but took
most of the quotations from older collections.[11] These, in turn, are to
a great degree based on collections of quotations from predecessors.
The *Collectio Tripartita B*, for example, is excerpted from the *Decretum*
of Ivo of Chartres, dated at the end of the eleventh century.[12] The *Decretum Gratiani* assembles the tradition known up to that point and serves as
the foundation for diverse theories of the just war; these extend from the
first commentary on the *Decretum*, the *Summa* of Rufinus (written
around 1164), to the authoritative work on European international
law, *De iure belli ac pacis* (1625) of Hugo Grotius, and even to the current

---

9 For the background of the following cf. Roland Kany, "Zitat." In *Historisches
   Wörterbuch der Philosophie*, vol. 12 (2004), 1344–55, 1346 f.
10 *Decretum Gratiani* C. 23, particularly q. 1 (*an militare peccatum sit?*) and q. 2
   (*quod bellum sit iustum, et quomodo a filiis Israel iusta bella gerebantur?*) (Friedberg I, 889–895). Cf. Stephan Kuttner, Gratien. Canoniste du XIIe siècle. In
   Dictionnaire d'Histoire et de Géographie Ecclésiastique, vol. 21 (1986), 1235–39.
11 Recent scholarship questions the plausibility of many of the traditional assumptions about the historical Gratian, the purported compiler, commentator, rubri-
   cator, and reviser of the *Decretum Gratiani*. Cf. John T. Noonan, Jr., "Gratian
   Slept Here: The Changing Identity of the Father of the Systematic Study of
   Canon Law" *Traditio. Studies in Ancient and Medieval History, Thought, and Religion* 35 (1979): 145–172.
12 Cf. Peter Landau, "Das Dekret des Ivo von Chartres." *Zeitschrift der Savigny-Stiftung für Rechtsgeschichte. Kanonistische Abteilung* 70 (1984): 1–44; Ch. Rolker,
   Canon Law and the letters of Ivo of Chartres (Cambridge 2009).

secondary literature in theology and political science.[13] The doctrine of Thomas Aquinas on the just war is only one of these theories, but presumably the most influential.

The provenance of the quotations alone clearly indicates that, in his tractate on the just war, Thomas Aquinas does not approach Augustine's works as an exegete, but simply presents the final, canonized version of a long series of florilegia on this topic. The underlying technique of discriminate selection from Augustine's vast oeuvre was, of course, not only utilized for the doctrine of the just war but for dogmatic, spiritual, and philosophical purposes as well. This technique had already been initiated during Augustine's lifetime: Prosper of Aquitaine had collected excerpts from various Augustinian texts, and around 500 Eugippius compiled an even more comprehensive collection. In this manner the gradual reception of Augustine in the form of excerpts developed, divorced from Augustine's original arguments and from the original context of his writings.[14] This particular form of the reception of Augustine became dominant in the Middle Ages.

For reasons of brevity I will not examine all the quotations from Augustine found in the *Quaestio de bello* of Thomas Aquinas; I have limited my discussion to those quotations related to the *sed contra* and the *corpus articuli*.

2 Augustine and Pacifism

Thomas Aquinas outlines the counterposition to the four pacifistic arguments solely with the following statement: "On the other hand Augustine says, in a sermon on the centurion's son, *If Christian teaching forbade war altogether, those looking for the salutary advice of the Gospel would have been told to get rid of their arms and give up soldiering. But instead they were told, Do violence to no man, be content with your pay. If it ordered them to be satisfied with their pay, then it did not forbid a military career.*"[15] These sentences are quoted from a letter written by Augustine at the end of 411 or 412 and are also included in the *Decretum Gratiani* under the same (in-

---

13 Cf. fn. 5.
14 Cf. Vittorino Grossi, "La recezione 'sentenziale' di Agostino in Prospero di Aquitania. Alle origine delle 'frasi' sentenziali attribuite ad Agostino." In *Traditio Augustiniana. Studien über Augustinus und seine Rezeption,* Festschrift Willigis Eckermann (Würzburg: 1994), 123–140.
15 Luke 3:14. *S. th.* II-II, 40, 1, trans. T. Heath, 81.

appropriate) title, *Sermo de puero centurionis*; The *Decretum Gratiani*, however, cites a much longer passage from Augustine's letter, apparently taken from the *Collectio* of Anselm of Lucca (1083) or the *Polycarpus* of Gregory of San Crisogno compiled approximately twenty years later.[16]

What was the topic of Augustine's long letter, in which this brief quotation initially appeared? The addressee was the *tribunus et notarius* Flavius Marcellinus, a high-ranking Roman official.[17] In 410 Marcellinus had been invested with extensive authority and dispatched to Africa as imperial commissioner by Emperor Honorius to stabilize the country by resolving the conflict between Catholics and Donatists once and for all. Marcellinus presided at the momentous Conference of Carthage in 411 and remained in the city until his death there in 413, the victim of a fatal intrigue. After Alaric's troops had plundered Rome in August 410 and withdrawn to the north, northern Africa had become a refuge for many Roman citizens, particularly for aristocratic families with African landholdings. These notabilities imported certain aspects of the religious diversity and intellectual ambience of Rome to Africa. Carthage, with the seat of the *proconsul Africae*, numerous government agencies, military bases, and schools and institutions of higher learning dedicated to the study of philosophy, languages, and comportment, was considered the African Rome[18]; it became the center of an equally elegant and reactionary paganism[19] as well as the center of a deeper, ascetic Christianity embraced above all by the female members of the nobility. Spiritual advisors such as Pelagius were among the exiles. Marcellinus and his wife considered themselves Catholics, and approached the two most important living theologians of the Latin West, Jerome and Augustine, with questions under discussion in these circles at the time, questions which they posed in spoken or written form. Marcellinus frequented the salon organized by Volusian daily, where pagan, Catholic, and incipient Pelagian arguments were openly debated. Volusian was the member of

---

16 *Decretum Gratiani* C. 23 q. 1 c. 2 (Friedberg I, 890–892 with sources) = Augustine, *Epistula* 138, ii, 12–15 (CSEL 44, 138, 5–141, 16). Thomas Aquinas quotes only the ending in *S. th.* II-II, 40, 1 s.c. (CSEL 44, 141, 10–16).

17 For a summary of the information about him: André Mandouze, *Prosopographie de l'Afrique chrétienne* (303–533), Paris 1982, 671–688.

18 Salvianus of Marseille, *De gubernatione Dei VII*, xvi, 67 f. (CSEL 8, 177, 11–25).

19 Claude Lepelley, *Les cités de l'Afrique romaine au Bas-Empire*, vol. 1 (Paris 1979), 359.

an aristocratic Roman family.[20] His mother and sister were pious Christians, while he himself maintained the slightly arrogant scepticism of the intellectual toward Christianity. In his circle theological issues were examined in detail, occasionally with an ironic undertone, for example, the question whether it is truly plausible to assume, as Christians do, that the Pantokrator, the ruler of the world, persevered for many months in the womb of a pregnant virgin.[21] Political issues were also discussed there.

Serious reservations about the plausibility of Christianity were essentially due to the shock effected by the fall of the city of Rome. Was this disaster not the equally sad and logical consequence of almost a century of Christian imperial rule? In one of his own letters to Augustine, Volusian avoided mentioning these political implications and raised only the more theological questions, which Augustine replied to in a detailed letter.[22] However, Marcellinus informed Augustine of Volusian's political reservations about Christianity. The teachings of Christ, in Volusian's opinion, directly contradict the exigencies of the state. If one is no longer allowed to counter evil with evil, if one offers the other cheek and allows the person, who wants to take the shirt off one's back, to take one's coat, too, this conflicts strongly with the interests of the state. Who could allow the enemy to take something belonging to him, or who would not avenge the plundering of a Roman province with war?[23] Augustine was confronted with reproaches questioning Christianity in general, which was being held responsible for the decline of the Roman Empire. His letter to Marcellinus is intended to provide the Christian politician with arguments for the debates with the governing elite.[24] This was initial preparation for his later work, *De civitate dei*, which Augustine dedicated to Marcellinus.

Augustine's remarks on military service, which Thomas Aquinas quotes, are situated in this apologetic context. In the relevant section of his letter to Marcellinus, Augustine first refutes the pagan criticism of Christianity by arguing that the leniency or mercy which Christians show toward their enemies actually corresponds to an ancient Roman

---

20 André Chastagnol, "Le sénateur Volusien et la conversion d'une famille de l'aristocratie romaine au Bas-Empire." *Revue des Études Anciennes* 58 (1956): 241 – 253.

21 Volusianus, within the corpus of Augustine's *Epistulae*, 135, 2 (CSEL 44, 91, 11 – 13).

22 Volusianus, ibid. (CSEL 44, 89 – 92); Augustine, *Epistula* 137 (CSEL 44, 96 – 125).

23 Marcellinus, within the corpus of Augustine's *Epistulae* 136 (CSEL 44, 93 – 96).

24 Augustine, *Epistula* 138 (CSEL 44, 128 – 148).

principle. This principle is the explanation for Rome's greatness, namely, that principle recounted by Sallust: "they 'preferred to pardon an injury received rather than to avenge it'"[25]; even Caesar, according to Cicero, tended "to forget nothing but injuries".[26] Augustine quotes both these passages.

Subsequently, in his letter to Marcellinus Augustine attempts to comprehend the Christian conception of love for one's enemies not simply as a commandment prescribing outward conduct: in actuality, it is a question of inner liberation from vindictiveness and vengeance, which are much viler than the external, political enemies. Jesus does not turn the other cheek, when the servant of the High Priest strikes him in the face, but answers: "*If I have spoken evil, rebuke me for the evil, but if I have spoken well, why do you hit me?*"[27] For Augustine it is thus a matter of reducing the evil in the world and not of defenselessly allowing evil to spread. Analogously, a just father does not punish his son out of a lack of love, but, on the contrary, in order to exercise influence on his son's values. A peace-loving state, established on Christian principles, will similarly demonstrate benevolence toward the enemy even in war and generally ensure that evil is contained. For precisely this reason, Augustine argues, John the Baptist advised the soldiers, who asked him what they should do, to conduct their work with propriety, and did not advise them to change professions.[28]

Significantly, Augustine implies that something similar holds for all other members of human society: a state would derive considerable ethical benefits from having Christians at all levels of society, from the government to the individual families. What Augustine teaches in this letter to Marcellinus is neither a position against pacifism nor a legitimation of war, but an apologetically motivated rejection of the conception that Christians are doomed to idly stand by and allow injustice and barbarity to spread, imperiling the state. Augustine's refutation is undoubtedly informed by the political and military catastrophe of the Christianized

---

25 C. Sallustius Crispus, *De Coniuratione Catilinae* ix, 5; Augustine, *Epist.* 138, ii, 9 (CSEL 44, 134, 7 f.) (English translation: Saint Augustine, *Letters* 100–155, ed. B. Ramsey/trans. R. Teske, II/ 2, A translation for the 21st Century (Hyde Park 2003) 230).

26 Cicero, *Pro Q. Ligario Oratio xii*, 35; Augustine, *Epistula* 138, ii, 9 (CSEL 44, 134, 9 f.), 230.

27 John 18:23; Augustine, *Epistula* 138, ii, 13 (CSEL 44, 138, 16 f.), 232.

28 Luke 3:14.

Roman Empire. Augustine does not advocate pacifism but a pacification of the means of averting evils.

3 Augustine and the Three Criteria for the Just War

In the *corpus articuli* Thomas Aquinas formulates the three conditions for a just war. The first requirement is the *auctoritas principis*, the authority of the sovereign, who commands that war be waged. Private persons are not allowed to wage war, because the judgment of a higher instance, a superior court of justice, is responsible for the enforcement of the rights of individuals. Responsibility for the entire state, however, is entrusted to the ruler, and just as he (or she) is to punish the disruption of internal order with force, with "the sword", according to Romans 3:14, he (or she) must also protect the state from disruption by external parties with the "sword of war". "Hence Augustine writes, *The natural order conducive to human peace demands that the power to counsel and declare war belongs to those who hold the supreme authority.*"[29]

This quotation is excerpted from Augustine's text attacking the Latin Manichean Bishop Faustus of Milevis, which was probably written between 397 and 399. The same quotation is already found in the *Decretum Gratiani*,[30] which quotes the original context more extensively than Thomas Aquinas does in the *Quaestio de bello*. Faustus had written a work in which he aspired to prove that Manicheanism was the true Christian religion in its pure and unadulterated form. He rarely based his argumentation on Manichean texts but primarily on the Bible. In the course of his argument, Faustus primarily polemicized against the Old Testament, which he did not hold to be a work of divine inspiration, but, on the contrary, a work manifesting evidence of immorality and absurd belief in rites. In his refutation, the lengthiest of all his anti-Manichean writings, Augustine above all attempts to establish the complementarity and unity of the Old and New Testaments. Book XXII of Augustine's work is directed against Faustus' attacks on the purported amorality of the Old Testament patriarchs. One example is the series of plunderings of the Egyp-

---

29 *S. th.* II-II, 40, 1c; trans. Heath, 83.
30 *Decretum Gratiani* C. 23 q. 1 c. 4 (Friedberg I, 892 f.) = Augustine, *Contra Faustum* XXII, 74 f. (CSEL 25/1, 672, 5–674, 6). Gratian does not quote Augustine's text verbatim but summarizes it directly after the sentence quoted by Thomas Aquinas (CSEL 25/1, 673, 11–13).

tians, which the Israelites carried out under Moses' leadership.[31] To Faustus these are obviously injust acts. Augustine, however, emphasizes that they ensue on God's command and, consequently, are inevitably just acts. Moreover, he shows that this is not essentially different from the New Testament, since Jesus, too, for example, orders the demons to possess the swine, which then plunge into the sea; there the damage is also extensive, yet appropriate, since it allows the healing of the possessed persons.[32] In this context the problem of the wars in the Old Testament becomes the focus of attention. Augustine argues that Moses is by no means cruel in his warring behavior but obedient to God, who had commanded this action, just as Abraham was obedient to God in his willingness to kill his son Isaac as God had commanded. Augustine then reformulates this thought as a generalization to demonstrate that Moses' obedience is not unique to either the Old Testament or even to the Bible: wars are always declared by an authority. What makes a difference is why and on the basis of whose authority people wage war. While Augustine had previously mentioned the wars in the Old Testament, which, according to the Bible, had been commanded by God, he now explains – using the formulation cited by Thomas Aquinas – that the social and political order requisite for the peace of mortal human beings demands, as is generally known, that authority (*auctoritas*) and the decision to declare war are matters within the jurisdiction of the ruler. Since, as Augustine infers from Romans 13, there is no authority other than that of God, no one, who carries out a military command, should be criticized. Not even if the commander is "godless" – and Moses, even less so, since he was acting on God's command.

At this point in time – shortly before 400 – Augustine had a relatively positive opinion of the Roman Empire. As Robert Markus has convincingly shown, Augustine shared in the widespread optimism during and briefly following the reign of Theodosius I (Theodosius the Great) (379–395).[33] Approximately a decade later, Augustine will develop a profound scepticism toward the Roman Empire. However, his position on war will scarcely change, although its context shifts, as had already

---

31   Exodus 3:21 f.; 11:2 f.; 12: 35 f.

32   Matthew 8:31 f. Cf. Augustine, *c. Faust.* XXII, 71 f. (CSEL 25/1, 668, 8–670, 24).

33   Robert A. Markus, "Saint Augustine's Views on the 'Just War.'" In *Studies in Church History 20* (1983), 1–13. Cf. Marie-François Berrouard, "Bellum." In *Augustinus-Lexikon*, vol. 1 (1986–94), 638–645.

been implied in the letter to Marcellinus: the Christian theologian – qua apologist – will then challenge the reproach that his religion is to blame for the political and military decline. Around 399, in contrast, in the work against Faustus, the self-assured follower of a successful religion inveighs against the Manichean, who criticizes the Old Testament and its nexus between religion, war, and politics. Once again, it becomes evident that Augustine's sentence quoted by Thomas as an authority for the first requirement for a just war is obviously not intended to define a general criterion for the just war but to preserve the unity of the Old and New Testaments.

The second criterion for a just war which Thomas specifies is the just cause *(causa iusta):* "namely that those who are attacked are attacked because they deserve it on account of some wrong they have done. So Augustine, *We usually describe a just war as one that avenges wrongs, that is, when a nation or state has to be punished either for refusing to make amends for outrages done by its subjects, or to restore what it has seized injuriously.*"[34] The quotation is taken from the sixth book of Augustine's *Quaestiones* on the Heptateuch, which was written around 419 and focuses on the Old Testament book of Joshua. The *Quaestiones* are not a systematic commentary on the Bible but exegetical scholia formulated by Augustine, that is, predominantly brief observations on selected Biblical passages. In contrast to the *Summa* of Thomas Aquinas, the *Decretum Gratiani* presents Augustine's complete scholium on Joshua 8:2. The only commentaries that the *Decretum Gratiani* provides on quotations are brief titles and introductions; in this case it follows Augustine's text closely and aptly emphasizes that Augustine's scholium is less concerned with the definition of a just war than with the following principle: "The justness [of a war] is not determined by the fact whether someone fights openly or lies in ambush."[35] In the preceding chapter the *Decretum Gratiani* gives a definition of the just war under the heading *quid sit iustum bellum,* but quotes the definition of a just war not from Augustine but from a passage in Isidore of Seville.[36]

---

34 *S. th.* II-II, 40,1, transl. Heath, 83.
35 *Decretum Gratiani* C. 23 q. 2 c. 2 (Friedberg I, 894 f.) = Augustinus, *Quaestiones in Heptateuchum* VI,x (CChr.SL 33, 318 f., 252–266). Thomas Aquinas quotes only lines 259–262 (with a simplification in the wording).
36 *Decretum Gratiani* C. 23 q. 2. c. 1 (Friedberg I, 894) = Isidorus, *Etymologiae* XVIII, i, 2: Iustum est bellum quod ex edicto (praedicto) geritur de rebus repetendis (repetitis) aut propulsandorum hominum (hostium) causa (the formulations by Isidore are in parentheses).

What is Augustine's topic of inquiry in his scholium on Joshua 8:2? In the relevant Biblical passage God directs Joshua to take his soldiers to Ai and to set up an ambush "behind [at the back of] the city" in order to capture the inhabitants, the city, and the surrounding land.[37] Here Augustine is confronted with a military stratagem expressly ordered by God. However, the question which Augustine contemplates is not the same question which Thomas Aquinas had raised, namely, whether there can be just wars or what justifies a war. What preoccupies Augustine, who had devoted an entire tractate – *De mendacio* – to subterfuge and untruthfulness two decades earlier, is the problem of how to reconcile the justification of the undeniably reprehensible methods of ambush and subterfuge in this Biblical passage with fundamental, recognized ethical principles. In the book of Joshua it is God himself, who commands the preparation of the ambush.[38] Apparently imagining a conversational partner who sees an implicit contradiction to Roman ethics, Augustine formulates the following reply: even from the Roman perspective, in a just war it has no bearing on the issue of justice whether the war is waged openly or with recourse to subterfuge. This in effect answers the question about the general consensus on what constitutes a just war. Here Augustine introduces that definition which I have already quoted in English translation, and which Thomas Aquinas quotes, but which Augustine gives as the prevailing opinion to support his line of argumentation: *Iusta autem bella ea definiri solent quae ulciscuntur iniurias*. "*We usually describe a just war as one that avenges wrongs*".[39] Augustine adds that those wars, too, are just, which God himself commands, since God never acts unjustly.

Through his use of the verb *solere* in this quotation —"We usually describe a just war as one that avenges wrongs" – Augustine introduces a definition of the just war, which he characterizes as usual or customary. It is not his actual intention to present this theory here; he has recourse to it in order to show that the Biblical passage does not contradict the Roman position.

In any event, the definition, in Augustine's formulation, became perhaps the most important principle of the medieval theory of war.[40] Just

---

37 Joshua 8:2.
38 For the background cf.: Eberhard Schockenhoff, "List und Lüge in der theologischen Tradition." In *Die List, ed.* Harro von Senger (Frankfurt 1999) 156–175.
39 English translation by Heath, *S. th.* II-II, 1, 40, 1, 83.
40 F. H. Russell, *The Just War in the Middle Ages*, 18.

wars, the definition states, avenge or punish injustice. Augustine's exact source cannot be ascertained, yet his definition is extremely close to Cicero's formulations in his work on the state. In the third book of Cicero's *De re publica,* there must have been a passage on war that is no longer completely extant in the only existing manuscript of the work, the famous fragmentary palimpset of the Vatican Library. Isidore of Seville cites from this passage: *Illa iniusta bella sunt quae sunt sine causa suscepta. Nam extra ulciscendi aut propulsandorum hostium causa bellum geri iustum non potest.*[41] Unjust are those wars which are undertaken without cause. For a just war can only be waged to take revenge or to repel enemies. This passage proves the incorrectness of the following assertion in a recent study: that for Cicero war "only serves the compensation of the legal infringements of rights suffered by the party waging war and not, however, the punishment of the enemy", while for Augustine war serves "the expiation of injustice," indicating that war serves a more compensatory function for Cicero in contrast to a more punitive function for Augustine.[42] In actuality, Augustine bases his argument for both functions on no one other than Cicero.

For Augustine the injustice to be punished encompasses – among other things – the failure of the enemy "to reconstitute what has been unlawfully appropriated."[43] Cicero provides a catalog of the requirements for the just war: *nullum bellum iustum habetur nisi denuntiatum, nisi indictum, nisi de repetitis rebus.*[44] No war can be considered just, which is not announced in advance, formally declared, and waged in order to effect the restitution of property. The third, the "compensatory" criterion specified by Cicero in this list, is the equivalent of the compensatory criterion given by Augustine. In this ostensibly major passage of his presumed doctrine on the just war, Augustine by no means aspires to put forth his own doctrine but to demonstrate that the Bible is in accordance with the established, recognized doctrine of Cicero on the just war. The question does arise, however, whether Augustine's supplementary con-

---

41 Cicero, *De Republica III,* 24 (23, 35) (= Isidorus, *Etymologiae* XVIII, i, 3).
42 Christoph A. Stumpf, "Vom heiligen Krieg zum gerechten Krieg. Ein Beitrag zur alttestamentlichen und augustinischen Tradition des kanonistischen Völkerrechts bei Gratian." *Zeitschrift der Savigny-Stiftung für Rechtsgeschichte. Kanonistische Abteilung* 87 (2001): 1–30, 12–16, who only consults Cicero, *De officiis* I, xi, 36, but not the fragment from *De republica* quoted directly beforehand.
43 Augustine, *Quaestiones In Heptateuchum VI,* x (CChr.SL 33, 319, 262).
44 Cicero, *De republica III,* 24 (23,35) (= Isidorus, *Etymologiae* XVIII, i, 3), similar *De officiis* I, xi, 36.

struct that a war is also just, if it is commanded by God, does not actually explode the Ciceronian criteria for a just war. However, to the best of my knowledge, Augustine restricts this argument to Biblical wars. He apparently did not consider the possibility that wars waged during his own lifetime could be wars commanded by God. In my opinion, Augustine is not the father of a Christian ideology of the holy war.

Thomas Aquinas names a third criterion for a just war: the right intention (*intentio recta*) of the party waging war, specifically, either to promote the good or to avoid evil. Conversely, a war can be unjust, even if it has been lawfully declared and if its cause is also legitimate: "So again Augustine says, *The craving to hurt people, the cruel thirst for revenge, the unappeased and unrelenting spirit, the savageness of fighting on, the lust to dominate, and suchlike – all these are rightly condemned in wars.*"[45] This passage from Augustine's work directed against Faustus, the Manichean, mentioned earlier in my lecture, states that a military act can become censurable through the manner in which it is conducted. Here the question arises whether every war even in Augustine's time did not involve those elements of cruelty, savagery, and irreconcilability which, in Augustine's own words, reveal it to be an unjust war.[46] In reality it was probably the experience of the total war in the twentieth century, which led certain theologians to come to this conclusion and to teach that the question of the just cause of war and the formally correct declaration of war is no longer tenable given the modern forms of warfare, so that in practice it can no longer be considered permissible to declare war on any state at all.[47] In a certain respect the germ of an idea radically questioning the realizability of just wars is present in Augustine's works, even if Augustine did not come to this conclusion himself.

---

45 *S. th.* II-II, 40, 1 c., (here trans. Heath, 83) = *Decretum Gratiani* C. 23 q. 1. c. 4 (Friedberg, I, 892) = Augustinus, *Contra Faustum* XXII, 74 (CSEL 25/1, 672, 8–10).

46 Adrian Keith Goldsworthy, *The Roman Army at War 100 BC-AD 200* (Oxford: 1996), describes the reality of war in antiquity, although only until the end of the second century.

47 Franziskus Maria Stratmann, *Weltkirche und Weltfriede. Katholische Gedanken zum Kriegs- und Friedensproblem* (Augsburg: 1924), 75–104; Alfredo Ottaviani, *Institutiones Iuris Publici Ecclesiastici*, vol. 1 (Rome: 1947), 151–155.

4 War and Peace

Thomas Aquinas supports his third criterion for a just war, the right intention, with another quotation by Augustine, which is also attributed to Augustine in the *Decretum Gratiani* but is no longer attributed to Augustine today: *Apud veros Dei cultores etiam illa bella pacata sunt quae non cupiditate aut crudelitate, sed pacis studio geruntur, ut mali coerceantur et boni subleventur.*[48] For true venerators of God, wars, too, promote peace, in that they are not waged out of greed or cruelty but out of a zeal for freedom, in the hopes that the wicked will be defeated and the righteous will prevail. The quotation is close to Augustinian thought as developed in the nineteenth book of *De civitate dei*. While in all the passages previously discussed Augustine generally touches on the topic of war marginally and in highly specific contexts, in this particular book of the *City of God* war is discussed and evaluated within a systematic framework. There Augustine writes, *Pacis igitur intentione geruntur et bella:* wars, too, are waged with the intention of peace.[49] This, too, has been a traditional view since antiquity, which Augustine encountered in the works of pagan Latin authors and scholars such as Varro or Cicero; earlier Aristotle had also taught that wars are to be waged for "the sake of peace."[50]

In Augustine's work *De civitate dei* it becomes clear, however, that this does not adequately justifiy wars that only serve the purpose of a future peace. There Augustine demonstrates the absolute deficiency of war in comparison with peace by emphasizing the asymmetry between both entities: "For every man seeks peace by waging war, but no man seeks war by making peace. For even they who intentionally interrupt the peace in which they are living have no hatred of peace, but only wish it changed into a peace that suits them better."[51] Even the evildoer loves his unjust

---

48 *S. th.* II-II, 40, 1 c. = *Decretum Gratiani* C. 23 q. 1 c. 6 (Friedberg I, 893) = *Collectio Tripartita* B 3.20.35 (ed. Brett, http://knowledgeforge.net/ivo/) = Ivo of Chartres, *Decretum* X, 105 (PL 161, 724).

49 Augustine, *De civitate Dei XIX*, xii (CChr.SL 48, 675, 7 f.).

50 Aristotle, *Politica 7*, 14 (1333 a 35) (English trans. *The Politics*, ed. S. Everson, trans. B. Jowett/J. Barnes (Cambridge: 1988, 177); *Ethica Nicomachea* X, 7 (1177 b 4–12). On Augustine's sources cf. Harald Fuchs, Augustin und der antike Friedensgedanke. Untersuchungen zum neunzehnten Buch der Civitas Dei, Berlin 1926, Reprint with Preface by W. F. Bense (New York/London: 1973).

51 Augustine, *De civitate Dei XIX*, xii, (St. Augustin's City of God and Christian Doctrine, ed. P. Schaff , trans. M. Dods, NPNF, vol. 2, Grand Rapids 1979, 407).

peace, but he loves peace and consequently witnesses the unshakable order of the universe, where every element ultimately strives to attain its appropriate position. The peace of all things lies in the tranquillity of order: *pax omnium rerum tranquillitas ordinis. Ordo est parium dispariumque rerum sua cuique loca tribuens dispositio.*[52] The disturbance of this order leads to conflicts such as those wars, which are nothing other than sad indications of the sinfulness of this world, *huius saeculi.* "But, say they, the wise man will wage just wars. As if he would not all the rather lament the necessity of just wars, if he remembers that he is a man...."[53] In marked contrast to his letter to Marcellinus, written at least a decade earlier, Augustine abandons his apologetic efforts to promote the recognition of the Christian as a responsible citizen of the Roman Empire. Even the just war is nothing other than a sign of the imperfection of this world, and peace as the aim of war proves to be only a pale reflection of that one, true peace, which cannot be attained in this world.

Augustine was not a pacifist; this is clear from his earliest to his latest works. He lived in a society, in which wars were an integral part of everyday life. In the context of such a society, however, Augustine's statements on war are to be read differently than in the context of a society in which peace is the the normal reality. If one takes this into consideration, the fact that Augustine develops his theory of war within the framework of a comprehensive view of peace in *De civitate dei* acquires particular significance. The three criteria for a just war, however, which have been interpretatively distilled from essentially marginal observations in totally different works of Augustine since the Middle Ages, without consideration of their original contexts, these three criteria for a just war divert one's attention from Augustine's conception of peace. By appealing to these specific quotations from Augustine and by broadening particularly the idea of injustice to be punished, the doctrine was even propagated in the ethics of the wars of conquest in the sixteenth century that it could be a mortal sin not to wage war, and that even a war of aggression could be imperative from a moral perspective.[54]

Of course, one can speculate whether Augustine theoretically could not have propagated a pacifism that was not simply resigned to the reality of wars. Perhaps Augustine was a realist on this issue, precisely because he

---

52 Augustine, *De civitate Dei XIX*, xiii (CChr.SL 48, 679, 10–12).
53 Augustine, *De civitate Dei XIX*, vii, trans. Dods, 405.
54 Joseph Höffner, *Christentum und Menschenwürde. Das Anliegen der spanischen Kolonialethik im Goldenen Zeitalter* (Trier: 1947), 255 f.

knew that this world together with its history is the place of human action in responsibility to God and man, but is not to be seen as the ultimate reality.[55]

55 I am grateful to Jo Ann Van Vliet for the translation of my paper into English.

Augustine: Peace Ethics and Peace Policy

Johannes Brachtendorf

1 The Dimensions of Meaning of the Augustinian Concept of Peace

1.1 The Metaphysical Concept of Peace: Inner Unity

To Saint Augustine, peace is not only an ethical and political concept but also a metaphysical one. The ethical and the political concepts of peace arise from the metaphysical concept of peace, which will be elaborated upon to begin with.

According to Saint Augustine, peace is a general characteristic contained in every existing object in addition to unity, truth and ingrained good.[1] In this context, peace is to be understood as inner unity. Every existing entity, be it a lifeless rock, a living animal or a human being, manifests a unity of parts. Peace among the parts is the prerequisite of the maintenance of order of the whole, for that what loses its peace, loses its unity and collapses. Inner peace is thus a condition of existence for every entity composed of parts.

To Saint Augustine, reality confronts us with a hierarchy with lifeless objects at the bottom, living creatures at the centre and God at the very top. As the inner order of the living object becomes more complex and the parts become more strongly integrated, the degree of peace increases. Every form of existence possesses thus its own unique degree of peace. The intensity or ranking of peace increases from the bottom to the top. At the very top of the pyramid stands God as the ultimate form of Being, Unity and Peace. Every finite form of life obtains its existence, its unity and its peace through its share ('participatio') in God as the highest and most complete reality.

---

1 See *De civitate dei XIX* 12 – 13, in Sancti Aurelii Augustini *De civitate Dei Libri I-XI XI-XXII*. Pub. Bernard Dombart/Alphons Kalb (CCL 48). 2 volumes (Tournhout: 1955), 675 – 680. In this specific context, Trancendentials are traditionally referred to.

Every form of existence contains a natural aspiration for self-fulfilment or, at least, self-perpetuation. Saint Augustine defines this as a striving for preservation or reconstruction of inner peace. As every finite form of existence constitutes a unity of parts, it is alterable and transitory. However, that which is damaged or destroyed does not lose its peace entirely, as it does not dissolve into nothingness, but simply moves downwards in the hierarchy of being, unity and peace to the level of the fragments into which it disintegrates. A building, for example, is more highly integrated than the bricks it consists of. If the building, however, is destroyed it does not simply disappear, but falls into parts that, in turn, contain a unique (if lower) degree of unity and peace.[2] To Saint Augustine, God has created reality according to an 'eternal law',[3] a hierarchical order of being. Within this order there is creation and decay, and no form of existence can escape this order. That which cannot maintain its status in the hierarchy does not dissolve into nothingness but finds itself on a lower level of that hierarchy.

1.2 The Ethical Concept of Peace: The Highest Good

As reality in its entirety strives for peace by its tendency for self-perpetuation and self-fulfilment, so aspires a human being – a creature capable of rational action – to peace. Peace is both the motif and the goal of all human activity. The highest degree of peace available to human beings lies with God. This peace is the 'summum bonum', the highest good of a human being, who derives perfect happiness from this possession.[4] "All humans want to be happy", reads a maxim of Hellenistic ethics which Saint Augustine regularly refers to in order to explain that human beings, in their quest for goals, ultimately strive for happiness.[5] Since this happiness can also be described as peace, this implies that the human desire for peace surpasses all desires for other inferior goods.

---

2 Saint Augustine uses the metaphor of a decomposing corpse that loses its organic unity and descends onto the level of hummus. See *De civitate dei XIX* 12 (footnote 1), 675–678.

3 See *De civitate dei XIX* 12 (footnote 1), 675–678; "De libero arbitrio" 1 15,48; 30,101–34,114. In *Sancti Aureli Augustini Opera Sect. VI Pars III: De libero arbitrio libri tres,* pub. William M. Green (CSEL 42) (Vienna: 1956), 15, 30–36.

4 See *De civitate dei XIX* 11 (footnote 1), 674 f.

5 See "De trinitate XIII" 8,11. In *Sancti Aurelii Augustini De trinitate libri XV* (libri XIII-XV). Pub. W.J. Mountain (CCL 50a), (Turnhout: 1968), 396–398.

However, even though every human being strives for happiness, he can be wrong about what goods actually give him happiness. He, who desires money, glory or lust as the highest good and does not strive for God, will only find unhappiness. Inspired by antique philosophy, Saint Augustine relates the moral distinction between good and bad to the distinction between goods that produce happiness and those goods that fail to do so. He, who acts correctly by aspiring to the true goods, gains inner unity, peace and happiness. He, who acts poorly by striving for worldly goods, loses his inner unity, damages his soul and finds only unhappiness. Although bad deeds may be directed at the finding of happiness, they ultimately lead to unhappiness. While a good person can achieve the highest level of peace that is possibly attainable for human beings, a bad person falls behind and remains on a lower level of peace.[6]

1.3 Peace as a Category of Redemption: Sin and Salvation

According to Saint Augustine, the existence of human kind was characterised by complete peace prior to the fall of man. Humans lived at peace with God (love for God) and at peace with each other (love of neighbor) and with themselves, thus in accordance to the order of creation. With the fall of man, however, humankind turned its back on God. Humans lost their original perfection and, consequently, fell back to a lower level of peace in accordance to the 'eternal law'. Disease and death came about, which Saint Augustine regards as turmoil inside the body, and as the disintegration of the unity of body and soul respectively. To Saint Augustine, the creation of the passions arouse from the inability of human rationality to conquer his lower instincts ('passiones'). In the fallen man, libido takes control and manifests itself in the human desire to dominate ('libido dominandi') and to harm ('libido ulciscendi'). Mankind, burdened by sin, becomes distracted from its goal to reach absolute peace in God, because it is led by 'libido dominandi' in its desire to conquer and destroy others. Consequently, the fall of man also weakens social peace. Battles and war come about. While peace was protected by love prior to the fall of man, it may have to be defended by force in its after-

---

6   Saint Augustine focuses on this falling behind when he depicts evil as the lack of good (privatio boni). See Johannes Brachtendorf, *Augustins Confessiones* (Darmstadt: 2005), 136–142.

math. This implies that all of mankind has fallen back onto a lower level of unity and peace due to the fall of man.

Jesus Christ appeals to the tranquillity, patience and love for the enemies of those men and women who are led by 'libido dominandi'.

"But I say to you, That you resist not evil: but whoever shall smite you on your right cheek, turn to him the other also. And if any man will sue you at the law, and take away your coat, let him have your cloak also. And whoever shall compel you to go a mile, go with him two." (Matthew 5,39–41)

According to Saint Augustine, man is not capable of ridding himself of libido. Only through his belief in Jesus Christ can he attain God's mercy, which frees him from the burden of libido and enables him to be guided by the love for God and neighbor and thus become peaceful. However, in Saint Augustine's eyes, even he, who acts out of love for God, is still susceptible to the temptations of libido. Man's mental condition is, therefore, characterised by a struggle between his virtues and his passions.[7] Perfect peace with God, others and himself can only be attained in the afterlife.

From a metaphysical point of view, nothing can escape the order of God, as anything that proves to be unable to remain at the same level of existence will simply find itself on a lower level. According to Saint Augustine, the 'eternal law' of the world order also contains an educational dimension, as it perfectly portrays not only the sovereignty of God as the world architect, but also His love and justice. All of mankind suffers from war and violence and is thus punished for its sins. This suffering enables man to contemplate the possible causes of his pain and allows him to come to terms with his inborn sinfulness. God's omniscience entails a strategy of healing, because, first of all, sin entails punishment, and, secondly, the suffering inspires man to change his ways. Thirdly, Saint Augustine believes that God imposes suffering on any person who is in need for 'correctio' as a result of committed sins, his desire for worldly goods, or haughtiness, which is found even among Christians. When a Christian has to endure violence and war (both just and unjust), he can assume that his suffering is not meaningless, but imposed upon him by God for his

---

7   See *De civitate dei XIX* 4 (footnote 1), 664–669; see "Confessiones X" 28,39–39, 64. In *Sancti Aureli Augustini Confessionum libri tredecim*, pub. Pius Knöll (CSEL 33) (Prague/Vienna/Leipzig: 1896), 255–275.

own good.[8] This is, of course, not to be seen as a justification for brutality and war. God is not the source of sin, but because of His omniscience, He can turn the negative consequences of sin into beneficial and potentially redemptive lessons for mankind.

2 The State and its Function as a Guarantor of Peace

The social categories of order that Saint Augustine pays most attention to are the family (including the house slaves) and the state. The family was part of the order of creation (Adam and Eve were married, so to speak) and the state, too, as an orderly unity of men and women, designed to overcome the human state of nature, is not to be disregarded. This community of human beings arises naturally from the perfect love for God and for each other. Thus, the family and the state are not consequences of the fall of man. The penal power of the family in addition to the penal power and the military might of the state are, however, results of the fall of man.[9]

Do a family and a state as such correspond to the will of God or are they mere results of the fall of man? On the one hand, the non-coercive state embodies the full degree of peace attainable for mankind. On the other hand, the coercive state lessens the degree of peace. As man proved himself incapable of maintaining the social order of love, the degree of peace available to him became reduced to an enforceable order. Prior to the fall of man, humanity constituted an ethical community. In its wake, humanity formed a legalistic community. Thus, both the head of a family endowed with penal power and the coercive state exist in accordance to divine premonition. For if an order of love becomes impossible, the enforcement of peace guarantees a minimum degree of social order,

---

8   See *De civitate dei I* 8–18 (footnote 1), 7–20, concerning the question why Christians, too, were robbed, raped and murdered during the conquest of Rome. Saint Augustine writes: "…et omnis victoria, cum etiam malis provenit, divino iudicio victos humilitat vel emendans peccata vel puniens." (And every victory, even when achieved by the wicked, is a divine judgement designed to humiliate the defeated, be it to cleanse them of their sins, be it to punish their sins.) (*De civitate XIX* 15 [footnote 1], 682).

9   The most comprehensive and most sophisticated work concerning this topic is Timo J. Weissenberg's, *Die Friedenlehre des Augustinus. Theologische Grundlagen und ethische Entfaltung* (Stuttgart: 2005). I (the author of this essay) gained a great deal of inspiration from this book.

which keeps humankind from losing more unity and peace and descending into chaos.

Consequently, a legal order is an important tool of the state, which through the threat of coercion and punishment, guarantees a minimum degree of peaceful human coexistence. A minimal state as such abstains from making moral claims, but attempts to impose legality. Wicked people, who strive for material goods and power, also need laws that prohibit crimes, such as theft – even if the love of the rightful owner for his possessions is morally despicable.[10] According to Saint Augustine, state law does not condemn the desire for material goods, but punishes theft and the unlawful deprivation of others. Out of fear of punishment, humans maintain a level of social cohesion that is essential to the order of the state.

To Saint Augustine, the mere regulatory function of the state is, in itself, praiseworthy. This, however, does not imply that the minimal state cannot be surpassed. For even if the worst state fulfils a regulatory function and is thus to be chosen over statelessness, a good state takes the greater public good into account, very much like a father caring for the well-being of his family. In a good state, and that to Saint Augustine is a Christian one, coercion is not only used for the maintenance of order but also for the containment of human passions. Moreover, the coercive power of the state should be characterised by punishments aimed at the correction ('correctio') of the offender.

This entails certain demands on the attitudes of those who are in charge of the exertion of coercion. They must have the right intentions and be inspired by their love for the offender and their wish to change his ways. They must not be guided by 'libido dominandi' or 'libido ulciscendi'. There must not be punishment without the attempt to correct the offender.[11] Saint Augustine elaborates in his 'mirror of princes'[12] on Christian emperors who punished not out of revenge but out of hope for betterment. They governed not out of greed but aspired to eternal blessedness and preferred to rule over their passions rather than over foreign nations. "If the true believers, who live a good life, understand, at

---

10   See *De libero arbitrio I* 33, 112 (footnote 3), 33.
11   See Weissenberg, *Friedenslehre* (footnote 9), 133 f.
12   *De civitate dei V* 24 (footnote 1), 160.

the same time, the art of ruling nations, then there is no greater good for mankind than the divine bestowment of rule upon them."[13]

Whereas 'libido dominandi' is condemnable in itself, the exertion of coercion in the face of the real conditions in a post-lapsian world is not necessarily despicable. It can serve bad as well as good purposes. Coercion in order to dominate others is reprehensible, whereas coercion used as an educational tool designed to protect others from wrong-doing can serve the public good.

3 The Doctrine of War

3.1 War as an Evil of Mankind

According to Saint Augustine, war represents an evil that dramatically portrays human suffering in the post-lapsian world. No one could regard the 'monstrous, horrifying, disastrous evil'[14] of wars without experiencing tremendous emotional pain. To Saint Augustine, even the benefits of the 'pax romana' diminish in the face of the horrors of war. The domination of the Roman Empire was "just, but achieved by how many terrible wars, by what massacres, what bloodshed!"[15] Moreover, the sheer size of the Empire conjured up the civil wars "from which mankind continues to suffer."[16] In Saint Augustine's opinion, all wars, including the just ones, caused suffering: "But the wise man, they say, will wage just wars. As if

---

13 "Illi autem, qui vera pietate praediti bene vivunt, si habent scientiam regendi populus, nihil est felicius rebus humanis, quam si deo miserante habeant potestaem." (*De civitate dei V* 19 [footnote 1], 156). Saint Augustine argues that Constantine and Theodosius were such regents.

14 "Haec itaque mala tam magna, tam horrenda, tam saeva ..." (*De civitate dei XIX* 7 [footnote 1], 672).

15 "Verum est; sed hoc quam multis et quam grandibus bellis, quanta strage hominum, quanta effusione humani sanguinis comparatum est?" (*De civitate dei XIX* 7 [footnote 1], 671).

16 "Tamem etiam ipsa imperii latitudo peperit peioris generis bella, socialia scilicet et civilia, quibus miserabilius quatitur humanum genus..." Saint Augustine goes on to say: "Quorum malorum multas et multiplices clades, duras et diras necessitates si ut dignum est eloqui velim, quamquam nequaquam sicut res postulat possim: quis crie prolixae disputationis modus?" (If I wanted to describe the manifold evil, all the pressing and onerous grievances resulting from it – a deed I am indeed incapable of – how would I ever come to an end?) (*De civitate dei XIX* 7 [footnote 1], 672).

he would not all the more, if he remembers his humanity, deplore his being compelled to engage in just wars."[17]

3.2 Just War (iustum bellum)

Although all wars represent a deplorable evil, Saint Augustine differentiates between unjust wars, led out of imperiousness, greed for worldly commodities (i. e. raw materials) or expansionist ambitions, and just wars, triggered by an apparent violation of the law or led by decree of God. Saint Augustine considers most wars led by the Roman Empires to be unjust.

Saint Augustine himself did not produce a disquisition on the just war theory. There are but a few comments in his work, mostly in the context of an interpretation of the Old Testament or, respectively, in his defence of the Old Testament against the Manicheans.[18] On the one hand, Saint Augustine attempts to defend his interpretation of Christianity against the Manicheans and their notion of pacifism by construing the Old Testament in a way that deprives the narrations about God's decreed wars of their potentially offensive nature. He depicts the Old Testament as the harbinger of the New Testament, which contains the secrets of salvation in disguised form. The Old Testament is but a symbol of the New Testament and must be interpreted as such. On the other hand, Saint Augustine confronts those Romans who claim that the Sermon on the Mount (and thus Christianity in its entirety) could not become part of the political discourse of that time. The Romans argued that Christianity with its pacifist doctrine posed a threat to the 'res publica' whose founding principles were defended by martial law. In their opinion, the 'res publica' could not be governed, let alone be expanded, if committed

---

17 "Sed sapiens, inquiunt, iusta bella gesturus est, quasi non, si se hominem meminit, multo magis dolebit iustorum necessitatem …" (*De civitate dei XIX* 7 [footnote 1], 672).

18 In spite of their conciseness and remoteness, these two passages were equally well-received. Gratian and Thomas Aquinas (see *Summa Thelogiae* II-II q. 40, a.1) contributed to their impact, which allowed Saint Augustine to emerge as the intellectual father of the just war theory; see *Die deutsche Thomas-Ausgabe. Vollständige, ungekürzte deutsch-latainische Ausgabe der Summa theologica*, vol. 17b, *Die Liebe* (2. part) – *Klugheit* (II-II, 34–56), pub. Joseph Endres (Heidelberg/Graz/Vienna/Cologne: 1966).

crimes were forgiven rather than punished.[19] Saint Augustine countered this critique of Christianity by arguing that the Sermon on the Mount was not absolutely pacifistic, but actually allowed for the use of coercion in the context of a just war. The Christian state morally surpassed the Roman Empire, because it refused to engage in unjust wars but also because it was led by the motif of 'correctio' when engaged in just wars.

3.2.1 Just War as a Result of a Violation of International Law

Saint Augustine distinguishes between two kinds of just war. The first kind is directed at the punishment of a crime, the second kind is conducted upon the will of God. The Quaestiones in Heptateuchum offer a concise description of the first kind of just war:

> Just wars are defined as such if they punish injustice when a people or a state, that is to be warred against, does not live up to its responsibility to do so, when their members must be punished for their wicked deeds, or when that which has been unlawfully taken must be returned.[20]

We can only speak of a just war if it is justified by 'iusta causa', that is an 'iniuria' or an 'iniquitas'[21] committed by the opposing side.[22] Unfortunately, Saint Augustine offers hardly any concrete examples. One example is the war of Israel against the Amoritans (No 21, 21–25), who refused

---

19 See Epistula 138 to Marcellinus. In *S. Aureli Augustini Hipponiensis Episcopi Epistulae*. Pars III. Pub. Al. Goldbacher. (CSEL 44) (Vienna/Leipzig: 1904), 126–148.

20 "Justa autem bella ea definiri solent quae ulciscuntur iniurias, si qua gens vel civitas, quae bello petenda est, vel vindicare neglexerit quod a suis inprobe factum est vel reddere quod per iniurias ablatum est." Quaestiones in Heptateuchum VI 10 (Liber Sextus. Quaestiones Iesu Nave). In *Sancti Aurelii Augustini Quaestionum in Heptateuchum Libri VII*. (CCL 33.) (Tournhout: 1958), 318 f. The corresponding passage by Cicero reads: "illa iniusta bella sunt, quae sunt sine causa suscepta. Nam extra ulciscendi aut propulsandorum hostium causa bellum geri iustum nullum potest." Cicero, "De re publica III" 35. In *M. Tulli Ciceronis scripta quae manserunt omnia*. vol. 39, *De republica. Librorum sex quae manserunt*. Pub. K. Ziegler. (Bibliotheca scriptorium Graecorum et Romanorum Teubneriana, Fasc. 39.) (Leipzig: 1929). See the comments on martial law in Cicero, "De officiis I" 34–37. In *M. Tulli Ciceronis scripta quae manserunt omnia*, vol. 48, *De officiis*. Pub. C. Atzert (Bibliotheca scriptorium Graecorum et Romanorum Teubneriana, Fasc. 48. (Leipzig: 1932/1975), where it reads: "quare suscipienda quidem bella sunt o beam causam, ut sine iniuria in pace vivatur..." (I 34).

21 *De civitate dei XIX* 7 (footnote 1), 671 f.

22 See Epistula 138 (footnote 19), 139 f.

to authorize the peaceful march-through of the Israelites, "which should have been open to them by the natural law of human society."[23]

Externally, just wars restore the relations between states and thus correspond internally to the regulatory function of the law. Both kinds of just war are conducted to restore minimal standards of peace, which are a prerequisite of human co-existence. Bad states, too, which strive merely for material goods, can lead just wars with 'iusta causa'. However, if a just war is led by a Christian state, it will be inspired by educational factors, emphasizing the 'correctio' of the enemy. Thus, good states, when at war, do not know "the desire to harm, the cruelty of revenge, the unforgiving nature and brutality of a strike-back."[24] They protect their enemy as much as possible and aspire to peace, even though they are at war. They are not led by 'libido dominandi et ulciscendi', but strive for the elimination of 'iniquitas' in order to bring about the self-improvement of the opposing forces. Whereas Saint Augustine assented to the right of authorities to impose the death penalty, as a bishop he disapproved of it because it deprived the offender of his chance to change his ways. A war of annihilation is thus equally undesirable. He writes "This is why wars are to be led compassionately by the good and virtuous, if that is possible at all, in order to shake off the burdens that must be repressed and exterminated by a just empire through the taming of base human passions."[25] To lead a just war 'misericorditer' means not only to restore peace, but also to allow the enemy to extricate himself from his unrighteousness, overcome his desire for worldly goods and recognise God as the highest good.

However, is a Christian state actually allowed to declare war? Does this notion not contravene the demands of the New Testament not to retaliate a crime with a crime? According to Saint Augustine, the instructions put forth in the New Testament do not relate to outer actions

---

23 *Quaestiones in Heptateuchum IV* 44 (footnote 20), 263 f.

24 "Nocendi cupiditas ulciscendi crudelitas, inpacatus atque inplacabilis animus, feritas rebellandi." Contra Faustum XXII 74. In Sancti *Aurelii Augustini* De utilitate credendi/ De duabus animabus contra Fortunatum/ Contra Adimantum/ Contra epistulam fundamenti/ Contra Faustum. Pub. Joseph Zycha. (CSEL XXV, Sect. VI, Pars 1), (Prague/Vienna/Leipzig: 1891), 672.

25 "Misericorditer enim, si fieri posset, etiam bella gerentur a bonis, ut licentiosis cupiditatibus domitis haec vitia perderentur, quae iusto imperio vel extirpari vel premi debuerunt." (Epistula 138,14 [footnote 19], 141). Pub. Al. Goldbacher.

but to inner attitudes, to 'praeparatio cordis'.[26] Jesus Christ demands patience and benevolence towards the unrighteous. A good person is to turn the other cheek "in order to conquer human evil with human good and allow man to better himself out of inner conviction rather than as a result of outer intervention."[27] He, who conquers evil with good, teaches the wicked to resist worldly goods for the sake of true peace and justice, and the wicked will ultimately learn from his enemy how unworthy the objects of his desire, which inspired him to commit a crime, truly are. The offender is thus not defeated by the strength of the soldier, but by the benevolence of his victim.[28] According to Saint Augustine, the righteous believer must patiently endure the cruelty of those who he desires to overcome their wickedness.

He, who wholeheartedly believes in 'patentia' and 'benevolentia' will not retaliate evil with evil. According to Saint Augustine, one must confront the evil-doer with a 'certain benevolent sternness' and act against his will, for the ultimate goal is the betterment of the wretched, not the assertion of his will. Christ Himself did not turn the other cheek when the servant of the high priest slapped him, but answered instead: "If I have spoken wrongly, testify of the wrong; but if rightly, why do you strike Me?" (John 18,23). Christ was not only willing to turn the other cheek, but also to die on the cross. However, it was more beneficial for the servant to be confronted by Jesus in order to be prevented from doing more harm.[29] The punishment imposed by parents, teachers and rulers thus corresponds to the commandments of Christ, as long as the punishment against the wrong-doer is inspired by benevolence. For sometimes a doctor can only heal by causing more pain, and he, who is violently prevented from doing wrong, is defeated for his own good. The Christian doctrine thus does not condemn all wars, only the unjust ones and those that are fought out of hatred and greed. John the Baptist did not appeal to the soldiers who came to him to leave the military service (Luke 3,14), and Christ did not command the centurion to quit soldierhood (Matthew 8,9–10).

---

26 See *Contra Faustum XXII* 76 (footnote 24), 674 f.
27 "…ut vincatur bono malus, immo in homine malo vincatur bono malum et homo liberetur a malo non exterior et alieno sed intimo ac suo …" (Epistula 138,11[footnote 19], 136).
28 Epistula 138, 11 (footnote 19), 136 f.
29 Epistula 138, 13 (footnote 19), 138 f.

Saint Augustine responds to the Romans, who declared Christianity to be the enemy of 'res publica' due to its doctrine of peace, in the following way: "They should put together an army that is in accordance with the teachings of Christ, such soldiers, governors, married couples, parents, sons, masters, slaves, kings, judges, debtors, donors – then they would understand that this would be the salvation of the 'res publica'.[30]

If the 'res publica' abided by the commandments of Christ then wars would not be fought without 'benevolentia'. They would be fought in order to create an improved society imbued by piety and justice.

The prerequisite of a just war is 'iusta causa'. A severe violation of the law qualifies as such. This may raise the question whether these 'iniquitas' and 'iniuria' relate only to a specific violation of international law or if the mere wickedness of a nation or a state suffices as a legitimate reason to declare war. Also, does idolatry qualify as a 'iusta causa' for a religious war? The first question is to be answered in the negative. There is no evidence that Saint Augustine regarded the moral improvement ('correctio') of a people as a legitimate reason to declare war. Neither is the moral depravity of a citizen a just cause for punishment in the absence of a committed crime. According to Saint Augustine, 'correctio' does not qualify as a potential 'causa' for a just war but belongs to the realm of intention and motivation out of which a war, caused by 'iniquitas' (that is a material violation of the law), is fought. The question relating to the religious war is to be answered in a similar fashion. There is no evidence, either, that Saint Augustine considered idolatry to be a 'iusta causa' for a war against a nation. The righteous worship of God also belongs to the realm of motivation, insofar as moral good is only achieved through the worship of the true God. According to Saint Augustine, a war only qualifies as a just war if it is fought to restore a minimum inter-state 'ordo'. This does not apply to religious or moral warfare.[31]

---

30 "Proinde, qui doctrinam Christi adversam dicunt esse rei publicae, dent exercitum talem, quales doctrina Christi esse milites iussit; dent tales provincials, tales maritos, tales coniuges, tales parentes, tales filios, tales dominos, tales servos, tales reges, tales iudices, tales denique debitorum ipsius fisci redditores, quales esse praecepit, doctrina christiana, et audeant eam dicere adversam esse rei publicae, immo vero dubitent confiteri magnam, si ei obtemperetur, salute esse rei publicae." (Epistula 138, 15 [footnote 19], 141 f.).

31 See Weissenberg, *Friedenslehre* (footnote 9), 163–165.

3.2.2 Just Wars by Command of God

Another kind of 'iustum bellum' is a war fought by command of God. To Saint Augustine, the destruction of the city of Ai by the Israelites under Joshua (Joshua 8, 1–29)[32] serves a good example. God orders Joshua to organise an ambush, which turns out successfully. The Israelites conquer the city, burn it down, kill all citizens (12 000!) and nail the king to a tree. They take the livestock as a spoil of war. Saint Augustine elaborates on the issue of just wars by decree of God and the divinely authorized use of violence in the book 22 of 'Contra Faustum', Saint Augustine's long discussion with the Manichean Bishop Faustus.[33] The Manicheans claimed that the God of the Old Testament was an evil God, who could not be identical to the God described in the New Testament, for He ordered pacifism, whereas the God of the Old Testament loved violence. Faustus regarded the heinous crimes committed by the patriarchs by decree of the God of the Old Testament as supportive arguments for this claim.

Saint Augustine is convinced that God does order man to go to war, and actually did so in the case of the people of Israel. Whereas Faustus regards this order to pick up arms as a form of divine injustice, Saint Augustine argues differently: God is the only entity incapable of unjustifiably doing harm. Therefore, the peoples defeated by Moses and Joshua deserved divine punishment and, ultimately, a violent death. As God could not be unjust, wars commanded by God could only be just wars.[34]

---

32 *Quaestiones in Heptateuchum VI* 10 (footnote 24), 428 f.; Jos 8,–1–29.

33 See *Contra Faustum XXII* 70–79 (footnote 24), 666–682.

34 Saint Augustine has a critical perspective on the incidents of murder and theft in the Old Testament. Abraham was indeed asked by God to sacrifice his son Isaac (see Gen. 22, 1–19). He, thus, deserved praise, not blame, for his willingness to obey God's command. Whether Jiftach actually acted on behalf of a divine decree when he sacrificed his only daughter (see Book of Judges 16,29–40), however, was questionable, according to Saint Augustine. Even more questionable was the deed of Samson, who buried himself and numerous Philistine rulers beneath the ruins of a house (see Book of Judges 16,23–31). In order to justify Samson's actions, one would have to assume that he acted on behalf of a secret plan revealed to him by the Holy Spirit (see *De civitate dei I* 22 [footnote 1]). According to Saint Augustine, Moses's murder of an Egyptian (Ex 2,11–12) as well as Peter's use of violence during the arrest of Jesus (see John 18,10) are blameworthy (*Contra Faustum XXII* 70 [footnote 24], 666 f.) The theft of gold and silver items committed by the Israelites during their flight from Egypt (Ex 12,35 f.) was certainly allowed by God. However, He may have given permission to steal from the Egyptians rather than an order to do so. Moreover, it may be possible that the

Can a divine command then qualify as a justification for war? According to Saint Augustine, it could, but only in pre-Christian times. God did indeed order wars in the Old Testament. In the New Testament, however, He orders patience and peace. The wars in the Old Testament were to demonstrate that earthly goods, such as kingdoms and victories over one's enemy, lie in the hands of God. With the New Testament the truth emerged that there was a life after death that made life on earth seem insignificant. For there was a heavenly kingdom and in quest of it the attacks against earthly empires were to be patiently endured.[35] The patriarchs, for example, owned earthly empires and demonstrated that these empires could be given and taken by God. Conversely, the apostles and matyrers owned no earthly empires and thus implied that the heavenly kingdom was more desirable.

> The duty of the worshippers of the Old Testament, who were also harbingers of the New Testament, was to kill sinners; the duty of the worshippers of the Old Testament, who were also the teachers of the New Testament, was to die at the hands of sinners. Yet both served a God who ruled in different ways, depending on the time, that finite goods are to be resented and that worldly worries are sent by Him and must, therefore, be endured.[36]

The Israelites were initially well-inclined towards material goods. This is why the promise of heavenly goods appeared to them in the form of earthly goods. The divine secrets of heavenly goods were disguised by the veil of earthly promises. However, the New Testament reveals the message of the heavenly kingdom that surpasses all earthly empires and renders all material goods insignificant. According to Saint Augustine, the times in which God demonstrated His reign over earthly goods through His war commands have been overcome because God no longer gives signs, but actually reveals the truth. He now orders mankind to as-

---

People of Israel did not act out of obedience but out of greed, which would, of course, qualify as a sin (see *Contra Faustum XXII* 71 [footnote 24], 668 f.).

35 *Contra Faustum XXII* 78 (footnote 24), 628.

36 "Servierint dispensatores veteris testamenti idemque praenuntiatores novi testamenti peccatores occidendo, servierint dispensatores novi testamenti idemque expositores veteris testamenti a peccatoribus moriendo, deo tamen uni utrique servierunt per diversa et congrua tempora docenti bona temporalia et a se petenda et propter se contemnenda, molestias temporales et a se posse inperari et propter se debere tolerari." (*Contra Faustum XXII* 79 (footnote 24], 680). See also the conflict with the Manicheans in Confessiones III 7,13–14, where Saint Augustine explains that the same notion of justice can allow for permission as well as prohibition, depending on the circumstances and the context.

pire to His heavenly kingdom by renouncing material goods rather than fighting wars in quest of them. To Saint Augustine, the divine war commands of the Old Testament belong to an era that has long been overcome. The birth of Christ initiated a new era, the final stage of the human story that ultimately proclaims the necessity of patience and a doctrine of peace.

4 Christians as Soldiers

May a Christian become a soldier and fight in a just war? According to Saint Augustine, he doubtlessly may do so if he is led by patience and benevolence. The military service shall only be open to moral and pious men, for they will not only bring about just peace through minimal use of violence, but they are also less susceptible to hatred and revenge when fighting the enemy.[37] Saint Augustine thus puts a great deal of faith in Christian military leaders such as Marcellinus, Bonifatius and Darius.[38]

It becomes more complex when a Christian soldier serves under a heathen king. With reference to Paul (Rom 13,1) Saint Augustine claims that the soldier is obliged to obey:

"There is no authority except that which God has established. The authorities that exist have been established by God."

There are, however, exceptions. Saint Augustine writes:

"If a just man serves under a heathen king he can act under his orders without committing a violation against justice by helping to protect the public order of peace and as long as the command of God is not violated or if it is not certain if the command of God is violated. It is possible that, by his orders, the king may turn into the culprit, but the chain of command is evidence of the soldier's innocence.[39]

37 See Weissenberg, *Friedenslehre* (footnote 9), 407.

38 Saint Augustine praises him because he negotiated a peace agreement with the Vandals instead of fighting against them; see Epistula 229,2. In *S. Aureli Augustini Hipponiensis Episcopi Epistulae Pars IV.* Pub. Al. Goldbacher. (CSEL 57), (Vienna/Leipzig: 1911), 497 f.

39 "Non est enim potestas nisi a Deo (Rom 13,1), sive iubente sive sinente. Cum ergo vir iustus, si forte rub rege homine etiam sacrilego militet, recte poscit illo iubente bellare civicae pacis ordinis servus; cui quod iubetur, vel non esse contra Dei praeceptum certum est, vel ultrum sit, certum non est, ita ut fortasse reum regem faciat iniquitas imperandi, innocentem autem militem ostendat ordo serviendi." (*Contra Faustum XXII* 75) (footnote 24), 673 f.

The function of the state to promote and protect peace and order is to be respected even if it involves fighting on the side of a heathen king. The refusal to do so is permitted, and at the same time required, if the orders of the king contradict the commandments of God. This is always the case when they openly contravene the Christian doctrine by, for example, proclaiming idolatry. Saint Augustine writes the following about the Christian soldiers in the army of the heathen Emperor Julian:

> Christian soldiers served under the unfaithful king. When it came to Christ, they only recognised God, who resides in heaven. As long as the king ordered them to worship idols, to burn incense they preferred God over him. As soon as he said: Pull your sword, fight that people – they obeyed. They differentiated between the eternal master and the finite master, and yet they were, for the sake of the eternal master, subordinate to the finite master.[40]

Unfortunately, Saint Augustine does not provide his readers with more concrete reasons for disobedience. One can only assume that blatantly felonious and unjust wars violate the commandments of God, thus allowing a Christian soldier to disobey.

Saint Augustine regards the participation of Christians in the state-sanctioned use of violence as reasonable, be it directed at criminals or in the context of just wars. He holds a more strict view, though, when it comes to the individual citizen. The law does permit the killing of a thief who has attacked a traveller, or the murder of a rapist out of self-defence. Saint Augustine asks, however, whether the taking of another man's life simply to protect one's property or physical integrity can be reconciled with the true hierarchy of values.[41] Saint Augustine appeals to Christians to analyse the Sermon on the Mount not only in relation to 'praeparatio cordis', but also in relation to their actions. Any criminal offender will thus understand by the reaction of his victim how little worth worldly goods contain and, ultimately, evil will be defeated by good. Henceforth, Saint Augustine distinguishes between the Christian as a public figure (emperor, military leader, soldier, etc.) and the Christian as a private

---

40 "Milites christiani servierunt imperatori infideli; ubi veniebatur ad causam Christi, non agnoscebant nisi illum qui in caelo erat. Si quando volebat ut idola colerent, ut thurificarent, praeponebant illi deum; quando autem dicebat; producite aciem, ite contra illam gentem, statim obtemperabant. Distinguebant dominum aeternum a domino temporali; et tamen subditi errant propter dominum aeternum, etiam domino temporali." Enarrationes in Psalmos 124,7. In *Sancti Aurelii Augustini Enarrationes in Psalmos CI-CL*. Pub. Eligius Dekkers/Johannes Fraipont (CCL 40), (Tournhout: 1956), 1841 f.
41 See *De libero arbitrio I* 9–13 (footnote 3), 9–15.

person. Both, of course, are concerned with the betterment of the unjust, and both shall act out of love, not hatred. Evil must not be retaliated with evil. However, he, who acts on behalf of the law, may apply violence and, as a last resort, kill, for he is obliged to fulfil the function of the state to promote and protect peace and order. Conversely, the private man, who does not have to fulfil such a function, must implement the Sermon on the Mount in a more literal and direct fashion.

5 The Donatist Conflict: 'Compelle intrare' as the Origin of the Religious war?

We must differentiate between the religious war of one state against another and the question of religious legislation within the Roman Empire. Saint Augustine acknowledges the capacity of the emperor to make religious legislation. According to Saint Augustine, the Christian emperors, especially Theodosius, rightly criminalised and punished idolatry, such as public acts of heathen worship.[42]

The case of the Donatist schism is different. It occurred within the Empire and under Christian rule. After some struggle, Saint Augustine supported the state-sanctioned measures designed to repatriate the Donatists into the Catholic Church.[43]

The Donatist schism occurred during the first decade of the fourth century. Of contentious theological nature was the different understanding of the church and the sacraments. According to the Donatists, the validity of the sacrament depended on the moral integrity of the donator. According to the Catholic Church, however, it stemmed from the virtue of Jesus Christ. The Donatists considered the church as the community of those true and pure Christians, who were willing to die as martyrs.

---

42 Saint Augustine welcomes the imperatorial prohibitions of heathen worship that were repeatedly passed since the year 399 (see Robert Dodaro, "Auseinandersetzung mit dem Heidentum." In *Augustin Handbuch,* ed. Henning Drecoll, (Tübingen: 2007), 203–205. However, these prohibitions do not qualify as a religious war, but as administrative measures. Regarding Saint Augustine's perspectives on Judaism see Thomas Raveaux, *Augustin und die Juden.* In ibid., 212–218. Saint Augustine opposes the use of violence against Jews, as they propagate the Old Testament, which, according to Saint Augustine, reveals the truth about Christianity around the globe.

43 See Ernst Ludwig Grasmück, "Coercitio: Staat und Kirche im Donatistenstreit." *Bonner historische Forschung*, vol. 22, (Bonn: 1964).

Their opponents, especially Saint Augustine, stressed that the church encompassed the whole world and harboured both good and evil, which will be eschatologically separated just as the net filled with 153 fishes (John 21, 1–4) was laid out before the Lord. Another point of contention was the consecration of Bishop Caecilian of Cathargo in 312. The opponents of Caecilian claimed that the consecration was invalid, as the bishops involved in it had allegedly handed over books and items of worship to the state during the Diocletianic prosecution of Christians ('traditores'). This group consecrated a different Bishop, Majorinus, who was soon succeeded by Donatius whom the movement was named after. The Donatists turned to Emperor Constantine, who, however, was more inclined towards the Catholic Church. In the time to come, more and more imperatorial edicts against the Donatists were passed, most of which, however, were not implemented. Only Emperor Julian (Apostata) supported the Donatists, probably in order to promote his pagan restoration policy through a schism of the Christian Church. Donatism remained confined to North Africa, where it flourished and temporarily constituted the main religion in spite of the imperatorial edicts. The so-called Circumcellions posed yet another challenge. They were a group composed of the socially and economically disadvantaged rural population, who, on the one hand, were the ideological foundation of Donatism. On the other hand, they were a burden to the Donatist Church because of the numerous violent attacks they committed against Catholic priests and bishops. Donatists and Circumcellions maimed and murdered, stole and ousted clerics from their churches.

The Catholic side appealed to the state to persecute and punish the perpetrators of these crimes. Rather critical, however, was the question whether the mere belonging to the Donatist Church should be punished as a crime in order to pressure Donatists into returning to the Catholic faith.

During Saint Augustine's lifetime, some Donatists argued that state power had nothing to do with religious matters and could thus not be used against them by the Catholics. Neither the Gospels nor the Letters of the New Testament contained a case in which the church turned to an earthly king in order to conquer its opponents.[44] According to Saint Augustine, however, this was because there actually were no Christian kings in New Testament times the church could have appealed to. Conversely,

---

44 Epistula 93,9. In *S. Aureli Augustini Hipponiensis Episcopi Epistulae*. Pars II. Pub. Al. Goldbacher (CSEL 34), (Vienna/Leipzig: 1989), 453 f.

the Old Testament contained examples of how kings used their power for the true faith.[45] Thanks to the Christian emperors of the Roman Empire, the prophesy of Psalm 72,11 – "And let all kings bow down before him, All nations serve him" – had come true. The appeal of the Catholics to the emperor was just biblically justifiable. According to Saint Augustine, the emperor was indeed responsible for religious matters. He was to punish sacrilege and prosecute the infidelity to God to the same extent that he prosecuted marital infidelity.[46] Nonetheless, Saint Augustine opposed religious coercion within his North African episcopate. He wanted to win people over by means of argument and disputation. His reasons for doing so were both of a principled and a pragmatic nature. Saint Augustine principally believed that no one can be good against his will. Nobody can be coerced into being righteous,[47] for the ultimate truth can only be accepted voluntarily. Of a rather pragmatic nature is his argument that a forced unification of Donatists and Catholics would ultimately result in the transformation of heretics into false Catholics, who avowed themselves to the Catholic faith not out of conviction but in order to eschew state-sanctioned punishment.[48]

Whereas the older bishops pledged for religious coercion, Saint Augustine and the younger bishops, who made up the majority, opposed them. This situation remained the same until the year 404 when the regional bishops sent a delegate to Emperor Honorius with the plea to apply the Theodosian heretics laws to Donatist bishops in order to prevent violent attacks against Catholic clerics. Saint Augustine wanted to ensure that Catholic priests could preach freely and that those Donatists, who were willing to convert, did not have to fear acts of retaliation.[49] Theodosius had intended to impose a fee of 10 pounds of gold on every heretic bishop.[50] Supported by the majority of his bishops, Saint

---

45   For example, Nebukadnezar II. in Dan. 3,1–21; 91–96; see also Epistula 185,19 (footnote 38), 17 f.

46   Epistula 185,20 (footnote 38), 18. Saint Augustine points out that the Donatists themselves repeatedly turned to the state in order to solve questions concerning the church. At the beginning of the schism they turned to Emperor Constantine, then to Emperor Julian, when they wanted to get his support to overcome the inner-Donatist schism and force dissidents to repatriate.

47   See Epistula 93,5; 16 (footnote 44), 449 f.; 461.

48   See Epistula 93,17 (footnote 44), 461 f.; Epistula 185,25 (footnote 38), 23 f.

49   See Epistula 185,24 (footnote 44), 461 f.; Epistula 185,25 (footnote 38), 22 f.

50   See Codes Theodosianus 16,5,2. In *Theodosiani libri XVI cvm constitvtionibvs Sirmondianis et Leges novella ad Theodosian*, vol. 1,2, *Codex Theodosianus. Textus cum apparatu.* Pub. Theodor Mommsen (Berlin: 1963), 862–863.

Augustine wanted to persuade the emperor to impose the same fee on those Donatist bishops and clerics whose parishes were prone to attacks against Catholics. Saint Augustine thus pled for an imperatorial guarantee for unrestricted religious practice for Catholics.

The emperor had, however, already taken action before the delegate reached the imperial court. In response to a complaint filed by the Catholic bishop Maximianus of Bagai, who had been ousted from his church and abused by Donatists, the emperor had promulgated a law that classified the Donatist schism as heresy because of the baptismal re-enactment. Any person who agreed to a second christening would lose all of his or her assets, and the places of Donatist worship would go to the state. Anyone who underwent a second christening or approved of it by remaining in the community of Donatists was prohibited from signing any form of contract and, consequently, from making a legally binding will. State authorities were charged a penal fee of 20 pounds of gold if they did not implement the new laws.[51] These laws criminalised the belonging to the Donatist Church and thus coerced Donatists into returning to the Catholic faith. Punishment consisted of dispossession and expulsion only. Torture or capital punishment was not applied.

After Emperor Honorius had implemented the new law in North Africa in 405, Saint Augustine changed his opinion and supported the imperatorial decree. Once again we have to distinguish between his pragmatic and principled contemplations. Contrary to his initial concerns, the new law did not produce a vast number of false Catholics. Saint Augustine was under the impression that many Donatists welcomed the op-

---

51 See Grasmück, *Coercitio* (footnote 43), 203. In the year 407, more imperatorial edicts against Manicheans, Priscillianists, and heathens were to follow. Heathen temples were to be deprived of their revenues. Idols had to be removed. Altars were destroyed and the celebration of heathen holidays was prohibited. In 409, Emperor Honorius, however, passed an edict of tolerance, that was applied to both heathens and Donatists. In 410, this edict was revoked and the former anti-Donatist laws put in place again. At the same time, a religious dialogue between the Catholics and the Donatists was initiated. In 411, Honorius passed a law that imposed a penal fee on those who refused to renounce the Donatist faith. The amount of the fee depended on the status of the offender. Illustres had to pay 50 pounds of gold, senators 30 pounds, plebei 5 pounds and Circumcellions 10 pounds of silver. Women had to pay an extra fee. If a person refused to pay, he or she lost all of her assets. Slaves had to endure beatings if they refused to repatriate into the Catholic Church. All Donatist clerics were expelled from North Africa and their churches and property were turned over to the Catholic Church.

portunity to return to the Catholic faith without having to fear violent acts of retaliation. Thus, whole cities, including Saint Augustine's home town Thagaste, converted to Catholicism.

Saint Augustine held on to his belief that nobody could be coerced into being good and accepting the truth, for true creed always rested upon true conviction and could thus not be externally imposed. It remained unquestionable that bringing men and women closer to God through doctrine ('doctrina') was ultimately more rewarding and worthwhile than coercing them through punishment and fear. However, the fact that indoctrination was more appropriate did not necessarily mean that the threat of punishment was futile.[52] For fear could serve as an occasion for one who – due to his upbringing, for example – remained ignorant of the truth to search for the truth. Many Donatists explained that they did not know the truth but had begun aspiring to it in the wake of the implementation of the new laws. There were, of course, also those who already knew the truth, but bad habit kept them from living in accordance with it.[53] Fear could inspire to give up 'animositas',[54] overcome habit[55] and translate the knowledge of the truth into action.[56] Although Saint Augustine considers friendliness and patience to be more appropriate educational tools, fear must not be underestimated according to him. It is, however, only a temporary solution, for the ultimate goal of the indoctrination is the discovery of one's love for moral good, and love is irreconcilable with fear; in fact, perfect love conquers fear.[57]

Saint Augustine offers biblical evidence relating to his conviction that verbal indoctrination does not always suffice but must occasionally be complemented by threat or use of violence. Saint Augustine quotes the following biblical passages: "The stubborn slave will not change through words; for even if he understands them, he will not obey."[58] This slave is coerced into obedience through a beating. Or: 'Do not spare the knave a beating. If you beat him with a stick he will not die.'[59] Moreover, while

---

52 Epistula 185,21 (footnote 38), 19 f.
53 Epistula 93,18 (footnote 44), 462 f.
54 Epistula 93,16 (footnote 44), 461.
55 Epistula 185,18 (footnote 38), 16 f.
56 Epistula 185,21 (footnote 38), 19 f.
57 1 Joh 4,18; Epistula 185,21 (footnote 38), 19 f.
58 "Verbis non emendabitur servus durus; si enim intellexerit, non obediet." (Proverbs 29,19; Epistula 185,21 (footnote 38), 20).
59 "Tu quidem percutis eum virga, animam vero eius liberabis a morte." (Proverbs 23,13; Epistula 185,21 (footnote 38), 20).

Christ admonished Peter and the other disciples only verbally, he did not only speak to Saul but pushed him to the ground and blinded him in order to turn him into Paul (see Acts 9,1–21).[60] Finally, Saint Augustine invokes the parable of the feast (Luke 14,15–24), in which the host politely issues an invitation. When his invitation is ignored, he sends off his servants with the order: Force them to enter – "compelle intrare"[61] – in order to better those whose stubbornness could not be conquered by words through severity and castigation ('aliquantula severitate disciplinae').

The ultimate goal of the state-sanctioned use of force against the Donatists is the same as the goal of a just war, namely the 'correctio' of one's opponents. Nonetheless, one cannot deduce from the case of the Donatists that Saint Augustine considers opposing religious beliefs as a just cause to declare war. Thus, the coercion of the Donatists does not qualify as a religious war but as an administrative measure consisting of the imposition of fines and exile. The Donatist schism could not have served as a ground for just war. However, Saint Augustine did see in it an imperative for police action.

---

60 More examples can be found in John 6,44: "No one can come to me unless the Father who sent me draws him", as well as the expulsion of Hagar and her son Ismael by Abraham's wife Sara (Gen. 21,9–21). In Saint Augustine's exegesis Sara and Isaac embody the spiritual human being, Hagar and Ismael represent the physical human being.
61 Epistula 185,24 (footnote 38), 19 f.; 22 f.; Epistula 93,5 (footnote 44), 430.

Thomas Aquinas and Humanitarian Intervention*

Gerhard Beestermöller

> "Rescue the poor: and deliver the
> needy out of the hand of the sinner"
> (Ps. 82:4).

This passage from the Psalms occupies a central place in the Thomist doctrine of war. Aquinas uses it to justify (at least this is my thesis) the obligation of Christian princes to stand up for the rights of Christians beyond the reach of Christian jurisdiction if these Christians are unable to receive any legal protection from the authorities directly in charge. Thomas reads the passage as a direct, divine instruction to the princes: "Hence [in the Psalm] it is said to those who are in authority: 'Rescue ...'"

The Thomist doctrine of just war, accordingly, cannot be captured using our categories of war and intervention. The decisive variable shaping political order in our modern thinking, the state, does not loom on the medieval horizon. For Thomas, rather, the decisive political unit is represented by the respublica fidelium, the political-secular unit of Christendom. The task of the Christian princes is to protect Christendom as a whole and its individual members. This task can include taking action against heathen princes if, for example, they attack Christendom, or if they do not guarantee proper legal protection to Christians within their jurisdiction. The ultimate thrust of the Thomist bellum-iustum doctrine is, in this respect, an interventionist ethic – as understood in the categories of political order from his time.

Developing this thesis has presented a kind of intellectual travelogue for me personally. In 1990 I submitted my dissertation on the Thomist doctrine of war.[1] During the time I was working on the dissertation, hardly anyone gave any thought to the collapse of the Eastern bloc and the dissolution of the Soviet Union, in other words, to the disappearance

---

* First published in German in: Nils Goldschmidt et al. (eds.), *Die Zukunft der Familie und deren Gefährdungen. Norbert Glatzel zum 65. Geburtstag,* (Münster: Lit-Verlag, 2002), 401–419; trans. Jeremiah Riemer.

1 Gerhard Beestermöller, *Thomas von Aquin und der gerechte Krieg. Friedensethik im theologischen Kontext der Summa Theologiae* (Bachem: 1990).

of the parameters defining the Cold War order. It was certainly not apparent that the period of the "classic type of war, where regular armies of hostile states fight against each other" was drawing to a close and that "in its place" there would be an increase in "violent conflicts within states" that would be "sharp in number, duration, and intensity."[2]

At that time I had thought about (though without really thinking this through to the end) an interpretation that tried to construe the Thomist doctrine of the just war beyond our understanding of war as a large-scale, cross-national, bellicose conflict. It was not until NATO's military action against Yugoslavia in the spring of 1999 raised questions about the ethics of law – questions of who, when, and to what end (relevant to the protection of fundamental humanitarian goods) militarily intervention in another state may be justified – that my eyes were opened more widely to the matter of Thomist war doctrine (without excluding, needless to say, subsequent progress in our understanding of just war).

1 "In order for a war to be just, three things are necessary."

The crucial Thomist text about the conduct of war may be found in that section of the Summa Theologiae[3] that one might, somewhat anachronistically, characterize as applied ethics (Sth II-II). Here Aquinas treats the subject in the context of the God-given virtue of love of God and of one's neighbor. He is dealing with the question of whether conducting a war contradicts or is in keeping with this love.

In order for a war to be just, according to Thomas, it requires approval from the authority of the prince (or what the standard English Dominican translation calls the "supreme authority"), a just cause, and the right intention of the belligerents. The content of these demands frequently imposes puzzles on the literature. That is why, in the following remarks, I will be citing the Thomist text more comprehensively, relying here on the standard (English Dominican) translation.

2　Sekretariat der Deutschen Bischofskonferenz (Ed.), *Gerechter Friede: 27. September 2000.* (Die deutschen Bischöfe 66) (Bonn 2000).

3　Beestermöller (1990), 58–61.

1.1 Those in (supreme) authority (the princes)

In the interpretation of the first criterion we find the key to understanding the two others. On this point Thomas explains:

"In order for a war to be just, three things are necessary. First, the authority of the sovereign (auctoritas principis) by whose command the war is to be waged. For it is not the business of a private individual to declare war, because he can seek for redress of his rights from the tribunal of his superior. Moreover it is not the business of a private individual to summon together the people (multitudo), which has to be done in wartime. And as the care of the common weal (respublica) is committed to those who are in authority (principibus), it is their business to watch over the common weal of the city (civitas), kingdom (regnum) or province (provincia) subject to them. And just as it is lawful for them to have recourse to the sword in defending that common weal against internal disturbances (interiores quidem perturbatores), when they punish evil-doers, according to the words of the Apostle (Romans 13:4): 'He beareth not the sword in vain: for he is God's minister, an avenger to execute wrath upon him that doth evil'; so too, it is their business to have recourse to the sword of war in defending the common weal against external enemies. Hence it is said to those who are in authority (Psalm 81:4): 'Rescue the poor: and deliver the needy out of the hand of the sinner'; and for this reason Augustine says (Contra Faust. xxii, 75): 'The natural order (ordo naturalis) conducive to peace among mortals demands that the power to declare and counsel war should be in the hands of those who hold the supreme authority (principes).'"[4]

According to a widespread reading, Thomas prohibits the "private citizen" from protecting his rights with force, since he can "make an effort to obtain a judgment from a higher authority." But since states are not subject to any "higher-ranking legal authority,"[5] resort to force is all that is left to the state in order to defend itself against injustice. "The government's mission and duty is to protect the common weal against sinners from the outside."[6]

This interpretation poses three problems. Two are of a nature intrinsic to the text. It is, first of all, not clear why Thomas invokes two different Biblical passages (Romans 13 and Psalm 82) for the safeguarding of rights and the external defense of the state. "[F]or his line of argument

---

4   Sth II-II, q. 40, a. 1, resp.
5   Paulus Engelhardt, "Die Lehre vom gerechten Krieg in der vorreformatorischen und katholischen Tradition." In Reiner Steinweg (Ed.), *Der gerechte Krieg: Christentum, Islam, Marxismus*, (Suhrkamp: 1980) 72–184, 85.
6   Ernst-Josef Nagel, *Friedensförderung im Gesamtkontext der kirchlichen Friedenslehre* In Ernst-Josef Nagel (Ed.), *Dem Krieg zuvorkommen. Christliche Friedensethik und Politik* (Herder: 1984) 7–35, 19.

follows a common principle," namely "the protective function against internal and external threats to the common weal."[7] Secondly, one cannot identify any explanation for why Thomas uses the corroborative "quidem" instead of an explanatory "qua".

In terms of content, there is the problem that Thomas (if one follows this interpretation) would be legitimating a kind of international right to wage feuds without showing any prospect for overcoming such a right to feuding. Is it conceivable, for Thomas, that supernatural love would acquiesce in such a world order?

The fundamental problem with this interpretation is that the modern category of the state is being read into the Thomist text. The following observations, however, speak against this present-day projection back onto the medieval outlook. In the just quoted q. 40, a. 4 resp., Aquinas talks about the "respublica fidelium," in other words, about the political unit of the faithful encompassing the entirety of Christendom. Furthermore, one notices a flaw in the translation, minor at first glance, in the above-cited passage invoking the authority of the princes. The English version of Aquinas translates "*materialis gladius*" as "*sword*". But in this translation the allusion to the medieval two-swords doctrine ceases to apply. The proper background becomes tangible again in Sth II-II, q. 40 a. 2. ad 1, where it says that prelates should "*not ... [be] having recourse themselves to material arms (materialibus armis)*", but should rely instead on the secular authorities or princes.

In the horizon of the medieval orbis christianus, then, the quote from Augustine at the end of Thomas's remarks on authorization for waging war also acquires a new dimension of depth, with Aquinas getting around to a discussion of the ordo naturalis along the lines of the Church Father The issue for Thomas (this is where my interpretation is heading) is the authority of Christian princes outside the orbis christianus on the basis of universal human reason. Thomas is not, therefore, dealing with the question: Under what conditions may one state wage a war against another? Rather he wants to legitimate the Crusades, which in his day was regarded as a "*bellum iustissimum*".[8]

The Thomist line of argument may be divided into two parts. The first part deals with the question of why waging war is not a matter

---

7   Thomas Hoppe, *Friedenspolitik mit militärischen Mitteln: Eine ethische Analyse strategischer Ansätze* (Bachem: 1986), 19 ff.

8   Frederick H. Russell, *The Just War in the Middle Ages* (Cambridge University Press: 1975), 199.

for a private individual. The second step establishes the war-waging authority of the princes. Let us being with the second.

1.1 In his argument in favor of the princes' authority to wage war, Thomas answers two questions: Why may Christian princes act against heathen princes (1.1.1.)? How is the unity of authority in the office of the prince preserved in view of a multitude of office holders (1.1.2.)?

1.1.1 The argument begins with the sentence *"And as the care of the common weal ..."* and goes on, by the end of the section, to discuss the war-waging power of the prince (the "supreme authority"). In order to develop my interpretation, I must first put forward some thetic assertions so that the issue as a whole may be recognized, and then I shall work through the argument in detail. The problem Thomas confronts emerges from his schema of levels concerning nature and grace. Grace surpasses not only the nature of the individual human being but also that of the community. The problem with this approach is that Thomas wants to link together two different sets of order or regulation that cannot so easily be made congruent with each other.

Thus the regulating principle of nature is territory, whereas the ordering principle of grace is confession or belief. The two elements happen to coincide in the idea of the Occident as orbis christianus.[9] But Christians living under heathen rule constitute a problem. Here the two principles move apart. Thomas wants to show that the Christian prince, on the basis of the worldly sword he wields owing to his confession of faith, has the right and the duty to safeguard the rights of Christians on the fiefdom of heathen princes if the latter fail to do so.

The argument for the text just cited may be reconstructed as follows: Christian princes have been entrusted with responsibility for the *"respublica fidelium"*[10] in its entirety. This assignment includes protecting order in the component parts of Christendom – city, kingdom – and, beyond that, in subjugated provinces.

This responsibility also includes the obligation to act against one of these political sub-units when it no longer serves the public welfare of Christendom as a whole, but only its own interests. This is precisely the issue at stake when Thomas speaks of the princes acting against *"interiores quidem perturbatores"*. The term *"interiores"* refers to the "principes," not to the city or the kingdom. To defend the *"respublica fidelium"*

---

9 I am leaving out the entire problem of the Jews living in the Occident.
10 Sth II-II, q. 40, a. 4., resp.

in this comprehensive sense, namely against those who commit injustice, the princes wield the gladius materialis of the Church.

At this point a question is bound to strike the reader of today: Is the issue here legitimating a war or an intervention? In other words, are the princes permitted to defend their special sphere of accountability against attacks from somebody else in their circle, or might they even be required to intervene in the other party's domain if he has failed to discharge his office properly at home? But Thomas does not actually make this distinction between home and abroad within Christendom. He is only concerned about whether princes act against one of their own if that other party, in whatever manner, *disturbs the peace of Christendom.*

Up to this point Thomas is still not drawing any conclusions; instead he merely introduces something hardly controversial as an argument for what he will conclude. The conclusion consists in a kind of argument by analogy. Thomas reaches it by indicating the rationale for why Christian princes may gain authority over another one of their own should that other prince be creating disorder rather than order. This ratio is found in the citation from Paul (Romans 13). The basic meaning of the power of the sword per se consists in taking action, in the name of God, against those who "do evil." When, in other words, a Christian prince does evil, he ipso facto falls under the Church's power of the sword, which is there in order to act against injustice. Thereby a prince who is a perpetrator of injustice falls under the authority of the others.

This line of argument (and this is crucial) is not tied to Christian belief and therefore not to the domestic territory of the "*respublica fidelium*". For non-Christians are also moral subjects who can distinguish between good and evil at the level of natural morality and who commit crimes that need to be punished. Hence there is also authority of lordship outside of faith. In just this way it is also possible for rulers outside of Christendom to fail in exercising the duties of their office and then become subject eo ipso to the official authority of other princes.

This brings the third question, the sword of war, into view. Just as the Christian prince has responsibility for defending the "*respublica fidelium*" against other Christian princes, he also has to defend this respublica against heathen princes. At this point, the distinction between defending the respublica as a whole against external attacks and standing up for individual Christians who are suffering injustice in the fiefdom of heathens where the heathen princes do not provide justice becomes a relevant distinction for Thomas. This is so because, for Thomas, Christian princes are not obligated, on the basis of their office grounded in a confessional order, to provide comprehensive subsidiary legal protection inside heathen territories: "*Wars are lawful and just in so far as they protect the poor and the entire common weal from suffering at the hands of the foe.*"[11]

When Christian princes wage war against heathen rulers, there is just as little injustice done to the heathen rulers as to Christian rulers who do not attend to the duties of their office. The only issue is what "*the natural order (ordo naturalis) conducive to peace among mortals*" demands and which is therefore binding on all human beings.

The key to this exegesis is supplied by the interpretation of "*interiores quidem perturbatores*" ("internal disturbances"), which I should like to render as "one's peers, who prove to be troublemakers themselves." Two things need to be demonstrated for the sake of my interpretation. First, I must make good on my assertion that, for Thomas, the princes have, so to speak, a collective responsibility for all of Christendom. When this has been demonstrated, secondly, it can be shown that it is reasonable to apply the category "*interiores*" not to the inhabitants of cities, kingdoms, or provinces, but to princes ("those who in authority" in the English Dominican translation).

a) The crucial sentence at issue here reads like this in the Latin original: "*Cum autem cura reipublicae commissa sit principibus, ad eos pertinet rem publicam civitatis vel regni seu provinciae sibi subditae tueri.*" (Sth II-II, q.40, a.1, resp.)

The English Dominican translation renders this as follows: "*And as the care of the common weal is committed to those who are in authority, it is their business to watch over the common weal of the city, kingdom or province subject to them.*"

The translation suggests a presumption that there is a plurality of different respublicae – city, kingdom, province – each of which is subject to the authority of a prince who is responsible for maintaining public order. Initial doubts about this translation, and hence about the interpretation, are raised by the sentence's very construction. The translation has "sibi subditae" referring not only to the provinces, but also to the city and the kingdom. That is, at the very least, not compelling.

Militating against this translation and exegesis are three passages in which Thomas reveals, almost in passing, what he means by "*respublica,*" "*unitas,*" "*multitudo,*" "*populus,*" "*civitas,*" and "*regnum.*" The first passage immediately precedes the sentence from q. 40 to be interpreted here.

---

11 Sth II-II, q. 40. a. 2., obj. 1.

It is "*not the business of a private individual to summon together the people [multitudinem, accusative for multitudo], which has to be done in wartime.*"

If it were correct to interpret the city or the kingdom as a self-con-
tained respublica, then each would have a "multitudo" of its own. But
militating against this interpretation is the following quote: "*Sedition is
contrary to the unity of the multitude (multitudo), viz. the people (populus)
of a city (civitas)*[12] *or kingdom (regnum).*"[13] [See Note 14 for Latin terms
in their original declensions.]

There is, therefore, an overarching multitudo of the respublica. The
populus of the city and of the kingdom are parts of this multitudo, so
that the city and the kingdom are part of the respublica. If things
reach the point of sedition in a populus, then this amounts to sedition
in the entire respublica. Ultimately it is not the city or the kingdom
that is summoned to war, but the multitudo of the respublica.

Which respublica is meant here? At this point, the third passage continues:

> "*Sedition differs from schism in two respects. First, because schism is opposed to
> the spiritual unity of the multitude, viz. ecclesiastical unity, whereas sedition is
> contrary to the temporal or secular unity of the multitude, for instance of a city or
> kingdom. Secondly, ...*"[14]

Here Thomas is talking about the unity of Christendom. Spiritually, this
finds institutional expression in the overarching unity of the ecclesia. It is
the same unity (or entity) of christianitas, and not a natural-political entity with which people affiliate by joining forces, not manifested in a political institution, but which instead is subdivided into city and kingdom.
For humankind outside of Christendom may constitute a unity grounded
in nature, but not a secular-temporal unity. A second argument points in
the same direction. If Thomas were not speaking of Christendom here,
then the reference to city and kingdom would have a different status in
the logic of argumentation. Thomas would then no longer be naming
the basic categories one finds to denote the orbis christianus. He
would, rather, be representing the thesis that there are more elements

---

12   For reasons that are incomprehensible, the German edition of Thomas (DThA)
     translates "civitas" here as "Staat" ("state") rather than (as it does elsewhere) as
     "Stadt" ("city").
13   "Seditio opponitur unitati multitudinis, idest populi, civitatis vel regni" (Sth II-
     II, q. 42, a. 2, resp.).
14   Sth II-II, q. 42, a. 1, ad 2. English Dominican translation.

of political order than just cities and kingdoms, without providing a rationale for this thesis.

It is manifest, therefore, that the respublica whose responsibility is assigned to the princes, and whose multitudo is summoned to war, designates the "*respublica fidelium*"[15] as a whole. It follows that the princes have responsibility for the respublica christiana in its totality. This point is also supported by the way that city and kingdom, both in this passage and in q. 42, are mentioned in the singular. Thomas designates the basic categories in which the respublica realizes itself, a respublica to which, in its totality, no single institution corresponds. Hence, responsibility for the respublica of believers in Christ is manifested in care or concern for the elements in which it subsists. It follows that the "*interiores*", who demarcate the radius of the materialis gladius, do not refer to the citizens of a particular polity, but to all Christians.

One question, admittedly, remains open. Why, in the last two passages just cited, does the concept "*provincia*" not appear, a concept found in q. 40? A province could mean a sphere of accountability outside the christianitas, in other words beyond that domain in which Christianity has come to power completely. What province might Thomas have had in mind? The Crusader states with their significant Muslim populations? Or the territories in the east that were transferred to the Teutonic Knights in order to conduct missionary work there?[16] One may also ask if Thomas was not thinking about several provinces. In that case, province as well as city and kingdom would have been introduced as basic categories of which there are several examples. These questions need not be answered conclusively here.

b) If respublica does not refer to the parceled-out entities of city and kingdom, then an entirely different light is also cast on the formulation "*interiores quidem perturbatores.*" The conventional interpretation sees this formulation referring to the citizens of a city or kingdom to the extent that they commit a breach of the peace. This interpretation cannot be sustained after what has just been explained. Only two possibilities re-

---

15 Sth II-II, q. 40, a. 4., resp.

16 "Frederick II's Golden Bull of Rimini (1226) authorized the [Teutonic] Order to exercise sovereign rule in the territory to be conquered, and the Grand Master became an Imperial Prince. The Order's land '[as] right and possession of St. Peter's' was 'given over to the Order for eternal and free ownership' by Gregory IX (1234)." Hans Wolter, *Der Kampf der Kurie um die Führung im Abendland (1216 bis 1274)*, In *Handbuch der Kirchengeschichte*, Vol. III / 2, 2nd ed., Hubert Jedin (Ed.) (Herder: 1985) 273–296, 280.

main. The term "*interiores*" refers either to all citizens or to the princes. In the first instance the reference group would be the "*multitudo*", in the second case the "*principes*".

In favor of the first variant is the way that Thomas occasionally uses the concept "*perturbare*" in a general sense to mean a breach of law.[17] In opposition to this interpretation is the use of "*quidem.*" This would not make sense if referring to all Christians. Thomas would then have used a "*qua*" – that is, he would have written "*interiores qua perturbatores.*" In terms of content, the ultimate thrust of the entire line of argument, to legitimate an intervention into the sovereign territory of heathen princes, would not apply if "interiores" were understood to mean the personae privatae of Christendom.

One argument that can be advanced on behalf of the second variant, namely the interpretation of the "*interiores*" as princes, is that "*quidem*" as used here can be well understood as a corroborating "the princes for their part." One then also reaches the conclusion that the Christian prince can act against heathen princes in the same way he would act against his (Christian) peers should they abuse their office.

Another point in favor of this interpretation is Thomist linguistic usage surrounding q. 40. In q. 42 "perturbatio" designates disturbing a government or rule: "*[T]here is no sedition (seditio) in disturbing (perturbatio) a government of this kind (…a tyrannical government)… Indeed it is the tyrant rather that is guilty of sedition (seditiosus).*" Tyrants are therefore the real "*perturbators*" who disturb their own rule. A tyranny is distinguished by being "*directed, not to the common good, but to the private good of the ruler*".[18]

This interpretation finds additional confirmation in Article 2 of quaestio 40, where Thomas asks if clerics may perform military service. The answer is negative. Clergy may not have "*recourse themselves to material arms*"; instead they have the materialis gladius. But this does not mean that they only defend the herd when it is oppressed in a spiritual regard. They also use their own weapons – "*salutations, devout prayers, and … excommunication*" – to act against "*the pillager and the oppressor*".[19]

---

17 "For the end of human law is the temporal tranquility of the state (temporalis tranquillitas civitatis), which end law effects by directing external actions, as regards those evils which might disturb (perturbare) the peaceful condition of the state." Sth I-II, q. 98, a. 1, resp.

18 Sth II-II, q. 42, a. 2, ad 3.

19 Sth II-II, q. 40, a. 2, ad 1.

By mentioning *"the pillager and the oppressor"*, Thomas is picking up on the distinction between the two swords. The gladius materialis is directed against tyrants who oppress the herd from within, the *"gladius bellicus"* against the tyrants who oppress the herd from without.

To sum up, the Thomist argument may be outlined this way: Whoever shares the view that the Christian prince is responsible not only for safeguarding the law within Christendom as a whole, but also vis-à-vis his (Christian) peers, cannot also ignore the argument that the job of defending sovereign Christian territory externally also includes responsibility for obtaining justice for Christians wherever they encounter injustice under heathen rule. Though this does pose the question of who has binding authority to decide when a prince is abusing his authority.

1.1.2. One of the difficult questions posed by the Thomist doctrine of just war entails the manner in which spiritual power is involved in the conduct of just wars. There is a host of reasons indicating that just wars always constitute a collaborative or community action.[20] Q. 40 already points in this direction. To begin with, there is the term *"materialis gladius"*, which refers to the worldly power of the Church.

Worldly power according to Thomas, furthermore, is subordinated to spiritual power *"even as the body is subject to the soul"*[21] in everything that involves human salvation. But human salvation is at stake in the safeguarding of peace. For every breach of the peace is an injustice and, as such, a sin that imperils the salvation of the perpetrator and of others who might be tempted to imitate this breach. For that reason Thomas sees *"punishment"* as having *"medicinal properties in checking sin"*.[22] Accordingly, just wars are oriented toward *"the Divine spiritual good"*.[23]

Finally, it is important to recall once more the formulation that clerics do not *"[have] recourse themselves to material arms"*[24]. This, too, points in the direction of worldly power driving war at the behest of spiritual power. Against this interpretation, Thomas's heavy emphasis on the authority of the princes in q. 40 may be adduced. One is therefore on safer ground assuming that just wars are conducted by the spiritual and

---

20 Cf. Beestermöller (1990), 88–119.
21 Sth II-II, q. 60, a. 6, ad 3.
22 Sth II-II, q. 43, a. 7, ad 1.
23 Sth II-II, q. 40, a. 2, ad 3.
24 Sth II-II, q. 40, a. 2, ad 1.

the worldly power acting jointly. Thus *"it is the duty of clerics to dispose and counsel other men to engage in just wars"*[25].

No just war, even in a cautious interpretation of the great medieval theologian's thinking, can be conducted without or against the authority of the spiritual power. There even seems to be some evidence indicating that wielding the two swords of the Church must be preceded by a kind of verdict from the Church about the princes against whom war is to be conducted. Thus, *"this right of dominion or authority [sc. of unbelievers or heathens over the Christian faithful] can be justly done away with by the sentence or ordination of the Church who has the authority of God"*[26]. This means that, after all, it is ultimately the spiritual authority, with the Pope at the top, that decides whether a war is just. For Thomas, therefore, there can be no such thing as a just war on both sides.

In light of the interpretation offered here, the Thomist rationale stating that princes are to conduct just wars may be expressed this way:

> *"And as the care of the common weal (respublica) is committed to those who are in authority, it is their business to watch over the common weal of the city, kingdom or province subject to them. And just as it is lawful for them to have recourse to the material sword (materialis gladius) in defending that common weal against one's peers, who prove to be troublemakers themselves (contra interiores quidem perturbatores), when they punish evil-doers – according to the words of the Apostle (Romans 13:4): 'He (the authorities) beareth not the sword in vain: for he is God's minister, an avenger to execute wrath upon him that doth evil' – so too, it is their business to have recourse to the sword of war in defending the common weal against external enemies. Hence it is said to those who are in authority (Psalm 81:4): 'Rescue the poor: and deliver the needy out of the hand of the sinner'; and for this reason Augustine says (Contra Faust. xxii, 75): 'The natural order conducive to peace among mortals demands that the power to declare and counsel war should be in the hands of those who hold the supreme authority.'"*[27]

1.2. Continuing with this interpretive approach also reveals the substance of the argument Thomas uses to prohibit private persons from conducting wars. The passage says:

> *"… it is not the business of a private individual to declare war, because he can seek for redress of his rights (ius suum) from the tribunal of his superior (iudicium superioris). Moreover it is not the business of a private individual to summon together the people (multitudo), which has to be done in wartime."*[28]

---

25   Sth II-II, q. 40, a. 2, ad 3.
26   Sth II-II, q. 10, a. 10, resp.
27   Sth II-II, q. 40, a. 1, resp.
28   Sth II-II, q. 40, a. 1, resp.

In q. 42, a. 2, Thomas explains wherein the unity of the *multitudo* consists. It is a *"unity of law and common good"*. Whoever destroys this unity by sedition violates *"justice"* and the *"common good"*[29]. Illegitimate sedition is to be distinguished from legitimate rebellion against a tyrant. Legitimate rebellion is directed not against legitimate but against arrogated authority, which in reality destroys unity in justice and the common good. But the violent overthrow of an authority, no matter how unjust, is to be condemned if *"the tyrant's rule be disturbed so inordinately, that his subjects suffer greater harm from the consequent disturbance than from the tyrant's government"*[30].

Both aspects, the right of the individual and good order for society as a whole, also show up in the passage just cited on the authority to wage war. Thomas is concerned that war be conducted in such a manner that both the rights of the individual and the unity of the people are continually and simultaneously observed. This happens, for one thing, because the right of the individual is protected by a higher authority whenever the initial authority who had immediate jurisdiction has failed and, for another, because there is an orderly procedure.

In this interpretation I interpret *"iudicium superioris"* as the "verdict of a higher judicial authority." This is covered by Thomist linguistic usage. Thus, in the lex tractate (the *Summa's* Treatise on Law) it says that in the Old Testament it was possible to appeal to a highest-level judicial authority, i.e. to *"the chief judge of the people relating to the judgments (iudicia) of men:*[31] *just as even now cases are taken from a lower to a higher court (superiores) either by appeal or by consultation"*[32].

It is, then, part of good order in the *"respublica fidelium"* that responsibility for safeguarding the rights of each individual Christian should reside with Christian princes when they become the superorindate authority after a heathen prince has failed in the exercise of his office. This means, for one thing, that an individual person is not authorized to safeguard justice by using force – neither for himself nor for another person. This would be tantamount to anarchy. *"[I]n matters of justice, there is further need for the judgment of a superior, who is 'able to reprove both, and to*

---

29 Sth II-II, q. 42, a. 2, resp.
30 Sth II-II, q. 42, a. 2, ad 3.
31 To which disputes about customs in religious services constitute the complimentary element.
32 Sth I-II, q. 105, a. 2, ad 7.

put his hand between both' (Job 9:33)."[33] This argument, too, is not tied to religious belief; it applies to all human beings because they are human. *"[I]n human society (societas hominum) no man can exercise coercion except through public authority."*[34] But a stipulation like this is only meaningful if it can be guaranteed that nobody can achieve satisfactory justice for himself or others only by self-assisted force. *"As regards princes, the public power is entrusted to them that they may be the guardians of justice."*[35]

Safeguarding the unity of the multitudo also includes making sure that good order continues to be maintained in the commonwealth. For this reason legislative power resides, as a matter of principle, with the public authorities.

> *"A law, properly speaking, regards first and foremost the order to the common good. Now to order anything to the common good, belongs either to the whole people, or to someone who is the viceregent of the whole people. And therefore the making of a law belongs either to the whole people or to a public personage who has care of the whole people."*[36]

For this reason, too, declaring a state of war and mobilizing an army ("*convocare multitudinem*") cannot be a private matter for an individual.

The quote from Augustine that Thomas uses to conclude his remarks on the war-making authority of the prince ties together all of these aspects. The individual Christian acting as a private person may not, and does not need to, wage war. The prince must provide justice, if need be by way of war, for all entrusted to him by virtue of their membership in the respublica fidelium, and in a manner that does not damage society as a whole: "'*The natural order (ordo naturalis) conducive to peace among mortals demands that the power to declare and counsel war should be in the hands of those who hold the supreme authority [principes – the princes].*'"[37]

One can certainly presume, on the one hand, that Thomas intended to give short shrift to phenomena like the Children's Crusade or pillaging hordes of Crusaders. But he also provides immediate exoneration for the conscience of Christians living under Muslim rule. They are not ipso facto under a permanent summons to resistance. Moreover, Thomas appeals to the conscience of dilatory princes who are adept at surveying the

---

33　Sth II-II, q. 60, a. 1, ad 3.
34　Sth II-II, q. 66, a. 8, resp.
35　Sth II-II, q. 66, a. 8, resp.
36　Sth I-II, q. 90, a. 3, resp.
37　Sth II-II, q. 40, a. 1, resp.

enormity of a crusade and are constantly trying out new excuses to escape this obligation to wage war when a just cause is at hand.

2 "'A just war is wont to be described as one that avenges wrongs …' (Augustine)"

This Thomist claim about a just cause has also proved unwieldy for his interpreters. Let us take a look at the translations (English Dominican and DThA German) of the relevant passage:

> "*Secondly, a just cause is required, namely that those who are attacked, should be attacked because they deserve it on account of some fault (propter aliquam culpam). Wherefore Augustine says (QQ. in Hept., qu. x, super Jos.): 'A just war is wont to be described as one that avenges wrongs, when a nation or state has to be punished, for refusing to make amends for the wrongs inflicted by its subjects, or to restore what it has seized unjustly.'*"

> "*Zweitens ist ein gerechter Grund verlangt. Es müssen nämlich diejenigen, die mit Krieg überzogen werden, dies einer Schuld wegen (propter aliquam culpam) verdienen. Deshalb sagt Augustinus: 'Unter gerechten Kriegen versteht man solche, durch welche Unrecht geahndet wird; so wenn ein Volk oder eine Stadt zu strafen ist, weil sie entweder versäumt haben, das zu ahnden, was von ihren Bürgern frevelhaft verübt wurde, oder versäumt haben, das zurückzugeben, was ungerechterweise geraubt wurde.*"[38]

According to a widely accepted interpretation, what Aquinas wants to say here is "that there has to be a real fault on the adversary's side"[39]. This poses the problem that "the wording 'propter aliquam culpam' [is] so vague as to encompass flagrant aggressors as well as heretics and heathens"[40]. "One is entitled to ask whether the generality with which Thomas treats the subject of a just cause for war does not practically beg to be given such an extensive interpretation."[41] At the very least, then, the Doctor of the Church might be said to have acted negligently by the underdetermined way he treated the question of just cause.

---

38 Sth II-II, q. 40, a. 1, resp.
39 Anselm Hertz, *Die Lehre vom gerechten Krieg als ethischer Kompromiss*, In *Handbuch der christlichen Ethik*, Vol. 3, Anselm Hertz (Ed.) (Herder/Gütersloher Verlagshaus: 1982) 425–448, 436.
40 Wolfgang Lienemann, *Gewalt und Gewaltverzicht: Studien zur abendländischen Vorgeschichte der gegenwärtigen Wahrnehmung von Gewalt* (Kaiser: 1982), 132.
41 Hoppe (1986), 21.

Here, too, it is worthwhile to quote the Latin original (or at least the first sentence):

"Secundo, requiritur causa iusta, ut scilicet illi qui impugnantur propter aliquam culpam impugnationem mereantur."

The problems raised by this passage arise because of the way the German and English version of the *Summa* has translated it with an interpretive twist that is by no means compelling. The first thing that strikes one about these translations is how they read an explicative and therefore definitional meaning into the sentence that does not correspond to the *"ut"* with the subjunctive phrase that follows. In view of the German version it is striking, furthermore, that Thomas does not even speak about a *"bellum"* or *"bellare"* in the Latin original. In the original text we find only the concepts *"impugnatio"* and *"impugnatur"*. Only the special reading corresponding to the German translation and following that translation gives rise to the impression that Thomas would be offering a criterion here for which condition needs to be fulfilled so that war can be waged.

But if one reads *"ut"* along with the subjunctive phrase that follows, and if one reads this so that the *"impugnatio"* really does refer to fighting, then an entirely different meaning is indicated. This could be expressed roughly this way: There has to be a just cause so that the soldiers one is fighting deserve to be fought owing to a fault of their own. The problem for Thomas (so my thesis goes) is that, although abuse of office by a prince can legitimate his punishment, such misfeasance can not justify punishing his soldiers.

But since soldiers get wounded or killed in battle, and since it can be anticipated that serious damage will be inflicted on them, that eventuality can only be deemed legitimate if it is though their own fault that they deserve to be fought. For *"it is unlawful to do a person a harm, except by way of punishment in the cause of justice"*[42]. Whereas *"it is in no way lawful to slay the innocent"*[43].

Two quotations from Augustine employed by Thomas in this context also point in the same direction. The first one was just cited and is used by Thomas to elucidate his requirement for a just cause. According to this Augustinian citation, a people or a city do not deserve a war because they have committed injustice, but rather because they have not punished injustice.

---

42 Sth II-II, q. 65, a. 2, resp.
43 Sth II-II, q. 64, a. 6, resp.

The second citation is found in the Reply to Objection 2 from Question 40, a. 1. Here the issue is the relationship between nonviolence and the use of force. In that passage Thomas refers to Augustine as he takes the view that it is laudable under certain circumstances to refrain from defending one's own life. But this restraint does not apply when the common good is at stake and also not when the cause is *"for the good of those with whom ... a man ... is fighting"*[44]. Hence, Augustine says:

> *"Those whom we have to punish with a kindly severity, it is necessary to handle in many ways against their will. For when we are stripping a man of the lawlessness of sin, it is good for him to be vanquished, since nothing is more hopeless than the happiness of sinners, whence arises a guilty impunity, and an evil will, like an internal enemy."*[45]

A war is therefore only just if it also pursues the welfare of those against whom it is waged. The underlying idea is that *"integritas bonitatis"*, or being *"good in every respect"*, is an inherent part of any morally good act.[46] A war can be thought of as act of impartial, supernatural love only if it is not accomplishing something for the particular good of one's own group at the expense of others' welfare.

One would be over-interpreting Thomas if one believed that, for him, the subjects of a prince who abuses his office deserved to have war waged against them simply because they failed to instigate an uprising. Militating against this interpretation is the Thomist claim that a private person may not proclaim a war. What really matters to Thomas is the following: When there is just cause for a war against a prince, then those who nonetheless remain loyal to him and fight along with him incur blame for that reason alone, so it is just for the prince's followers to be opposed in combat.

I therefore propose the following translation:

> *"Secondly, a just cause will be required, namely so that those against whom the battle is aimed deserve this combat on account of some fault."*

---

44 The DThA translates *"bonum ... illorum cum quibus pugnatur"* as "[those] with whom one is fighting" ("mit denen man kämpft" in German). This leaves it open as to whether fellow combatants (comrades) or soldiers in the opposing party are meant. This is clarified by how Thomas takes up the formulation for a causa iusta here – *"illi qui impugnantur"* – and by how the ensuing citation from Augustine also unequivocally refers to those against whom one is fighting.

45 Sth II-II, q. 40, a. 1, ad 2.

46 Sth I-II, q. 20, a. 2, resp.

(In German: „Zweitens wird ein gerechter Grund verlangt, damit nämlich jene, gegen die sich der Kampf richtet, diese Bekämpfung einer Schuld wegen verdienen.")

The problem of concern to Thomas here is that, to begin with, a subject is obligated to remain loyal to his master, most especially when the latter is attacked. When, therefore, the injustice of his prince is not apparent to a subject, there is a great danger that he will take his master's side and so participate in a bad thing as well. But then the war would achieve the opposite of that for which it was undertaken, namely to combat sin:

"But if it is evident that the infliction of punishment will result in more numerous and more grievous sins being committed, the infliction of punishment will no longer be a part of justice."[47]

In the requirement for a just cause, therefore, the issue is about when a *"a man's crime"* in need of punishment *"is so publicly known, and so hateful to all, that he has no defenders, or none such as might cause a schism"*. In this case, *"the severity of discipline should not slacken"*[48]. So for a just cause to exist in the first place, the injustice against which the just war is aimed needs to be blatant and unequivocal. It is not enough for the prince to have committed an injustice. The wrong must also have been committed "flagrantly" ("frevelhalft" in German [although the standard English Dominican translation of Aquinas about "wrongs inflicted" does not include any such adjective conveying the point so strongly – Trans.]), and it must clearly have been inflicted "unjustly"[49]. If this is not the case, then people should keep their distance from warfare:

"...his sin [sc. the sin of "the sovereign (principis)" to whom the multitudo is obliged] should be borne with, if it cannot be punished without scandal to the multitude."[50]

Thomas seems to be of the opinion that this clarity or obviousness is something that results, above all, from the Church taking sides. He makes this clear, expressis verbis, with regard to apostasy:

"... as soon as sentence of excommunication is passed on a man on account of apostasy from the faith, his subjects are 'ipso facto' absolved from his authority and from the oath of allegiance whereby they were bound to him."[51]

---

47 Sth II-II, q. 43, a. 7, resp.
48 Sth II-II, q. 10, a. 8, ad 1.
49 Sth II-II, q. 40, a. 1, resp.
50 Sth II-II, q. 108, a. 1, ad 5.
51 Sth II-II, q. 12, a. 2, ad 1.

In sum, the requirement for a causa iusta has to do not only with the princes one is opposing in combat having failed in their office, but also with the soldiers who obey these princes' orders therewith committing a reprehensible injustice. This is the case when the injustice of the prince against whom war is to be waged is an obvious wrong.

3 "Thirdly, it is necessary that the belligerents should have a rightful intention."

The third requirement for a just war also poses problems of interpretation. The Thomist passage reads as follows:

> "Thirdly, it is necessary that the belligerents should have a rightful intention, so that they intend the advancement of good, or the avoidance of evil. Hence Augustine says: … 'True religion looks upon as peaceful those wars that are waged not for motives of aggrandizement, or cruelty, but with the object of securing peace, of punishing evil-doers, and of uplifting the good.' For it may happen that the war is declared by the legitimate authority, and for a just cause, and yet be rendered unlawful through a wicked intention. Hence Augustine says: … 'The passion for inflicting harm, the cruel thirst for vengeance, an unpacific and relentless spirit, the fever of revolt, the lust of power, and such like things, all these are rightly condemned in war."[52]

The passage poses two problems. First of all, it must be asked how we are to understand that a wicked intention renders a war impermissible. Does this mean that an otherwise just war becomes impermissible owing to the unethical intention of a single soldier (3.1)? The second problem relates to what should be understood by a rightful intention. Isn't the Thomist requirement tantamount to "placing oneself on the standpoint of morality in the first place"[53]? But then why should Thomas raise this requirement when, after all, the question of criteria for a just war presupposes this very point of view (3.2)?

3.1 The problem of collective intention can be solved if by "*the belligerents*" ("bellantes" in the nominative plural) one understands not the soldiers but rather the princes whose mandate authorizes the waging of war. There are four reasons speaking for this interpretation.

a) The passage on just war in Sth II-II q. 40, a. 1 is strictly parallel in its construction. Corresponding to the requirement or stipulation about

---

52 Sth II-II, q. 40, a. 1, resp.
53 Hoppe (1986), 22.

the prince's authority is the first reply, which has to do with authorizing soldiers. Corresponding to the causa iusta is the second reply, where the subject is discovering the reasons for whatever circumstances Christians might have for resorting to force. Finally, the third reply deals with soldiers' motives. This indicates that Thomas uses the third stipulation to address the intentions of princes.

The thesis of parallel construction is also supported by the use of language. In the third reply Thomas does not talk about "*bellantes*" but instead about those who wage war ("*bella gerunt*"). In so doing he adopts the same linguistic usage he used to introduce the authority of the princes, namely "by whose command the war is to be waged" ("*bellum gerendum*"). In the third reply, therefore, he is discussing the intention of those who follow the summons to war. This indicates that bellantes means the princes who declare war.

b) In the Latin version of the text it is striking how Thomas formulates this passage in a peculiarly passive way. The translation does not properly capture this passive formulation: "*qua scilicet intenditur vel ut bonum promoveatur, vel ut malum vitetur*".

So what's being stipulated is not the intention to advance good and avoid evil, but rather the intention to have good advanced and evil avoided. This indicates that the one whose intention is the issue at hand and the one who carries out the action are different persons. The stipulation for a correct intention, therefore, aims at prescribing only those actions through which good is advanced and evil avoided.

c) In another passage Thomas returns once more to the intention of soldiers in war. At that place in the text it says that "*they who are engaged in a just war may sin in taking spoils through cupidity arising from an evil intention, if, to wit, they fight chiefly not for justice but for spoil*"[54]. Here it is assumed that that a just war does not become unjust owing to the bad intention of soldiers, even though they are sinners. If, therefore, one wishes to give the *Summa* a coherent interpretation, then the stipulation for a proper intention cannot mean that of the soldiers.

d) Thomas treats war under the category of "*vices contrary to peace*"[55]. But subjecting war as a whole to an ethical evaluation presupposes that there is a subject that assumes full responsibility. The intention of this agent finds its way into the moral constitution of the action as a whole, whereas the deeds of the executor constitute a moral act of

54 Sth II-II, q. 66, a. 8, ad 1.
55 Sth II-II, q. 39, prolog.

their own. *"It is just as if the servant [minister] of some man were to carry alms to the poor with a wicked intention, whereas his master had commanded him with a good intention to do so."*[56]

This differentiated view distinguishing between the intentions of princes and soldiers corresponds to the Thomist requirement for a just cause. Here, too, the issue is the distinction between the misdeeds of the princes and of those doing military service in his retinue. Only if the misdeeds of both are reprochable injustices may war be waged. But if a war is ordered by the proper authority with a just cause and proper intention, it is not made unjust by the sinful intention of soldiers. When, however, the proper intention of the prince is absent, then the war is a sin, even if soldiers go to war out of motives that are good. What, then, is the substance of a proper intention?

3.2 Here, too, at the outset, it makes sense to take a close look at the text: *"Tertio, requiritur ut sit intentio bellantium recta, qua scilicet inteditur vel ut bonum promoveatur, vel ut malum vitetur."*

And here, too, it is not the case that Thomas is presenting a definition of *"intentio recta"* (right or proper intention). Rather, he is establishing a consecutive relation. When a proper intention is present, then we can be assured that the paramount rule of natural law has been fulfilled: *"Good is to be done and pursued, and evil is to be avoided."*[57]

Here what matters to Aquinas is the following problem: The most paramount and general principle of ethics is one that is valid always and everywhere. Located between this highest principle and the concrete norm are principles of gradated generality. The next stage of concretion below the highest principle is constituted by general statements, of which no single one can claim validity without exception. Thomas elucidates this using the example of the tension between the prohibition on doing harm and the commandment to punish:

> *"Some things are therefore derived from the general principles of the natural law, by way of conclusions; e. g. that 'one must not kill' may be derived as a conclusion from the principle that 'one should do harm to no man': while some are derived therefrom by way of determination; e. g. the law of nature has it that the evildoer should be punished; but that he be punished in this or that way, is a determination of the law of nature."*[58]

---

56 Sth III, q. 64, a. 10, ad 3.
57 Sth I-II, q. 94, a. 2, resp.
58 Sth I-II, q. 95, a. 2, resp.

The tension is resolved because the only person to whom harm may be done is someone who has deserved punishment by committing a wrongful act. When, therefore, there is a case like this in which action is taken against somebody, this kind of action continues to fall under the highest ethical command. This also applies to war.

> *"The slaying of a man is forbidden in the decalogue, in so far as it bears the character of something undue: for in this sense the precept contains the very essence of justice. Human law cannot make it lawful for a man to be slain unduly. But it is not undue for evil-doers or foes of the common weal to be slain..."*[59]

The first and second requirements for a just war are meant to guarantee that martial force is not used against any human being who does not deserve it. But it is not just the proper subject and the proper object of an action that are incorporated into the constitution of a moral act; the intention of the actor is as well. Two acts that look the same on the surface can have opposing qualities in the moral order. When, therefore, the prince in charge uses a just cause as a pretext but is imbued with an intention to promote evil and prevent good, then the war is unjust. What kind of intention that can lurk behind war-waging constitutes a species in the genus of the morally good intention?

The man who is deservedly killed owing to his deeds is certainly also violating his human dignity as a moral subject – namely to be one who *"is naturally free, and exists for himself"* – but he does not lose this status entirely. Hence one may inflict damage on him only to the extent that this is necessary in order to ward off the peril. Thus, one may kill him like a wild animal, yet one may never rear him like cattle or instrumentalize him like livestock.[60] Accordingly, the intention of the prince who orders war is only good when he is exclusively concerned with the betterment of those against whom he is acting – to the extent that this is possible – and with the protection of the others:

> *"If ... the avenger's intention be directed chiefly to some good, to be obtained by means of the punishment of the person who has sinned (for instance that the sinner may amend, or at least that he may be restrained and others be not disturbed,*

---

59 Sth I-II, q. 100, a. 8, resp.
60 *"By sinning man departs from the order of reason, and consequently falls away* [the German DThA version translates "recedere" as "abfallen" – "falling off" in English – which is too strong] *from the dignity of his manhood, in so far as he is naturally free, and exists for himself, and he falls into the slavish state of the beasts ... yet it may be good to kill a man who has sinned, even as it is to kill a beast."* Sth II-II, q. 64, a. 2, ad 3.

that justice may be upheld, and God honored), then vengeance may be lawful, provided other due circumstances be observed."[61]

The state of will in which man does harm to someone else in order to win back that person to peace is righteous anger. While the lover affirms the beloved and wishes him or her something good, and while hatred rejects the hated and wishes to inflict evil on him or her (wenn, dann auch consequent.), righteous anger is directed toward a person who has acted unjustly and is rejected as such, even as this is an anger that strives for the restoration of justice.[62] The angry person, therefore, inflicts damage on another human being only *"in so far as it has an aspect of good, that is, in so far as he reckons it as just … Because to wish evil to someone under the aspect [ratio] of justice, may be according to the virtue of justice, if it be in conformity with the order of reason…"*[63] When, therefore, worldly authority wages a just war, it acts as *"'God's minister, an avenger to execute wrath upon him that doth evil.'"*[64]

The exegesis proposed here has solved all the difficulties that the interpretation has with the Thomist text, with one exception. Is not the defense of the respublica fidelium against Christian princes and its defense against heathen princes one and the same principle, namely the prince's protective function for the commonwealth? Militating against this conjecture is the way the text speaks ad intram about *"punire"* and ad extram about *"tueri."* The solution may be found in the distinction between territorial reign based on nature and the gladius materialis grounded in Christianity.

The worldly sword of the princes is there in order to punish Christian believers to the extent that they break the law. In this way they are meant to be dissuaded from taking the wrong path. *"In the infliction of punishment it is not the punishment itself that is the end in view, but its medicinal properties in checking sin…"*[65]

Penal power in this sense presupposes that a person has subjected himself to the salvation and care of the Church by accepting its faith.

---

61 Sth II-II, q. 108, a. 1, resp.
62 *"Hence the movement of anger has a twofold tendency: viz. to vengeance itself, which it desires and hopes for as being a good, wherefore it takes pleasure in it; and to the person on whom it seeks vengeance, as to something contrary and hurtful, which bears the character of evil."* Sth I-II, q. 46, a. 2, resp.
63 Sth I-II, q. 46, a. 6, resp.
64 Sth II-II, q. 40, a. 1, resp.
65 Sth II-II, q. 43, a. 7, ad 1

To be sure, the great medieval theologian was convinced that a refusal to accept the faith could only be thought of as a sin. For this offer of faith accords so closely with man's inner longing that this medieval Aristotelian could not imagine how a man can shut himself off from this offer in good faith.[66]

But should one wish to punish rejection of the faith, one would have to force faith on the sinner, if punishment is really going to serve the purpose of preventing sin. Yet this would be diametrically opposed to the voluntary character of adopting faith. Hence the course of action for princes to take against heathens is confined to defending Christian believers from the negative effects of the heathens' sins, especially the sin of refusing the faith:

"Among unbelievers there are some who have never received the faith ... and these are by no means to be compelled to the faith, in order that they may believe, because to believe depends on the will: nevertheless they should be compelled by the faithful, if it be possible to do so, so that they do not hinder the faith, by their blasphemies, or by their evil persuasions, or even by their open persecutions."[67]

Aquinas the Dominican, however, certainly does believe that it is highly advisable to punish the sin of heresy and lapse of faith. For both the heretic and the apostate have voluntarily subjected themselves to the Church's responsibility for salvation and its regulations:

"Nevertheless a man who sins by unbelief may be sentenced to the loss of his right of dominion... Now it is not within the competency of the Church to punish unbelief in those who have never received the faith ... She can, however, pass sentence of punishment on the unbelief of those who have received the faith ..."[68]

It can be seen, therefore, that the protective function for the commonwealth that the prince is required to heed both domestically and externally represents only one aspect of the gladius materialis. The other consists in justice toward those against whom the sword is wielded. The duty arising from Romans 13 to act against those who do bad manifests itself within Christianity in the entire severity of penal power. The same duty toward those who never found their way to faith, however, is restricted to fending off reproachable dangers to the faith of Christendom.

---

66   Cf. Beestermöller (1990), 175 ff. and Gerhard Beestermöller, *Heilsbotschaft und Weltverantwortung. Der Weg zu einer christlichen Sozialethik als theologischer Partner im pluralistischen Dialog*, In *Theologie und Philosophie* 72 (1997) 527–552.
67   Sth II-II, q. 10, a. 8, resp.
68   Sth II-II, q. 12, a. 2, resp.

Let us sum up: The ultimate thrust of the Thomist doctrine of just war is an ethic of intervention. The Christian princes – they and only they – are justified and obligated to defend the respublica fidelium as a whole, but also its individual members, against heathen princes when their members are forced to suffer injustice under heathen rule and the public authorities in charge fail to enforce justice on their behalf.

To be sure, the injustice suffered by Christians does not quite justify the application of military force. This is only legitimate when one can count the resistance of those being fought as an act of injustice itself. Ultimately, waging a just war is only a morally good act when the prince who pleads for the war is imbued with righteous anger and not with hatred, a craving to do harm, or other base motives. Acting out of righteous or just anger, he finds no joy in the suffering of those on whom he wages war; rather, his action finds its aim in the restoration of justice and peace.

4 A brief concluding outlook

Can the Thomist doctrine of just war help in any way when it comes to solving our contemporary questions, especially with regard to an ethic of humanitarian intervention? I invite the reader to entertain a momentary thought experiment. Try replacing just once (experimentally, as it were) Christian faith in the thought of Aquinas with the idea of human rights. Would one not then find oneself squarely in the middle of our modern debate about the ethics of humanitarian intervention?

I should like to undergird my justification for posing this question – n.b., a question, not a thesis – with two highlights. In his article about NATO's Kosovo deployment, Jürgen Habermas discusses whether the Western alliance should have been allowed to impose ethically motivated human rights on the Serbs without a UN mandate. For him, the problematic aspect of this action was that Yugoslavia had subjugated itself to UN regulations, but not to the jurisdiction of NATO. "Even nineteen undoubtedly democratic states remain a partial actor, if they legitimate their intervention for and by themselves… To this extent they are acting paternalistically."[69] Habermas believes, nevertheless, that NATO's action

---

69 Jürgen Habermas, *Bestialität und Humanität. Ein Krieg an der Grenze zwischen Recht und Moral*, In Reinhard Merkel (Ed.), *Der Kosovokrieg und das Völkerrecht*, (Suhrkamp: 2000) 51–65. (An English translation may be found at <http://www.theglobalsite.ac.uk/press/011habermas.htm>.)

was the right thing to do. "If there is no other way out, democratic neighbor states have to be permitted to intervene with emergency relief based on a legitimization by international law."[70]

In our thought experiment we would find that Thomas, who was concerned about intervening in the Islamic world in order to protect the human rights of Christians living there, and Habermas are discussing questions that are barely distinguishable from one another. Habermas solves his problem of not being allowed to do what needs to be done by invoking the exceptional nature of the required action.[71] Thomas, however, advocates the thesis that an intervention can only be legitimate when it can also be justified to the victims of an act of force.[72] But then there must also be a tertium between an ethos that has a purely moral grounding and legal norms that are reached through consensus. Is not Thomas the more consistent and rigorous thinker here?

A second highlight: The two Höffe students Jean-Christophe Merle and Alessandro Pinzani venture quite a ways forward to develop an ethics of humanitarian intervention: "We see no reason in principle why only states and not, say, organizations like Amnesty International or Doctors Without Borders should be authorized to intervene or participate in an intervention."[73] What Thomas says is that "a religious order may be fittingly established for soldiering, not indeed for any worldly purpose, but for the defense of divine worship and public safety, or also of the poor and oppressed, according to Psalm 82 (81):4: 'Rescue the poor, and deliver the needy out of the hand of the sinner.'"[74]

Don't the reflections of Merle and Pinzani amount to a new knightly order, and didn't this kind of thinking have its origins in the orders for nursing care? Is not the entire ambivalence of the humanitarian impulse revealed here?

---

70 Habermas (2000), 64. (The translation here departs slightly from <http://www.theglobalsite.ac.uk/press/011habermas.htm>.)

71 "NATO's self-empowerment should not become the rule." Habermas (2000), 64.

72 To this extent, I agree with the critique that Hajo Schmidt has made of the Habermas article: "Hence, instead of arguments from discourse ethics, it is arguments from the philosophy of history that shape Habermas's core argument." In Hajo Schmidt, Wie weiter? Rechtsethische Erwägungen gelegentlich des Kosovo/a-Krieges, In Gerhard Beestermöller (Ed.), Die humanitäre Intervention – Imperativ der Menschenrechtsidee? (Kohlhammer: 2003) 101–122, 111.

73 Jean-Christophe Merle / Alessandro Pinzani, Rechtfertigung und Modalitäten eines Rechts auf humanitäre Intervention, In Vierteljahresschrift für Sicherheit und Frieden 18, no. 1 (2000) 71–75, 73.

74 Sth II-II, q. 188, a. 3, resp.

These parallels could be continued almost indefinitely. What follows from this? To begin with, it gives us quite a lot of food for thought! What consequences follow from the return of the discriminating war, the war of justice against injustice, of those who are good[75] against those who are evil? Can we prevent a repetition of the slide into the Thirty Years War, of a war that destroyed practically everything, when the imbalance of power might no longer be so clear? These questions really do call out to be read merely as questions. Perhaps the separation of truth and power that took place along with the establishment of the absolutely sovereign state was a great historical error, a wrong track that was corrected first by human rights movements within states, then curbed by collective security, and finally overcome by humanitarian intervention from outside the states?

Questions of this kind must be left to other studies. But there is one thing one may confidently assert here. Thomas derives the authority to intervene from the obligation of Christian princes to act against their counterparts when the latter abuse their office. It will hardly be possible for a group of states to invoke the great Doctor of the Church if this coalition does not decisively stand up for the value of human rights on its home territory before making a military commitment to enforce them inside the borders of another state.

---

75 Christian Tomuschat sees NATO as "an alliance of states that selflessly aspire to serve the protection of human rights…" Christian Tomuschat, *Völkerrechtliche Aspekte des Kosovo-Konflikts,* In *Die Friedenswarte* 74, no. 1–2 (1999) 33–37, 37. Does this show that the category of humanitarian intervention is incapable of being thought of coherently on its own, without the requirement for recta intentio?

Forerunners of Humanitarian Intervention?
From Canon Law to Francisco de Vitoria

James Muldoon

In the past century, as mankind has became more interconnected and as globalization has become one of the most important themes in public policy debates, reconsideration of the concept of an international legal order has become increasingly important. Since the seventeenth century, the work of the Dutch jurist Hugo Grotius (1583–1645) has dominated the discussion of international law, so much so that Grotius is often identified as the Father of International Law. His work and that of a number of lawyers, legal theorists, and public officials who followed in his footsteps created a legal order often termed the Grotian system that has dominated international law thinking from the seventeenth century to the twenty-first.[1]

The Grotian legal system developed in conjunction with efforts to end the religious wars that wracked Europe in the sixteenth and seventeenth century and also with the attempts to create a legal regime for regulating relations among the emerging European overseas empires. The Peace of Westphalia (1648) that ended the religious wars set "down the political and religious conditions for allowing the European powers to start building a new international legal order", a secular order based on agreements among sovereign states. This order replaced the hierarchical medieval international order headed by the pope.

The refusal to allow a papal representative to participate in the negotiations that led to the Peace of Westphalia symbolized the end of what has been termed the "religious, cultural and, to a certain extent, political and juridical unity, often referred to as the *respublica Christiana*" that included the numerous "political entities in the Latin world … in a greater hierarchical and juridical *continuum* under the supreme, if theoretical,

---

1 For a brief introduction to the Grotian tradition: see Cornelius F. Murphy, Jr., "The Grotian Vision of World Order." *American Journal of International Law 76* (1982): 477–498; Headley Bull, "The Importance of Grotius in the Study of International Relations." In *Hugo Grotius and International Relations*, eds. H. Bull, B. Kingsbury, A. Roberts (Oxford: 1992) 65–93.

leadership of the pope and the emperor."[2] This meant that the "claims of the papacy to be a super-state institution with a right to pronounce on the validity of treaties concluded among Christian powers were explicitly rejected."[3] The Grotian theory of international law and the Westphalian structure of international order dominated the theory and the practice of international relations since the seventeenth century.[4]

Since the beginning of the twentieth century, however, the Grotian notion of a world legal order and the Westphalian structure of international relations has come under attack on several fronts. One line of criticism, stemming from the work of James Brown Scott (1866–1943), a founder of the study of international law in the United States, has been to assert the priority of other thinkers, especially the Spanish scholastic philosophers of the sixteenth and seventeenth centuries who formed the so-called *scholastica secunda*.[5] Scott focused attention not on Grotius but on Francisco de Vitoria (1480–1546) whose *De Indis* and related works had examined the legitimacy of the Spanish conquest and occupation of the Americas.[6] In effect, he argued that in the early modern world

---

2 Randall Lesaffer, "Peace Treaties from Lodi to Westphalia." In *Peace Treaties and International Law in European History from the Late Middle Ages to World War One*, ed. Randall Lesaffer (Cambridge: 2004) 9–44 at 11.

3 Headley Bull, "The Importance of Grotius" 77.

4 See in particular the work of Randall Lesaffer on the pre-Grotian development of international law: "The Grotian Tradition Revisited: Change and Continuity in the History of International Law." In *British Yearbook of International Law 73* (2002) 103–139. There is now a journal dealing with the early development of international law, the *Journal of the History of International Law* (1998).

5 On the second scholasticism and the role of these thinkers in the development of the debate about the right of the Spanish to occupy the Americas: see Anthony Pagden, "The 'school of Salamanca' and the Affair of the Indies", *History of Universities*, vol. I, *Continuity and Change in Early Modern Universities* (Avebury, Eng.: 1981) 71–112; Thomas F. O'Meara, O.P., "The Dominican School of Salamanca and the Spanish Conquest of America: Some Bibliographical Notes." *The Thomist 54* (1992): 555–582. On James Brown Scott: see James Muldoon, "The Contribution of the Medieval Canon Lawyers to the Formation of International Law.," *Traditio 28* (1972): 483–497, esp. 486–487; Christopher R. Rossi, *Broken Chain of Being. James Brown Scott and the Origins of Modern International Law* (The Hague: 1998).

6 Scott arranged for the publication of translations of several pre-grotian writers who contributed to the development of international law in The Classics of International Law series published by the Carnegie Endowment for Peace. These included one medieval author, John of Legnano (d. 1383), and two sixteenth-century scholastic philosophers, Francisco de Vitoria, and Francisco Suárez (1548–1616). These writers provided the foundation of what Scott labeled as

two lines of thinking about international law developed, the older Catholic tradition rooted in the Middle Ages and the Grotian line that professed to reject that tradition.

One of the fundamental differences between the Catholic and the Grotian approaches to international law concerned the nature of a global society. The Catholic tradition was hierarchical and moralistic, envisioning a world legal order based on the medieval papacy's claims to universal jurisdiction. As Walter Ullmann pointed out many years ago, the Middle Ages had seen an extraordinary attempt to create a society based on moral principles and to unite mankind not by force but by the employment of law. In his opinion, the papacy and its lawyers attempted "to direct Europe … by means of an idea enshrined in a universally binding law."[7] In order to do this, there had to be a recognized legal order with clear-cut rules the violation of which could be punished by competent authority. Eventually, canon lawyers expanded the papal role to cover not only Christians and even non-Christians living within Christian societies, they also extended papal jurisdiction to all mankind.

On the other hand, the Grotian tradition of international law rejected any claims to universal jurisdiction by the popes or anyone else.[8] Instead, the Grotian order assumes the existence of sovereign states whose leaders would work together to regulate international relations and set out the legal terms that would insure that this effort succeeded. These states would be sovereign that is legally subject to no external power making universal jurisdictional claims, specifically the papacy and the Holy Roman emperors. Above all, the Grotian-Westphalian world order would not recognize any claims to universal jurisdiction that would authorize intervention in the internal operation of any state.[9]

The Spanish Conception of International Law and of Sanctions (Washington, D.C 1934). There is now a new translation of Vitoria's work: *Francisco de Vitoria. Political Writings*, eds. Anthony Pagden and Jeremy Lawrance (Cambridge: 1991).

7   Walter Ullmann, *The Growth of Papal Government in the Middle Ages*, 2nd ed. (London: 1962), 448.

8   Grotius's first public work was an explicit rejection of papal claims to regulate the sea: see Hugo Grotius, *The Freedom of the Seas*, ed. James Brown Scott, trans. Ralph van Deman Magoffin (New York: 1916); see also James Muldoon, "Who Owns the Sea?" In *Fictions of the Sea: Critical Perspectives on the Ocean in British Literature and Culture,* Bernhard Klein (Aldershot, Eng.: 2002) 13–27.

9   On the development of the concept of sovereignty in the Middle Ages: see Kenneth Pennington, *The Prince and the Law: Sovereignty and Rights in the Western Legal Tradition* (Berkeley: 1993).

The Grotian-Westphalian conception of an egalitarian world order of sovereign states remained dominant until after World War II in spite of challenges. The era of decolonization that followed the war as the European empires collapsed began with the assumption that the former colonies would soon join the ranks of sovereign states. The optimistic hopes that accompanied decolonization were in many cases frustrated. While membership in the United Nations grew from 51 states in 1945 to 191 in 2004, providing public recognition of the sovereignty of many of the new states, many of these new countries became what are now labeled 'failed states' or 'quasi-states', whose sovereign status is questionable. They are "juridical more than empirical entities", often former European colonies now recognized as sovereign states and therefore the legal equals of the older European nation-states even though they "are limited in their capacity or desire to provide civil and socioeconomic goods for their populations."[10] Efforts to employ outside force, even under the aegis of the UN, to impose order on a "failed state" and end a civil war or to force the government of such a state to protect an oppressed minority raises charges of neo-imperialism and violation of a state's sovereignty.[11]

The existence of failed states and the development of internationally recognized standards of behavior has encouraged the development of the theory of humanitarian intervention, the use of military power to force the leaders of failed states to adhere to recognized standards of behavior. This concept has added a new element to discussions of the just war. Traditionally, discussion of the just war has fallen into two categories that scholastic philosophers, theologians, and canon lawyers had created in an attempt to regulate warfare in medieval Europe. The first category concerns those "concepts relating to the justification for going to war,

---

10 Robert H. Jackson, *Quasi-States: Sovereignty, International Relations, and the Third World* (Cambridge: 1990) 5, 9; see also his "Surrogate Sovereignty? Great Power Responsibility and 'Failed States'". *Institute of International Relations, The University of British Columbia, Working Paper No. 25* (1998).

11 Some observers have even suggested re-establishing some form of imperial control over failed states: see Christopher Dickey, "The Empire Burden: Why It's So Hard to Get Out of Iraq, Afghanistan or … The Comoro Islands." *Newsweek International, June 22*, (2009). "It's rare, in fact, that imperial powers decide on their own to give up any fragment of their foreign territories or influence. The British, for instance, 'regarded long-term occupation as an inherent part of their 'civilizing mission', 'the Harvard historian Niall Ferguson wrote in 2003. A self-described neo-imperialist, Ferguson supported the invasion of Iraq then taking place …"

gathered together under the traditional rubric *jus ad bellum* ...."[12] The second category concerns "the *jus in bello*, or law of war, has to do with restraint or limiting of war once begun." As Frederick Russell has pointed out, the "scholastic position ... justified all hostile acts in defense of justice." Stated this way, the concept of the just war would seem simple and clear cut. The only just war would be a defensive war but, as Russell also pointed out, "the concepts of avenging injuries, punishment and defense are often explicitly conflated. In an actual situation it is psychologically very difficult for the aggrieved party to distinguish lust for vengeance from defense of his own rights or even defense of the vaguely-defined moral order...."[13] Does a claim to a just war of defense actually mask a desire to wage an aggressive war for immoral ends?

The medieval concept of the just war assumed that in any war one side was right and the other wrong, one side was legitimately defending itself from the aggressive actions of the other side. At least in theory, that made matters clear and simple, although the reality was much more complicated. Furthermore, the medieval theorists did not consider what has become an important theme on modern discussion of the just war, "intervention by an impartial third party", that is humanitarian intervention, that is the use of force by an outside power to provide effective government when the indigenous government has lost the capacity to do so.[14]

In recent years, humanitarian intervention has emerged as an important issue when considering the current state of international affairs. According to Alex J. Bellamy writing in 2004: "The idea that there is a limited right of intervention in supreme humanitarian emergencies is today well-established in international society and widely recognised by scholars...."[15] Humanitarian intervention differs from the other two categories of analysis of the just war in that it does not focus on wars of defense, the

---

12 James Turner Johnson, Just *War Tradition and the Restrain of War: A Moral and Historical Inquiry* (Princeton: 1981), xxii–xxiii; see also his other works: *Ideology, Reason, and the Limitation of War* (Princeton: Princeton University Press, 1975); *The Quest for Peace. Three Moral Traditions in Western Cultural History* (Princeton: 1987). The fundamental book on the medieval development of these concepts is Frederick H. Russell, *The Just War in the Middle Ages* (Cambridge: 1975).

13 Russell, *Just War* 305, 307.

14 Russell, *Just War* 305.

15 Alex J. Bellamy, "Motives, Outcomes, Intent and the Legitimacy of Humanitarian Intervention." *Journal of Military Ethics 3* (2004): 216–232 at 217. He attributes the term to Nicholas J. Wheeler, *Saving Strangers: Humanitarian Intervention in International Society* (Oxford: 2000), 1–2.

use of force to protect oneself and one's society from violence from out-side. Instead, humanitarian intervention refers to the use of armed force in a positive, even aggressive, manner, to protect the members of another society from oppression by their rulers or from one another in a civil war. Such intervention is justified as fulfilling a moral responsibility for assist-ing those in need so that failure to do so could be construed as a moral failure.

Labeling such military action as 'humanitarian' might preclude any serious discussion of the military action involved because after all who could object to a humanitarian action aimed at protect the defenseless from harm?[16] The obvious question is who decides that the intervention is truly humanitarian and not simply a ploy to mask aggression or impe-rialistic expansion? Furthermore, by precluding careful analysis of the sit-uation, even a truly humanitarian motive for intervention could lead to the creation of a worse situation than had existed before the intervention. More than any other stage of just war thinking, humanitarian interven-tion requires the exercise of the virtue of prudence.

Humanitarian intervention exists at the intersection of three distinct intellectual traditions: the philosophical theory of the just war, the legal theory of state sovereignty, and the moral tradition of assisting those in need of help. Is it possible to create a legal regime that accommodates the three distinct traditions and develop a system of international law and relations that implements them in a coherent fashion? The problem is not simply an academic issue, the subject of learned articles and books, but an immensely practical one, a matter of intense public debate about foreign policy in many countries at the moment.[17]

The theory of humanitarian intervention assumes that it is possible for state or group of states to judge another state as 'failed' and in need of assistance or correction. This assumes of course that there are uni-versal standards of acceptable behavior and also institutional structures capable of implementing such judgments. In practice, this assumes the existence of a hierarchical world order that is – or should be – moving toward the creation of a universal egalitarian moral and political order.[18]

---

16 Daniel Schwartz, "The Principle of the Defence of the Innocent and the Con-quest of America: 'save Those Dragged Towards Death.'" *Journal of the History of International Law 9* (2007): 263–291 at 263.

17 See for example: Gary J. Bass, *Freedom's Battle: The Origins of Humanitarian In-tervention* (New York: 2008).

18 The theory of stadial development developed in the seventeenth and eighteenth centuries supported the notion of a universal course of development proceeding

Although scholars generally see the concept of humanitarian intervention as a modern development, a product of the collapse of the colonial empires, in fact it is an old justification in a new guise. The Roman poet Virgil (d. 19 BC) announced Rome's humanitarian mission two millennia ago:

> Roman, remember by your strength to rule
> Earth's peoples – for your arts are to be these:
> To pacify, to impose the rule of law,
> To spare the conquered, battle down the proud.[19]

In effect he was proclaiming a kind of humanitarian intervention on the part of the Romans. The Romans would bring peace, order, and stability to unruly mankind. It is difficult to imagine that many Romans actually believed that they were engaged in a humanitarian mission to bring peace and order to mankind.[20] In the sixteenth and seventeenth centuries, the supporters of the emerging European overseas empires often quoted Virgil in defense of their activities. In effect, the English and the Spanish were the new Romans.[21]

The notion of humanitarian intervention received fuller development during the Middle Ages as the papacy asserted its claim to be the supreme moral authority not only in Christian Europe but over all mankind.[22] When Francisco de Vitoria discussed the legitimacy of the conquest the Americas he was building on the medieval conception of universal order, an order that did not include a notion of sovereignty in the Grotian sense. That is, while Catholic thought recognized the autonomy of states,

---

at different rates in different societies: see Bruce Buchan, "The empire of political thought: civilization, savagery and perceptions of indigenous government." *History of Human Sciences 18* (2005): 1–22.

19 Virgil, *The Aeneid*, trans. Robert Fitzgerald (New York: 1983), 190 (book 6, lines 854–857).

20 Russell, *Just War* 7.

21 On the use of Virgil and other Roman models: see David A. Lupher, *Romans in a New World, Classical Models in Sixteenth-Century Spanish America* (Ann Arbor, Michigan: 2003); Sabine MacCormack, *On the Wings of Time: Rome, the Incas, Spain, and Peru* (Princeton: 2007).

22 There was the fading notion of the Holy Roman Emperors possessing some kind of universal jurisdiction, a concept that lawyers of the emerging European kingdoms increasingly rejected, arguing that the king in his kingdom had the same authority as the emperor in the empire and was therefore exempt from any overarching universal imperial jurisdiction in temporal matters: see James Muldoon, *Empire and Order: The Concept of Empire, 800–1800* (New York: 1999), 97–98.

it also asserted the right of the pope to order armed intervention into a state whose rulers would not or could not govern effectively, who oppressed their subjects, or who tolerated violations of the natural law. In effect, the papacy had long claimed a right to intervene in the internal operations of states in a manner similar to the modern concept of humanitarian intervention. One of the reasons that Vitoria's work has attracted attention in recent years is that his discussion of an early version of humanitarian intervention. Vitoria was after all the proponent of a concept of a hierarchical world order that justified the use of armed force against other states in the pursuit of moral goals, the concept of international order that Hugo Grotius challenged.[23]

The Catholic concept of international order justified such intervention because of the responsibility of the pope to protect mankind not only from oppression by wicked rulers but also from cultural practices that would endanger their salvation. The actual work of intervention would be carried out by Christian rulers acting under papal authorization. In the mid-fifteenth century, Nicholas of Cusa's *Christian Concordance* sketched a coherent picture of an all-embracing world order under papal headship, a conception that underlay subsequent visions of world order such as Francisco de Vitoria was to envision in his writings.[24]

The development of the papal theory of humanitarian intervention began in the mid-eleventh century as a line of reform minded popes and canon lawyers strove to reform the Church by creating a strong, centralized administrative structure separate from the secular government but possessing the moral responsibility to insure that secular rulers adhered to Christian moral principles.[25] Building on this base, Catholic thinkers eventually formulated a theory of universal papal jurisdiction and created the legal institutions that would implement this theory.[26]

Included within these legal developments was discussion of the Just War as one aspect of the relations among the nations of the world. For the most part, the Just War was seen as defensive in nature. Christians

---

23 On the Grotian order: see Edward Keene, *Beyond the Anarchical Society* (Cambridge: 2002), 40–41.

24 Nicholas of Cusa, *The Catholic Concordance*, ed. Paul E. Sigmund (Cambridge: 1991).

25 On the Gregorian reform movement: see Uta-Renata Blumenthal, *The Investiture Controversy: Church and Monarchy from the Ninth to the Twelfth Century* (Philadelphia: 1988); also see Harold Berman, *Law and Revolution: The Formation of the Western Legal Tradition* (Cambridge, Massachusetts: 1983).

26 Walter Ullmann, *Medieval Papalism* (London: 1949), 1.

would resort to arms only as a last resort and only in defense of their life and liberty, and they would stop their military efforts when these interests were secure. Furthermore, they would employ weapons, tactics and levels of force appropriate to the situation. The capstone of the papal and canonistic theory of society was the claim that the papal court was the ultimate court for adjudicating conflicts between Christian rulers. Christian rulers were encouraged to seek papal mediation as a means of preventing war between Christian states rather than engaging in conflict.[27]

The papacy also encouraged Christian rulers to employ force in the achievement of ecclesiastically determined goals within Christendom. For example, the successful implementation of the ecclesiastical reforms demanded by the Gregorian reformers of the eleventh and twelfth centuries often required the armed support of rulers. William the Conqueror's invasion of England in 1066 and Henry II's entry into Ireland in 1173 benefited from papal support gained by promises to reform the Church in England and Ireland.[28] The papal bull *Laudabiliter* (1155) authorized the English king to enter Ireland

for the purpose of enlarging the borders of the Church, setting bounds to the progress of wickedness, reforming evil manners, planting virtue, and increasing the Christian religion" doing so for God's honour and the welfare of the same.[29]

Although *Laudabiliter* did not use the phrase humanitarian intervention, the call to reform the "evil manners" of the Irish was clearly a forerunner of later calls to civilize the barbarous peoples of the world for their own good.

To a large extent the medieval Church-State conflict revolved around the question of the proper balance of power between the two institutions. Ultimately, the peace and order of Christendom relied on their willingness to work cooperatively with one another in order to achieve their respective goals. Expansion-minded rulers such as William the Conqueror and Henry II could request papal approval for conquests on the grounds that they would be bringing the benefits of reformed Christianity to peo-

---

27 Walter Ullmann, "The Medieval Papal Court as an International Tribunal", *Virginia Journal of International Law 11* (1971): 356–371.
28 On William the Conqueror: see David Douglas, *William the Conqueror* (London: 1964), 317–345. For the papal role in the English entry into Ireland: see John Watt, *The Church and the Two Nations in Medieval Ireland* (Cambridge: 1970), 35–41.
29 "Laudabiliter." In *Irish Historical Documents 1172–1922,* eds. Edmund Curtis and R. B. McDowell (London: 1943; reprint ed. New York: 1968) 17–18.

ple whose rulers had failed them in this regard. Furthermore, bringing barbarous peoples, that is hunter-gatherers and semi-nomadic pastoralists, under Christian control would lead to their becoming settled agriculturalists and therefore both Christian and civilized.[30]

Popes could also call upon Christian rulers to use force against enemies on the frontiers of Christendom. Beginning with Urban II's call for a crusade in 1095 popes legitimated violence against the Muslims in order to defend Christendom from Islamic expansion, the traditional war of defense. Urban also, however, called on Christian rulers to liberate the oppressed Christian inhabitants of the East from Muslim rule, what Jonathan Riley-Smith described as crusading as an act of love, intervening in the internal operations of another state to protect the oppressed. To go on crusade to assist the oppressed Christian of the Near East was to express "love of one's neighbour as well as love of God" in a concrete way.[31]

In the fourteenth and fifteenth centuries the expansion of Christendom at both extremities generated new interest in papal claims to universal jurisdiction. At the Council of Constance (1414–1417), German and Polish lawyers debated the status of the Lithuanians and the possession of their lands. Could the Germans claim possession of Lithuania on the grounds that the inhabitants being infidels could not legitimately possess their lands? Did legitimate rule depend on being in the state of grace?[32] Did the marriage of the heiress to the Polish throne, Hedwiga, to the Grand Duke Jagiello of Lithuania in 1386 and the Duke's subsequent baptism end any basis for German claims to possess Lithuania? The Pope and the Council serving as the supreme court of Christendom were expected to resolve the legal issues involved. At the core of the debate was not simply the issue of possession of territory but, from the papal perspective, the best way to insure the preaching of Christianity

---

30   Christianizing a people inevitably required the formation of a settled agricultural population living in villages centered on a parish church: see Amy Turner Bushnell, "'None of These Wandering Nations Has Ever Been Reduced to the Faith': Missions and Mobility on the Spanish-American Frontier." In *The Spiritual Conversion of the Americas,* ed. James Muldoon (Gainesville, Florida: 2004) 142–168.

31   Jonathan Riley-Smith, "Crusading as an Act of Love." In *History 65* (1980) 177–192 at 182.

32   On Paulus Vladimiri: see Stanislaus F. Belch, *Paulus Vladimiri and His Doctrine concerning International Law and Politics,* 2 vols. (The Hague: 1965); Frederick H. Russell, "Paulus Vladimiri's Attack on the Just War: A Case Study in Legal Polemics." In *Authority and Power: Studies on Medieval Law and Government,* eds. Brian Tierney and Peter Linehan (Cambridge: 1980) 237–254.

among the Lithuanians in order that they might gain eternal salvation, the most humane of bases for intervention in the conflict.

At the other end of Christian Europe, the Portuguese capture of Ceuta (1415) on the coast of North Africa, the first successful European colony in Africa, marked the beginning of continuous European expansion beyond the traditional boundaries of the Mediterranean-centered Christian world. Portuguese and Spanish sailors moved down along the coast of Africa, out into the Atlantic islands, the Azores, Madeira, Cape Verde, and, eventually, into the Americas. This expansion posed a new problem for European rulers, ecclesiastical officials, and intellectuals. Although Africa was a part of the known world and could be fitted into the existing model of the world, the islands, with the exception of the Canaries, had been entirely unknown to Europeans.[33] The Azores, Cape Verde, and Madeira, were unoccupied so they posed no problems for theologians or philosophers to consider as the papacy claimed jurisdiction over men's souls but not over land. The Canary Islands, however, were inhabited by people living at a very primitive level. Could the papacy authorize Christian rulers to support missionary and other efforts among the Canarians, efforts that might lead to violence and the conquest of the Canarians?[34] The numerous papal bulls, more than 100 of them (many devoted to the Canaries), issued in connection with this phase of European expansion indicate that in addition to attempting to convert the Canarians to Christianity, the missionaries would also strive to raise them from their primitive level of existence.[35]

In effect, the papacy saw the role of Christians in the newly discovered lands as both spiritual and cultural in nature. That being the case, the papacy sought to insure that the entry of Christians into the islands was done in the most peaceful and orderly fashion possible, respecting the

---

33 As far back as the eleventh century, the papacy had negotiated with the rulers of various parts of North Africa: see M. L. de Mas Latrie, ed., *Traités de paix et de commerce et documents divers concernant les relations des Chretiens avec Arabes de l'Afrique Septentrionale au moyen age*, 2 vols. (Paris: 1865–1868; reprint ed., New York n.d. (1964)).

34 On the Canary Islands: see Anthony M. Stevens-Arroyo, "The Inter-Atlantic Paradigm: The Failure of Medieval Spanish Colonization of the Canary and Caribbean Islands." In *Comparative Studies in Society and History* 35 (1993) 515–543.

35 For these bulls see: D. J. Wölfel, "La Curia Romana y la Corona de España en la defensade los aborigines Canarios." In *Anthropos* 25 (1930) 1011–1083.

rights of the inhabitants but also insuring that they were offered the bless-
ings of Christianity and a civilized way of life.

The entry of Europeans into the Canary Islands, however, generated
some discussion about the legitimacy of occupying the islands, a forerunner of the extensive debate about the legitimacy of the conquest of the
Americas that was to occupy the Spanish intellectual world in the sixteenth and seventeenth centuries. In the fifteenth century the Spanish
and the Portuguese were competing for possession of the Canaries. At
one point, King Duarte of Portugal (1433–1438) asked Pope Eugenius
IV (1431–1437) about the right of the Portuguese to occupy the Canary
Islands. In his letter, the king pointed out that the Canarians were "nearly
wild men who inhabit the forests" and that they are not united by a common religion, nor are they bound by the chains of law" and that they are
lacking normal social intercourse, living in the country like animals." The
king proposed that the pope authorize him to occupy the islands in order
to protect the inhabitants from attacks by cruel adventurers and to give
them "civil laws and an organized form of society" so that they might develop a civilized society.[36] By occupying the islands and Christianizing
and civilizing the Canarians the Portuguese would be training them to
defend themselves against slavers and freebooters, certainly from the Portuguese perspective a humanitarian activity.

The pope requested opinions from two noted lawyers who answered
in the affirmative.[37] Their responses re-stated Innocent IV's assertion that
all rational human beings had the right to self government. On the other
hand, they also argued that all mankind came under papal jurisdiction so
that a pope could order a Christian ruler to intervene in an infidel society
if the people blocked the entrance of Christian missionaries or if they
were violating the natural law.

Pope Eugenius's response to King Duarte reflected the views of his
legal advisors. He justified the entry of the Portuguese into the Canary
Islands on the grounds that it was ultimately to their spiritual advantage
to accept Christian missionaries. He also added, again reflecting a point
that the Portuguese monarch had made, that if a Christian ruler was not
authorized to enter the Canary Islands, then unscrupulous men, slavers

---

36 James Muldoon, *The Expansion of Europe: The First Phase* (Philadelphia: 1977)
    54–56 at 54–55.
37 James Muldoon, "A Fifteenth-Century Application of the Canonistic Theory of
    the Just War." In *Proceedings of the Fourth International Congress of Medieval
    Canon Law* (Vatican City: 1976) 467–480 at 473.

and murderers, would attack the defenseless native population. In other words, the long-term security of the Canarians would depend on the Portuguese intervening to assist them.[38]

The long line of papal bulls that accompanied European expansion into the Atlantic and the commentaries of canon lawyers continued to reflect the practical application of a broad theory of universal papal jurisdiction over both Christians and non-Christians that had been in process of development since the twelfth century.[39] The core of this theory first appeared in a commentary on a decretal letter of Pope Innocent III (1198–1216) involving participation in the crusades. About 40 years later, the noted canon lawyer Sinibaldo Fieschi, better known as Pope Innocent IV (1243–1254), the leading legal mind of the papacy according to Frederic Maitland, in a commentary on his predecessor's letter, raised an issue that no one else appears to have raised.[40] Having disposed briefly with the specific issue that generated the decretal, Innocent IV asked the obvious question: by what right did Christians engage in the Crusades at all? By what right did they invade and seize the lands of the Muslims? He concluded that it was legitimate to invade the Holy Land where Christ had lived or other lands once possessed by Christians but now in Muslim hands because the Muslims had seized them in an unjust war.[41] In addition Christians had the right to defend themselves from further Muslim expansion and also the right to liberate their fellow Christians living under the Muslim yoke. They had no right, however, to seize other lands that the Muslims had acquired legitimately, because all men had the right to *dominium*, that is the right to posses property and to govern themselves.

---

38 Muldoon, "A Fifteenth-Century Application", 471, 478–479.
39 Luis Weckmann, "The Alexandrine Bulls of 1493: Pseudo-Asiatic Documents." In *First Images of America*, Fredi Chiappelli, ed., 2 vols. (Berkeley: 1976) 201–9; *Las Bulas Alejandrinas de 1493 y la Teoriá Política del Papado Medieval* (México City: 1949); *La herencia medieval de Mexico*, 2 vols. (México City: 1984). For the list of bulls relating to expansion into the Atlantic: see Charles Martial de Witte, "Les bulles pontificales et l'expansion portugaise au XVe siécle." *Revue d'Histoire ecclésiastique 48* (1953): 683–718; 49 (1954): 438–461; 51 (1956): 413–453, 809–836; 53 (1958): 5–46, 443–471.
40 Frederic W. Maitland, "Moral Personality and Legal Personality." In *The Collected Papers of Frederic William Maitland*, ed. H. A. L. Fisher, 3 vols. (Cambridge: 1911) 3:304–320 at 310.
41 Innocent IV, *Commentaria Doctissima in Quinque Libros Decretalium* (Turin: 1581) ad 3.34.8 (fols. 176–177). There is a translation of part of this commentary: see Muldoon, *Expansion*, 191–192.

Innocent IV's position on the right of all mankind to possess *dominium* was not unchallenged. His student, the distinguished canonist Cardinal Hostiensis, normally a devoted follower of his master's views, took the opposite opinion. He argued that the coming of Christ eliminated the natural right to *dominium* so that only those in the state of grace could legitimately claim it.[42] Although some scholars subsequently identified this position as the official Church position on *dominium,* it was not.[43] In the fifteenth century, John Wyclif (d. 1384) and John Hus (d. 1415) were condemned at the Council of Constance for holding this opinion. If the opinion of Hostiensis had been accepted, Christians could legitimately claim possession of the entire world, setting Christendom against all mankind, clearly not an acceptable situation.

While recognizing the legitimacy of the *dominium* of infidels, Innocent IV also asserted papal jurisdiction over them, assigning all mankind to one of three legal regimes: canon law, the Law of Moses, and the natural law, with the pope as the supreme judge in each of these legal regimes. Each one regulated the lives of those subject to it, emphasizing their duties and responsibilities. Within Europe, for example, popes had ordered the burning of the Talmud by Christian rulers on the grounds that it contained errors in Jewish teaching and slandered Christians. When the leaders of the Jewish community refused to end the use of the Talmud, it was the responsibility of the pope to act in their place for the spiritual welfare of the Jewish community.[44]

Innocent IV's commentary also at least hinted at the possibility of humanitarian intervention as a basis for Christian military intervention in an infidel society: "I believe that if a gentile, who has no law except the law of nature [to guide him], does something contrary to the law of nature, the pope can lawfully punish him...." Furthermore, if infidel rulers such as Muslims "molest unjustly the Christians who are their subjects" or if they "treat Christians badly the pope can deprive them of the jurisdiction and sovereignty they possess over Christians by judicial sen-

---

42 Hostiensis, *Lectura quinque decretalium*, 2 vols. (Paris: 1512), ad 3.34.8 (2:124–125). There is a translation of this commentary in Muldoon, *Expansion*, 192–193.

43 J. H. Parry, *The Age of Reconnaissance: Discovery, Exploration and Settlement: 1450–1650* (London: 1963; reprint ed. London: 2000), 303–304.

44 Benjamin Z. Kedar, "Canon Law and the Burning of the Talmud." In *Bulletin of Medieval Canon Law*, n.s. 9 (1979) 79–82; see also Amnon Raz-Krakotzhin, *The Censor, the Editor, and the Text: The Catholic Church and the Shaping of the Jewish Canon in the Sixteenth Century* (Philadelphia: 2007).

tence…." Finally, if infidel rulers "prohibit preachers from preaching" Christian doctrine, the pope could punish them, because in such cases the infidel ruler was interfering with his subjects' opportunity to hear the words of salvation and accept baptism.[45] In other words, the pope can order the use of force for the moral well being of infidels as well as for Christians.

By the time that Pope Alexander VI (1492–1503) responded to the request to establish a line to divide Spanish and Portuguese zones in the Atlantic after Columbus's first voyage he could respond in terms of the three-centuries long body of legal theory and papal practice. The famous legal debate that accompanied the conquest of the America, what Lewis Hanke described as "The Spanish Struggle for Justice in the Conquest of America", was rooted in that medieval legal tradition.[46]

Discussion of the legitimacy of the conquest of the Americas was invariably associated with the revival of interest in scholastic philosophy and theology, although interestingly not canon law, the *secunda scholastica* associated especially with the University of Salamanca during the sixteenth century. The Spanish experience in the Americas generated an extensive literature about war and conquest that has yet to be fully examined. The work is difficult for modern scholars to appreciate because those involved in the great debate did not restrict their arguments to materials in a single discipline. To understand and appreciate what scholars such as Vitoria wrote it is necessary to recognize that they drew promiscuously on scripture, theology, philosophy, and law, Roman and canon.

At the beginning of his discussion of the legitimacy of the conquest of the Americas Vitoria raised the question of why he, a theologian, was writing on an issue that would seem to belong to the lawyers. He observed that "it is not the province of lawyers, or not of lawyers alone, to pass sentence in this question" because the relation of the Spanish to the inhabitants of the Americas "is a case of conscience, it is the business of priests, that is to say of the Church, to pass sentence upon it" because "jurists are not sufficiently versed to form an opinion on their own."[47] In making this point, Vitoria was not denying that there was a role for lawyers and jurists in the discussion of the Americas, only that each discipline had a specific role to play. In defining the role of each discipline and im-

---

45 Muldoon, *Expansion*, 192.
46 Lewis Hanke, *The Spanish Struggle for Justice in the Conquest of America* (Philadelphia: 1949).
47 Vitoria, 238–239.

plicitly ranking them, placing theology above law, Vitoria was not only making a claim about the situation in the Americas, he was participating in an old debate between theologians and canon lawyers about the relative importance of their respective disciplines.[48]

Paradoxically, however, for the past 100 years or so Vitoria's reputation has been based on his role in the development of international law, a claim that has led to a fruitless debate about whether the Spanish Dominican or the Dutch lawyer, Hugo Grotius, or someone else for that matter, was indeed the Father of International Law.[49] While the theological system to which Vitoria contributed is now generally considered to be irrelevant to the secular affairs of mankind, his thinking about the nature of relations among the nations of the world is relevant to some of the political problems facing the modern world. It is interesting to note that in the sixteenth century while the theologians and philosophers, especially Spanish ones associated with the *secunda scholastica*, devoted an enormous amount of attention to the moral problems that the discovery of the New World created, the canon lawyers did not.[50]

The fundamental problem with which Vitoria was concerned was the question of whether the Spanish occupation of the Americas was just. At the outset he stated the issues involved:

… by what right (*ius*) were the barbarians subjected to Spanish rule? Second, what powers has the Spanish monarchy over the Indians in temporal and civil matters? And third, what powers has either the monarchy or the Church with regard to the Indians in spiritual and religious matters?[51]

Thus the question of the legitimacy of the Spanish conquest of the Americas rested on the question of whether the Spanish use of violence in the Americas occurred within the parameters of the concept of the

---

48 Canonists placed their scholarship "on a pedestal" from which they "looked down on all other branches of learning and human knowledge, including theology, with that feeling of superiority that springs from the deep conviction of possessing inherent and intrinsic value." In the opinion of the canonists, their learning "towers high above the humble civil knowledge and takes theology under its protective wings.

    Ullmann, *Medieval Papalism*, 26–28.

49 Muldoon, "The Contribution", 483–497 at 486–488.

50 On the later development of canon law: see Charles Donahue, Jr., "A Crisis of Law? Reflections on the Church and Law over the Centuries." In *The Jurist* 65 (2005): 1–30.

51 Vitoria, 233.

Just War that had been developing for several centuries.[52] Complicating matters was the fact that the Americas were inhabited by vast numbers of people who lived at a variety of levels of existence from the sophisticated societies of the Aztecs and the Incas to the most primitive, such as the inhabitants of Patagonia. None of these people had ever attacked Christendom, so there was no basis for a just war of defense in the Canaries or in the Americas. Would it be possible to justify the conquest of these people in terms of the just war? The arguments that Vitoria presented for and against the legitimacy of the conquest in the *De Indis* were his response to that question.

The intellectual framework within which Vitoria presented his work was fundamentally legal, specifically property law. That is, while the fundamental issue was one of moral theology, he presented his discussion of the legitimacy of the Spanish occupation of the New World in terms of lawful possession of property: "it remains to consider by what title we Christians were empowered to take possession of their territory." He proposed to examine the question in terms of the "seven irrelevant titles, and seven or perhaps eight just and legitimate ones". Title obviously means 'heading' but also contains the implication of a claim to property.[53] The legitimacy of Spanish possession of the Americas rested on the justice of the campaigns that were waged in the course of acquiring the Americas. If the means employed were unjust or illegitimate then the possession was illegitimate. The crucial point in Vitoria's argument was the assertion "that the barbarians undoubtedly possessed as true dominion, both public and private, as any Christians." Dominion, *dominium* in Latin, referred to the legitimate possession of property and government.[54]

If the inhabitants of the Americas did possess legitimate *dominium*, what would justify the Spanish conquest of the Americas? By the time that Europeans were encountering the Americas for the first time, it was the received opinion that *dominium* did not depend on being in the state of grace, so that if the Spanish were to claim legitimate posses-

---

52 Causa XXIII of the Decretum, the first volume of the *Corpus Iuris Canonici*, dealt specifically with the question of the use of violence drawing heavily on the writings of St. Augustine: see Russell, *Just War*, 55–57.

53 Vitoria, 251–252.

54 Vitoria, 250.

sion of the Americas they would have to explain why they could override the legal rights of the indigenous population.[55]

Among the arguments that Vitoria discussed as a plausible argument in support of the conquest was: "Question 3, Article 5: fifth just title, in defence of the innocent against tyranny".[56] Could the Spanish legitimately enter the Americas in order to protect the oppressed peoples of the New World from their wicked rulers, that is, could they defend their conquest on the grounds of humanitarian intervention? The answer to the last question resided in the legal structure that Innocent IV had erected to encompass all mankind. The natural law, the fundamental rules for the moral operation of human society, was accessible to all rational creatures so that even the infidels could not claim ignorance of the terms of that law. Their failure to adhere to the natural law could, therefore, justify their conquest in order to coerce them to fulfill those responsibilities.[57] Elsewhere, in a discussion of cannibalism, Vitoria's discussion of the natural law took an ironic twist when he presented the arguments for and against the basis for just war against infidels who violated the natural law by committing the sins of "idolatry or pederasty or buggery...." If this line of argument was accepted, then Christians would have the right to wage war against "all unbelievers, since they are adulterers or fornicators, perjurers or thieves" and "all these things are against natural law...." Furthermore, if Christian rulers could legitimately punish infidels for violations of the natural law, so too infidel rulers could punish Christians who violated the natural law, not a position that many Christians would care to defend.[58]

The collective theme of Vitoria's dismissal of the arguments that he rejected was that claims to universal political jurisdiction based on Roman law or on the New Testament were invalid. The ancient Romans had no right to make such a claim and the responsibility of the Church to preach Christ's message to all mankind did not authorize the conquest of non-believers because the acceptance of baptism had to rest on the voluntary act of the convert, not on fear of physical punishment.

---

55 Innocent IV's opinion was an important part of Vitoria's discussion: See James Muldoon, "A Canonistic Contribution to the Formation of International Law." In *The Jurist 28* (1968): 265–279.

56 Vitoria, 287.

57 James Muldoon, "Extra ecclesiam non est imperium: The Canonists and the Legitimacy of Secular Power." In *Studia Gratiana 9* (1966): 553–580.

58 Vitoria, 218.

The key to understanding Vitoria's notion of international order is the first claim to occupy the Americas that Vitoria recognized as legitimate, the right to travel everywhere in peace. Vitoria asserted that "Amongst all nations it is considered inhuman to treat strangers and travellers badly without some special cause, [and it is considered] humane and dutiful to behave hospitably to strangers." Even the "division of property", that is the creation of private property by the ius gentium, was not designed "to prevent men's free mutual intercourse with one another...."[59] Thus, Spanish merchants have a natural right to engage in trade with the people of the New World and Christian missionaries have the right to preach the Gospel without fear of reprisal.[60] Should the infidels not allow merchants and missionaries to travel in peace, then Christian rulers would have the right to protect their subjects who were engaging in these activities. This could lead to the conquest of the entire country but presumably only in order to insure that the people and their rulers behave according to the universal principles of human behavior.

In Vitoria's eyes, however, there was a possible limitation on the right of peaceful Christian penetration of the Americas. The pope might limit the exercise of this right to the subjects of a particular Christian ruler, in the case of the Americas to the Spanish, "if this is convenient for the spreading of the Christian religion, because he has the power to order temporal matters for the convenience of spiritual ones." In making this assertion, Vitoria was providing a theoretical justification for the division of the Atlantic world into two spheres, one assigned to the Spanish, the other to the Portuguese. The aim was to prevent "an indiscriminate rush to the lands of these barbarians from other Christian countries" lest "the Christians might very well get in each other's way and start to quarrel." If that happened, peace "would be disturbed, and the business of the faith and the conversion of the barbarians upset."[61] In other words, the papacy could play a regulatory role in the relation among the Christian nations engaged in overseas trade and colonization and a similar role with regard to Christian relations with the native peoples for the moral good of all concerned.

---

59 Vitoria, 278.
60 This line of argument can be found in Innocent IV's commentary as well. Innocent however would forbid the preaching of Islam is Christian states.
61 Vitoria, 284–285.

Finally, there was the question of whether Christians could lawfully conquer an infidel land in order to protect the subjects of a tyrannical ruler from his cruelty, on the basis of what Vitoria described as "defence of the innocent against tyranny."[62] Would it be lawful to wage war on such a basis? Given the current interest in the legitimacy of humanitarian intervention, this title is of special interest. Vitoria's response to this question is quite blunt: *"in lawful defence of the innocent from unjust death, even without the pope's authority, the Spaniards may prohibit the barbarians from practising any nefarious custom or rite."* The reason for this is that the "barbarians are all our neighbours, and therefore anyone, and especially princes, may defend them from such tyranny and oppression."[63] In other words, the nature of the situation itself, the sight of such "nefarious" customs and rites, would justify the use of force by any responsible rule. There is no need for seeking authorization from any universal authority such as the pope or the Holy Roman Emperor because the defense of the innocent is a responsibility that human beings owe to one another, "an affirmative precept pertaining to natural law."[64]

Vitoria's broad statement about the right to intervene in the activities of another state raised an obvious question. What if the people who engage in these practices do not wish to end them? In his opinion, it "makes no difference that all the barbarians consent to these kinds of rites and sacrifices, or that they refuse to accept the Spaniards as their liberators in the matter."[65] In other words, the barbarians should be defended even from themselves if necessary. Such practices were clearly violations of the natural law so that those who engaged in them, rational human beings, were capable of seeing and correcting their erroneous cultural practices and so were guilty of willful rejection of the natural law if they did not correct such practices. That being the case, would it be enough to defeat such a society in battle, set the ruler and the people on the right path, and then withdraw? If it is not enough, Vitoria argues that "their masters may be changed and new princes set up."[66]

Vitoria's reference to the possibility of establishing new rulers as a consequence of intervention raises an issue that neither he nor most others who have written on the topic of humanitarian intervention have con-

---

62 Vitoria, 287.
63 Vitoria, 288.
64 Schwartz, "The Principle", 290.
65 Vitoria, 288.
66 Vitoria, 288.

sidered. How long should the interventionist power remain in place to ensure that the evil rulers do not return or to prevent the people from reverting to their evil ways? Does military victory automatically guarantee long-term political and cultural change?[67] At what point would short-term humanitarian intervention become long-term imperial conquest?

Finally, do Vitoria and other theorists of social and political development assume that there is ultimately a single acceptable form of such development leading to a particular form of government, social structure, and code of moral behavior?[68] In the contemporary world, the use of terms such as developed and underdeveloped states suggests that there is some form of natural course of development that states can be expected to follow so that humanitarian intervention might be necessary to remove the obstacles that hinder the full development of an underdeveloped society. Does the removal of such obstacles require only short military actions or would it require the long-term presence of the interventionist power until the society was ready to follow the expected course of development? Would such use of force be in keeping with the principles of the just war and how can it be reconciled with the legal notion of sovereignty?

At this point, we may turn to the question raised earlier: is Vitoria primarily a moral theologian or an early example of what we would term an international lawyer? Those terms create a somewhat crude basis for considering the significance of his work and its relation to the concept of the just war. After all, the sharp disciplinary boundary lines that characterize modern universities, generating turf wars and other academic guerrilla actions, did not exist in the sixteenth century, as the wide range of citations found in his work demonstrate. Vitoria reflects an effort to draw upon long-standing theological, philosophical, and legal traditions in order to deal with a situation that while similar to some European experience posed old questions in new contexts. His interest in the issues that the discovery of the New World generated stemmed from the pastoral concerns of a moral theologian as befitted a priest. He then drew

---

67   Some have called for the restoration of imperial control over failed states in order to prepare these states for full participation in the international community: see for example Niall Ferguson, *Colosseus: The Price of America's Empire* (New York: 2004) 169–199. This plan would re-establish something like the mandate system that was applied after World War I: see also Brett Bowden, *The Empire of Civilization: The Evolution of an Imperial Idea* (Chicago: 2009) 193–199.

68   Francis Fukuyama advanced such a position in his *The End of History and the Last Man* (New York: 1992).

on the legal tradition, especially the canon law, for some specific applications of theological principles. Central to the entire effort was the concept of God as lawgiver whose creation operated according to laws that men could comprehend in order to create a rightly ordered society that replicates God's law. Law in practice represents the effort to institutionalize moral principles and humanitarian intervention is an instrument that might be required to achieve that goal in some cases.

Francisco de Vitoria:
Just War as Defense of International Law

Heinz-Gerhard Justenhoven

"bellum nullum argumentum est
pro veritate fidei Christianae"[1]

The Dominican scholar Francisco de Vitoria (1483–1546) is one of the best known figures in the history of the just war theory. Quite often his contribution in this regard is reduced to his lecture *de iure belli*, where he indeed deals with the questions of the *auctoritas legitima, causa iusta* and questions of *the ius in bello*. It is not by chance, though, that the lecture *de iure belli* is the second part of the lecture *de indis*. The overall subject of these two lectures is the question, by what law the American Indians came under the dominion of the Spanish king. Part of that investigation is the question, of the Spanish king fought a just war against the Indians. As both texts are a unit, they have to be read as one. It goes without saying that these two lectures have to be analyzed within the body of Vitoria's other lectures on political and ethical matters.

In the first place I will argue that Vitoria's examination on just war has to be understood as part of his debate on international law. This is why most of my presentation will deal with international law, not with just war. Secondly I will make an argument that Vitoria is not a lawyer but a theologian and this fact does have consequences for the interpretation of what he is saying. And finally I will place his arguments into the historical setting: Much of what Vitoria said and wrote will be clarified if put on the historical and intellectual stage of the 16th century.

Vitoria, a Dominican priest, was born in 1483 in Burgos in northern Spain and studied in Paris, the intellectual center of the early 16th century. Through his teacher Peter Crockaert he became familiar with the theology of Thomas Aquinas and together with Crockaert he prepared one of the first editions of the *Summa Theologiae*. Back in Spain, Vitoria

---

1   Francisco de Vitoria, "De Indis." In *Francisco de Vitoria, Vorlesungen I*, eds. Ulrich Horst, Heinz-Gerhard Justenhoven, Joachim Stüben (Stuttgart: 1995), (hereafter Vitoria, Vorlesungen II) 446.

was appointed to the chair of theology first in Valladolid, later in Salamanca, where he read and explained the *Summa Theologiae* of Thomas Aquinas with his students.[2] At the end of each academic year, Vitoria delivered a lecture on current political issues such as the Spanish war against the Indians or the highly political divorce of the King of England, Henry VIII., which caused the separation of the Anglican Church from Rome. Within his more than twenty years as a professor of theology he became one of the decisive theologians of Thomistic renaissance.[3]

The event that had deeply changed the world of late Medieval Christianity was the discovery of the New World. Within one generation, Spanish soldiers discovered and conquered half of the American continent. The Indian peoples were made subjects of the Spanish Emperor Charles V. The contemporaries of Vitoria had little time to understand what had happened. They found themselves in the midst of epochal changes. Besides the conquest of the new world, Europeans witnessed deep changes in their own continent:

France under the reign of its mighty King Francis I. successfully challenged the Habsburg-Emperor Charles V., a struggle that weakened the Empire and strengthened the upcoming states of the early modern age. At the same time the unity of the Latin Church broke apart: Martin Luther initialized the reformation in Germany. The English King Henry VIII. broke with the Pope to establish the Anglican Church. In sum these changes open up a new epoch, definitely overcoming an old one: the medieval ideal of one Christian community with the Emperor being responsible for the temporal wellbeing under the spiritual and ultimate political leadership of the Pope.

While the struggle in Europe was going on and the outlines of a new European order were only about to emerge, the conquest of the New World on the other side of the ocean brought pagans and – in Spanish eyes – wild peoples under the reign of the Christian Emperor. The intellectual debate of the early 16th century, confronted with the uncivilized Indians of the Carribeans, questioned whether these Indians were slaves by nature in the sense of the Aristotelian definition: that there are

---

2   For further bibliographical details see: Ulrich Horst "Leben und Werke Francisco de Vitorias." In *Vitoria, Vorlesungen I* (Stuttgart: 1995/1997) 13–99.

3   Vitoria's lectures were long forgotten and we are indebted to scholars like the Belgian international lawyer Ernest Nys (*Le droit de la guerre et les précurseurs de Grotius* (Bruxelles: 1882)) and the American James B. Scott (*The Spanish Origin of international law* (London: 1934)) that there has been intensive research on Vitoria within the last decades.

human beings without any civilization, that live like wild animals and therefore could be treated like slaves. It was a comfortable position justifying the Spanish conquest and cruelties against the Indians.

That position was challenged by Dominican missionaries, who had baptized many Indians and pointed to the Christian Empereor's responsibility to protect his Indian subjects. Some of them had already become Christians, others were yet to be confronted with the Gospel of Christ. But how could missionaries bring the message of the Saviour's love, as long as Christian soldiers were only interested in conquest, gold and slaves and therefore slaughtered and suppressed the Indian population.

As professor of theology, the Dominican priest Francisco de Vitoria was in the midst of this debate. He understood that the discovery of the New World had confronted European Christianity with questions that could not be answered within the traditional framework. Dealing with ethical problems implies an understanding of what is called into question. It was not the discovery of formerly unknown countries as such. The discovery of unknown parts of the African or Asian continent was nothing unusual to Europe of the early modern age. Hence the discovery of America in 1492 had been more: it was the discovery of a New World that within little more than a generation came under the dominion of the Spanish king. The Scottish theologian John Mair initiated the debate of who these Indians were and how to deal with them.

1 The conquest of the New World as a theological issue

While Vitoria usually is looked at as being an early international lawyer, I am convinced that first of all he was and remained a theologian. It is no wonder that the Indian question for Vitoria was a theological one and he tried to solve it with theological categories: The experience, the Dominican missionaries had made with the Indian population, became the decisive hint and the starting point of Vitoria's deliberation of the Indian problem. Quite a number of the Indians professed their faith in Christ, once the missionaries had preached the Gospel. The Indian people were obviously able to believe in Christ. This could only be possible, Vitoria concluded, if the Creator had furnished the Indians with the ability to do so. From here, Vitoria could go back to Aquinas' theology of a cosmos in complete harmony that the Creator had aligned to himself. Within the order of the cosmos it is the destination of humankind to respond to God's call to salvation. Being an image of God, every human being is able to understand and accept faith by reason, once the Gospel is preached to him. As images of God the Europeans are able to respond the call to salvation. The Dominican missionaries reported that some Indians had responded to God's call and had already confessed the Christian faith. The Thomistic distinction between nature and grace is of great value at this point. It is Vitoria's merit to have seen its political implications in his time.[4] According to Aquinas, grace does not change but fulfill nature, being based on it.[5] Regarding the Indian question the thomistic distinction leads Vitoria to the argument, that the Indian's nature can be fulfilled by Gods grace as well: Dignity and value of the Indian nature are based in the disposition of each human being's nature which can be fulfilled by God's grace. Or in other words: The fact that the Indians are able to convert to Christendom, Vitoria concludes, shows that God by creation has given them a nature that is open for his grace. The Indians must have the same nature by creation as the Europeans as they obviously are gifted with sufficient reason to understand the sense of the gospel. As humankind is gifted with reason by his nature not by civilization, there can be no difference between Spaniards and Indians in this regard: the Indians are obviously gifted with reason by nature in the same way.[6] Having a nature that is obviously gifted with sufficient reason to understand the sense of the gospel and therefore being images of God is the foundation of the Indians human dignity and rights.[7] With this thesis Vitoria could negate claims that the Indians for spiritual reasons were to be made subject and civilized by the Spanish conquerors.

Vitoria's comprehension on the Indian peoples as possessing human dignity and rights[8] challenged the position of the conquerors and their intellectual representatives as Juan Ginés de Sepulveda.[9] Sepulveda stated

---

4   Cf. Ulrich Matz, "Vitoria." In *Klassiker des politischen Denkens I* (München: 1968), 277.

5   Cf. Thomas von Aquin, *Kommentar zu den Sentenzen des Petrus Lombardus III*, dist. 29,1,7.

6   C.f. Brian Tierney, *The Idea of Natural Rights*. Studies on Natural Rights, Natural Law and Church Law 1150–1625 (Atlanta/GA: 1977), 271.

7   Cf. Heinz-Gerhard Justenhoven, *Francisco de Vitoria zu Krieg und Frieden* (Köln: 1991), 60 f.

8   Anselm Spindler distincts Vitorias concept of "rights" from Thomas Aquinas; c.f. Anselm Spindler, "Vernunft, Gesetz und Recht bei Francisco de Vitoria." In *Die Normativität des Rechts bei Francisco de Vitoria*, eds. Kirstin Bunge, Anselm Spindler, Andreas Wagner (Stuttgart-Bad Cannstatt: 2010) 39 f.

9   C.f. Stephen F. Brett, *Slavery and the Catholic Tradition. Rights in the balance* (New York: 1994), 111.

that the Indians had to be civilized and learn to develop their rational ability first, before they could claim any rights. According to him, it was up to the Spanish to take care of the education that would first civilize and later christianize the Indians. Therefore the Indians would have to live under Spanish dominion and to work for their masters. This position allowed the Spanish king to reign over his Indian colonies and enjoy the respective benefits.

Vitoria, having started that discussion, had to argue precisely whether the Spanish conquest had violated the rights of the Indian peoples. Doing so, Vitoria had to argue, which rights the Indians had at all. Yet there was no generally accepted moral and juridical foundation covering the Old continent and the New World. The political order reflected in Thomas Aquinas *Summa Theologiae* was the *orbis christianus*, one Christian community, the *respublica fidelium*, the Church with the Pope as the spiritual leader. Within this universal Church, the Emperor would have to care for the secular order. Yet the framework of medieval political thinking could not serve to integrate the political questions of the early 16th century after reformation had taken place, modern states were emerging and a New World had been incorporated into the Spanish kingdom.[10]

2 Developing the modern notion of international law

Vitoria pointed out two related questions to be answered: First: Which are the political rights of the Indian peoples and have these rights been violated? Or did the Spaniard have a right to wage war against the Indian peoples? Second: How to define the relation between the Old and New World in a moral and juridical sense as the medieval framework of the Thomistic political philosophy did not apply any more?

It was a decisive point in the early 16th century discussion, whether the Indians were able to organize a state. Sepulveda or the Scottish scholar John Mair argued that the Indians lacked the ability to build up states

---

10 In his Commentary to Thomas Aquinas Summa Theologia Vitoria developed his theory that he later applied in his lectures. Some of his commentaries are being newly edited: Francisco de Vitoria "De Lege – Über das Gesetz." *Series: Political Philosophy and Theory of Law in the Middle Ages and Modernity. Texts and Studies,* ed. Joachim Stüben, vol I,1 (Stuttgart-Bad Cannstatt: 2010); Francisco de Vitoria "De Iustitia I– Über die Gerechtigkeit." *Series: Political Philosophy and Theory of Law in the Middle Ages and Modernity. Texts and Studies,* ed. Joachim Stüben, vol I,3 (Stuttgart-Bad Cannstatt: 2012).

and pointed to the low degree of civilization especially of the wild Caribbean Indians. But since Hernán Cortés had conquered the highly civilized Aztec Empire and Francisco Pizarro the Inca Empire, the Old World had learned that there were civilized Indian peoples as well. On the basis of this knowledge Vitoria could declare, that "they have some order (*ordo*) in their affairs: they have properly organized cities, proper marriages, magistrates and overlords (*domini*), laws, industries, and commerce, all of which require the use of reason."[11] Reason as prerequisite to organize states is obviously given to the Indian people by nature, in the same way as it is given to the European people.

With his argument of the natural rights of the Indians and their ability to understand the Christian faith Vitoria could negate claims that the Indians for spiritual reasons were to be made subject and civilized by the Spanish conquerors. Stating the dignity of the Indian nature and political communities, Vitoria had the fundamental argument to reject papal or imperial claims for world sovereignty, arguments that allowed to subdue the Indian people.

Vitoria is an early era representative of the doctrine of the sovereignty of the people, which he became aquainted with at the University of Paris. According to this doctrine it is not the prince, who is originally bearer of the politicial power. Political power has its foundation in the people. Following Aristotle, Vitoria states that man is a social being and therefore joins together in communities. "A civil society (*societas civilis*) is one which most aptly fulfils men's needs. It follows that the civil society (*societas civilis*) is, if I may put so, the most natural community, the one which is most conformable to nature."[12] Therefore, according to Vitoria, states are not inventions of humankind but founded in human nature: Wherever humankind lived, they had to meet their necessities and form states and in that way corresponded to their nature. Whatever is necessary for humankind in that way is founded in natural law. The Dominican concludes that the Indian and European states in the same are based on natural law and because of this foundation, Indian and European states enjoy equal rights.

The plurality of positions and interests in a state has to be aligned to the common good; this is the task of the state authority (*potestas civilis*). According to Vitoria, there is no reason, to grant privileges to anybody in

---

11 Vitoria, *On the American Indians*, (Edition Pagden) 250.
12 Vitoria, *On Civil Power*, (Edition Pagden) 8 f. Pagden translates *societas civilis* with "civil partnership" and "city".

that regard, "because by natural law all men are equal and nobody was prince by natural law"[13]. Originally the people is the bearer of the political authority. But as it is impossible that the people itself exercises political power, it has to transfer the authority to the government by consensus or at least by approval of the majority.[14] Even though Vitoria admits, that democracy can be one possible form of governing a state, the 16th century Dominican prefers monarchy.

As far as I can tell it is because of this preference that Vitoria only talks about the *princeps* as political authority. He is *princeps* only through his election by the people. He has to exercise his political power in orientation of the common good. Vitoria thinks more of a virtual election than of a real one, but he wants to stress the point that it is not the *princeps* himself, but the people, where political power originates. Only if he administrates the state in leading the partial interests towards the common good, does he use the political power legitimately. It is a consequence of the doctrine of the sovereignty of the people that the laws the *princeps* enacts as head of state, obligate him as well. If he does not subordinate himself under the law, he is a tyrant and the political power falls back to the people, who can dismiss him.

Regarding the Indian question, Vitoria can point out that the Indian peoples have states and are governed by legitimate *principes*. The Indian states are founded on natural law as necessary communities for the Indians to meet the necessities of their nature which they have been given by creation. Regarding their natural law basis, these states differ in no way from the European states. As Indian and Spanish states in principle have equal rights, it is still in question, whether the Spanish conquerors had violated Indian rights or conducted a just war. To deal with this problem, Vitoria still needs a basis to describe the moral and juridical relationship between the conquered Indian states and their Spanish conquerers. He will use the idea of a fundamental unity of humankind before the division in nations and states existed.

The idea of the unity of humankind can be traced back to the philosophy of the classical antiquity. The intellectual world of the early

---

13 Cf. Francisco de Vitoria, *Commentarios a la Secunda secundae de Santo Tomás*, V. Beltrán de Heredía, vol. 3 (Salamanca: 1934) (hereafter ComSTh II.-II., Vol. 3) q. 62 a.1 n.21.

14 A. Brett shows that according to Vitoria it is the *auctoritas*, not *potestas* that is transferred; cf. Annabel S. Brett, *Liberty, Right and Nature. Individual rights in later scholastic thought* (Cambridge: 1997) 136.

16th century was fascinated by this idea. It was a reaction to the numerous wars of their time that especially the Renaissance humanists were looking for peace-concepts. Thomas Morus for example published his *Utopia* in 1515/16, which is about the idea of a fundamental equality of all human beings. Vitoria, having studied in Paris, was influenced by this intellectual movement. Humankind, according to Vitoria, is a "natural society and community"[15]. He states that the idea of unity is implicitly present in the right to hospitality, as "amongst all nations it is considered inhumane to treat strangers and travelers badly without some special cause"[16]. Trade between nations and the freedom of travel point into the same direction: The human nature's social orientation is not limited to the family, the tribe or the nation; it is universally oriented. Arguing phenomenologically, according to Vitoria, freedom of travel and trade between nations are indications of the unity of humankind. This means, Vitoria concludes, that the unity of humankind is founded in natural law, i.e. a principle that is founded in the Creator's will, that can be understood by all human beings and that obligates the positive law of all states. I think this is the setting in which Vitorias famous quote has to be understood: "*totius orbis … aliquomodo est una respublica*" ("the whole world …somehow is a commonwealth"[17]). Vitoria is the first to use the notion *orbis* to describe the whole world in the modern sense: It includes the Old World as well as the known parts of Africa and Asia and the newly discovered continent, later called America, the New World.[18] Originally the term *orbis* was used to describe the universal empire: The Roman Empire of the classical antiquity was called the *orbis*, and the medieval Emperor was called "*dominus et monarcha totius orbis*". Using the classical term *orbis*, Vitoria could make sure that his contemporaries understood that he was talking about the New World in a sense that it was to be part of the same community as the Old

---

15 Pagden translates Vitorias "*naturalis societatis et communicationis*" with "natural partnership and communication", which does not grasp the idea of a natural community; c.f. Vitoria, *On the American Indians*, (Edition Pagden) 278. For the Latin text c.f. Vitoria, *Vorlesungen II*, 460.

16 Vitoria, *On the American Indians*, (Edition Pagden) 278.

17 Vitoria, *On Civil Power*, (Edition Pagden) 40.

18 C.f. Kirstin Bunge, "Das Verhältnis von universaler Rechtsgemeinschaft und partikularen politischen Gemeinwesen: Zum Verständnis des *totus orbis* bei Francisco de Vitoria." In *Die Normativität des Rechts bei Francisco de Vitoria*, ed. K. Bunge (2010).

World. Old and New World, this is Vitoria's key message, are to be understood as one community in a similar way as the old *orbis* was.

Vitoria does not see a contradiction between the fundamental unity of humankind and its division in nations and states, as "the peoples never intended to end their mutual communication"[19]. In fact the question is how to regulate peaceful communication and interaction between states: The states of the early modern era had liberated themselves from the universal powers and were in no longer ready to submit to the Emperor or to the Pope. The heads of these states like the English King Henry VIII. or the French King Francis I. regarded themselves as supreme judges in their own states, independent – the notion sovereign was not used yet – from other political entities. While the evolving European states had liberated themselves from the universal powers, the Indian states had never been under their jurisdiction. With this situation the ideal order of a *ius commune* with a supreme judge was obsolete.

3 Just War as defense of international law

How could Vitoria discuss the moral issues of the Spanish conquest of the Indian states? What was the overarching moral and legal order embracing Old and New World, embracing the larger *orbis?* Vitoria seeks the answer in re-interpreting the classical Roman law term *ius gentium:* The "body of Roman law that applied to all non-Romans in the empire as well as to the relationship between Romans and non-Romans was called *jus gentium*, or law of tribes… it was based on norms and concepts common to the various groups throughout the Roman Empire."[20] According to Thomas Van Dervort, *ius gentium* "came to be viewed by early writers and jurists as universal in applicability because it consisted of norms common to divergent groups who may not have had contact with one another."[21] In this sense Vitoria understands the term *ius gentium* as applicable to a law common to all peoples in the larger world. Vitorias wellknown defintion of *ius gentium* reads: "*Quod naturalis ratio*

---

19   "*Numquam enim fuit intentio gentium per illam divisionem tollere hominem invicem communicationem …*" Vitoria, "De indis III,1." In *Vitoria, Vorlesungen II,* 460 f. Pagden translates "communication" with "intercourse" instead of "communication"; c.f. Vitoria, *On the American Indians,* (Edition Pagden) 278.

20   Thomas R. Van Dervort, *International Law and Organization* (Thousand Oaks: 1998), 5.

21   Thomas R. Van Dervort, 5.

inter omnes gentes constituit, vocatur ius gentium." (What natural reason has established among all nations is called law of the nations)[22]. This definition differs only in one word from the classical definition of the Roman jurist Gaius. According to Gaius *ius gentium*, is called "what natural rationality constitutes with all men (*inter omnes homines*)".[23]

According to Vitoria, *ius gentium* includes the law that is common to all peoples or nations and originates in reason. I have already pointed out that Vitoria includes the right to hospitality, freedom of travel and trade between nations and states into the *ius gentium*, as they are common to all peoples. Vitoria enumerates further norms of the *ius gentium:* Most of them are consequences of his idea of a fundamental unity and communication between the peoples of the world: Free access to all countries of the world (*ius peregrinandi*), free trade (*ius negotiandi*), the right to become citizen of another state and diplomatic immunity. Vitoria faces much criticism from some of his modern interpreters who presume that he opened the door wide for the justification of the conquest of the Indian states with this argument.[24] While I can't argue at length against this interpretation, I would like to quote Vitoria himself at this point:

"…if the barbarians attempt to deny the Spaniards in these matters which I have described as belonging to the law of nations (*ius gentium*), that is to say from trading and the rest, the Spaniards ought first to remove any cause of provocation by reasoning and persuasion, and demonstrate with every argument at their disposal that they have not come to do harm. But wish to dwell in peace and travel without any inconvenience to the barbarians. And they should demonstrate this not merely in words, but with proof… But if reasoning fails to win the acquiescence of the barbarians, and they insist on replying with violence, the Spaniards may defend themselves, and do everything needful for their own safety… Hence,

---

22 C.f. Vitoria, *On the American Indians*, (Edition Pagden) 278.
      Johannes Thumfart gives evidence in his dissertation that Vitoria relies with this new interpretation of *ius gentium* on his contemporate Miguel de Ulzurrun, Catholicum opus imperial regiminis mundi (1525), cf. J. Thumfart, Die Begründung der globalpolitischen Philosophie. Francisco de Vitorias Vorlesung über die Entdeckung Amerikas im ideengeschichtlichen Kontext, Berlin 2012.
23 Cf. *Institutions I*, 2, 1.
24 Cf. James Muldoon, "Francisco de Vitoria and the Humanitarian Intervention." *Journal of Military Ethics* 5 (2006): 128–143, 139.

if war is necessary to obtain their rights (*ius suum*) they may lawfully go to war."[25]

Vitoria's position was voiced publicly after the fall of the Indian States through the hand of men like Cortés and Pizzaro whos cruelties were made public through Bartholomé de Las Casas vocal criticism. On the background of the Dominican friar's criticism Vitoria's words sound almost ironic: everybody knew the very facts: While the Spanish could of course make use of the right to travel and trade, they had shown a very different behavior than Vitoria demanded and therefore no right to go to war.[26]

But what about the right of the Christians to preach the gospel, which Vitoria emphatically argues for.[27] For Vitoria it is obvious that human beings are in search for the truth. According to the Christian theologian Vitoria, the truth in Jesus Christ has to be preached to whoever is willing to listen. It is up to the Spanish Christians to preach the gospel to the Indians. Is this the loophole by which a sinister just war reasoning on behalf of the Spanish conquest could come in?

First of all, Vitoria states, "that it is not sufficiently clear to me that the Christian faith has up to now been announced and set before the barbarians in such a way as to oblige them to believe it under pain of fresh sin"[28]. Then he clarifies, saying that even if the Christian faith were announced adequately and then rejected by the Indians, "this is still no reason to declare war on them"[29].

In case a good part of the Indian population converted to Christendom, according to Vitoria the Pope could replace the pagan *princeps* in favour of a Christian one. While we strongly reject this argument, according to Vitoria the temporal power within the state has to be oriented to the spiritual end of humankind as it is announced in the Christian gospel. Vitoria, no question, is neither advocating religious freedom nor a secular state; he is a theologian of the early modern age, not of the 21st century.

According to Vitoria *ius gentium* is related to the natural law and to the positive law as well. It is part of the natural law, in so far as it is in

---

25 Vitoria, *On the American Indians*, (Edition Pagden) 281 f. For the discussion of Vitorias ideas in Domingo de Soto and Luis Molina see: Bernice Hamilton, *Political Thought in Sixteenth century Spain* (Oxford: 1963), 101 ff.

26 C.f. G. Scott Davis, "Conscience and conquest: Francisco de Vitoria on Justice in the New World. " *Modern Theology* 13 (1997): 485.

27 Cf. Vitoria, *On the American Indians*, (Edition Pagden) 284 f.

28 Vitoria, *On the American Indians*, (Edition Pagden) 271.

29 Ibd.

accordance with men's nature in aligning humankind to peace.[30] In difference to natural law the norms of *ius gentium* are a human decision either by custom or by a virtual legal act of the international community. In other words: The *ius gentium* includes the common law of humankind and Vitoria provides the case that the international community enacts new norms as international legislator by consensus. If the majority of the nations agree, the new norms are binding for all nations, not because the majority wants it, but because of the necessity to align the international community to the common good, where peace is a part of it.

The Vitorian definition of *ius gentium* is not yet comparable to the modern understanding of international law and I did not translate it, to stress this distinction.[31] It was the Jesuit Francisco Suárez who in 1612 took the decisive step to distinguish the term *ius gentium* into *ius gentium inter se,* the law between states from *ius gentium intra se,* the civil law[32] and excluded questions like those of private property, which according to Vitoria were part of the *ius gentium.*[33] With this distinction Suárez had formed the modern term of international law, the starting point for Hugo Grotius.

After having heard the terminological clarification of his international law as a juridical basis between Old and New world, we are likely to question the Dominican scholar, about the value of his concept of international law, as long as there is no supreme international judge, who would protect peace between the nations and states and enforce international law. As a thomistic scholar, Vitoria had this problem in mind. He states that the "world (*orbis*) could not exist unless some men had the power and authority to deter the wicked by force from doing harm to the good and the innocent".[34] An international authority to punish the wicked is as necessary for the *orbis* to exist, as it is for a state, Vitoria argues. According to him, some sort of international political authority is founded in natural law, as the political authority is within the state. Lack-

---

30 Cf. Vitoria, *ComSTh II.-II.*, Vol 3, q.57 a.3.
31 C.f. Stefan Kadelbach, "Mission und Eroberung bei Vitoria. Über die Entstehung des Völkerrechts aus der Theologie." In *Die Normativität des Rechts bei Francisco de Vitoria*, ed. K. Bunge (2010) 283.
32 Suárez, *De Legibus*, lib. II, cap. 19 n.8.; cf. Markus Kremer, *Den Frieden verantworten. Politische Ethik bei Francisco Suárez (1548–1617)* (Stuttgart: 2008) 126 ff.
33 Cf. Daniel Deckers, *Gerechtigkeit und Recht. Eine historisch-kritische Untersuchung der Gerechtigkeitslehre des Francisco de Vitoria* (Freiburg: 1991) 372 f.
34 Vitoria, *On the Law of War*, (Edition Pagden) 305.

ing an universal power in this new *orbis*, Vitoria abstains from asking for a universal monarch, as the Italian humanist Dante Alighieri does[35] and sticks to the realities of his time.

The *principes* of the states of the early modern era are those effectively in power. Vitoria obligates these *principes* to achieve not only the common good for their own state, but also to achieve the international common good and protect the international community from those violating international law:[36] "If the commonwealth has these powers against its own members, there can be no doubt that the whole world has the same powers against any harmful and evil men. And these powers can only exist if exercised through the princes of commonwealths."[37] The Spanish war against the Indians is the case with which Vitoria had to develop his theory: The Spanish King Charles I. could only fight the Indian states legitimately, if the Indians had violated international law. Being responsible not only for his own state but likewise for peace and security of the international community – not as Emperor Charles, but as King Charles of Spain –, he had to conduct war not only for the benefits of his own state, but in a way that peace and security of the international community would be achieved. This is, of course, the implicit answer to the question, whether or not the Spanish were fighting a just war against the Indian states.

4 Can war be just on both sides?

At the same time Vitoria realizes that his concept of each *princeps* being responsible for the common good in the same way and having the authority to use force in defending the international common good evolves a new issue: two princes may judge differently on the same matter. Therefore Vitoria asks, "wether war can be just on both sides"[38]. Other than the earlier tradition, Vitoria realizes that diverging judgments emerge from a

---

35   Cf. Ernst Ludwig Grasmück, "Dante Alighieri: De Monarchia. Zur politischen Idee vom Kaiser als Garanten des Friedens." In *Friedensethik im Spätmittelalter,* eds. Gerhard Beestermöller/Heinz-Gerhard Justenhoven (Stuttgart: 1998) 64–78.

36   C.f. Laura Purdy, "Vitoria's Just War Theory: Still relevant Today?" In *The Just War and jihad. Violence in Judaism, Christianity and the Islam,* ed. R. Joseph Hoffmann (New York: 2006) 255–276, 259.

37   Vitoria, *On the Law of War,* (Edition Pagden) 305 f.

38   *On the law of war* (Edition Pagden) 312.

different knowledge or interpretation of an issue or simply by an error. Therefore two *princeps* may believe to have a just cause and send their soldiers to war. Vitoria's solution to this dilemma is the obligation to the *princeps* to be most careful in their judgment on the case in the first place. Acknowledging the subjectivity of any judgment, the *princeps* is obliged to consult "reliable and wise men who can speak with freedom" and "also listen to the arguments of the opponents"[39]. While the head of state and his counselors bear this responsibility, the simple citizen or a trooper is responsible for the cause of the war (only) in as much as they are able to oversee the case. Vitoria concludes that a trooper may run into a situation where he believes to fight for a just cause without understanding the injustice of the war he is fighting – with insurmountable ignorance from his side.[40] Only in this case he may be excused, not his *princeps* or his advisor who could have known better. In any case of doubt they may not wage a war.[41]

As Vitoria sticks to his idea of the responsibility of each *princeps* for the international community, he demands him to pass judgment over the loser after the war has ended. The *princeps* who won the war, has to deliver his judgment not in prosecuting the loser, but as an impartial judge above the partial interests; a judge, who bears the responsiblity for the common good of the international community. But what happens, if the wrongdoer wins the war? Vitoria does not give an answer to this question and this is probably the weakest point in his just war thinking.

5 Limitations of force in a just war

Thomas requests in his treatise "de bello" that a war has to be fought with the "intentio recta". Vitoria translates the "right intention" into the challenge "not to harm out of greed"[42]. It seems obvious, that the 16th century soldiers requested a more specific advice than to have the right intention in waging a just war. The issue at stake was to know precisely of how to act externally when trying to have the right intention. The reference to

---

39 *On the law of war* (Edition Pagden) 307.
40 C.f. Bernice Hamilton, *Political Thought in Sixteenth century Spain*, 147.
41 C.f. *On the law of war* (Edition Pagden) 309 ff.
42 Cf. "Et ita Sanctus Thomas ponit…quod non (fiat) nocendi cupiditate." Francisco de Vitoria, "Comentarios a la Secunda Secundae de Santo Tomás." vol. 2, ed. Vicente Beltrán de Heredia (Salamanca: 1932) 279.

the right intention as such seemed no longer enough in a time that produced a number of new ethical questions of the conduct of war. Therefore, "Thomas sixteenth and seventeenth century successors insisted on more externalized, objective standards", as LeRoy Walters noted.[43]

The question of legitimate harm and or how much is enough seems to be a pressing one in the early 16th century, as Vitoria puts an enormous emphasise on it.

The starting point of his reasoning is Augustine's axiom of "peace and security of the commonwealth being the aim of any war"[44]. Any action taken in a war has to be seen in relation to this final goal of the war: Is it serving or undermining peace and security of the state that is defending itself – and is it serving peace and security of the *orbis*, the international community? Whatever soldiers do in a war can only be serving peace and security according to Vitoria if is adequate to this ultimate goal. Having stated this Vitoria is now able to advise warriors of his time. The issues he deals with mirror the reality of the war of the early the 16th century: The retrieval of lost property like cities or provinces, where the will of the people living there does not seem to matter; the treatment of prisoners in the brutal wars with the Saracens, who quite so often were killed for deterrence; the shooting of cities with the newly invented canons killing civilians and soldiers likewise.

---

43 LeRoy Walters, *Five Classic Just-War Theories: A Study in the thought of Thomas Aquinas, Vitoria, Suarez, Gentili and Grotius* (New Haven: 1971) 354.

44 Pagden translates "finis" as purpose, but in ethical reasoning the finis indicates the aim of an act. C.f. *On the law of war* (Edition Pagden) 309 ff; see the Latin text: "finis belli est pax et securitas reipublicae" ; De iure belli, in: Vitoria, *Vorlesungen II*, 546.

Martin Luther on Peace and War:
A Systematic Approach

Volker Stümke

These theses are the attempt to represent systematically the main aspects
from the political ethics of Martin Luther, developed especially between
1523 and 1526.[1] I focus Luther's ethics on the debate of peace and war and
may do this without touching the historical dimension.

1. Martin Luther does not take up the scholastic debates on just war. He
   instead develops his point of view of peace and war biographically as
   well as theologically, starting with his understanding of justification by
   God and going back to the Bible as the fundamental authority.

   a. Biographical view: The development of Luther's theology took
      place in the surrounding of a monastery even beyond his Refor-
      mation break-through, and not at the court of the Elector nor at the
      copper mine of his father. Accordingly his perception is mainly
      guided by his religiousness and derived from it through a concen-
      tration on personal aspects also in his ethics.

Luther's biographical development is well known just as his critical look at
the influence through the monastery, so that I may restrict to a quotation,
showing his concentration on personal aspects. At the end of „The Freedom
of a Christian" Luther describes the moral attitudes of a Christian: „For a
Christian, as a free man, will say, 'I will fast, pray, do this or that as men
command, not because it is necessary to my righteousness or salvation; but
that I might show due respect to the pope, the bishop, the community, a
magistrate, or my neighbor, and give them an example. I will do and suffer
all things, just as Christ did and suffered far more for me, although he
needed nothing of it all for himself, and was made under the law for my
sake, although he was not under the law.' Although tyrants do violence or
injustice in making their demands, yet it will do no harm as long as they

---

1 I would, in particular, like to thank Pastor John W. Siegmund for his help with
   translating my thoughts into English.

demand nothing contrary to God"[2]. The first sentence emphasizes the priority of justification before any good work, even before the possibility to do good works, thus marking Luther's decisive soteriological conclusions. Only the Christian, who in his faith is freed from his sins, can do good works, for which the second sentence gives examples. That Luther will fulfil works for the Pope's sake, although he, as a tyrant, has no right to demand them of him, shows how dominant Luther's personal view is. The Pope is not faced as a dignitary, but as just one concrete person whom a Christian could serve.

> b. Theological view: Luther in search for the graceful God facing his own and invincible sins, recovered the Gospel which speaks of justification only through faith without any works (Rom 3,28). This led him to a reserved and even a declining attitude toward human actions. Luther looks at works with this soteriological background and therefore rejects them as the wrong way to salvation. Only for the faithful works receive subaltern an ethical connotation[3].

In correspondence with the ecclesiastical tradition Luther notices that every man is an sinner and therefore cannot stand before God. He emphasizes man being connected in the history with God, thus practically avoiding an ontological definition of man[4]. To be more precise Luther interprets sin as

---

2   Jaroslav Pelikan and Helmut T. Lehman, eds., *Luther's Works*, hereafter LW (Philadelphia), vol. 31, 370 (= WA 7, 37, 8–15: „Ein freier Christ spricht so: Ich will fasten, beten, dies und das tun, was geboten ist, aber nicht weil ich dessen bedarf oder dadurch fromm oder selig werden wollte. Sondern ich will es dem Papst, dem Bischof, der Gemeinde oder meinem Mitbruder, meinem Herrn zu Willen, Exempel und Dienst tun und leiden, so wie mir Christus viel größere Dinge zu Willen getan und gelitten hat, was ihm viel weniger nötig war. Und wenn schon die Tyrannen Unrecht tun, dies zu fordern, so schadet es mir doch nicht, weil es nicht gegen Gott ist.").

3   Cf. LW 31, 361 (*The Freedom of a Christian*, 1520): „Consequently it is always necessary that the substance or person himself be good before there can be any good works, and that good works follow and proceed from the good person." (= WA 7, 32, 15–17: „Also muss der Mensch in der Person zuvor fromm oder böse sein, ehe er gute oder böse Werke tut").

4   Cf. LW 34, 139 (*The Disputation Concerning Man*, 1536): „Paul in Romans 3 [: 28], 'We hold that a man is justified by faith apart from works,' briefly sums up the definition of man, saying, 'Man is justified by faith.'" (= WA 39 I, 176, 33–35: „Paulus fasst in Röm 3, [Vers 28, wo es heißt:] wir erachten, dass der Mensch durch Glauben unter Absehen von den Werken gerechtfertigt wird, in Kürze die Definition des Menschen dahin zusammen, dass der Mensch durch Glauben gerechtfertigt werde"). – This definition is formal striking. Man is not defined with „to be" (esse), instead his nature develops from the meeting with God, where

the self-idolization of man[5]. From this follows first that man's depravity is to become selfish, being turned inwardly to himself[6], twisting God's spiritual goods for his own selfishness. Second, he lowers God to the level of a junk-dealer[7], because he does not trust the Gospel, but wants to earn God's grace with his works instead of accepting it as a present. Thirdly, sin messes up the world, because it mixes up the competences and tasks of God and man. This third implication of sin is politically relevant. One aspect of the self-idolization, following Luther, is, that man even presumes to be the final judge and reclaims the authority to judge and to punish, although God has reclaimed this competence in Rom 12,19 for himself. Since

---

something happens to him. Therefore his nature can only be defined in a narrative way, but not statical with a description of his condition. Cf. Albrecht Peters, *Der Mensch* [HST 8], vol. 2, (Gütersloh: 1994), 29: „Diese umfassende und erschöpfende 'Definition' (Th.20) menschlicher Existenz lässt sich nur als ein Weg ausschreiten, nur als eine Geschichte erzählen; hierzu muß der Horizont dieses todverfallenen Erdenlebens radikal aufgesprengt werden".

5   Cf. LW 31, 10 (*Disputation Against Scholastic Theology*, 1517): „Man is by nature unable to want God to be God. Indeed, he himself wants to be God, and does not want God to be God." (= WA 1, 225, 1 f: „Der Mensch kann von Natur aus nicht wollen, dass Gott Gott ist; er möchte vielmehr, dass er Gott und Gott nicht Gott ist").

6   Cf. to the „homo in se incurvatus" LW 25, 345 (*Lectures on Romans*, 1515/16): „And this is in agreement with Scripture, which describes man as so turned in on himself that he uses not only physical but even spiritual goods for his own purposes and in all things seeks only himself." (= WA 56, 356, 4–6: „Und dies bestätigt die Schrift, die den Menschen beschreibt als so sehr in sich verkrümmt, dass nicht nur die leiblichen, sondern auch die geistlichen Güter sich verbiegen und er sich selbst in allem sucht").

7   Cf. LW 44, 32 f (*Treatise on Good Works*, 1520): „That is the reason I have so often spoken against the display, magnificence and multitude of such works and rejected them. It is as clear as day that these works are not only done in doubt or without the faith we are talking about, but that there is not one in a thousand who does not put his confidence in the works and presume that by having done them he wins God's favor and lays claim to his grace. They turn the whole thing to a fairground. God cannot tolerate this: God has promised his grace freely, and wills that we start by trusting his grace and perform all works in that grace, whatever those works may be". (= WA 6, 211, 29–36: „Das ist die Ursache, warum ich so oft gegen den Pomp, die Pracht, die Menge solcher Werke geredet und sie verworfen habe. Es liegt hell zutage, dass sie nicht bloß im Zweifel oder ohne solchen Glauben geschehen, sondern dass auch unter tausend nicht einer ist, der nicht sein Vertrauen auf sie setzte und vermeinte, dadurch Gottes Huld zu erlangen und seiner Gnade zuvorzukommen. So macht man einen Jahrmarkt daraus, was Gott nicht dulden kann. Denn er hat seine Huld umsonst zu schenken versprochen und will, dass man bei dieser anhebe mit seiner Zuversicht und in ihr alle Werke vollbringe").

Luther understands war as well to be a measure of the judging God, his interpretation of Rom 12,19 is important for his critical look at the doctrine of the just war. He leads this argumentation only indirectly. We will refer to it in the next thesis.

For the faithful good works express the cooperation that God wants from them[8], so that the three characteristics of sin reverse. First, the Christian is orientated not towards himself, but towards the benefit of his neighbours[9]. So secondly he conforms with God, whose given grace he accepts cheerfully and complies with God's two main commandments (i. e. to love God and his neighbours), freed from the self-fixation on his own spiritual welfare[10]. Thirdly, his cooperation does not infringe upon God's competences, but does whatever he finds before his eyes and is not concerned with the valuation criteria of the world[11]. This third aspect becomes

---

8 Cf. LW 44, 52 (*Treatise on Good Works*, 1520): „But you might ask, 'Why does God not do it all by himself, since he is able to help everyone and knows how to help everyone?' Yes, he can do it; but he does not want to do it alone. He wants us to work with him. He does us the honor of wanting to effect his work with us and through us". (= WA 6, 227, 28 – 31: „Sprichst du aber: Warum tut's Gott nicht allein und von selber, wo er's doch kann und einem jeden zu helfen weiß? Ja, er kann es wohl, er will es aber nicht allein tun. Er will, dass wir mit ihm wirken und tut uns die Ehre an, dass er mit uns und durch uns sein Werk wirken will").

9 Cf. LW 31, 365 f (*The Freedom of a Christian*, 1520): „Here [i.e. in Phil 2,1 ff] we see clearly that the Apostle has prescribed this rule for the life of Christians, namely, that we should devote all our works to the welfare of others, since each has such abundant riches in his faith that all his other works and his whole life are a surplus with which he can by voluntary benevolence serve and do good to his neighbor". (= WA 7, 35, 9 – 12: „Sieh da [in Phil 2,1 ff] hat Paulus ein Christenleben deutlich so zusammengefasst, dass alle Werke dem Nächsten zugute ausgerichtet sein sollen, weil jeder für sich selbst an seinem Glauben genug hat und alle Werke und das Leben ihm überlassen sind, seinem Nächsten damit aus freier Liebe zu dienen").

10 Cf. LW 45, 118 (*Temporal Authority: To What Extent it Should be Obeyed*, 1523): „For cursed and condemned is every sort of life lived and sought for the benefit and goods of self; cursed are all works not done in love. They are done in love, however, when they are directed wholeheartedly toward the benefit, honour, and salvation of others, and not toward the pleasure, benefit, honour, comfort, and salvation of self". (= WA 11, 272, 1 – 5: „Verflucht und verdammt ist alles Leben, das sich selbst zu Nutzen und zugute gelebt und gesucht wird, verflucht alle Werke, die nicht in der Liebe gehen. Dann aber gehen sie in der Liebe, wenn sie nicht auf eigene Lust, Nutzen, Ehre, Ruhe und Heil, sondern auf anderer Nutzen, Ehre und Heil von ganzem Herzen gerichtet sind"). – Cf. furthermore: Michael Trowitzsch, *Gott als ‚Gott für dich'. Eine Verabschiedung des Heilsegoismus* (München: 1983), 82 ff.

11 Cf. LW 44, 26 (*Treatise on Good Works*, 1520): „In this faith all works become equal, and one work is like the other; all distinctions between works fall away,

deepened through Luther's understanding of vocation (Beruf). The Christian remains in his vocation and duty, accepting God's vocation and works for the benefit of his neighbours.

2. The „doctrine of the just war", strictly spoken, does not receive additions from Luther, but is reduced to the legitimacy of a solely defensive war. Luther's two new impulses about peace and war are on one hand his doctrine of the two governments (Zweiregimentenlehre), on the other hand his understanding of vocation (Beruf) in connection with his view of the three classes in society (Dreiständelehre).

   a. Luther accepts as natural law the insight that defence with military instruments is legitimate (vim vi repellere licet[12]). In addition he interpolates three further conditions to delimitate even the defensive war. First, the causes and the aims of the war must be secularly assignable and must not be loaded religiously. Secondly, negotiations must be conducted and therewith means of de-escalation must have been brought into operation. Thirdly, the claimed will is to accept the rules of law and to compromise[13], as far as this averts a further escalation of the war.

---

whether they be great, small, short, long, many, or few. For the works are acceptable not for their own sake, but because of faith, which is always the same and lives and works in each and every work without distinction, however numerous and varied these works always are, just as all the members of the body, live, work, and take their name from the head, and without the head no member can live, work, or have a name. It further follows from this that a Christian man living in this faith has no need of a teacher of good works, but he does whatever the occasion calls for, and all is well done". (= WA 6, 206,33–207,5: „In diesem Glauben werden alle Werke gleich und ist eins wie das andere; es fällt aller Unterschied der Werke dahin, sie seien groß, klein, kurz, lang, viel oder wenig. Denn nicht ihrer selbst wegen sind die Werke Gott angenehm, sondern des Glaubens wegen, welcher als ein und derselbe in allen und jeglichen Werken ohne Unterschied ist, wirkt und lebt, wie zahlreich und unterschiedlich sie immer seien: so wie alle Glieder vom Haupt ihr Leben, ihr Wirken und ihren Namen haben und ohne das Haupt kein Glied leben, wirken oder einen Namen haben kann. Daraus folgt dann weiter, dass ein Christenmensch, in diesem Glauben lebend, keines Lehrers bedarf guter Werke, sondern was ihm vorkommt, das tut er").

12 Cf. LW 46, 120 (*Whether Soldiers, Too, Can Be Saved*, 1526): „Self-defense is a proper ground for fighting and therefore all laws agree that self-defense shall go unpunished". (= WA 19, 647, 8–10: „Wehren ist eine redliche Ursache zu streiten! Darum billigen es auch alle Rechte, dass Notwehr ungestraft sein solle").

13 Cf. WA Br 10, 35, 128–133 (*Sendbrief in der Wurzener Fehde*, 1542): „Ich trete, sage ich, in dem Fall zu dem Teil, der Recht und Frieden anbietet und leiden kann oder begehrt. Denn wenn gleich der andere Teil das höchste Recht hätte und billig

With the first condition Luther rejects any kind of religious war. This already implies a refusal of the just war doctrine, since these wars were legitimated by theological-ethical arguments. In contrast Luther accents that solely the defence as a secular and political sanction can legitimate a war. The second and the third condition limit the defensive war procedural. An attack must not immediately be answered in a military way. It must rather be tried to border the conflict and to avert a war with negotiations[14] and the willingness to compromise, especially in the acceptance of a settlement by arbitration[15].

These arrangements indicate that the law occupies for Luther a central position. With his theological ethics Luther has supported the build-up of constitutional conditions leaning towards the establishment of the governmental monopoly on legitimate use of physical force, as concluded

---

    Zorn verwenden könnte, so verdammt er sich doch selbst damit, dass er Gott in seine Gewalt eingreift, selbst Richter und Rächer sein will und damit die Gegenseite zur Notwehr zwingt". ‒ Not translated in LW.

14 Cf. LW 46, 40 (*Admonition to Peace, A Reply to the Twelfe Articles of the Peasants in Swabia*, 1525): Luther appeals at both parties in the beginning Peasants' Wars: „For God's sake, then, take my advice! Take a hold of these matters properly, with justice and not with force or violence and do not start endless bloodshed in Germany". (= WA 18, 329, 6‒9: „So lasst euch um Gottes Willen belehren und beraten und greift die Sachen an, wie solche Sachen anzugreifen sind, nämlich auf dem Rechtsweg und nicht mit Gewalt oder mit Kampf, damit ihr nicht ein unendliches Blutvergießen anrichtet in deutschen Landen").

15 This term (acceptance of an arbitrament) shall combine the following references of Luther.

    First, the cue to the proportionality of means: „A prince must punish the wicked in such a way that he does not step on the dish while picking up the spoon, and for the sake of one man's head plunge country and people into want and fill the land with widows and orphans" (LW 45, 124 = *Temporal Authority: To What Extent it Should be Obeyed*, 1523). (= WA 11, 276, 13‒16: „So muss auch ein Fürst die Bösen so strafen, dass er nicht einen Löffel aufhebe und eine Schüssel zertrete und um eines Schädels willen Land und Leute in Not bringe und das Land voll Witwen und Waisen mache").

    Second, the control of the own emotions: „He cannot govern who cannot wink at faults" (LW 45, 124). (= WA 11, 276, 20 f: „Wer nicht kann durch die Finger sehen, der kann nicht regieren").

    Third, compliableness considering the exceeding worth of peace: „Thus a certain peasant in the neighboring village of Dabrun said that a man who has two cows should contribute one of them to keep the peace. It is better to have one cow in peace than to have two cows in war (=LW 8, 279 = *Lectures on Genesis*, 1535/45). (= WA 44, 784, 17 f = „Wer zwei Kühe hat, soll die eine darum geben, dass der Friede erhalten werde. Es ist besser, eine im guten Frieden als zwei im Krieg zu besitzen").

in the „Ewige Landfriede" from 1495, together with the prohibition of personal vendetta[16].

    b. All ongoing considerations about a just war of aggression are ge-nerally rejected by Luther[17], without entering decidedly into the scholastic debates. Axiomatically and without exception the rule applies: „Whoever starts a war is in the wrong"[18].

By referring to the legitimacy of defensive wars exclusively on the grounds of both natural justice and jurisdiction, Luther substitutes the law for the ethical criteria of the just war. Thereby there is no place for these criteria in his political ethics, although the main terms may be discovered[19]. The word justice (Gerechtigkeit) means for Luther in secular and political contexts rights, laws and jurisdiction[20]. According to that Luther analyses war in legal diction. Right and command are necessary for a just war[21].

---

16 Cf Herfried Münkler, „Politisches Denken in der Zeit der Reformation." In *Pipers Handbuch der politischen Ideen Band 2*, ed. Iring Fetscher and Herfried Münkler (München: 1993) 615–683 and Gerta Scharffenorth, „Luthers Lehre vom weltlichen Regiment Gottes. Die Reichsverfassungsreform als Problem des Frie-densauftrags der Christen." In *Den Glauben ins Leben ziehen … Studien zu Luthers Theologie*, Gerta Scharffenorth (München: 1982) 205–313.

17 Cf. LW 45, 63 (A Sincere Admonition by Martin Luther to All Christians to Guard Against Insurrection and Rebellion, 1522): „I am and always will be on the side of those against whom insurrection is directed, no matter how unjust their cause; I am opposed to those who rise in insurrection, no matter how just their cause, because there can be no insurrection without hurting the innocent and shedding their blood". (= WA 8, 680, 32–35: „Ich halte und will es allezeit halten mit der Seite, die Aufruhr erleidet, wie unrecht ihre Sache auch sein mag, und will wider die Seite sein, die Aufruhr macht, wie recht ihre Sache auch immer sei, weil Aufruhr nicht kann ohne unschuldiges Blut und Schaden geschehen").

18 LW 46, 118 (*Whether Soldiers, Too, Can Be Saved*, 1526). (= WA 19, 645, 9: „Wer Krieg anfängt, der ist im Unrecht").

19 Reading Luther from the scholastic doctrine of the just war, emerges the following result: The right intention (recta intentio) of the belligerent power lies in the concentration on secular aims, in particular the reconstitution of peace and alignment. That the war must be forced (debitus modus) and is therefore the last resort (ultima ratio) Luther has taken up with insisting on negotiations. The au-thority of the sovereign (auctoritas principis) is strengthened by Luther with his doctrine of the two governments, likewise it is relativized through his reference to the law and his demand for willingness to compromise. The only convincing reason (causa iusta) is the state of defence.

20 Cf. LW 46, 95 (*Whether Soldiers, Too, Can Be Saved*, 1526): „In the second place I want you to understand that here I am not speaking about the righteousness that makes men good in the sight of God. Only faith in Jesus Christ can do that; and it is granted and given us by the grace of God alone, without any works or merits of our

Occasionally Luther speaks about punishment and vengeance in connection with war, thus using terms that are common to the doctrine of just wars. However, Luther reproduces, first of all, the Biblical findings from Rom 13,4 (the governing authority being God's servant, an agent of wrath to bring punishment on the wrongdoer) and Deut 32,35 („vengeance is mine, and recompense", says God). The main point of his remarks is that he delegates these acts to God and combines them with the policy of the law. „Paul says in Romans 13 [: 4]: that it is the duty of the sword to protect and punish, to protect the good in peace and to punish the wicked with war. God tolerates no injustice and he has so ordered things that warmongers must be defeated in war"[22]. Thereby he invokes Rom 12,19, in accordance with Paul Luther holds firm that God has reserved punishment and revenge for himself, so that they do not belong to mankind's power of

---

own, as I have written and taught so often and so much in other places. Rather, I am speaking here about external righteousness which is to be sought in offices and works. In other words, to put it plainly, I am dealing here with such questions as these: whether the Christian faith, by which we were accounted righteous before God, is compatible with being a soldier, going to war, stabbing and killing, robbing and burning, as military law requires us to do to our enemies in wartime. Is this work sinful or unjust? Should it give us a bad conscience before God?" (= WA 19, 624, 30–625, 7: „Aufs zweite schicke ich hier voraus, dass ich für diesmal nicht rede von der Gerechtigkeit, die vor Gott eine gerechtfertigte Person macht; denn dies tut allein der Glaube an Jesus Christus, ohne alle unsere Werke und Verdienste, aus lauter Gnade Gottes geschenkt und gegeben, wie ich das sonst so oft und manches Mal geschrieben und gelehrt habe. Sondern ich rede hier von der äußerlichen Gerechtigkeit, die in den Ämtern und Werken besteht und vor sich geht; das heißt, auf dass ich es ja deutlich sage, ich handele hier davon, ob der christliche Glaube, durch welchen wir vor Gott als gerechtfertigt erachtet werden, auch neben sich dulden kann, dass ich ein Kriegsmann bin, Krieg führe, würge und steche, raube und brenne, wie man dem Feind in Kriegsverläufen nach Kriegsrecht tut, obgleich solche Werke auch Sünde oder Unrecht sind, woraus man sich ein Gewissen zu machen hat vor Gott").

21 Cf. LW 46, 170 (*On War Against the Turk*, 1529): „In the first place, the Turk certainly has no right or command to begin war and to attack lands that are not his. Therefore his war is nothing but an outrage and robbery". (= WA 30 II,116, 9–11: „Weil das sicher ist, dass der Türke gar kein Recht noch Befehl hat, einen Streit anzufangen und die Länder anzugreifen, die nicht sein sind, ist sein Kriegführen ohne Zweifel ein reiner Frevel und Räuberei").

22 LW 46, 118 (*Whether Soldiers, Too, Can Be Saved*, 1526). (= WA 19, 645, 16–19: „Das Amt des Schwertes sei es, zu schützen und zu strafen – zu schützen die Rechtschaffenen in Frieden und zu strafen die Bösen durch Krieg. Und Gott, der Unrecht nicht duldet, fügt es auch so, dass die Kriegführenden bekriegt werden müssen").

disposition[23]. More precisely Luther gives this restriction two interpretations. Beside the eschatological restriction, that God is judge on the Day of Judgement, there is the institutional restriction saying that God has directly constituted the secular authorities and mandated them here on earth to carry the sword, whereas neither the subjects (for example, the peasants) nor the clergy have this warrant[24]. So Luther's thoughts on war lead to his doctrine of the two governments, where they are theological substantiated.

3. The doctrine of the two governments forms together with the concept of vocation the central idea of Luther's political ethics. This doctrine implies that God as the Lord of this world has instituted two governments to carry out his will in the world[25]. The spiritual government shall lead the Christians with proclamation of God's Word to salvation and eternal life. The secular government shall keep peace with the sword and justice and by this means organise the external life

---

23 Cf. WA Br 10, 33, 50–58 (*Sendbrief in der Wurzener Fehde*, 1542): „So hat wahrlich Gott auch die Rache hart verboten in Röm 12,19: ‚Die Rache ist mein, ich will vergelten'. Wer nun Gott das Gericht und die Rache nehmen will, den wird sein Urteil treffen nach Röm 13,2. Und wenn mir jemand meinen Vater und Bruder erschlüge, so bin ich dennoch über den Mörder nicht Richter noch Rächer. Und wozu bedarf man der Rechte und der Obrigkeit, ja wozu bedarf man Gottes, wenn ein jeder selbst Richter, Rächer, ja Gott selbst sein will wider und über seinesgleichen oder seinen Nächsten, besonders in weltlichen Sachen"? ~ Not translated in LW.

24 I must admit that Luther concedes – again according to the bible – exceptions from the governmental monopoly on legitimate use of physical force: the directly from God appointed judges in the Old Testament, for example Samson (cf. LW 46, 110 = *Whether Soldiers, Too, Can Be Saved*, 1526 = WA 19, 641, 14–21). But Luther completes that these exceptions are seldom and that anyone, who refers to this, must do it with eschatological seriousness and must verify the divine vocation objective (with a sign from God) and subjective (through his moral conduct). „Therefore first become like Samson, and then you can also do as Samson did" (LW 45, 104 = *Temporal Authority: To What Extent it Should be Obeyed*, 1523). (= WA 11, 261, 24 = „Darum werde zuvor wie Simson, so kannst du auch tun wie Simson").

25 Cf. LW 45, 91 (*Temporal Authority: To What Extent it Should be Obeyed*, 1523): „For this reason God has ordained two governments: the spiritual, by which the Holy Spirit produces Christians and righteous people under Christ; and the temporal, which restrains the un-Christian and wicked so that – no thanks to them – they are obliged to keep still and to maintain an outward peace". (= WA 11, 251, 15–18: „Darum hat Gott zwei Regimente verordnet: das geistliche, welches Christen und fromme Menschen macht durch den heiligen Geist, unter Christus, und das weltliche, das den Unchristen und Bösen wehrt, dass sie äußerlich Frieden halten und still sein müssen, ob sie wollen oder nicht").

of society. Both governments are in like manner directly appointed by
God and receive their assignments from Him. They both fight together
with God against sin and evil, but with different means and clearly
marked functions[26]. For the individual Christian the obedience to both
God and to the secular authority is therefore compatible.

    a. Luther's reception of Augustine's doctrine of the two realms in his
       treatise „Von weltlicher Obrigkeit" stresses neither the cosmological
       nor the philosophic-historical connotations, but instead emphasises
       the soteriological and ethical aspects. Hence, not the fight of the two
       realms is the centre stage, but God's government over the whole of
       creation.

For Luther the heathen powers are not the main enemy of the living
Christian faith, but rather sin. This enemy has indeed been defeated
through Jesus Christ. The forgiveness of the sins, that he has obtained, is
effectively addressed to the Christians through the Gospel. However Luther
had to face that the distribution of this Gospel in the form of the New
Testament, which he had translated, was forbidden by some territorial
lords[27]. Thus the question arose for him about the functions and the authority of the secular government. Exactly this question, as evident in the
title of his treatise „Von weltlicher Obrigkeit, wie weit man ihr Gehorsam
schuldig sei" from 1523 is answered in it.

    b. By emphasizing God's direct institution of both governments, Lu-
       ther overcomes the dispute about the hierarchical relationship of the
       two swords. At the same time he supports thereby the distinction
       between religion, politics, moral and justice. As a result for Luther
       the secular authority becomes relatively autonomous. It receives
       from God its assignments, namely external peace and societal life
       under just conditions, and is apart from that responsible for its
       politics.

---

26 Cf. LW 45, 92 (*Temporal Authority: To What Extent it Should be Obeyed*, 1523):
    „For this reason one must carefully distinguish between these two governments.
    Both must be permitted to remain; the one to produce righteousness, the other to
    bring about external peace and prevent evil deeds. Neither one is sufficient in the
    world without the other". (= WA 11, 252, 12 – 14: „Darum muss man die beiden
    Regimente sorgfältig voneinander unterscheiden und beide bleiben lassen: eines,
    das fromm macht, das andere, das äußerlich Frieden schafft und bösen Werken
    wehrt. Keins reicht ohne das andere aus in der Welt").
27 Cf. LW 45, 83 f (*Temporal Authority: To What Extent it Should be Obeyed*, 1523).
    (= WA 11, 246 f). Bans were enacted by the Bavarian dukes, the prince-elector
    Joachim I from Brandenburg and duke Georg from Saxony.

The controversy in the late Middle Ages about the exegesis of Luke 22,38 was focussed on the question, who had at first received the two swords from God and had kept one for himself and delegated the other one. The Curial standpoint, as expressed in the bull „Unam Sanctam", as well as the opposite standpoint, as expressed by Marsilius from Padua, connected this with a hierarchical structure of the corresponding institutions church and state (or the persons: Pope and King)[28]. In contrast Luther claims the coexistence of both governments under the guidance of God. Both have different tasks to fulfil and therefore cannot compete with each other[29]. In particular the governmental monopoly on legitimate use of physical force counts among the means God has delegated to the secular authority. This also includes defensive war, limited of course by the standards set by God.

As a result in view of war two important consequences arise. For one thing Luther has, as already mentioned, rejected any religious justification of a war – be it by the secular or the spiritual government – because both of them would become intermingled and corrupted. For another thing Luther has not accepted an intrusion by force of the state in religious matters, not only in case of the forbiddance of the Bible[30], but as well in regard to the

---

28 Cf. Volker Mantey, *Zwei Schwerter – zwei Reiche. Martin Luthers Zwei-Reiche-Lehre vor ihrem spätmittelalterlichen Hintergrund* (Tübingen: 2005) and Arnold Angenendt, Geschichte der Religiosität im Mittelalter, vol. 2. revised (Darmstadt: 2000), 311–325.

29 Cf. LW 45, 107 (*Temporal Authority: To What Extent it Should be Obeyed*, 1523): „Besides, we cannot conceive how an authority could or should act in a situation except where it can see, know, judge, condemn, change and modify". (= WA 11, 263, 26–28: Grundsätzlich gilt für Luther, „dass jede Gewalt nur da handeln soll und kann, wo sie sehen, erkennen, richten, urteilen, wandeln und ändern kann").

30 Cf. LW 45, 111 f (*Temporal Authority: To What Extent it Should be Obeyed*, 1523): „If your prince or temporal ruler commands you to side with the pope, to believe thus and so, or to get rid of certain books, you should say: It is not fitting that Lucifer should sit at the side of God. Gracious sir, I owe you obedience in body and property; command me within the limits of your authority on earth, and I will obey. But if you command me to believe or to get rid of certain books, I will not obey, for then you are a tyrant and overreach yourself, commanding where you have neither the right nor the authority". (= WA 11, 267, 1–8: „Wenn nun dein Fürst oder weltlicher Herr dir gebietet, es mit dem Papst zu halten, so oder so zu glauben, oder dir gebietet, Bücher abzugeben, sollst du so sagen: Es gebührt Luzifer nicht, neben Gott zu sitzen. Lieber Herr, ich bin euch schuldig zu gehorchen mit Leib und Gut; gebietet mir nach dem Maß eurer Gewalt auf Erden, so will ich folgen. Befehlt ihr mir aber, zu glauben und Bücher abzugeben, so will ich nicht gehorchen. Denn da seid ihr ein Tyrann und greift zu hoch, gebietet, obwohl ihr weder Recht noch Macht habt").

public handling of people of a different creed, namely heretics and Jews: „Gedanken sind zollfrei"[31] (Thoughts are duty-free). The idea of religious freedom as well as the insight that religion may evoke or amplify acts of war, if religion is not restricted to its duties and means, can therefore be found in Luther's writings. With this, Luther stresses the individual freedom of conscience.

Despite the theological upgrading of the secular authority to an institution on equal footing beside the church Luther does not suggest this government to assume an independent existence that completely makes its own laws. With it's monopoly on physical force it remains nevertheless restrained by the rule and sovereignty of God. And the spiritual government has to remind the state time and again critically of God's pretences – sine vi sed verbo (without force, but proclaiming the Gospel). Luther's numerous letters to the dukes and princes are the best evidence for his definition of the two governments and their tasks[32]. Thus the obedience of the Christians to the secular government is limited. In nearly all writings concerning political ethics Luther refers back to Acts 5,29 („We must obey God rather than men"). The disobedience of the Christians however is also limited. He is not allowed to get around the stately monopoly on physical force and is therefore restricted to forms of passive resistance.

   c. Initial point of the doctrine of the two governments is the question
      how Math 5,38 (renunciation of violence) and Rom 13,1 f (use of

---

31 Cf LW 45, 108 (*Temporal Authority: To What Extent it Should be Obeyed*, 1523): „Thoughts are tax-free". (= WA 11, 264, 28 f). – Regarding the Jews cf. Luthers scripture „That Jesus Christ Was Born a Jew" from the same year (LW 45, 199–229 = WA 11, 314–336). At the end of this text, having argued heavily against the Jewish exegesis of the Old Testament, Luther accounts that no stately violence is allowed against the Jews. The citizens should accept them friendly, allow them to work and earn and let them stay – even if some of them are obstinate and will not proselytise to the Christian faith. – Regrettably Luther has later on cancelled this position and formulated awkward sentences against the Jews and enforced political sanctions that are beyond the pale and are diametrically opposed to his doctrine of the two governments. Even making reference to his possibly senile stubbornness cannot exculpate these statements; cf. furthermore: Walther Bienert, *Martin Luther und die Juden. Ein Quellenbuch mit zeitgenössischen Illustrationen, mit Einführungen und Erläuterungen* (Frankfurt/Main: 1982), 115–178.

32 Cf. Eike Wolgast, *Die Wittenberger Theologie und die Politik der evangelischen Stände. Studien zu Luthers Gutachten in politischen Fragen* (Gütersloh: 1977) and Hermann Kunst, *Evangelischer Glaube und politische Verantwortung. Martin Luther als politischer Berater seiner Landesherrn und seine Teilnahme an den Fragen des öffentlichen Lebens* (Stuttgart: 1976).

force) are consistent in the Christian's perspective. Against the hierarchical grading in two levels of ethics Luther distinguishes two relations of any Christian: For himself (as a private person) he has to bear misery, for others (as a civil servant) he must not tolerate it, but has to fight against the inflicted injustice[33].

The monastic differentiation between generally binding commandments (praecepta) and the Gospel's recommendations (consilia) Luther has rejected[34], because they falsify the Gospel to commands, as well as establish gradations in faith which threatens the certainty of salvation. His basically relational understanding of being Christian leads him to the distinction between private person and civil servant in order to specify the relationship between renunciation and use of force[35]. In the office of civil servant the Christian is not only allowed to use force but must in some cases use it, not as an end in itself, but as an expression of brotherly love which manifests itself in protecting the victims. Not self-defence but emergency relief legitimises the civil servant's use of force. With this Luther assumes that the civil servants, when using force, correspond to the commandment of Christian love, even if there are from time to time (private) persons that execute their office badly[36]. These thoughts Luther has unfolded in his

---

33 Cf. LW 45, 96 (*Temporal Authority: To What Extent it Should be Obeyed*, 1523): „In what concerns you and yours, you govern yourself by the gospel and suffer injustice toward yourself as a true Christian; in what concerns the person or property of others, you govern yourself according to love and tolerate no injustice toward your neighbor". (= WA 11, 255, 17–20: „An dir und an dem Deinen hältst du dich nach dem Evangelium und leidest Unrecht als ein rechter Christ für dich. An dem andern und an dem Seinen hältst du dich nach der Liebe und leidest kein Unrecht für deinen Nächsten").

34 Cf. LW 45, 87 f (*Temporal Authority: To What Extent It Should Be Obeyed*, 1523). (= WA 11, 249, 9–23).

35 Cf. LW 31, 304 f (*Two Kinds of Righteousness*, 1519). (= WA 2, 150 f).

36 Cf. LW 46, 94 (*Whether Soldiers, Too, Can Be Saved*, 1526): „The occupation of a judge is a valuable divine office. This is true both of the office of the trial judge who declares the verdict and the executioner who carries out the sentence. But when the office is assumed by one to whom it has not been committed or when one who holds it rightly uses it to gain riches or popularity, then it is no longer right or good. The married state is also precious and godly, but there is many rascals and scoundrels in it. It is the same way with the profession or work of the soldier; in itself it is right and godly, but we must see to it that the persons who are in this profession and who do the work are the right kind of persons, that is, godly and upright". (= WA 19, 624, 22–29: „Ein Richteramt ist ein köstliches, göttliches Amt, sei es der Mundrichter oder der Faustrichter, welchen man Scharfrichter nennt; aber wenn es einer vornimmt, dem es nicht aufgetragen ist, oder wenn der, der den Auftrag dazu

doctrine of the three classes in society and applied in his understanding of vocation.

4. Luther has developed his understanding of vocation from 1.Cor 7,20 and John 21,19–24 and has connected it with Plato's doctrine of the three classes in society. Plato's doctrine, as a pattern for society, together with the corresponding understanding of vocation that applies it to the individual, open up active cooperation for the Christian in politics and even in the army as a possible and equal scope for brotherly love.

    a. The three classes and the variety of tasks are predefined by God to arrange the communal life in society[37]. Whereas the secular authority in the doctrine of the two governments is concentrated on the state and focussed upon the monopoly of force, the word about the armed forces (politeia) emphasizes the societal function of political rule. It is seen in the doctrine of the three classes as part of society beside „oeconomia" (economy) and „ecclesia" (includes education and religion).

Only by reducing Luther's political ethics one-sidedly on the two governments and not including the three classes, can one name him a supporter of a strong state and align him with Bismarck and even Hitler, as Karl Barth has done[38]. It may be true that Luther supported at the threshold of the modern era the strengthening of the state. In addition he concentrated the state on persons (and not on institutions or functions)[39]. But on the other hand Luther had always conceived it as constitutional state and by this means transferred with political reasoning the connection with God.

---

hat, es nach Geld und Gunst ausrichtet, so ist es schon nicht mehr recht noch gut. Der eheliche Stand ist auch köstlich und göttlich; dennoch gibt es manchen Bösewicht und Buben darin. Ebenso ist es auch mit dem Kriegsstand, -amt oder -werk, das an und für sich recht und göttlich ist; aber darauf muss man schauen, dass es auch die Person gibt, die dazu gehört, und dass sie rechtschaffen ist").

37 Cf. LW 3, 217 (*Lectures on Genesis*, 1535/45): „This life is profitably divided into three orders: (1) life in the home; (2) life in the state; (3) life in the church". (= WA 43, 30, 13 f: „Nützlicherweise ist dieses Leben in drei Stände unterteilt worden: der eine ist das haushälterische Leben [vita oeconomica], das andere ist das politische [politica] und das dritte ist das kirchliche [ecclesiastica] Leben").

38 Cf. Karl Barth, „How my mind has changed." In *Der Götze wackelt. Zeitkritische Aufsätze, Reden und Briefe von 1930 bis 1960*, ed. Karl Kupisch (Berlin: 1961), 181–209, 194; and Eberhard Busch, *Karl Barths Lebenslauf nach seinen Briefen und autobiographischen Texten*, vol. 5 (Gütersloh: 1993), 33.

39 Cf. Hans Richard Reuter, „Martin Luther und das Friedensproblem." In *Suche nach Frieden: politische Ethik in der frühen Neuzeit Band I*, eds. Norbert Brieskorn and Markus Riedenauer (Stuttgart: 2000), 63–82, 74.

And most notably Luther has required the collaboration of Christians in political offices and professions in which they can concretely form Christian love[40]. That this connection of office and Christian love needs a particular explanation in cases requiring force is, as has been presented, the occasion for the special analysis of secular government. For this reason Luther developed over and above Plato's doctrine his concept of the two governments.

b. Luther has definitively shaped the modern concept of vocation by dissolving it out of monastic constriction and adopting it to all ongoing human labours and works in society. More precisely he affirms a double equality of all professions in the face of God. On

---

40 Cf. LW 37, 364 f (*Confession Concerning Christ's Supper*, 1528): „But the holy orders and true religious institutions established by God are these three: the office of priest, the estate of marriage, the civil government. All who are engaged in the clerical office or ministry of the Word are in a holy, proper, good, and God-pleasing order and estate, sich as thoese who preach, administer sacraments, supervise the common chest, sextons and messengers or servants who serve those persons. These are engaged in works which are altogether holy in God sight. Again, all fathers and mothers who regulate their household wisely and bring up their children to the service of God are engaged in pure holiness, in a holy work and a holy order. Similarly, when children and servants show obedience to their elders and masters, here too is pure holiness, and whoever is thus engaged is a living saint on earth. Moreover, prinves and lords, judges, civil officers, state officials, notaries, male and female servants and all who serve such persons, and further, all their obedient subjects – all are engaged in pure holiness and leading a holy life before God. For these three religious institutions or orders are found in God's Word and commantment; and whatever is contained in God's Word must be holy, for God's Word is holy and sanctifies everything connected with it and involved in it". (= WA 26, 504, 30–505, 10: „Aber die heiligen Orden und rechten Stifte, die von Gott eingesetzt sind, sind diese drei: das Priesteramt, der Ehestand, die weltliche Obrigkeit. Alle, die im Pfarramt oder im Dienst des Wortes vorgefunden werden, sind in einem heiligen, rechten, guten, Gott angenehmen Orden und Stand – wie die, die predigen, die Sakramente reichen, dem allgemeinen Armenkasten vorstehen, Küster und Boten oder Knechte, die diesen Personen dienen. Dieses sind lauter heilige Werke vor Gott. Ebenso, wer Vater und Mutter ist, das Haus wohl regiert und Kinder erzieht zu Gottes Dienst, ist auch lauter Heiligtum und heiliges Werk und heiliger Orden. Desgleichen, wo Kinder oder Gesinde den Eltern oder Herren gehorsam sind, ist auch lauter Heiligkeit; und wer darin erfunden wird, der ist ein lebendiger Heiliger auf Erden. So auch Fürst oder Oberherr, Richter, Amtleute, Kanzler, Schreiber, Knechte, Mägde und alle, die diesen dienen, dazu alle, die untertan und gehorsam sind: Alles lauter Heiligtum und heiliges Leben vor Gott, weil diese drei Stifte oder Orden in Gottes Wort und Gebot gefasst sind. Was aber in Gottes Wort gefasst ist, das muss heilig sein, denn Gottes Wort ist heilig und heiligt alles, was an ihm und in ihm ist").

the one hand they are all unable to earn righteousness before God; on the other hand all of them afford the opportunity to express Christian love not only spontaneously but also in an organized way[41].

With it we return to the initial point of our deliberations: to Luther's starting-point with justification and to his laying great weight on personal constellations. For Luther vocation cannot compete with justification solely by faith. It can only be conceivable as God's mandate to Christians to give their collaboration a definitive form. And this can take place in all professions that correspond to God's commandments. So Luther holds the opinion of the negative as well as the positive equality of all vocations before God. He doesn't deny however that the world draws distinctions in the assessment of specific jobs and professions, but declares these differences for a Christian as being soteriologically as well as ethically irrelevant. Christians should not conform to the worldly esteem of a profession, but fill this job according to concrete social necessity[42].

This becomes valid also for the soldier. The Christian may practise this profession knowing that he can exercise Christian love by protecting the citizens and retaining or restoring civil peace, all this – of course in the

---

41 Cf. WA 10 I.1, 308, 6–12 + 14–20 (*Auslegung von Joh 21,19–24* in der Kir-
    chenpostille, 1522 Evang. am St. Joh Tag): „Du möchtest einwenden: Wenn ich
    nicht berufen bin, was soll ich dann tun? Antwort: Wie ist es möglich, dass du nicht
    berufen seiest? Du wirst ja immer schon in einem Stand sein, du bist immer schon
    Ehemann oder Ehefrau, Sohn oder Tochter, Knecht oder Magd. Nimm den ge-
    ringsten Stand für dich: Bist du ein Ehemann, meinst du, du habest nicht genug zu
    schaffen in diesem Stand? So Ehefrau, Kind, Gesinde und Güter zu regieren, dass
    alles im Gehorsam gegen Gott geschehe und du niemandem Unrecht tust? […]
    Ebenso wenn du ein Sohn oder eine Tochter bist, meinst du, du habest nicht genug
    mit dir zu tun, dass du züchtig, keusch und Maß haltend deine Jugend hältst,
    deinen Eltern gehorsam bist und niemandem mit Worten oder Werken zu nahe
    trittst? Weil man es verlernt hat, solche Befehle und Berufe zu achten, geht man
    statt dessen hin und betet Rosenkränze und tut dergleichen, was nicht dem Beruf
    dient, und keiner denkt daran, dass er seinen Stand wahrnehme". – Not translated
    in LW.
42 Cf. LW 45, 95 (*Temporal Authority: To What Extent it Should be Obeyed*, 1523):
    „Therefore, if you see that there is lack of hangmen, constables, judges, lords or
    princes, and you find that you are qualified, you should offer your services and seek
    the position, that the essential government authority may not be despised and
    become enfeebled or perish". (= WA 11, 255, 1–4: „Wenn du sähest, dass es am
    Henker, Büttel, Richter, Herrn oder Fürsten mangelte, und du dich geeignet dazu
    fändest, solltest du dich dazu erbieten und dich darum bewerben, auf dass ja die
    notwendige Gewalt nicht verachtet und matt würde oder unterginge").

framework God has set. Regarding his salvation the Christian will not employ his works as a self-portrayal in front of God, but rather as an expression of his collaboration with God, performing them for the sake of his neighbour. He will politically respect the limitations of his vocation and will therefore combat only in a defensive war, but in any other case he will put up passive resistance in reference to Acts 5,29. And as an individual he will not abuse his vocation, otherwise he would become a murderer.

Morality and Just War According to Francisco Suárez

Markus Kremer

Francisco Suárez (1548–1617) was a leader of Iberian silver-age scholastic natural law thinking. If natural law is, in the times of Suárez, to be understood as a 'theological' system of natural rights and obligations, this classification will be in principle correct.[1] Though, we have to consider that in the 16th century, the old paradigms of world order had begun to change, so that a too strong term of natural law (in the sense of concludent, logical) was no longer useful. While the (European) medieval unity of *sacerdotium* and *imperium*, carried by a closed Christian society (*respublica christiana*), had been abandoned and replaced by political and religious pluralism, the whole conception of the world totally changed for the reason of the new world's discovery. In consequence, the political ethics was challenged by new questions that required more differentiate answers than the previous natural law theory could give, and asked for a new language of natural rights. Especially the problem of particular subjective rules of action led to a moral casuistry which raised doubts about the importance of general moral principles.

In order to guarantee both, the general norm and its singular case, Suárez layed – within a Thomistic framework – new stress on virtue as a regulative of political action. While on the one side, morality consists in an external obedience against law, it demands on the other side, that the prescribed good is also done in a good manner.[2] By that, he understood an inner orientation of will (*intentio*) towards the good, which is identical with the will of God.

While the question, whether Thomistic ethics is basically virtue ethics or basically natural law ethics, remains hotly disputed by scholars,[3]

---

1 Cf. Suárez' definition of natural law: "Lex naturalis est lumen naturale intellectus repraesentans voluntatem Dei auctoris naturae, obligantem homines ad servandum, quod recta ratio dictat." (DL II, 6, 13).

2 "Ius naturale, quod praecipit facere actum honestum, praecipit etiam, ut studiose fiat." (DL II, 10, 13); "quia non satis ad virtutem honestum facere, nisi fiat honeste." (*ibid.* n. 2).

3 Cf. Jean Porter, *The recovery of virtue* (Louisville, 1990); and Bernice Hamilton, *Political thought in sixteenth-century Spain* (Oxford, 1963).

Suárez' political theology has to be understood as pleading for a morally filled up theory of action, in which commitment to natural law and to virtue are equivalent ideas. In concern of the question of just war, Suárez wanted to show that Christian charity and warfare were not longer contradictory actions.

1 Virtue and political ethics

Virtue ethics traditionally distinguishes between general virtues that are valid for everybody (the so-called 'cardinal virtues'), and virtues that depend on the grace of God and are consequently in force only among Baptized (the so-called 'theological virtues').

Before asking for their political impact, let's see what Suárez exactly comprehends under virtues: "Virtue is a *habitus*, that accomplishes the rational ability of man and does incline it in what is good."[4] This definition provided, virtuous behaviour covers only such actions that are intentionally good. In consequence, the good itself becomes the motive of human will. At the same time human reason has to assess the congruence of what will intends and what is compatible with human nature.

A second aspect of virtue affects the way *how* an action is done (the good intention provided). Not only the *bonum per se* is the object of virtue, but also the way it is realized. Virtue in this respect makes it easier to act morally well. In Suárez' words: "Virtue is a kind of mental force by which man becomes able and ready to act in a good way."[5] A moral (= virtuous) action therefore has to meet a good disposition of will as well as a good performance.

The distinction between virtues in general and specific Christian virtues follows the logic of creational order that doesn't require faith to make man act morally good. At the same time the question raises, how nature and grace are related to each other according to Suárez. While Aquinas pleaded for a two-steps-concept, wherein grace perfects the deficient human nature with regard to salvation without abandoning it, Suárez

---

4   "Virtus est habitus perficiens rationalem potentiam et inclinans ad bonum."
    (Tractatus quinque IV, disp. III, 1, 1).
5   "Virtus significat vim quamdam animi, qua homo fit aptus et idoneus ad opera
    sua bene praestanda." (Tractatus quinque IV, disp. III, 1, 1); cf. Aristotle who
    said: "If somebody possesses virtue, he himself and his deeds become good."
    (Nicomachean Ethics II, 5 f).

claims a complementary assignment of two independant sectors: In principle – and that is the lesson Suárez learned from hundreds of years of religious and confessionel quarrel – every man, despite wether he believes in God or not, should be able to lead a morally honest life. But this idea is only compatible with a theological ethics (that interpretes moral actions in view of God's commandments), if human will must not longer considered to be directed to God intentionally, but only 'interpretatively'. That means, that actions have not to intend God actually as ultimate goal (*finis ultimus simpliciter*), if only directed to the good (*bonum per se*). "Whoever acts morally, acts for God's sake, although formally not intended."[6]

However, Suárez preserves the transcendality of the moral act by attributing it to man's rational nature. In consequence – and that's the innovation Suárez invented – even good actions of unbelievers may fit to God's will. Thus, the semantics of just war, formerly understood as a mean of punishing the sinners (Augustine, Aquinas), changes radically: War remains part of a natural permission, but becomes at the same time subjected to human morality in general, characterized by justice, law and virtue. Accordingly, Suárez defines war not only under a legal, but also under a moral point of view: "War is not principally evil, but can even be a means of true peace, if conducted honestly."[7]

2 War as part of natural law and of international law (*ius gentium*)

In order to make precise moral distinctions, Suárez distinguishes between violence that is naturally permitted, and violence that needs a special authorization by positive law. The first coincides with self-defense respectively defensive war, which covers all measures that serve the salvation of one's own or another person's life or goods. "Defensive war is [in terms of natural law, MK] not only allowed, but sometimes necessary."[8] An imperative to defend might result from charity, if to protect innocent people. Additionally, the direct revision of unlawful occupation, and the

---

6   Johannes Brachtendorf, "Die Finalität der Handlung nach F. Suárez." *Theologie und Philosophie* 76 (2001): 530–550, 550.

7   "Bellum simpliciter nec est intrinsece malum, sed potius medium ad veram et tutam pacem, … si honeste gereatur." (DB I, 2 et 3).

8   "Bellum defensivum non solum est licitum, sed interdum etiam praeceptum." (DB I, 4).

defense of fatherland and of public welfare may be just aims of defensive war, that has no punitive character at all. While the right of defense belongs to natural law, aggression is part of the (positive) international law (*ius gentium*), which requires the institutions of states and whose goal is the welfare of all nations (not that of a single state). Suárez tries to seperate *ius gentium* from natural law more clearly than the tradition he finds. On his behalf *ius gentium* neither is derived from national law (Aquinas), nor does it simply contain more conclusions than natural law (Covarruvias), nor is it more complex (de Soto). On the contrary, Suárez considers *ius gentium* as proper human positive law which is based on the fact, "that mankind, although divided in different nations and peoples, is bound to a political and moral unity".[9] Although each state may be perfect, independant and self-sufficient in itself, it remains part of the community of nations, because they all depend from each other for reason of better life (*ad melius esse*). "In consequence, we need a legal order, by which communication and cooperation between the nations can be regulated."[10] Because a mere natural law cannot be sufficient for this purpose, certain norms have been invented by human reason, which can be found among all nations (*ius gentium intra se*) or which settle their international relations (*ius gentium inter se*).[11] The 'legislator' of such international law therefore is the community of sovereign nations. Matters of international law are diplomacy, war, cease-fire, peace treaties, trade and travelling, slavery.[12] Additionally, international law may also include bilateral treaties that are not binding to other states (e. g. no slavery between Christian nations). These positive human norms are based upon a natural faculty (*ius naturale dominativum*). As an instrument of settling legal relationships between sovereign states, international law expresses their mutual political and moral commitment and responsibility. Differently from natural law,

---

9 "Ratio autem huius partis et iuris est, quia humanum genus quantumvis in varios populos et regna divisum, semper habet aliquam unitatem non solum specificam, sed etiam quasi politicam et moralem." (DL II, 19, 9).

10 "Hac ergo ratione indigent aliquo iure, quo dirigantur et recte ordinentur in hoc genere communicationis et societatis." (DL II, 19, 9).

11 It follows that *ius gentium* must be understood in a double sense: "First as law which all peoples respect in their mutual relations; second as law which is obeyed in every single state." – "Duobus modis dici aliquid de iure gentium: uno modo quia est ius, quod omnes populi et gentes variae inter se servare debent; alio modo quia est ius, quod singulae civitates vel regna intra se observant. Per similitudinem autem et convenientiam ius gentium appellatur." (DL II, 19, 8).

12 However, *ius gentium intra se* contains norms with concern to leasing, construction, marriage, inheritance, settlements, finances, sale and purchase.

ius gentium seems to be more variable, which means it can be easier changed.

Although natural law permits punishment in cases of violation of rights, the way of penalty mustn't be violent, "because it is impossible that the creator of nature has left the human affairs, so that litigations between princes and states are only to be solved by war";[13] however may war be a naturally embodied mean of justice in the relations between states. While defense reacts to an action in progress (*iniuria in fieri*), aggression requires the accomplishment of an injury (*iniuria facta*). Suárez counts among 'just causes': the occupation of territory, the disregard of international law (esp. against the immunity of legates or the freedom of passage) and the violation of good reputation.[14] All military measures that serve the subsequent satisfaction for an injury already concluded, belong to aggression. "Such an [offensive] war can be necessary for a state in order to avert injuries and to put the enemy in his place. Otherwise the nations couldn't preserve themselves in peace."[15]

It is important to know, that war as a legitimate way of punishment is no necessary, but a customary mean of solving conflicts, introduced by the common will of all nations. "As soon as the laws of war are based on punishment or on satisfaction, claimed legitimately by a sovereign state for the reason of an injury suffered by another, they belong to international law. Only by order of reason it wasn't necessary to ascribe this right to each single state, so that man could have chosen any other kind of atonement or transferred this faculty to a neutral arbiter."[16] Thus, the right to punish springs from natural law, but only positive law can define who gets to do the punishing and in which way. In

---

13 "Nam impossibile est auctorem naturae reliquisse res humanas ... ut omnes lites inter principes supremos et respublicas nonnisi per bellum terminari debeant." (DB VI, 5); cp. DB VII, 3.

14 Cf. DB IV. 3.

15 "Ratio est, quia tale bellum saepe est reipublicae necessarium ad propulsandas iniurias et coercendos hostes, neque aliter possunt respublicae in pace conservari. Est ergo hoc iure naturali licitum ..." (DB I, 5).

16 "Ideo censeo de iure belli: quatenus fundatur in potestate quam una respublica vel monarchia habet ad puniendam vel vindicandam, aut reparandam iniuriam sibi ab altera illatam, videtur proprie esse de iure gentium. Nam ex vi solius rationis naturalis non erat necessarium ut haec potestas esset in republica offensa: potuissent enim homines instituere alium modum vindictae, vel committere illam potestatem alicui tertio principi, et quasi arbitrio cum potestate coactiva." (DL II, 19, 8).

every case does an aggression need a jurisdiction over the culprit and is consequently permitted only to a public authority.

3 Authority as condition of just punishment
(*legitima potestas vindicandi*)

Besides just cause, offensive war needs as second condition, that there is an instance judging the claims of the conflicting parties. "Just as inside a state, in order to preserve peace, a legitimate power is necessary to punish an offence, a similar power is required in the whole world, so that the single nations can live together in peace and harmony."[17] Asked what Suárez exactly understands under *potestas legitima*, his classic definition must be quoted: "The highest power is one that is not subjected to any other power of the same order."[18] Suárez explains further, what 'of the same order' means, namely an earthly human superior.[19] In *De bello* Suárez makes it more precise: "The highest prince is the one who is not subordinated to another temporal leader."[20] Such a highest prince is to be recognized by his power to decide all cases in final instance: "Sign of a highest jurisdiction is, if there is a final court which judges all cases of its dominium without the possibility to appeal to a higher instance."[21]

    In order to understand how sovereignty originates, it may be helpful to see, how Suárez imagines the development of political life. In this respect he acknowledges different kinds of communities:

    (1) The fundamental community, called *communitas generis humani*, springs from the common natural rationability of all man.[22] It is directed by the *lex naturalis* which has to be considered as a law directly known by

---

17 "Sicut intra eamdem rempublicam, ut pax servetur, necessaria est legitima potestas ad puniendam delicta, ita in orbe, ut diversae respublicae pacate vivant, necessaria est potestas puniendi iniurias unius contra aliam." (DB IV, 5).
18 "Suprema potestas dicitur, quae in eodem ordine seu materia alteri subiecta non sit." (DEF III, 5, 2).
19 "Intelligitur autem de superiore in terris, seu humano (…) Excluditur ergo per negationem illam subiectio ad superiorem hominem mortalem." (DEF III, 5, 1).
20 "Supremum princeps [est] qui superiorem in temporalibus non habet." (DB II, 1); by that Suárez divides the secular from the spiritual sphere.
21 "Signum supremae iurisdictionis est, quando apud talem principem rempublicamque est tribunal, in quo terminantur omnes causae illius principatus, neque appellatur ad aliud tribunal superius." (DB II, 4).
22 "Hominem esse animal sociale et naturaliter rectaque appetere in communitate vivere." (DL III, 1, 3).

everybody through the light of reason. Lacking this natural bound of reason, mankind would only be a mere quantity of people without any legal capacity.[23]

(2) Furthermore, there is a community that arises out of a particular act of will, which brings about a special moral conjunction of its members (*coniunctio specialis*) and constitutes the unity of the whole. Such an association (*foedus*) may come into being either by human (*communitas politica*) or by divine will.[24] The following elements are necessary to transform the natural human community into a political one: deliberate union on the base of law (*se foedere, instituere, congregare*), orientation towards a common goal (*in ordine ad finem = bonum commune*), direction by a highest power (*sub aliquo capite*). A political community therefore is distinguished from the mere human community by the consensus of its members (citizens) who try to achieve the common good under the leadership of a ruler (*princeps*).[25]

(3) It is important to know that the so called political community is not yet a state (*respublica*), although it contains a political power which means nothing else than the ability to enact laws to which the subordinates feel obliged. Unless this 'potential power' has not been transformed into a certain kind of government, according to the will of the people which is the original carrier of sovereignty, there won't be no rule in a strict sense.[26] Let's resume: community (*societas*) results from *consensus*, rule (*potestas*) from contract. By this, Suárez has often been considered to be an early representative of contract theory on the grounds of a natural human fondness for unification.[27] As a third-grade community, *respublica* means that the original power has actually been carried into rulership. If the ruler is primarily committed to public welfare, he needs to have the means to protect it. This is the reason why a government

---

23 "Potestas condendi leges non est in singulis hominibus per se spectatis nec in multitudine hominum aggregata solum per accidens, sed est in communitate, ut moraliter unita et ordinata ad componendum unum corpus mysticum." (DL III, 11, 7).

24 On behalf of the terminus 'mysticum', that must be interpreted in the sense of a mysterious (transcendental) bound of the citizens united, cf. Markus Kremer, *Den Frieden verantworten. Politische Ethik bei Francisco Suárez* (Stuttgart: 2008), 116, footnote 189.

25 "Quia haec potestas est necessaria ad convenientem gubernationem reipublicae humanae." (DL III, 21, 8).

26 Cf. Reijo Wilenius, *The social and political theory of Francisco Suárez* (Helsinki: 1963), 37.

27 Cf. Josef Soder, *Francisco Suárez und das Völkerrecht* (Frankfurt: 1973), 79 f.

must be provided with coercive power (*vis coactiva*), of which the right of war was an important part.[28]

To the outside, sovereignty can be demonstrated by war, which is the prince's right on behalf of his vindictive justice that has to be exercised as commutative (compensation) as well as of distributive justice (punishment).[29] Presupposed that in every case the evil-doer has become guilty, vindictive justice has to be accompagnied by the jurisdiction over the culprit. While in internal affairs such a jurisdiction principally exists through the natural power of the ruler, it must externally be constituted even *ex causa delicti*: "Because there has no better way of mediation been invented", says Suárez, "vindiction seems to be a necessary means to run human affairs."[30] Already Augustine had underlined the vindicative character of war, but with a strong emphasis to its pedagogical function: The sense of punishment doesn't lie in deterrence, but in the conversion of the criminal.[31] Aquinas has stressed the relation of deed and punishment saying that those who are going to be punished for a guilt, should get the punishment they deserve.[32] The late scholastics, including Suárez, now reduced the (originally moral) guilt to an objective violation of laws by which the wrong-doer disturbes the natural order. Therefore, unbelief or heresy won't be just reasons for war any more. The capability of going to war belongs to the signs of every sovereign political community (*respublica*) without any difference whether it is Christian or not. Therefore, the religious confession of a prince or nation is of no importance in concern of international law (*ius gentium*) which applies to all nations in the same way.[33]

At the same time, the aspect of compensation becomes an eminent goal of vindiction. Suárez underlines, "that any injury can be faced by two ways: first by compensating all damages suffered, second by punish-

---

28 "Ratio a priori est, quia gubernatio sine potestate cogendi inefficax est, et facile contemnitur: coactio autem sine potestate obligandi in conscientia … est valde insufficiens, quia per eam non posset in multis casibus necessariis sufficienter reipublicae subvenire." (DL III, 21, 8); cf. Kremer, 117 ff.

29 "Quia potestas indicendi bellum est quaedam iurisdictionis, cuius actus pertinet ad iustitiam vindicativam, quae maxime necessaria est in republica ad coercendum malefactores." (DB II, 1).

30 "Quia actus hic iustitiae vindicativae fuit necessario humano generi et humano modo non potuit via ulla dari convenientor …" (DB IV, 7).

31 Cf. Augustine, *De civitate Dei XXII*, 22.

32 "Secundo requiritur causa iusta, ut scilicet illi qui impugnantur propter aliquam culpam impugnationem mereantur." (STH II-II, q. 40, 1).

33 Cf. Kremer, 126 ff.

ing the wrong-doer".[34] In concern of war, Suárez formulates as further condition, that a just cause for war might be, if the wrong-doer refuses to pay the satisfaction expected.[35] Typical for vindictive justice – and by the same reason critical within a Christian ethics – is "that it punishes an evil of guilt by an evil of punishment".[36] Thus, Suárez emphasizes, that, in order to be honest, "the act of punishment should be exercised in a manner that doesn't wish anything bad to the culprit, although he himself has done a wicked deed. And such an attitude belongs to charity."[37] That means that every punishment (which is, although part of justice, *in nuce* something evil) has to be considered with regard to a good, e. g. the reform of the wrong-doer or the satisfaction against the victim. What kind of punishment is equivalent to the guilt, can only be determined by a just judge. What seems to be crucial in Suárez' argument is the fact, that he considers the prince as an appropriate person to judge aggressions against himself respectively his country. Because Suárez presupposes the objectivity of law, he mustn't introduce a neutral arbiter, but confirms the "jurisdiction of the injured party, which probably is the most deeply controversial and contested claim in Suárez' doctrine: How does being injured give someone jurisdiction over the aggressor? Why should we allow at an international level, what we proscribe in a state's inner affairs, where no-one should be allowed to take the law in his own hands? Why cannot Suarez just admit that in the absence of a global public authority we permit private self-help by injured parties? He argues that "there is no higher authority than the sovereign himself. Therefore the power of punishing lies necessarily on the side of the in-

---

34 "Circa iniuriam illatam duo posse contendi: primum est, ut restituantur personae offensae damna illata ... alterum est, ut qui offenderit, debita poena puniatur." (DB IV, 4).

35 "Si alter vero neget satisfactionem, tunc poterit iuste bellum inchoare." (DB VII, 3).

36 "Quia hic affectus vindictae vere ac formaliter in Deo est, ut est certissimum, et vi proprii obiecti, quod est vindicare malum culpae malo poenae, habet honestatem respectu illius, qui potestatem et ius habet talem vindicationem faciendi, qui praecipue Deus est." (Opusc. theol. VI, 5, 3).

37 "Nam imprimis, ad honestatem illius actus [vindictae], necessarium est ut malum alterius per se non appetatur ut malum eius, etiamsi ipse nobis malum intulerit; et hoc munus spectat ad charitatem." (Opusc. theol. VI, 5, 7).

jured party, to whose will the culprit is subjected automatically by his crime."[38]

In order to understand Suárez in a correct way, we have to consider that he derives the prince's authority over another ruler not from his position of power, but from his commitment to public welfare (which includes the welfare of the community of nations, too). Admittedly, the ideal of an impartial judge, whose role the victimized prince should play – only committed to public (and international) welfare, free from selfish interests – seems to be unrealistic. But it fits to Suárez' concept of virtue: The decision to declare and to wage war (as a mean of punishing justice) must result from virtuous motives.[39] Against the (conventional) reading, that virtues are merely acquired dispositions to conform to natural law principles, the following explanations will give evidence that virtues (as a disposition of will) have to come up to moral actions, in order to make them good, and that 'principles without virtues remain impotent' (W. Frankena), although logically prior to them.

4 Justice and charity as norms of just warfare (*debitus modus*)

If virtue orientates human will towards what is essentially good, it will always play an important role within warfare, which is also subject of human morality. If carried out in an virtuous attitude – that means, that justice and charity will be regarded – war needn't to be unrigtheous: "Aggressive war might not be *per se* bad, but can even be honest and necessary."[40] The importance of how somebody acts, for the question of honesty turned out by the extansion Suárez deals with this question in *De bello*. The fact that the *debitus modus*-problem has apparently replaced the *intentio recta*, is no proof for any kind of positivism in Suárez legal

---

38 "Haec autem potestas non est in aliquo superiore, quia nullum habent, ut ponimus; ergo necesse est, ut sit in supremo principe reipublicae laesae, cui alius subdatur ratione delicti." (DB IV, 5).

39 Suárez solves the problem, that no one can be a judge in his own cause, by distinguishing the prince as a private person (who certainly cannot settle his own legal claims), from the prince as a public person who has to refrain from private interests; cf. Kremer, 122; 208 f.

40 "Bellum etiam aggressivum non est per se malum, sed potest esse honestum et necessarium." (DB I, 5).

theory.[41] The right way of acting must rather be seen as an effect of good will. Suárez can shift directly to concrete rules of warfare, because the correct behaviour does already include the right intention. That means, that the combatant is bound to justice and charity during the war. Otherwise he is guilty of violation of virtue. By introducing virtue into his just-war-doctrine, Suárez wants to show that a legitimate war does not already necessarily fit to the claims of Christian ethics, and therefore can be unjust. The difference made between the virtue of justice and that of charity lines out the difference between non-Christian and Christian princes. Let's see what this could mean in the context of war.

a) Justice

The necessity of war results from justice by which legal claims are to be satisfied and equality between conflicting parties is restored.[42] Justice serves to preserve peace between sovereign states that are bound to follow the rules of *ius gentium* in their mutual relations. Once introduced by international costum, the competence of punishment springs from the prince's responsability for public welfare, and not from his own (private) power. His role therefore must be that of an impartial judge, who punishes the law-breaker in order the restore justice. In an international context war seems to substitute the intra-state trial whereby an injury is atoned for.

An additional purpose of sanction is the protection from future misbehaviour. Consequently, sanction brings about honesty what is a precondition of the moral goodness of the war: "Vindiction is nothing else than retribution of something bad through something bad, what cannot be a matter of love. Only if considered in respect of just punishment

---

41 Soder, 351, mentions in this respect – besides "authors from the Dominican order" – Edgar Janssens and James Brierly. Edgar Janssens (*La coutûme, source formelle du droit, d'après St. Thomas et d'après Suárez* in: Revue Thomiste 1931, 681–726) and James Brierly (*Suárez' Vision of a World Community*, in: Actas del IV centenario del nacimiento de Suárez 1548–1948, tom.II, Madrid 1948, 259–267).

42 "Circa iniuriam illatam duo posse contendi: primum est, ut restituantur personae offensae damna illata … alterum est, ut qui offenderit, debita poena puniatur." (DB IV, 4).

and moral improvement of the wrong-doer, such a revenge might have an objective honest reason."[43]

Another reason for punishment is the debt of the law-breaker by which he owes compensation to the victim. This argument substantiates the duty of reparations by the defeated enemy. Estimating the right scale may be part of commutative justice, but is more of the legal justice that preserves the common interests of a political community.

Let's regard the concrete application of vindictive justice in war:

1) A first aspect is the princes duty to examine the just cause that has to be serious. "The king has to examine cause and legitimation of war carefully. Then, he may act according to the opinion he has formed by rational considerations. That's because war is one of the most grave enterprises. Reason requires to take advice and deals carefully with the matter."[44] Before all, war serves the restitution of a suffered injury and of all its consequences. "Whoever wages war without a just reason, has to compensate all damages suffered from such a war."[45] Adapted to the question of how injustices are to be compensated, Suárez explains, that everything must be done to offer the enemy a chance of satisfaction. That means, that already before war is declared, the affair has to be presented to the law-breaker, so that compensation can be given in due time. In case of refusal, war can be declared according to the norms of international law. At any time, also during the course of war, the enemy's offer has to be accepted. Suárez gives as reason, that the continuation of war must spring from a necessity, which lapses, if the opponent meets his commitments und fulfills the claims of the injured party.

In any case, the compensation has to meet the following conditions:
   – return of the misappropriated property,
   – refunding the costs on the part of the victim (indemnification),
   – additional reparations,

---

43 "Vindicatio autem est redditio mali pro malo, quae per se non est amabilis et charitati et rectae rationi contrarium est. Oportet ergo ut talis vindicatio seu mali redditio respiciatur sub ratione iustae poenae seu emendationis, ut honestam rationem obiecti habeat." (Opusc. theol. VI, 5, 5).

44 "Supremus rex tenetur ad diligentem causae et iustitiae examinationem, qua facta operare debet iuxta scientiam inde comparatam. Fundamentum prioris partis est, quia negotium belli est gravissimum; ratio autem postulat, ut in quovis negotio adhibeatur consultatio et diligentia qualitati eius accomodata." (DB VI, 1).

45 "Quia sine causa iusta bellum aggreditur, non solum contra charitatem, sed etiam contra iustitiam peccat; unde tenetur omnia damna restituere." (DB IV, 8).

– every measure that is necessary to guarantee peace in future.

All this extends first to the property of the guilty persons (= combat-tants + people able to fight), if sufficient for compensation. If the damage has been greater, all hostile possession can be included, even that of the innocent, because they belong to the hostile country (principle of collective liability).

2) Finally, justice affects the norms of combat: In a just war the prince can do any harm to the enemy, if necessary for gaining victory: "If the goals are honest, also are the means."[46] But every military action has to be exerciced in moderation, compared to the seriousness of the crime. It isn't allowed greater satisfaction than justice admits. See again Suárez' comparison to a just trial: "In times of war the same equality has to be considered as it is in a just sentence."[47] For the same reasons it is absolutely forbidden to do any harm to innocent people, whose death may only be acceptable under the conditions, that it is not intended directly, that it is necessary for victory, and that innocents cannot be discerned from the combattants.

b) Charity

Because war is attended by possible offenses against the 5th command-ment and by the danger of excessive violence, it might be an occasion of sin. That's why especially Christians are submitted to another virtue that doesn't apply equivalently to Non-Christians:[48] charity. Avoiding the risk of sin lies in the prince's responsability, not only on account of his own salvation, but of the care for his subordinates. By pointing out that love is an additional criteria of the moral quality of war, Suárez raises the question, wether Christians should anyway participate in such an un-dertaking, and – if yes – what they have to do to keep their souls free from sin.

Killing in times of war can be legitimized in two ways: (a) by the le-gality of the war itself, what is a matter of natural-law-arguments, and (b)

---

46 "Quia si finis licet, et media necessaria licent." (DB VII, 6).

47 "Nam in bello servanda est aequalitas, quae in iusto iudicio; in hoc autem puniri nequit reus omni poena, nec privari omnibus bonis sine mensura, sed pro qual-itate delicti." (DB VII, 7).

48 Of course may the heathen follow, what love requires, but if not, they cannot be blamed for.

by the goodness of the soldier's concrete behaviour, which is a matter of virtue. Charity, therefore, brings about the correction of what Suárez calls a 'deficit of mildness' (*defectus lenitatis*). Its main principle is, that the enemy will not be regarded with hatred.[49] It may occur that warfare seems to be legitimate in terms of justice, but isn't in terms of love, for instance because it is accompanied by cruelties or carried to excess. This taken into consideration, the sometimes heard statement, Suárez' just-war-theory treats the problem exclusively on the background of broken laws,[50] is obviously one-sided. Only a non-legalistic interpretation permits to understand legal conformity as a result of virtuous behaviour, wherein the intention to fulfill the precepts of law is already included. Whereas on a lower level of knowledge it is sufficient to observe what positive law lays down, virtue is necessary for moral perfection. This is relevant especially when someone holds a public function, bearing a responsability higher than the offcial's own interests. For a Christian prince war has ever to be seen in relation to charity, so that it must be not only legally, but also morally permitted without the danger of sin. Charity guarantees that politics is bound to the supernatural, spiritual dimension of human life. Without that, it is impossible to integrate a morally dubious action (war) into the universal order of salvation.

What consequences has an attitude of charity on the conduct of war?

1) Although punishment by war is a natural right, there is – especially for Christians – no duty to punish the wrong-doer at all, or to do it in a certain (esp. military) way. Charity even may demand to refrain from punishment and satisfaction, if therefore greater damage can be avoided. War is against love, if satisfaction is not absolutely necessary for the victim, i. e. if the wrong deed is trivial, or if compensation can be given only with a great disadvantage for the debtor. "If the hostile state is unable to pay the restitution demanded or could do this only with great disadvantage, the injured party would act against charity by insisting on satisfaction it hasn't to rely on."[51]

---

49 Whoever wages a just war, says Suárez (DB I, 3), doesn't detest the enemy, but his unjust deeds by which the unity of wills (= public order) is disturbed. This shows that virtue ethics are not limited to private behaviour, but have a public relevance as well.

50 Cf. Alfred Vanderpol, *Le droit de guerre d'après les théologiens et les canonistes do moyen-âge* (Paris: 1911).

51 "Sit tamen in casu aliquo non posset illa respublica vel satisfacere vel restituere sine magnis incommodis, neque esset necessaria satisfactio alteri principi, illam urgendo faceret plane contra charitatem." (DB IV, 8).

2) In concern of the conduct of war charity demands that no needless harm should arise to the persons involved. The background is that politics has to serve the human search for salvation. Hence, the Christian prince first of all has to examine the possible consequences of war:[52]

(a) If he reckons with a damage to the church, for instance if the enemies of faith will get stronger by the war, such a conflict will be considered as sin and therefore be prohibited.

(b) If a damage to the own country is probable, war is in contrast to justice and to charity. The prince namely is committed to public welfare and to the interests of his subordinates.

(c) Whether there will be any damage to the enemy is to a great extent irrelevant on reasons of guilt to which war must however be in right proportion.

3) Having permitted all means necessary for gaining victory, charity demands that there won't be any excessive and hateful use of violence.[53] "If sufficient for restitution and satisfaction, military actions have to be limited to the guilty persons."[54] This can include the death penalty, which isn't applicable to innocent people (here: persons who aren't able to or have not weared arms)[55].

However, Suárez' assessment of capital punishment is ambivalent. On the one side, killing hostile combattants in the course of war is possible without sin, if carried out to on the supreme authority's behalf, what contains the intention to punish the wrong-doer. If necessary for satisfaction, it might even be allowed to execute some few of the enemies for the purpose of deterrence, "when all other detriments are insufficient for the purpose of punishment".[56] On the other side, Suárez declares that, after having gained the victory, it isn't allowed to execute anybody who is not obviously guilty. Because the proofs must however be undeniable, the guilt of the delinquents has to be established within a just trial (and not by *ad-hoc*-tribunals). Charity rather suggests that, by reasons of uncertainty, the

---

52 Cf. DB IV, 8.
53 Cf. DB VII, 21.
54 "Si ad restitutionem et satisfactionem sufficiant damna nocentibus illata, non possunt iuste ad innocentes extendi." (DB VII, 11).
55 Cf. Kremer, 212 f.
56 "Si omnia praecedentia damna non videantur sufficientia pro delicti gravitate, posse etiam iuste post omnino finitum bellum aliquos occidi hostes nocentes, quamvis magna hominum multitudo non esset sine urgentissima causa interficienda." (DB VII, 7).

victor should refrain from applying the death penalty, since the aims of war have been already reached by the victory. Suárez' caution against capital punishment is also comprehensible by the fact that his theory of law is directed to the individual's happiness, so that the law-breaker shouldn't be generally deprived of the possibility of reform, repentence and pardon.

Between Christian nations, additional norms have been invented on the basis of charity: It is not usual to enslave Christian war prisoners (which right is also valid for heretics). Further, that clerics and goods of the church benefit of immunity. That's because the church is in a certain way a *respublica spiritualis* that differs from other (secular) human institutions.

By introducing virtue into the just-war-doctrine Suárez emphasizes that an apparently legitimate war must not be automatically in concordance with the precepts of a Christian ethics. Suarez obviously sees a tension between the demands of charity and the demands of natural justice, whether those demands are described in terms of principles or of virtues. In consequence, a just, but love-less war can be considered as morally inadmissable: "If all that is considered, what I mentioned above, and if the general conditions of justice are respected, then war won't be injust. However, it might infringe charity or any other virtue",[57] whose most important effect will be peace.

5 Peace as essential thought in Suárez' just-war doctrine

It has been shown that in the centre of Suárez' conception of political order stands the individual acting subject and his desire for happiness (salvation). The concentration on the individual, often been seen as typical for Jesuit thought, can be found in the introductional sentences to Suárez' *lex*-treatise: "For just as theologians should ponder concerning God for many other reasons, so also should they ponder concerning him for this reason: that He is the final end, towards the rational creatures direct their lives and what their happiness consists of."[58] This

---

57 "Si omnia haec, quae cavimus, in bello serventur, simulque adsint generales aliae conditiones iustitiae, bellum non erit iniustum; poterit aliquam habere malitiam contrariam charitati, vel alteri virtuti." (DB VII, 21).

58 "Deus enim, ut multis aliis titulis a theologo, ita illo expendi debet, quod ultimus sit finis ad quem tendunt creaturae rationis participes, et in quo unica illarum felicitas consistit." (DL prooem.).

short remark leads into the depth of Suárez' moral theology, where the single human being in his unique relation to God creator is to be found. If so, the Highest appears at the same time as inner principle of human actions, that must intend to be in accordance to God's will, irrespective of wether somebody is a Christian or not.[59] This presupposes the ability to restrain one's own passions, and implicates the social norm, that everybody must be allowed to seek his happiness. If we take it seriously that war should be a mean of true peace, a moral evaluation of war will be possible only under theological presumptions. Thus, in Suárez, we find a three-fold concept of peace:

1. *Peace as restraint of human passions:* That describes a level of character, where the perfect moderation of passions has been reached and where in a moral way any passionate war of desires is excluded.[60] By this definition Suárez joins Augustine's opinion who considered the moderation of carnal desires as a prerequisite for entering into the community with God.[61]

2. *Peace as unity of wills:* In this respect peace is a permanent disposition of will, as a result of which the harmony between one's own will and the will of his next occurs, wether that of God or that of other man. A peaceful person seeks the good order with God, with the fellow man, and of his own desires.[62]

3. *Peace as state of guaranteed rights:* As a political term peace is a condition of man's social existence. In this respect it is part of the governmental responsibility, that has to take action against the law-breaker: "War is often necessary for a state, so that it is able to prosecute injustices and to punish the enemies; otherwise the nations couldn't

---

59 Atheism has to be considered unknown to Suárez' thinking, whereas unbelief can be a possibility for him.

60 "Intelligenda ergo est de pace, quae ex perfecta moderatione passionum insurgit ... et quae morali modo anxietatem et contentiosum bellum concupiscentiae excludat." (DGr IX, 7, 19).

61 Cf. Augustine, *De civitate Dei, XIV,* 16–24.

62 "Respondetur pacem posse spectari vel in habitu, et quasi permanenter, atque ita nihil aliud est quam unio voluntatum, quam efficit charitas ... respectu quidem Dei, inclinando voluntatem hominis ad coniunctionem cum divina bonitate et voluntate, respectu vero aliorum hominum, inclinando ad concordiam et consensionem in rebus honestis." (DCh II, 1, 6).

preserve themselves in peace."[63] As a result, there cannot be any peace, if the legal claims of the citizens are ignored.

Although these understandings of peace lead from the inner conditions of human being to social ones, they remain focused on the singular person, her will and interests. As long as an action is directed towards the good (towards God), and unless it contradicts the reasonal judgement, it won't be a sin. This argument leads to the claim, that everything done in a good intention is morally acceptable and legitimate. If therefore moral actions, including war, are to be primarily considered as intrinsically motivated, and not as result of a natural law conclusion, the criteria of evaluating war must be different: We have to ask for the moral quality of individual behaviour of the people involved, and not for any kind of factual political constraint. The will to follow a (naturally founded) prescript must not only spring from obligation (external or internal), but also from the free decision of the individual actor. Then, natural law ethics, understood as the rational cognition of what is good or evil, won't be any longer inconsistent with a focus on the quality of the intentions.

To make it perfectly clear: A primacy of virtue over natural law within a theological concept of political ethics does not mean the irrelevance of the latter. On the contrary, natural law remains an essential, but not the only part of the moraliy of war. Natural law is the *conditio sine qua non* of any moral justification of war. And indeed, you will find all its elements in Suárez' war-treatise: power, sovereignty, jurisdiction, just cause, self defense, punishment and so on. In this respect Suárez joins the tradition. But he goes a step further: He declares the individual's happiness to be the main content of the order of charity that includes in a broader sense the social dimension of man's existence and finally the worldwide unity of mankind. This universal point of view is possible, because Suárez – different to Thomas – believes that peace is not an exclusive effect of love, but might also result from other virtues. This way, he affirms that peace is a possibility not only for Christians, but for all man who try to lead a virtuous life. Faith, therefore, is no necessary condition for peace at all, that should, in future, be able among every nation of the world and beyond the borders of religion or race. This thought (that has been completely new in the days of Suárez) had wide-ranging consequences for his own concept of international relations as well as for the follow-

---

63 "Bellum saepe est reipublicae necessarium ad propulsandas iniurias et coercendos hostes, neque aliter possunt respublicae in pace conservari." (DB I, 5).

ing philosophy of law (Christian Wolff, Hugo Grotius). Political peace, therefore, has to be functional to inner peace but not subordinate to it.

6 Conclusion

Suárez' conception of peace presupposes a political dimension, but cannot be reduced to it. Suárez places political peace (*pax temporalis*) into the perspective of salvation. It follows that offensive war shouldn't be undertaken carelessly, but only if deeply profounded. By infringing the order of creation (*lex naturalis*) or the precepts of virtue (*lex gratiae*), warfare becomes illegitimate. Suárez' conception of virtue doesn't replace natural law, but complements it. Thinking in categories of natural law is completely a matter of course for Suárez. He comments nearly all questions of natural law and exchanges views with his contemporaries. But he does also take into account the fact of God's revelation in Christ, which can't be without significance for how man live together.[64] The new way of life is founded on a theory of virtues that are valid for Christians (*caritas*) as well as for Non-Christians (*iustitia*).

Caritas obliges the Christian nations to apply the laws of war extremely carefully. War as a mean of punishment can be allowed to Christians without any danger of sin.[65] But on reasons of love they are particularly committed to respect the precepts of charity and of loving the enemy (Mt 5,44). By this, Suárez introduces additional moral criteria into the just-war-doctrine. In concrete terms does that mean, that the decision for war will be more difficult for the Christian prince and that, after having taken up military actions, mildness is advisable in any particular case (e.g. refraining from punishment or a human treatment of the enemy).

"War and peace are not morally equivalent. If peace as a self-performative expression of the moral unity of mankind should be realized, war has to remain a legal fiction."[66]

---

64 "Tale bellum est ergo hoc iure naturae licitum, atque adeo etiam lege evangelica, quae in nulla re derogat iuri naturali, neque habet nova praecepta divina, praeterquam fidei et sacramentorum." (DB I, 5).

65 Cf. DB I, 2.

66 Kremer, 264 f.

Abbreviations

DB =	De bello (= De charitate, disp. XIII)
DCh =	De charitate
DL =	De legibus
DEF =	Defensio fidei contra errores Angliae regis
Opusc. theol. =	Opuscula theologica
DGr =	De gratia

Suárez, Aquinas, and the Just War: Self Defense or Punishment?

James Bernard Murphy

In the classic tradition of Catholic just war doctrine, from Augustine to Suárez and beyond, the decision to wage war is justified by reference to two very different analogies: a just war is compared to the use of force in self-defense and to the use of force in punishing criminals. Is war more like private defense of one's self or like the public act of executing convicted wrongdoers? Following the lead of the classic theorists, I shall be focused mainly upon the moral justification for the decision to wage war (*ius ad bellum*), rather than the moral issues about how the war is conducted (*ius in bello*). We might well want to resist having to choose between these two plausible analogies, but our just war theorists developed these analogies into two mutually incompatible ethics of private and public killing. The analogies themselves are not incompatible, but the traditional interpretations of them are. Because of the very strong moral distinction drawn between private and public killing, and because war seems to be a paradigmatic example of public killing, the analogy between war and capital punishment became dominant in the tradition. The main exemplar of a just war in the Catholic tradition has always been an offensive and punitive war aimed to redress a past injustice. But during the 20th century, this ideal of offensive and punitive war has lost much of its appeal, both to international lawyers and to Catholic theologians and prelates. Moreover, the doctrine of punitive war was developed at a time when capital punishment was almost universally accepted as compatible with justice. As Catholics and others have very recently come to question the morality of capital punishment, the classic doctrine of punitive war has also come to be challenged. Of course, the fact that the doctrine of punitive war rests upon the presumed justice of capital punishment does not imply that a suitably revised doctrine of punitive war might well be compatible with a rejection of capital punishment.

I will explore these two analogies in relation to just war theory in Thomas Aquinas and Francisco Suárez. Each analogy both illuminates and obscures various aspects of the complex moral reality of war. Unfortunately, neither Aquinas nor Suárez analyzes the implications of these analogies adequately, so I shall pick up where they left off. Nor are these analogies mere relics of the past: I will also briefly discuss their use by two contemporary Christian just war theorists, Oliver O'Donovan and John Finnis. I will conclude by offering a few considerations for why the basis for the decision to wage war should shift from the paradigm of punishment to the paradigm of self-defense. My aim throughout is not exegetical but philosophical: I merely use exegesis as a way of framing the relevant issues and as a provocation for thought. I try to think with the tradition more than about it. We are now in a time of a radical challenge to the whole notion of a just war: the *philosophia perennis* ever changes. But, as we shall see, this classic tradition of just war theory has more than one strand; this rich body of thought includes the resources for its own fundamental transformation.

1 Punishment and Self-Defense in Aquinas

Suárez himself believed, and most of his commentators agree, that his thought is best understood in relation to that of Thomas Aquinas.[1] But there is no real agreement about how to characterize his relation to Aquinas. Suárez and his Jesuit commentators emphasize his continuity with many basic doctrines of Aquinas while Suárez's Dominican commentators and many lay Catholic philosophers and historians emphasize Suárez's innovative breaks with Aquinas. These disputes about whether or not Suárez was a good Thomist would be more illuminating if both sides were to acknowledge that Aquinas's own thought embodied ambiguities and tensions that anticipated and contributed to subsequent scholastic controversies. Nowhere is this more evident than in the contrasting and incompatible analogies of a just war that Suárez has inherited from Aquinas. Aquinas developed both a natural law theory of the just war and a Christian theory of the just Crusade; Suárez has much to say about

---

1   One scholar tabulated all of Suárez's citations in the *Metaphysical Disputations*, showing his overwhelming reliance on Aquinas; see John P. Doyle's edition of Suárez's *On Beings of Reason* (Milwaukee: Marquette University Press, 1995), 11, n. 65.

both of these theories, but we shall restrict our discussion to the natural law theory.[2]

Suárez begins his major discussion of war (De Bello: Disputation XIII of De Charitate) by explicitly referring to Aquinas's discussion of war in the *Summa Theologiae*, II-II, QQ. 40, 41, and 42[3]. These questions strongly contrast public killing in war with the private killing of sedition and violent quarrels, so Suárez signals here his reliance on the dominant paradigm of war as public punishment. But, as we shall see, Aquinas's discussion of private homicide and self-defense (ST II-II, Q. 64) will also turn out to be quite relevant to Suárez's analysis. We cannot tease out the ambiguities and tensions in Aquinas's treatment of the ethics of war until we first outline the principles he defends in a variety of kinds of killing. These various principles will force us to ask whether killing in war derives its justification from the specifically public authority of the state to kill convicted criminals or from the right of any private person to defend himself or others in his charge from unjust aggression.

We might want to resist having to choose between these two analogies. First, different kinds of just wars seem to share features both of capital punishment and of private self-defense. An offensive war to punish an unjust regime for crimes against its own citizens looks much like the execution of a criminal while a war to protect one's own polity from destruction looks much like private self-defense. Perhaps different kinds of just wars derive their justifications from different kinds of analogous cases. Second, perhaps the same war might have both justifications: we might declare war both to defend ourselves from attack and to punish the aggressor. Why cannot the justice of deciding to wage a war be overdetermined by different but mutually compatible justifications? But Aquinas forces us to choose between these analogies because of the very strong distinctions he makes between them. The principles that justify killing in self-defense are incompatible with the principles that justify killing as punishment.

---

2   LeRoy Brandt Walters shows that Aquinas has a well-developed theory of the just Crusade in his *Five Classic Just War Theories* (Ann Arbor, MI: University Microfilms, 1971) but Finnis denies that Aquinas has an account of the just Crusade in *Aquinas* (Oxford: Oxford University Press, 1998), 3.

3   For Aquinas, I have used the translations in Thomas Gilby's Blackfriars (1975) edition of the *Summa Theologiae*; for Suárez, I have used the translations from James Scott Brown's edition of "De Triplici Virtute Theologica" in *Selections From Three Works of Francisco Suárez* (Oxford: Clarendon Press, 1944).

What we find in Aquinas is less a unified ethics of killing and more a two-fold ethics of private and public killing. Roman law made a strong distinction between public and private law, between crimes and torts, between punishment and restitution, between corporations and partnerships, between war and brigandage. Augustine's treatment of killing and war reflected this Roman law distinction: Augustine seems to forbid killing in private self-defense but explicitly permits public authorities to kill criminals and to wage war.[4] Because the classic just war theorists so strongly distinguish what is permissible for private persons from what is permissible to public authority, we must decide whether war is ultimately a public or private act. If war is based on public authority, then the analogy to capital punishment seems inescapable.

The purpose of analogy is to use what is better understood to clarify what is less well understood. War is a complex moral, social, and political reality; perhaps we can clarify the moral obscurities of war by analogy to the simpler and better understood practices of punishment and self-defense? Unfortunately, punishment itself turns out to be a very complex and controversial practice: philosophers cannot agree about how to characterize the proper mix of purposes in the practice of punishment. We punish for many reasons, including protection, deterrence and retribution. So attempting to clarify the moral complexities of war by analogy to punishment just seems to land us in another set of moral obscurities. Nonetheless, if we restrict our inquiry to considering briefly what Aquinas and Suárez say about punishment, then perhaps we can understand better the point of this analogy. Although Aquinas's account of punishment includes elements of deterrence, remediation, protection, and rehabilitation, the core rationale for punishment is retribution. "The natural law prescribes that punishment be imposed for fault (*culpa*) and that no one may be punished without fault."[5] Punishment must be proportional, not so much to the amount of harm caused, but to the scale of the offender's moral fault. Still, as Finnis notes, "punishment, though merited, need not be imposed when its imposition would cause disproportionate harm to others."[6] As we shall see, this qualification will become important in Suárez's argument that justice sometimes must yield to peace even in a punitive war.

---

4   See *De Libero Arbitrio*, I, 5.11–6.15; *Contra Faustum*, XXII. 73–79.
5   Aquinas, cited in Finnis *Aquinas* (Oxford: Oxford University Press, 1998), 214n 160.
6   Finnis, *Aquinas*, 214–215.

In defining the just cause of a war, Aquinas always used the language of moral fault and punishment: an enemy can be attacked because of some fault (*culpa*).[7] In other words, the misdeed of the enemy is not merely involuntary or accidental: the enemy must be guilty of an offense, not merely the cause of an offense. Aquinas's concept of fault is conceptually bound to his concept of a penalty (*poena*): every fault merits a penalty and there should be no penalty without a fault.[8] Walters reformulates Aquinas's just cause formula as: "Those upon whom war is made merit the penalty of warfare because of some intentional and avoidable misdeed."[9] Just as the state may punish criminals for their misdeeds in the past, so the state may punish other states by launching a war to redress past misdeeds.

Aquinas agrees with Augustine that a private person may never intentionally kill anyone, guilty or innocent.[10] But Aquinas argues that using lethal force to defend oneself from attack need not involve an intention to kill, but only an upright intention to preserve one's own life.[11] A public official, however, may intentionally kill evildoers, as when an executioner kills by judicial order or when a soldier kills an officially-declared enemy.[12] This strong contrast between what is permitted to a private and a public person undermines any consistent ethics of killing in Aquinas. More precisely, Aquinas's general ethics of killing consists of just one norm binding on both public and private killing, namely the prohibition against directly killing the innocent, which, he says, admits of no exceptions.[13] If we assume, with all the classic just war theorists, that war necessarily involves the direct intention to kill the enemy, then the analogy to capital punishment is unavoidable.

Augustine and Aquinas also strongly distinguish the private good defended in self-defense from the common good defended in war. A private person rightly kills only to defend his own life while a public official kills

---

7   ST, II-II, q. 40, a. 1c. I have followed Walters' exposition of Aquinas on culpa and poena; see his *Five Classic Just War Theories*, 113.

8   ST, I-II, q. 105 a. 2 obj. 11.

9   Walters, *Five Classic Just War Theories*, 114. Walters notes the strong analogy to punishment: "It is therefore clear that Thomas' just-cause formula was couched in the language of punishment, although he carefully avoided the term 'punishment' as he had in his discussion of authority"(114).

10   ST, II-II, q. 64 a. 3 ad 3; q. 65 a. 2c; I-II, q. 100 a. 3c.

11   ST II-II, q. 64 a. 7c.

12   ST II-II, q. 64 a. 3c, q. 64 a. 7c

13   ST II-II, q. 64 a. 6c.

to defend, not himself, but others. So a private person is defending merely a private and personal good, while the public official is defending the common good: this is why, they argue, we permit public officials, but not private persons, to intentionally kill wrongdoers. If private killing in self-defense were indeed limited merely to defending one's own self, then the analogy to war seems remote; but the right of killing in self-defense is not so limited. By both morality and law, a private person may use force to repel force directed, not merely at himself, but against innocent third parties. A private person has a natural right, recognized by all modern legal systems, to use force to defend innocent strangers from direct attack. In his formal discussion of killing in self-defense, Aquinas never mentions the duty to defend innocent third parties, though he does refer to this duty elsewhere.[14] So the classic just war theorists generally reject the analogy between war and private self-defense because they wrongly describe the true scope of the right of private self-defense. If the just war theorists had rightly described the scope of legitimate private use of force, they might have seen a much closer analogy between war and self-defense.

Aquinas is so impressed by the public dimension of war and capital punishment, that he ignores some obvious similarities between war and private self-defense. The first condition for a just war, says Aquinas, is the authority of a sovereign who alone can declare war: "now a private person has no business declaring war."[15] But when American sailors were attacked in Pearl Harbor, they began waging war on the Japanese before Roosevelt could ask Congress to declare war. As Suárez will argue, a war of self-defense need not be declared because everyone preserves the right to defend himself from direct attack.

2 Punishment and Self-Defense in Suárez

As we shall see, Suárez's analysis of war will oscillate between these two analogies without much clarity about the tension between them. Aquinas did not explicitly distinguish between offensive and defensive wars, though his concept of a just cause for war certainly included both

---

14 Aquinas does not discuss this duty to third parties in his discussion of self-defense at ST II-II, q. 64 a. 7, but he does refer to it in his discussion of war at ST II-II, q. 40 a. 1 ad 2 and justice ST II-II, q. 60 a. 6 ad 2 and vengeance ST II-II, q. 108 a. 1 ad 2 and a. 2 and military religious orders ST II-II, q. 188 a. 3 ad 1.
15 ST, II-II, q. 40 a. 1c.

kinds of wars. Suárez makes the distinction between defensive and offensive war central to his analysis.[16] Defensive war is rooted in private self-defense while offensive war is rooted in public punishment. In the case of war for pure national defense, there is no distinction between the private and public ethics of killing. Resorting to the use of force in self defense is not only permitted but often required; and this is true equally of private individuals as of public officials.[17] A defensive war is justified by analogy to private self-defense "provided that it is waged with a moderation of defense, which is blameless."[18] Aquinas had argued that a moderate or proportional use of force in private self-defense was permissible because it reflected a licit intention of self-preservation rather than an illicit intention of destroying the aggressor. Suárez here applies the same analysis to justifiable self-defense in war.

So Suárez endorses the analogy between war and self-defense in the case of a defensive war, but he is primarily concerned to justify offensive war: "even when war is aggressive, it is not an evil in itself, but may be right and necessary."[19] What is the distinction between defensive and offensive war? Suárez concedes that the distinction is not always obvious. If the injury is about to take place or is now taking place, then my actions to stop it are defensive; but if the injury has already taken place, then my actions to redress it are offensive (DB, 1.6). But even this is too simple: if I have been wrongly barred from my property in my absence, then when I return and use force to reclaim it, my actions, he says are defensive, even though the injury was completed in the past (DB 1.60). Here Suárez is drawing upon legal distinctions between the power that private individuals (as well as states) have to defend themselves and their property from immediate threats and the power that the state reserves to itself to redress past wrongs and to punish past wrongdoers. Every war is either defensive or offensive, depending upon whether the cause is immediate or safely in the past: "The war was offensive or aggressive in the sense

---

16 Suárez actually uses the term "*aggressio*" for an offensive war, but since "aggressive war" is now a crime, it would be misleading to use "aggression" to translate what Suárez means by an offensive war. Today, all aggressive wars are condemned but not all offensive wars. I have not altered the use of "aggression," however, by the translators of the Scott edition of Suárez.

17 Suárez, DB 1.4.

18 Suárez, DB 1.6.

19 Suárez, DB, 1.5: "Our question [Who has the legitimate power of declaring war?] relates to aggressive war; for the power of defending oneself against an unjust aggressor is conceded to all" (DB 2.1). So much for Christian pacifism!

that it was not necessarily preceded by *military* action on the part of the enemy."[20] A private person may use deadly force against a wrongdoer in self-defense, but may not even fine him a penny in redress for a past wrong. The essence of a just offensive war, like the essence of punishment, is the redress of past wrongs.

In Suárez's view that a punitive war may be waged to redress past wrongs, we see that his theory of punishment is basically retributive. He frequently says that "the culprit may receive punishment suited to the nature of the crime."[21] According to England, Suárez's main addition to the theory of punishment in Aquinas is Suárez's focus on the contractual duty of a judge to the sovereign state to inflict punishments in proportion to moral fault.[22] However, it must be noted that there is no perfect duty to punish all crimes. Like Aquinas, Suárez concedes that sometimes retributive justice must yield to other requirements for the common good.[23] In the case of punitive war, this means that justice must sometimes yield to the demands of peace.

Suárez argues that only the sovereign may declare an offensive war (DB 2) because only the sovereign may redress past wrongs. A purely defensive war need not be declared by anyone because everyone has a natural right to self-defense (DB 2.1). Why is punishment restricted to public officials? If I may coerce a wrongdoer while he is attacking me, then why may not I punish him for his past injury? But Suárez very strongly rejects the whole idea of private punishment: "For a punishment inflicted by one's own private authority is intrinsically evil" (DB 2.2). Why? Suárez observes that were private persons permitted to punish wrongdoers, then tumults and wars would be frequently provoked within a state (DB 2.2). Indeed, a society in which private individuals were permitted to prosecute and punish wrongdoers for past offenses would quickly de-

---

20 Walters, *Five Classic Just War Theories*, 313.

21 Suárez, "Defense of the Catholic and Apostolic Faith" (In Brown): III, 23.18; 698.

22 Speaking of Suárez's theory of *vindicatio*, England says: "If it is applied by a judicial authority then it constitutes commutative justice, since the judge is duty bound to exercise penal jurisdiction in the framework of his assumed judicial task. The idea of a contractual or administrative judicial duty as an additional basis of commutative justice seems to be the original contribution of Suárez, since the traditional scholastic view referred the commutative dimension of revenge exclusively to the required equivalence between crime and punishment." Izhak England, *Corrective and Distributive Justice* (Oxford: Oxford University Press, 2009), 89.

23 See "On Law and God the Lawgiver" I, 7.15; 100 (In Brown).

scend into anarchy; and yet this is precisely what Suárez endorses for international society. Each sovereign prince is permitted to prosecute and to punish any other sovereign or subject in redress of past wrongs, where those wrongs cannot be avenged or repaired in any other way (DB 4.1).

Suárez notes that punitive justice stems from jurisdiction: a sovereign may punish those and only those subject to his jurisdiction. But here is where the analogy between war and punishment is severely strained, for the enemy attacked by a sovereign is not usually regarded as under his jurisdiction. But Suárez claims that by its fault, a sovereign state comes under the jurisdiction of the sovereign state whom it has injured (DB 2.1). But this seems like a mere legal fiction or even sophism: in what sense does a state come under the sovereignty of the nation it has wronged in the past? Indeed, sovereignty itself would vanish were it subject to such a principle, for what nation has not wronged its neighbors in the past?

Indeed, the whole notion of jurisdiction becomes irrelevant to the actual scope of justified offensive war, since on Suárez's account, I, as a sovereign prince, may launch a war not only on another sovereign who has injured me and whose injury has somehow put him under my sovereignty, but I may also launch a war on any sovereign who has injured anyone whom I consider a friend, including his own subjects—so long as those who are injured would be justified in seeking vengeance for a past injury and actually propose to do so. For, as Suárez quotes from Aristotle, "a friend is another self" (DB 4.3). True, Suárez rejects the view that a sovereign may roam the globe avenging any evils he wishes, but he permits sovereigns wide latitude to launch offensive war to avenge injuries on anyone who merits friendly assistance. What injuries are the causes of a just offensive war? They include unjust seizure of property, unwillingness to permit commerce and travel, damage to someone's reputation or honor. Nor need these be official or public injuries: it is sufficient for just war that the injuries be inflicted either on a sovereign or on any of his subjects (DB 4.3). Now Suárez insists that "not every cause is sufficient to justify war, but only those causes which are serious and commensurate with the losses that the war would occasion" (DB 4.2). Still, one wonders if any nation in history at any moment were immune from attack on such wide-ranging grounds.

Suárez's doctrine of justified offensive war is extended widely by him to permit myriad possible wars. But this extension is not limited to offensive wars. Suárez also argues that defensive wars may be fought, not only to defend one's own countrymen, but also innocent people under attack anywhere in the world (DB 5.8). So while offensive war may present unique moral hazards, defensive war can also be very permissive of war in the name of "humanitarian intervention."

Suárez is aware that there is something odd about a sovereign playing the role of both prosecutor and judge in his disputes with his neighbors. Indeed, it is a basic principle of natural law, enshrined in both Roman and English common law, that no one can be a judge in his own cause.[24] Suárez concedes that normally to conflate these two roles is contrary to natural law (DB 4.6). But in the absence of viable international institutions capable of punishing the crimes of sovereign states, Suárez sees a regime of punitive war as justified *faute de mieux*. Suárez seems rash in his judgment that no alternative to punitive war is even possible in human affairs (DB 4.7). Suárez considers the objection that if self-help is permitted in international society, then why not in domestic society? If public officials cannot or will not bring a wrongdoer to justice, then why cannot a private person? Isn't messy and informal justice better than no justice at all? But Suárez objects that punishment is a public, not a private, good, so that if a private person is denied justice he must simply endure his loss (DB 4.7). Of course, many theorists of international society see punitive war not as a form of public judgment and execution but as a form of self-help among private parties.

Suárez considers the objection that no prince should be permitted to be a judge in his own cause for the same reasons that no private person is permitted: "namely, that they would in practice exceed the bounds of justice" (DB 4.6). No party to a dispute can be expected to be impartial: he is very likely to exaggerate the fault of his opponent and minimize his own. Long and bitter experience of self-help in criminal law and custom has shown that parties to disputes cannot be trusted to assess blame accurately nor to exact punishment with restraint: "the same danger exists in the case of a prince who avenges himself" (DB 4.6). Suárez denies the analogy between private self-help and punitive war: he claims that while a private individual "is guided by his own judgment, and therefore will easily exceed the limitations of vengeance" public authority "is guided by public counsel, to which heed must be paid" (DB 4.7). Here we find echoes of Augustine's view that private persons kill out of blood lust (<u>libido dominandi</u>), while public officials kill out of love for the

---

24 This principle was the basis for Edward Coke's celebrated judgment in Dr. Bonham's Case, 8 Rep. 118a (1610).

common good.[25] Suárez hopes that princes will try to act as if they were judges in their disputes: "the sovereign ruler is bound to make a diligent examination of the cause and its justice, and that after making this examination, he ought to act in accordance with the knowledge obtained" (DB 6.1). In short, "a king ought to act as a just judge" (DB 6.2).

That Suárez remains worried about the capacity of a prince to play the role of judge in his own cause is evident by his strictures about referring these disputes to a genuinely impartial arbiter. Christian kings are bound to refer the causes of offensive wars to the decision of the Pope "which the parties are bound to obey, unless his decision be manifestly unjust" (DB 2.5). But a natural law principle cannot make reference to the authority of the Pope, so Suárez says that every prince is bound to seek an impartial arbiter to decide the justice of the case for war (DB 6.5). Since war must be avoided if possible, resort to an arbiter is required if feasible. But since arbiters function only with the consent of the parties, a prince is not bound by the decision of the arbiter: he is bound to seek it but not to follow it (DB 6.6). The moral burden of the decision to wage offensive war falls on the prince and no one else: he alone is bound in conscience to an investigation of the merits. Common soldiers have no duty to investigate the justice of war "but rather may go to war when summoned to do so, provided it is not clear to them that the war is unjust" (DB 6.8). Just as the duties of a prince are modeled on those of a judge, so the duties of a soldier are modeled on those of a subordinate officer of a court: an executioner "may execute a sentence without any previous examination, provided that the sentence is not manifestly unjust" (DB 6.8).

Suárez claims that to view offensive war as a mode of punishment will limit the injustice and cruelty of war. Just as we punish criminals, not for who they are, but for what they have done wrong, so punitive war is directed, not to destroy persons, but to chastise wrongful deeds. Punishment, both judicial and bellicose, hates the sin but loves the sinner (DB 1.3). Moreover, judicial punishment is always limited by the severity of the crime: the convicted person is not visited with every possible punishment but is punished in proportion to his crime. So punitive war may punish an enemy only in proportion to his fault (DB 7.7). Yet, in other places, Suárez develops a different principle for determining the limitations of punitive war, namely the "preservation of an undisturbed peace

---

25 "in killing an enemy the soldier acts as an agent of the law. That is why he can easily fulfill his duty without lust." Augustine, *De Libero Arbitrio*, I, 5.11.

in the future...since war is permissible, especially for this reason, namely as a way to an upright peace" (DB 7.20). What this means is that, like judicial punishment, bellicose punishment is not determined only by fault, but also by the more general requirements of the common good: "a just equality must be preserved, and a regard must be had for the future peace" (DB 7.7). In short, both in peace and in war, the larger demands of the common good may require us to forgo punishing wrongdoers. The enemy may well not get what he deserves because the larger aim of war is not punishment per se, but laying the foundations for a durable and just peace.

As we saw with Aquinas, one important consequence of the analogy of war to punishment is the view that public authorities have the right to intentionally kill people, a right strictly denied to private persons, even in self-defense. Suárez closely follows Aquinas by placing a huge moral weight on the distinction between public and private killing. Because the state defends the common good, which is higher than any private good, "it is not strange that more things are permissible to a state than to an individual" (DB 2.3). Only the state can intentionally kill criminals (DB 4.7). Although Aquinas asserts, following St. Paul, that evil may not be done even though good may come of it, Finnis argues that Aquinas nonetheless permits the state to inflict the evil of homicide on criminals for the common good. Suárez goes further than Aquinas by explicitly arguing that Paul's dictum applies to all evil except the evil inflicted by public authorities as punishment (DB 7.19). Nothing is more characteristic of the classic just war tradition than the doctrine that state officials are emancipated from the most basic norms of Christian morality. In the case of tyrannical oppression, for example, private persons retain the right to act in immediate self-defense, but they cannot organize an offensive campaign against a tyrant; only the state as a whole, acting with some kind of public authority, can wage war against a tyrant (DB 8.2). A duel organized by private parties is intrinsically evil, since no private person may kill except in self-defense or defense of property (DB 9.2); but a duel organized by public authority, as a mode of punishing a criminal or as an alternative to war, is permissible (DB 9.8, 9.9). So intentional killing is permitted under color of public authority, but, oddly, never lying or bad faith (DB 7.23).

All that remains of a general ethics of killing is the prohibition on direct, intentional killing of the innocent, whether by public or private agents (DB 7.15). But even here, the responsibility for the indirect killing of innocent persons is greatly reduced for public officials: direct killing of the innocent, he says "must be rejected when the slaughter is not necessary for victory (a condition which we have already assumed to exist), and when the innocent can be distinguished from the guilty" (DB 7.15). Suárez does not notice here the immense contrast between judicial and bellicose punishment: judicial punishment is always targeted solely at the guilty. Better that ten guilty men go free than one innocent person is punished is the implicit maxim of domestic criminal law. But bellicose punishment is almost always collective punishment: better one hundred innocent persons punished than one guilty person goes free is the implicit maxim of punitive warfare. As Suárez notes, "certain means essential to victory…necessarily involve the death of innocent persons, as in the burning of cities and the destruction of fortresses: for absolutely speaking, whoever has the right to attain the end sought by a war, has the right to use these means to that end" (DB 7.17). So in punitive war many innocent persons may be killed so that a few guilty ones are punished. Of course, Suárez is aware of the terrible collateral damage caused by war: that is why war must be a last resort in the redress of injustice. In punitive warfare, pulling up the tares also uproots much of the wheat. The doctrine of proportionality is meant to preserve a rough balance between the aims of pulling up the tares and preserving the wheat.

We saw that in his analysis of the ethics of self-defense, Aquinas introduced the principle of double-effect: a person may use lethal force in self-defense because his direct intention is to preserve his own life, not to kill his assailant. But Aquinas and Suárez make almost no use of this principle in their analysis of the ethics of war because public officials are permitted to intentionally kill the enemy, just as they are permitted to intentionally kill criminals. There is no need for recourse to indirect killing where direct killing is permitted. But in his discussion of killing innocent persons, Suárez argues that "the death of the innocent is not sought for its own sake, but as an incidental consequence…in like manner, a pregnant woman may use medicine necessary to preserve her own life, even if she knows that such an act will result in the death of her unborn child" (DB 7.17). It seems never to occur to Suárez, or to any of the classic just war theorists, that a soldier's rightful intention in combat is quite distinct from that of an executioner. As we have seen, the main concern of the theory of the just war is to endorse, with qualifications, offensive war. The ethics of self-defense seems irrelevant to such an exercise. If it were true that private persons were permitted to kill only to defend themselves, then any analogy with public officials would be remote. But had Suárez acknowledged that a private person is permitted to kill to defend innocent third parties, then we would see a much closer analogy between private and public killing.[26]

3 Punishment or Self-Defense: The Contemporary Debate

As we have seen, the classic tradition of Catholic just war theory, from Augustine to Suárez and beyond, defends offensive war as a kind of just punishment of wrongdoers. Resort to war in direct defense of the polity is taken for granted as a natural right; all the analysis and dialectic is devoted to elaborating the conditions in which offensive war to punish sovereign states is justified. But this classic defense of offensive war has lost much of its appeal in the 20th century, especially to international lawyers and to Catholic prelates. The first crime listed in the Nuremburg indictment of Nazi Germany was the crime of launching an "aggressive war": in that tribunal, the question whether that aggression was in the service of the just punishment of Stalin's regime was not regarded as germane![27] In a later UN resolution defining armed aggression as a crime, no moral or political justification of aggressive war is permitted as a defense.[28] So international law, if not international morality, has developed a strong presumption against any offensive war, no matter what its putative justification.

Ever since Pope Paul VI famously addressed the UN General Assembly in 1965 with the cry "No more war!", official statements of Popes, Vatican officials, and conferences of Catholic bishops have condemned virtually all recourse to war except in direct national defense. Indeed, conservative American Catholics have expressed great bitterness at what they see as the abandonment of the classic tradition of just war thinking by the contemporary Catholic hierarchy: they describe the recent prelates, with some justification, as merely using the language of the just war in defense

---

26 Suárez clearly rules out the possibility of a private person rightfully killing to protect an innocent person from attack: "the killing of any man on mere private authority is intrinsically wicked, except in the necessary defense of one's own person and property" (DB 9.2).

27 For the text of the first Nuremburg indictment, see: http://avalon.law.yale.edu/imt/count1.asp.

28 G.A. Res. 3314 (XXIX) (1974), G.A.O.R. 29th Sess., Supp. 31. "No consideration of whatever nature, whether political, economic, military or otherwise, may serve as a justification for aggression." (Art. 5).

of what amounts to pacifism.[29] But it would be more accurate to say that contemporary Catholic theologians and prelates are simply abandoning the punitive theory of a just war in favor of a much more restricted role for war, mainly limited to direct defense of the nation or innocent third parties. In the statement "The Challenge of Peace" (1983), the Conference of American Catholic Bishops explicitly distance themselves from the classic doctrine of punitive war: "War is permitted only to confront 'a real and certain danger' i.e. to protect innocent life, to preserve conditions necessary for decent human existence, and basic human rights. As both Pope Pius XII and Pope John XXIII made clear, if war of retribution was ever justifiable, the risks of modern war negate such a claim today."[30] The Catechism of the Catholic Church (1997) also limits war to national self-defense: "as long as the danger of war persists and there is no international authority with the necessary competence and power, governments cannot be denied the right of lawful self-defense, once all peace efforts have failed."[31]

In this movement, the Church is simply following the lead of the community of international lawyers, who have sought throughout the 20th century to find alternative ways to resolve disputes among nations. Moreover, the abandonment of the practice of capital punishment by virtually every advanced society calls into question the basic rationale of a punitive war. Now that even the Vatican attacks the morality of capital punishment,[32] it is difficult to see how the Church can continue to defend the classic doctrine of a punitive just war. If public authorities cannot intentionally kill wrongdoers by executing them, then how can they intentionally kill them in warfare? How could punitive war be permissible if capital punishment is not?

At the same time, however, the doctrine and the practice of defensive war have been extended beyond direct national defense to include the defense of innocent third parties from immediate threats. After all, the UN

---

29   See George Weigel's *Tranquillitas Ordinis: The Present Failure and Future Promise of American Catholic Thought on War and Peace* (NY: Oxford University Press, 1987).

30   See "The Challenge of Peace." In *Catholic Social Thought*, eds. David J. O'Brien and Thomas A. Shannon (Maryknoll, NY: Orbis Books 1992).

31   Here the Catechism is quoting from the Vatican II proclamation *Gaudium et Spes* (par. 79); for the Catechism, see http://www.scborromeo.org/ccc.htm.

32   The Church now claims that the state reserves the right to capital punishment but that its exercise is morally unacceptable where alternative ways to protect the common good are available.

Charter provides a mechanism, the Security Council, for the authorization of war quite apart from national defense; in principle, the Security Council could authorize the kinds of wars called "aggressive" by the classic just war theorists—though today if they are authorized by the Security Council they are technically no longer "aggressive". Yet, in practice, the Security Council is unlikely to authorize truly offensive wars for the redress of past wrongs. The Security Council does and will authorize wars, however, to defend innocent third-parties from terrorism, genocide, starvation, or ethnic cleansing. There is a very spirited debate among international lawyers and political theorists today about whether wars on humanitarian grounds can be justified even if not authorized by the Security Council, as in Kosovo. Requiring formal authorization is likely to lead to wrongdoers going unpunished while permitting unauthorized wars is likely to lead to innocents being punished.

These developments in Catholic doctrine and international law notwithstanding, the classic doctrine of the punitive just war is not lacking for contemporary defenders. Two leading contemporary theorists of the just war, Oliver O'Donovan and John Finnis, appeal to very different analogies. O'Donovan defends, with qualifications, the classic analogy to capital punishment, while Finnis attacks that analogy and seeks to replace it with the analogy to self-defense. O'Donovan begins his defense of the classic view by quoting Suárez's view that "war…has been instituted in place of a tribunal administering just punishment."[33] O'Donovan admits that there is something "paradoxical" about a sovereign acting as both plaintiff and judge, but he defends this use of war to punish wrongdoers as a necessity in those emergencies where other procedures for dispute resolution are not available.[34] O'Donovan lists two features of offensive war that strain the analogy to criminal punishment: "armed conflict typically extends a government's power beyond the limitations of its sphere of authority; secondly, it typically deploys force without judicial inquisition."[35] Still, O'Donovan defends this analogy by quoting Francisco Vitoria: "The victor must think of himself as a judge sitting in judgment between

---

33 Suárez, DB 4.5. O'Donovan quotes a parallel but more prolix passage from the same section.
34 Oliver O'Donovan, *The Just War Revisited*: "Justice in war stood in relation to the exercise of domestic justice as an emergency operation, performed in a remote mountain-hut with a penknife, stands to the same surgery performed under clinical conditions in a hospital", 18.
35 O'Donovan, *The Just War Revisited*, 19–20.

two commonwealths, one the injured party and the other the offender; he must not pass sentence as the prosecutor but as a judge."[36]

O'Donovan offers a critique of the alternative analogy according to which war is like ordinary private conflict and just war is limited to self-defense. Many modern natural law jurists have argued with Kant that in an international realm of independent sovereign states, no particular state can rightly claim public authority over other states. In Kant's words "no war of independent states against each other can be a punitive war."[37] According to O'Donovan, this view treats all war as private conflict, leaving no room for public authority: war is justified only as the universal right of self-defense. "From this arises the modern tendency to reduce the causes of war to the single cause of national self-defense." He is right that it is much more difficult to endorse the classic just war doctrine of offensive war if war is likened to private conflict, but many people today welcome this strong modern presumption against offensive war, even if O'Donovan regrets it. Moreover, O'Donovan argues that any analogy between just war and ordinary self-defense makes it harder for Christians to endorse war, since Christians have a duty or at least a counsel to avoid the use of force in personal self-defense. Here O'Donovan is clearly relying on Augustine, since Aquinas argues to the contrary that since grace does not supplant nature, the natural right to self-defense is not supplanted by Christian duties of charity. O'Donovan shows that he also misunderstands the true scope of the private right of self-defense: for even if a Christian ought to turn his own other cheek to an aggressor, a Christian cannot properly turn the cheek of an innocent third party to an aggressor. A private Christian has a duty to defend the innocent analogous to the duty of a Christian public official, but O'Donovan cannot see this because he limits the private use of force purely to defense of one's own self. Since O'Donovan believes that private self-defense is morally problematic for Christians, he permits Christian sovereigns to wage war only on the grounds that they are enforcing an implicit public structure of authoritative arbitration.[38]

John Finnis, by contrast, who seeks a consistent ethics of killing, defends the analogy between just war and self-defense and thus attacks Aquinas's distinction between public and private killing. He argues that the basic moral norm often affirmed by Aquinas, that "evil may not be

---

36   O'Donovan, *The Just War Revisited*, 22.
37   O'Donovan, *The Just War Revisited*, 22.
38   O'Donovan, *The Just War Revisited*, 22.

done, even though good may come of it," is not consistent with Aquinas's doctrine that public officials may intentionally kill evildoers to protect the common good.[39] In order to develop a consistent ethics of killing, Finnis argues that Aquinas would have to argue that capital punishment and war could be chosen without a specific intention to kill, but merely to preserve the common good. But executing someone involves inescapably a direct intention to kill. So Aquinas is right that the death penalty necessarily involves an intention to kill; Finnis concludes that the death penalty is therefore inconsistent with the first principle of a general ethics of killing, namely, that no one may be intentionally killed. The common good, says Finnis, can be protected without killing the evildoer: he may be imprisoned or deported. But this, of course, relies upon the contingent circumstances of institutions of long-term imprisonment and the feasibility of permanent exile. Whether the common good can be protected from evildoers in all circumstances without capital punishment seems doubtful.

What about war? Finnis acknowledges that Aquinas's discussion of war constantly draws upon the analogy to capital punishment.[40] But does the conduct of a just war necessarily involve a direct intention to kill the enemy? Aquinas claims that combat does necessarily involve an intention to kill, just as does capital punishment. But Finnis argues by analogy to killing in private self-defense that soldiers need only to intend to stop the enemy attack, not to kill the enemy soldiers. Of course, many common military tactics, ranging from orders to take no prisoners to reprisals to revenge atrocities to terror killing, would be excluded by this principle.[41] In this sense, combat seems less like capital punishment and more like private self-defense. Yet, soldiers use force, not to defend their own lives, but the lives of the noncombatants whom they are sworn to protect. Had Finnis properly described the true scope of the right that private persons have to defend the lives of innocent third parties, he would have greatly strengthened his analogy between war and self-defense. Of course, this analogy between combat and self-defense is plausible in the case of defensive wars. Whether it can be extended to the kinds of offensive and punitive war endorsed by classic just war theory is another question that Finnis does not address.

So the issues raised by the classic just war theorists about war, both defensive and offensive, remain vital and controversial. Certainly the doc-

---

39   Finnis, *Aquinas*, 282–283.
40   Finnis, *Aquinas*, 285–286.
41   Finnis, *Aquinas*, 286.

trine and practice of punitive war is more permissive: there are many crimes committed by sovereign states and few are ever punished. War in self-defense is much more restrictive: many wars have little direct relation to national survival. The doctrine of punitive war is likely to permit too many unjust wars while the doctrine of purely defensive war is likely to permit too few just wars. Conscientious people will always disagree about whether justice is more outraged by wrongs unpunished or by wrongful punishments. I will only observe that in the case of domestic justice, every democratic society organizes its law of criminal procedure on the presumption that it is better to let the guilty go unpunished than to punish the innocent.

Classic just war theory clearly exaggerated the analogy between judicial and bellicose punishment: punitive war usually involves no formal jurisdiction, no real inquisition, no impartial judge, no judicial finding. True, many wars are launched with punitive intention and certainly with punitive effect. The Allies in the Second World War fought for national defense certainly but also to punish the criminal German and Japanese governments. So war is often an instrument of punishment, sometimes even of just punishment. Yet, punitive war is constrained neither by statute nor by precedent. Domestic justice, for example, is severely limited by statutes of limitation, except for capital offenses; punitive war has no such limitations: a nation might be attacked to avenge an ancient crime. Domestic justice relies upon the judgment of prosecutors rather than the judgment of injured parties; we can only imagine what would happen were the allegedly injured parties permitted to initiate prosecutions, let alone administer punishments. In short, domestic justice attempts to insulate the whole legal process from the raw passion of aggrieved parties; the doctrine of punitive war can do little in this regard, other than recommend arbitration. Suárez and the other classic theorists also overlook the striking disanalogy between the rights of suspected criminals and the rights of enemy combatants. Aquinas and Suárez do not permit private individuals to use force to resist arrest or punishment, but Aquinas implicitly and Suárez explicitly permit enemy combatants to use at least moderate force against an army of just punishment (DB 7.19).

Perhaps the least persuasive aspect of the punitive analogy is the idea that an injured nation, by reason of its injury, acquires at least some limited sovereignty or jurisdiction over the nation at fault. For the essence of this analogy is the claim that a sovereign, in punishing a wrongdoer, acts on public authority; but since this claim of public authority is not recognized by other nations, in what sense is it public? It seems more honest to concede that in a conflict between independent sovereigns there is no public authority. But the lack of public authority does not mean that there is a legal or moral vacuum. Customary international law may well provide for mechanisms of self-help, in which nations are permitted to avenge wrongs as a last resort. A regime of self-help can empower states, as private parties, to make a finding of wrong and execute judgment or merely execute the judgment of an impartial court. But classic just war doctrine requires the claim of public authority in punitive war, so that a nation can intentionally kill the enemy—a deed forbidden to private authority.

Classic just war theory clearly understated the analogy between war and private self-defense. True, in the case of immediate attack, the just war theorists acknowledge the right of nations, like every person, to repel force with force. But it never occurs to them that this act of national defense might be like private self-defense in that it need not involve any direct intention to kill: while under attack, I may use deadly force to preserve my own life or my polity by stopping or deterring the enemy. I am delighted if my use of force causes the enemy to surrender rather than to die. Of course, some soldiers will always fight to kill: they will kill even harmless enemies; but studies show that most soldiers try not to kill the enemy but only to stop or deter him. Soldiers recognize the strong moral distinction between killing an enemy in the course of combat and simply executing him after he is captured. But all of this is equally true of private self-defense: most people attempt to flee or deter the aggressor rather than kill him. So war need not be like capital punishment, in which the executioner directly intends to kill a human being and fails if the condemned man flees or surrenders or is merely wounded. It is here on the central issue of specifying the moral act of homicide that the analogy between war and capital punishment fails catastrophically.

The just war theorists, starting with Augustine, argue that war is unlike self-defense because a person killing in self defense does so out of bloodlust while a prince who launches a war or a soldier who fights it does so out of a duty to protect the common good. Of course, these theorists acknowledged exceptions to this rule: Aquinas, though not Augustine, thought that killing in private self-defense need not stem from bloodlust; and all of them acknowledged that public authorities and soldiers do act sometimes from bloodlust.[42] In his discussion of private

---

42 Of public officers and soldiers, Aquinas says "and even such men sin if and to the extent that they are moved by some private passion." ST II-II, Q. 64, a. 7c.

brawling, Aquinas considers the objection that if brawling is always sinful, then why isn't war always sinful, since brawling is a mini war? He answers that private brawling stems from anger and hatred while war stems from public authority.[43] But whether a dispute originates in a private or a public context does not seem directly germane to the question of its moral restraint. A dispute between private persons that is referred to impartial mediation is less likely to result in killing from bloodlust than is a dispute between public sovereigns who eschew mediation. Indeed, the pressures of mass politics can often lead public authorities to depths of bloodlust and vainglory exceeding all private brawls. The just war theorists are again being unconsciously guided by the analogy to capital punishment: they imagine that punitive wars are launched and fought with the cold rationality of a public execution. But experience shows, I think, that wars are waged more with the violent passions of a private brawl than with the cold-blooded calculation of an execution.

The classic theorists of the just war forcefully reject the analogy between war and self-defense because they believe that justice requires resort to war not only to defend our own polity but also to defend our allies, friends, and other innocent victims of an aggressor. Why should we ignore our duty to champion the cause of justice, even where our own survival is not at stake? But our duties to resort to war to defend innocent third parties from aggression can be justified by analogy to our right to kill in self defense. As we have seen, the just war theorists wrongly describe the true scope of the right to self-defense. A private person can use force to repel force directed, not only at himself, but at an innocent third party. So by analogy, a sovereign state, subject to obvious qualifications, can wage war to defend an innocent third party from direct aggression, without any need to resort to a dubious theory of punitive war, of executing capital punishment against wrongdoers, or a right to intentionally kill the enemy. We can thereby avoid the dangerous doctrine that public officials are permitted to violate the most basic norms of Christian morality. A state merely has the same basic right that any person has to use force to stop aggression directed at innocent persons, where it is feasible to do so.

Thus, while forcefully rejecting the doctrine of punitive war, recent papal and episcopal statements have begun to assert a right of states to

---

43 Aquinas, ST II-II, Q. 41, a. 1 ob. 3 and ad 3. He also says here (a. 1c) that brawls "are like private wars, then, which private people get into, wars not declared by public authority but more from an undisciplined will."

use force to defend innocent third parties abroad, a right of humanitarian intervention. In *The Harvest of Justice is Sown in Peace* (1993) the American Catholic Bishops, quoting some statements of Pope John Paul II, defend the use of military force to defend innocent third parties: "military intervention may sometimes be justified to ensure that starving children can be fed or that whole populations will not be slaughtered. They represent St. Augustine's classic case: love may require force to protect the innocent. The just-war tradition reminds us, however, that military force, even when there is just cause, must remain an exceptional option that conforms strictly to just-war norms and norms of international policing."[44] Here we see the right to wage war in self-defense broadened to include the defense of innocent third parties: states thus have the same broad right to self-defense that private individuals have always enjoyed.

---

44 USCCB The Harvest of Justice is Sown in Peace: http://www.nccbuscc.org/sdwp/harvest.shtml.

Hugo Grotius: Just War Thinking Between Theology and International Law

Christoph Stumpf

Contemporary jurists praise Grotius as the father of modern public international law; numerous modern theologians continue to appreciate Grotius' contributions to the fields of exegesis and of early ecclesiastical history. However, the combination of jurisprudence on the one hand and moral theology and philosophy on the other in Grotius' work rarely attracted any keen interest by legal or theological scholars.[1]

Hence, I will endeavour to argue three different theses on Grotius' views on international law in general and the law of war in particular: First, I shall try to illustrate that Grotius does not, as many modern authors have claimed, separate law from theology or in any way 'secularise' natural law; instead, Grotius equates theological dogmatics as well as theological ethics with law in a genuine sense. Secondly, Grotius identifies objective legal principles, and also individual subjective legal obligations; a notion of subjective individual rights is, however, widely absent from his concept – therefore, Grotius does not so much propagate a theory of human rights, but rather a concept of human obligations. Thirdly, following an observation by Martin Wight[2], Grotius conceives of an international system of states grouped in two concentric circles: there is an inner circle of Christian states, which may in many ways be identified with the medieval concept of a *respublica Christiana*; and a wider circle, comprising all states, Christian and non-Christian alike, which are all bound by overarching principles of natural law, similar to the concept brought forward by the Spanish moral theologians of the school of Salamanca.

In the following, I shall first provide a brief sketch of Grotius' biography and his works most pertinent to this topic, before, secondly, an

---

1   Cf. D. M. Sprackling, *Divine and Human Law in Hugo Grotius* (1996), 81; C. A. Stumpf, *The Grotian Theology of International Law: Hugo Grotius and the Moral Foundations of International Relations* (2006), 3–4.
2   M. Wight, *Systems of States* (1977), 125–128.

analysis of his concept of law will be offered. Third, I shall try to present Grotius' views on the law of war.

1 Life and Work of Hugo Grotius

Grotius' overall views on international law are in many ways a consequence of his life, and the historic context within which he wrote down his thoughts.

1.1 Biographical Background

It is certainly impossible to accomadate in this place a full account of Grotius' life and works[3]. A few landmarks will have to suffice: Born in Delft in 1583, he attended the University of Leiden in 1594. At the age of 15 he joined a Dutch mission to King Henry IV. of France who referred to him as "le miracle d'Hollande"[4]; during this occasion he was awarded an honorary doctorate at the University of Orleans[5]. He then started to work as advocate in The Hague in 1599[6].

In 1613 Grotius became municipal attorney (*Syndicus*) of Rotterdam and consequently a member of the provincial states of Holland. It was this office through which Grotius was finally introduced as one the

---

3   For Grotius' biography and an introduction to his works cf. W. J. M. v. Eysinga, *Huigh de Groot* (1945); W. Fikentscher, "De fide et perfidia – Der Treuegedanke in den Staatsparallelen des Hugo Grotius, in Sitzungsberichte der Bayerischen Akademie der Wissenschaften", *Phil.-hist. Kl.* (1979), issue 1, 15 et seq.; W. S. M. Knight, *The Life and Works of Hugo Grotius* (1925); E. Wolf, *Große Rechtsdenker der deutschen Geistesgeschichte* (4th Ed., 1963), 263 et seq.; see also C. A. Stumpf, "The Christian Society and its Government", 151–175. In Stumpf/Zaborowski, Church as Politeia (2009), on which the following biographical sketch relies.

4   Cf. Ch. Link, *Hugo Grotius als Staatsdenker* (1983), 5.

5   There appear to be no reports about Grotius' legal training or, in fact, even of him receiving an "ordinary" degree at university. Referring to R. Feenstra, Link (Fn. 4), 5, Fn. 5, suggests that Grotius had received a bachelor's degree at Orleans together with his honorary doctorate.

6   Chapter 12 of the *De Iure Praedae Commentarius* was published anonymously in 1609; the whole manuscript did only appear in 1868; cf. for a discussions of the reasons for this G. Roelofsen, "17th-Century International Politics", 103–106 In Bull / Kingsbury / Roberts, *Hugo Grotius and International Relations* (1990), 108–109.

main actors to the religious and political controversies in the Netherlands between the Arminians or Remonstrants and the orthodox Calvinists or Counter-Remonstrants of that time. However, Grotius' engagement proved not to be successful: In 1617/18 at the Synod of Dort Prince Maurice of Orange as *Stadtholder* of the Netherlands managed to have the case decided in favour of orthodox Calvinism, and, in order to restore the religious peace in the Netherlands, Grotius, amongst others, was arrested, his estates were confiscated, and he was transferred to the Castle of Loevenstein[7].

Grotius managed to escape to France in 1621, where he was granted asylum by King Louis XIII. In 1634, after an unlucky attempt to return to the Netherlands and after a short stay in Hamburg[8], he accepted the offer of King Gustav Adolph to go back to Paris as Swedish Ambassador. This post Grotius held for ten years[9]. After the Swedish chancellor Oxenstjerna had lost his confidence in Grotius, Grotius resigned and travelled to Stockholm. After not having received any new orders by Queen Christine of Sweden, Grotius decided to leave Stockholm. Yet his ship got wrecked in the Baltic Sea, and though he managed to reach the coast he died in Rostock in August 1645 probably from exhaustion.

1.2 Pertinent Works

From the abundancy of theological and legal works written by Grotius, we will have to restrict ourselves in this context to certain main treatises:

The first major work of Grotius on the international law is *De Iure Praedae Commentarius*, written in 1603. It is written in defence of the Dutch East Indian Company that had used force against the Portuguese and Spanish fleet in the East Indies, which was criticised by the company's pacifist shareholders. Grotius here argues that there may be cases where force can be used legitimately, not only from a legal perspective, but also on moral grounds. During Grotius life time, only the chapter

---

7 During this time, Grotius started to work on theological works, e.g. on *De veritate religionis Christianae* (1627), as well as on a compendium to Dutch legal history, *Inleydinge tot de Hollandsche Rechtsgeleertheyd* (1631), in order not to await his release in idleness.

8 Cf. M. Grimm, "Hugo Grotius' Aufenthalt in Hamburg in den Jahren 1632–34." *Zeitschrift d. Vereins f. Hamburger Geschichte* 27 (1926): 130 et seq.

9 Cf. H. Hofmann, "Hugo Grotius." In *Staatsdenker im 17. und 18. Jahrhundert*, ed. M. Stolleis (1977), 57 s.

on the freedom of the seas, *De Mare liberum*, was published, albeit anonymously; the remainder of the book only resurfaced in the 19th century.

An apologetic theological work, *Meletius sive de Iis Quae inter Christianos Conveniunt Epistola*[10], written in 1611, followed.

In 1613, in the wake of the religious controversies in the Netherlands, Grotius' *De Ordinum Hollandiae ac Westfrisiae Pietas Vindicata* on the relationship between state authorities and religious affairs was published. It contains a rather polemic refutation of the attacks of Sibrand Lubbert on the States of Holland. Here Grotius is not so much concerned with theological questions or theoretical issues as such. Rather he endeavours to show that the States of Holland had the right to decide upon theological disputes, without interfering illegally in matters beyond their temporal concerns[11].

Also written in 1614, but only published in 1617 was Grotius' second treatise on the matter of the state's powers in ecclesiastical affairs, *De Imperio Summarum Potestatum circa sacra*[12]. In this treatise Grotius elaborates on the rôle and the powers of civil magistrates in spiritual matters in more sophisticated and eirenic way than had been done in *De Ordinum Pietas*[13].

In 1617 there followed an examination of the doctrine of atonement in *Defensio Fidei Catholicae de Satisfactione Christi*[14]. While this book may look purely theological at first glance, it is of some value for an assessment of Grotius' views on divine and natural justice.

During his imprisonment in Loevestein Grotius attended to the legal history of the Netherlands and published a book entitled, *Inleiding tot de Hollandsche Rechtsgeleertheyd*, in 1620.

---

10 Cf. Posthumus Meyjes and H. M. Guillaume, "Hugo de Groot's '*Meletius*' (1611), His Earliest Theological Work, Rediscovered", *Lias*, 11 (1984): 147–150.

11 Cf. H. Grotius, *De Ordinum Pietas* (ASD), 112 b et seq.

12 Cf. on the genesis of *De Imperio Summarum Potestatum circa sacra* H.-J. v. Dam, "De Imperio Summarum Potestatum circa Sacra." In *Hugo Grotius, theologian: Essays in honour of G. H. M. Posthumus Meyjes,* eds. H. Nellen and E. Rabbie (1994), 19 ss; A. Caspani, "Il De Imperio summarum potestatum circa sacra di Grozio." *Revista di Filosofia Neo-scolatica* 79 (1987): 218 et seq. (249), 382 et seq. (419).

13 A description of how Grotius endeavoured to return to a more mild and peaceful tone in *De Imperio*, in contrast to the more aggressive style exposed in *De Ordinum Pietas*, can be found in v. Dam (Fn. 12), 34 s.

14 Cf. E. Rabbie, "Some Remarks Concerning the Textual History of Hugo Grotius' De Satisfactione." *Grotiana*, 7 (1986): 99–120.

The most famous of Grotius' works is certainly *De Iure Belli ac Pacis libri tres*[15], which was written after 1623 and published for the first time in 1625.[16] It is a comprehensive treatise on the laws of war and peace, covering a number of legally and theologically relevant topics.

In 1627 there followed Grotius' apologetic work *De Veritate Religionis Christinianae*[17] which was also received quite enthusiastically and served, *inter alia*, as a text book for Christian missions overseas.

2 Categories of Law

Grotius had dealt with legal categorization repeatedly in his works, but his presentation in *De Iure Belli ac Pacis* is certainly the most elaborate one. While in terms of content, Grotius elsewhere is indebted to many of his forerunners, though typically without acknowledgement, like Vitoria, Suarez, and Gentili, his legal categorization may have been influenced by the Anglican theologian Richard Hooker, who had also been influential on Grotius with respect to his works on the powers of the state in the realm of spiritual affairs[18].

Grotius conceives of two main categories of law, namely divine law and human law. Each of these main categories contains a number of sub-categories.

---

15 Cf. P. Haggenmacher, "Grotius and Gentili: A Reassessment of Thomas E. Holland's Inaugural Lecture." In *Hugo Grotius and International Relations*, eds. H. Bull / B. Kingsbury / A. Roberts, (1990) 144 et seq.

16 Cf. on the genesis of De Iure Belli ac Pacis P. C. Molhuysen, "Over de editio princeps van Grotius' De Iure Belli ac Pacis", Mededeelingen der Koninklijke Akademie van Wetenschappen te Amsterdam, *afd. letterkunde* deel 60, serie B, no. 1 (1925): 1–8; J. S. Reeves, "The First Edition of Grotius' De Jure Belli Ac Pacis, 1625." *American Journal of International Law* 19 (1925): 12–23; for a comprehensive examination of Grotius' Just-War-Theory cf. P. Haggenmacher, *Grotius et la doctrine de la guerre juste* (1983).

17 Cf. F.-J. Niemann, "Die erste ökumenische Fundamentaltheologie", *Catholica* 37 (1983): 203–215.

18 Cf. C. A. Stumpf, "The Christian Society and its Government: A Comparison between the Theo-Political Concepts of Richard Hooker and Hugo Grotius." In *Church as Politeia*, eds C. A. Stumpf and H. Zaborowski (2004) 151–175; "Die Verfassung des Staates als Verfassung der Kirche: Richard Hooker und Hugo Grotius als Vorläufer des deutschen Territorialismus", *ZRG kan. Abt. 125* (2009) 437–456.

2.1 Divine Law

Divine law for Grotius is law set by God. God has granted laws first in creation, and then subsequently through revelation.

2.1.1 Natural Law

The first subcategory of divine law is natural law or the law of nature. Natural law is what reason prescribes, by indicating that an action is or is not in compliance with the rational nature and is therefore in itself either a moral turpitude or a moral necessity. If something is in itself a moral necessity it is commanded by God as author of nature; if it is a moral turpitude it is prohibited by him[19]. Therefore, natural law is in Grotius' views closely connected to the act of creation. It has been set into force by God with creation and, though God is in principle omnipotent, he cannot amend natural law subsequently. Moreover, natural law either prohibits or commands actions; it does not license actions explicitly other than by being silent. In other words, natural law does never grant subjective rights – there is no natural right to one's own life, just a natural law prohibition to kill someone else without there being any justification.

There are three main principles of natural law: Firstly, expletive justice, or justice properly so called[20]; this type of justice is concerned in particular with the restoration of rights: for example, a stolen good needs to be returned to the owner; a promise must be honoured; a claim must be fulfilled. For Grotius this is justice in the proper sense.

Secondly, there is attributive justice[21], which mainly is to govern the allocation of rights. It means that an office must be bestowed on the worthiest candidate. It also means that a punishment must be exerted according to the severity of the offence. Grotius calls attributive justice justice in a wider sense.

Both of these principles of natural justice would be valid, according to a famous remark of Grotius, even if one were to admit that there is no God. While the formula here used by Grotius "*etiamsi daremus Deum non esse*" had already been established in use by Scholastic authors from the

---

19 Cf. Grotius, *De Iure Belli ac Pacis*, I. i. x.
20 Cf. Grotius, *De Iure Belli ac Pacis*, Prolegomena 8; I. i. viii. 1.
21 Cf. Grotius, *De Iure Belli ac Pacis*, Prolegomena 9 s; I. i. viii. 1

middle ages onwards[22], it nevertheless inspired generations of later commentators who claimed that hereby Grotius intended to secularise natural law as such.

Nevertheless, Grotius is keen to point out that there is still a third principle of natural law, natural piety. It is already a principle of natural law to believe in one personified and intelligent God, who attends to the world and rewards and punishes compliance with or transgressions against his laws[23].

2.1.2 Arbitrary Divine Law

A second subcategory of divine law presented by Grotius is what may be translated as arbitrary divine law[24]. Arbitrary divine law finds its source in an explicit act of God's will, and is made known to man through divine revelation.

For Grotius, arbitrary divine law is only binding upon those to whom it has been given and been made known. Arbitrary divine law cannot contradict natural law, but it may reinforce rules of natural law, it may require higher standards than natural law, and, of course, arbitrary divine law may cover areas that are left unregulated by natural law. For example, natural law grants the permission to defend oneself against illegitimate attacks, even by killing the opponent, potentially even by killing innocent parties, not by granting a right to self defence, but by containing no explicit prohibition of self defence. However, arbitrary divine law curtails this implicit permission under natural law by requiring a higher degree of patience and restraint from the attacked party.

The most important piece of arbitrary divine law is the *lex Evangelica*, the law of the Gospel, which has been given to mankind through Christ. It covers all kinds of human conduct, in particular by imposing on Christians the twofold love commandment, which for Grotius is just as much a legal principle as a moral or theological principle. This is why Christians are expected to be more virtuous and more patient than heathens or Jews.

While Grotius certainly deems such arbitrary divine law and the law of the Gospel to be genuine law, he is, however, quite reluctant to acknowledge its consequent enforcement: As we have seen above, arbitrary

---

22 C. A. Stumpf, *The Grotian Theology of International Law: Hugo Grotius and the Moral Foundations of International Relations* (2006), 51–52; passim.

23 The scope of natural piety and the contents of natural religion are described by Grotius in more detail in his *Meletius* (1611).

24 Cf. Grotius, *De Iure Belli ac Pacis*, I. i. xv. et seq.

divine law is binding on anyone who has received knowledge of it. Nevertheless, Grotius strongly opposes its implementation through force, which is why he is, for example, strictly opposed to Christian proselytising with violence: Grotius claims that even if the Gospel were preached to heathens in the most convincing fashion, it could never be accepted without the secret assistance of the Holy Ghost, which assistance God granted or withheld according to his own secret reasoning. It was therefore not for man to impose it on his fellow men. It should be added that Grotius nevertheless held it possible for heathens to be punished if they were not faithful to their own Gods, seeing that any religion might contain at least a true nucleus of the general natural religion provided for under natural law.

2.2 Human Law

The second main category of law for Grotius is human law. Again he distinguishes between three different subcategories: National Law, international law, and the law of private households in the sense of household laws. Only the former two subcategories will be of interest to us.

2.2.1 National Law

A first subcategory of human law is human law which pertains to one state only. Grotius defines the state as a comprehensive association of human beings, which is established for their common use, and is aiming at securing their rights[25]. Grotius regards the state to be a merely human institution, which is not instituted or in any other way provided for by God, but just result of an institutionalisation of human society through a common human decision. By such human act a supreme power is installed as 'sovereign' and hence acquires the right to devise all laws on temporal as well as on spiritual matters.

Human law may not contradict divine law, be it natural law or arbitrary divine law. However, human actions can be defined by human law as well as by natural law or arbitrary divine law[26]. The law of God has priority over any human law. Hence, only those actions can be defined by human beings that have not already been defined by God[27]. If a

---

25 Cf. Grotius, *De Iure Belli ac Pacis*, I. i. xiv
26 Cf. Grotius, *De Imperio*, III. iii.
27 Cf. Grotius, *De Imperio*, III. iv.

state orders something contrary to divine law, *i. e.* natural law or arbitrary divine law, its subjects have to obey God rather than the state[28]. Moreover, though some acts are already morally defined in their substance, *e. g.* the profession of faith, their mode of performance is often left undefined. In this case, the human government may regulate such modalities.

Additionally, the human government may reinforce God's commandments and prohibitions. In this case it is a matter of the human government to exercise physical coercion or punishment. Yet, while rules of divine law may be reinforced by the human government, such reinforcement is not necessary. The government may decide to leave certain acts unpunished, even though they are contrary to the divine will. Notwithstanding this, the divine will will still be binding, with or without reinforcement by the human government.

2.2.2 International Law

International law is human law which has been agreed upon between two or more, rarely all, states. The same principles apply for international law as for human national law: International law may not contradict divine law, but it is possible that international law abstains from enforcing principles of divine law, e. g. by not providing for punishment of offences against divine law. In fact, that is what has happened in Grotius' opinion in respect of many fields of warfare: while international law here appears to be rather generous towards warfaring parties, divine law requires considerable moderation.

3 The Law of War

Grotius acknowledges that war may be a legitimate means to remedy breaches of law. Neither natural law, nor arbitrary divine law are overall contrary to war. However, both subcategories of divine law require a curtailment of warfare, in relation to the law to war (*ius ad bellum*) as well as the law in war (*ius in bello*). Overall, Grotius here follows the tradition of the classic just war doctrine.[29]

---

28 Cf. Grotius, *De Imperio*, III. v.
29 Cf. F. H. Russell, *The Just War in the Middle Ages* (1975), 155 et seq.

3.1 Law to War

In treating the different types of war as means to uphold the overall system of law, Grotius implicitly denies that there is any legitimate reason to wage war beyond the preservation and restoration of justice. In this sense there are only either just wars or unjust wars.

3.1.1 Just Authority

According to Grotius, the type of authority required to wage war legitimately depends upon the type of war that is to be waged. While for a private war no special authority is necessary at all – save for the absence of an effective jurisdiction to which recourse could be sought – in the case of a public informal or less formal war in principle any kind of public authority suffices. Yet, the use of force amongst private individuals or minor state authorities presents an exception from the ordinary means of jurisdiction provided within any established state. In his treatment on the law to war Grotius primarily focuses on the public formal war: a public formal war can only be initiated by the holder of the highest sovereign power of a state, as such a war is the only means to enforce rules of law in relation to sovereigns, and such rules can normally only be enforced legitimately by other sovereigns as their peers. Hence, a public formal war is a war between holders of sovereign authority.

Grotius makes it clear that, while a war is normally waged for one's own ends, one can also assist others in waging war or wage war on someone else's behalf.[30] It is possible for a sovereign ruler to assist another party in self-defence. There are various types of bonds amongst human beings, such as the bond between a state and its citizens[31], alliances[32], friendship[33], or family relations; if no other special bond can be drawn upon, there is yet the common nature of human beings which entitles any human being to render help to others.[34] Thus, interference of a third party on behalf of someone else does not need to be vindicated by a prior alliance; common human nature is enough to license such interventions.[35] Here Grotius follows Vitoria's thesis that sovereign rulers

---

30   Cf. Grotius, *De Iure Belli ac Pacis*, I.V.i.
31   Cf. Grotius, *De Iure Belli ac Pacis*, II.XXV.i.
32   Cf. Grotius, *De Iure Belli ac Pacis*, II.XXV.iv.
33   Cf. Grotius, *De Iure Belli ac Pacis*, II.XXV.v.
34   Cf. Grotius, *De Iure Belli ac Pacis*, II.XXV.vi.
35   Cf. P. Haggenmacher, *Grotius et la doctrine de la guerre juste*, 139 et seq.

exercise the power to wage war against other sovereign rulers on behalf of human society.[36] It is not a particular right that is enforced in war; rather any public war presents an act of asserting justice in the natural community of human beings. The entitlement to enforce justice in relation to sovereign rulers is, however, limited to sovereign rulers themselves.

The general admissibility to render assistance to others in warfare corresponds in Grotius' concept to a respective qualified obligation: the well-being of others does not have to be as close to our heart as our own.[37] The same applies to foreign citizens, who do not have to pursue the interests of a country other than their own.[38] This is again consistent with Grotius' more general notion of self-defence: though he seems to be in favour of a duty of the state to assist citizens who suffer violations of their individual rights – as the protection of individuals is the very purpose for which a state is normally established – Grotius would hardly go as far as to assert any obligation of individuals to assist other human beings that are attacked. Individuals are not under the same general obligation to protect their fellow-individuals as the ruler is in relation to his subjects.

3.1.2 Just Reason

The second prerequisite for a just war traditionally acknowledged by the just war doctrine is a just reason or a just cause. Grotius here points out that one has to make a distinction between causes which clearly justify a war because they are a consequence of a manifest breach of law on the one hand and causes which are mainly rooted in the desire for gain on the other, but which are not necessarily to be delineated from law. One might also call the latter incidents – as distinguished from a cause in the sense of just cause – that give rise to war. For Grotius the only just cause for war is an injustice.[39]

There are three types of injustice which Grotius conceives as possible causes for just wars, which correspond to the reasons for initiating legal actions in court: first the defence of what is ours, second the enforcement of a claim to what is due to us, and third the punishment of an offence.[40]

---

36 Cf. F. Vitoria, *De Iure Belli.*
37 Cf. Grotius, *De Iure Belli ac Pacis*, II.XXV.vii.
38 Cf. Grotius, *De Iure Belli ac Pacis*, II.XXV.viii.
39 Cf. Grotius, *De Iure Belli ac Pacis*, I.II.i.
40 Cf. Grotius, *De Iure Belli ac Pacis*, I.II.ii.

3.1.2.1 Defence

As regards the just defence of what is ours, Grotius first claims that we may defend our life even by taking the life of those who attack us.[41] However, self-defence exempts no one from the rule of law, so the strict limitations which govern the conduct of any human being in the course of war also apply to a person defending himself. Here Grotius follows the line set out by Suarez in relation to self-defence.[42]

However, the question whether it is permissible to kill an innocent person who intervenes and impedes one's flight or the defence necessary for escaping death remains a difficult one.[43] Grotius thinks that such killing is generally permissible under natural law, but not under the law of the Gospel, which commands us to love our neighbour as much as ourselves. Nevertheless, referring to Thomas Aquinas, Grotius claims that in the case of a true defence properly understood there is no intentional killing, because the death of the person attacking us is not the primary aim of the defence. Even so, Grotius regards it as preferable to seek other remedies for defence than killing the attacker, such as measures of deterrence or of weakening him.

Another problem arising in this respect is the question of whether measures of defence have to remain in proportion to the aim of the defence. Here natural law and arbitrary divine law come to different conclusions. For example, minor injuries, such as insults or the like, can serve as justification for the killing in defence under expletive justice and therefore under natural law if this is necessary to restore justice, but not under the law of the Gospel.[44] Similar principles apply to the violation of proprietary rights. Under the natural law principle of expletive justice it is permissible to kill a thief if this is necessary to preserve one's property. The difference between property and life is here equated for the benefit of the innocent and to the disadvantage of the offender.[45] Grotius then notes that Jewish law had differentiated between defence during the night on the one hand and defence during daytime on the other: the killing of a thief was therefore permissible if the thief was detected in the night, as the absence of witnesses at night time makes it more difficult to identify the thief later and to subsequently recover one's stolen

---

41 Cf. Grotius, *De Iure Belli ac Pacis*, I.II.iii.
42 Cf. F. Suarez, *Opus de triplici virtute theologica, fide, spe et charitate*, D. 13.
43 Cf. Grotius, *De Iure Belli ac Pacis*, I.II.iv.
44 Cf. Grotius, *De Iure Belli ac Pacis*, I.II.x.
45 Cf. Grotius, *De Iure Belli ac Pacis*, I.II.xi.

property. However, it was impermissible to kill a thief if he was detected during daylight or if there were witnesses.[46]

Grotius regards the situation under the law of the Gospel as more complex: while he claims that nearly all lawyers and theologians held that a human being may be killed in defence of one's own property, thus exceeding even what was allowed under Jewish law, Grotius thinks that under the law of the Gospel the prerequisites for defence against the violation of proprietary rights are to be interpreted much more strictly.[47] Thus, we may defend our property only with measures that stay below the threshold of killing a thief. Killing a thief can only be accepted under the law of the Gospel if the property to be stolen is necessary to sustain our own life or the life of our dependants, or if there is no hope that the good can be recovered with the assistance of the judge. Otherwise the property has to be abandoned. This is because man has been made in the image of God, wherefore the life of any human being is incalculably higher than any property whatsoever.

There remains the question whether it suffices that a particular human law, made by someone who has authority over life and death, allows a private person to kill a thief. Grotius replies in the negative[48]: First, civil laws could never have the power over life and death in relation to any type of offence, but only in relation to offences that deserve the death of the offender. Second, no civil law may allow for persons who are to be punished with the death penalty to be executed privately, unless in the case of the gravest offences. Thus, a human law may exempt the killer of the thief from punishment, but it cannot confer the right to execute someone to a private person.

3.1.2.2 Enforcement of a Claim

A claim that is held by any particular human being may be enforced by that person if there is no particular authority appointed which has a monopoly on the use of force.[49] In a state it will normally be for the court to assist individuals in enforcing their claims. Since between holders of sovereign authority there is no particular authority that could decide upon claims, the holders of sovereign authority will have to take charge of the enforcement of claims themselves.

---

46 Cf. Grotius, *De Iure Belli ac Pacis*, I.II.xii.
47 Cf. Grotius, *De Iure Belli ac Pacis*, I.II.xiii.
48 Cf. Grotius, *De Iure Belli ac Pacis*, I.II.xvi.
49 Cf. Grotius, *De Iure Belli ac Pacis*, I.IV.ii. et seq.

3.1.2.3 Punishment

Punishment is the third potential just cause for a war. It is of a different nature than self-defence and the enforcement of claims, as it is not rooted in subjective legal positions, but rather in the objective retribution for individual guilt of an offender according to the principle of attributive justice under natural law. Consequently, there is no particular right of anyone to punish someone else: under natural law it is possible for anyone to punish an offender, as long as one has not committed the same offence.[50] Nevertheless, as soon as the legal order of a state has been established, the holder of the sovereign authority has a monopoly to punish offenders who are subject to his authority. This authority to punish is then normally delegated to the judges.

While punishment exerted by God does not require any purpose to be achieved and thus no justification, punishment which is exerted by human beings requires a reason, as they may not punish merely out of sadistic impulses or because of a desire for revenge.[51] Human punishment thus needs to be measured according to the use which the offender has drawn from his offence, the interest of those for the benefit of whom the offence is prohibited, and the interest of anyone else.[52]

3.1.3 War as Appropriate Means

Even if sufficient cause can be found for a war and thus a just reason legitimates war in general, Grotius still argues for the necessity to check the appropriateness of war as measure to serve the cause. Grotius claims that there is an obligation to abandon the care for one's own life in order to care as much as one can for the life and the eternal salvation of others.[53] This is particularly true for Christians, to whom Christ has been the most perfect example. However, this still seems to be also an obligation under natural law for anyone, even if to a lesser degree.

According to Grotius, we should not pursue our rights and our claims in the course of a war if this necessarily implies great disadvantages to others. This is a most obvious case of applying attributive justice. In particular, a waiver of the right to exert punishment on those who have done

---

50 Cf. Grotius, *De Iure Belli ac Pacis*, II.XX.iii.
51 Cf. Grotius, *De Iure Belli ac Pacis*, II.XX.iv.
52 Cf. Grotius, *De Iure Belli ac Pacis*, II.XX.vi. et seq.
53 Cf. Grotius, *De Iure Belli ac Pacis*, II.XXIV.i.

wrong against us is to be considered[54]; mercy should be exercised where-ever possible.[55] The obligation to check the propriety of a measure, in particular of the use of force, is most clearly spelt out by arbitrary divine law, in particular by the law of the Gospel. However, this obligatory mod-eration of human conduct is also provided for by natural law, as here at-tributive justice may indeed require clemency and prudence. It can also be in our own best interest to abstain from waging war[56], in which case one has to compare advantages and disadvantages of warfare careful-ly.[57] Thus, attributive justice not only has an altruistic dimension: pru-dence as a virtue entailed by attributive justice is also to be applied to one's own affairs.

This means that even justice in the strict sense may have to give way to injustice; this is the case if the blind pursuit of one's right is to be ex-pected to cause more damage than gain from the war. The propriety of measures of war is a requirement which brings equity into play as a legal category. It is thus in the end attributive justice which provides a major check against inappropriate warfare. Grotius here claims that the cases in which a war could or should not be avoided are rare.[58] Thus a war may only be waged in case of great need, or because of a very impor-tant reason, and even then only if the situation looks favourable.[59] War as a means to enforce law obviously misses the point if the success of a mili-tary action is already improbable from the outset. Moreover, the rule of law does not need to be asserted in any case and under all circumstances.

It is interesting how Grotius here brings into play the requirement of the propriety of war in the light of the question of how to reconcile the strict necessity to uphold justice with the human inclination and Chris-tian counsel to exercise mercy and to forgive, which is inherently prob-lematic for any Christian theory of punishment. In Grotius' elaboration on punishment in *De Satisfactione*, he contends that a ruler is free to for-give an offence, like a creditor may waive his claim. This case is however different from that of a judge: the judge is not entitled to make disposi-tions on his authority.[60] Yet, while any ruler is entitled to administer his authority as he sees fit, no ruler may freely decide whether or not to ad-

---

54 Cf. Grotius, *De Iure Belli ac Pacis*, II.XXIV.ii.
55 Cf. Grotius, *De Iure Belli ac Pacis*, II.XXIV.iii.
56 Cf. Grotius, *De Iure Belli ac Pacis*, II.XXIV.iv.
57 Cf. Grotius, *De Iure Belli ac Pacis*, II.XXIV.v.
58 Cf. Grotius, *De Iure Belli ac Pacis*, II.XXIV.viii.
59 Cf. Grotius, *De Iure Belli ac Pacis*, II.XXIV.ix.
60 Cf. Grotius, *De Satisfactione*, II.

minister justice. It is a ruler's office to uphold justice; however, the ruler has relatively large leeway and does not necessarily have to resort to punishment.

3.1.4 Just Intention

Compared to other authors on the just war doctrine Grotius has surprisingly little to say about the just intention of the war-faring party with regard to its engagement in war. Traditionally, most lawyers concerned with the prerequisites of a just war held that a war is unjust even though all other conditions are fulfilled if the party having the just cause to wage war does so because of an unjust motivation.[61] There are two remarks by Grotius that shed some light upon his views in this respect.

First, Grotius adheres to the traditional idea that an erring consciousness obliges. Consequently, an act which is in itself just becomes wrong if it is performed by someone who holds this act in consideration of all aspects to be unjust.[62] From this it may also be concluded that a war for which the party in question has sufficient authority and good cause, and which also seems appropriate in light of the circumstances, is nevertheless unjust if the party waging the war is driven by an unjust intention.

A second remark of Grotius in his elaboration on dubious reasons for war is interesting in this respect. Taking up the traditional question of whether there is the possibility that a war is just in relation to all parties involved, Grotius distinguishes between various meanings of the term "just".[63] If one applies "just" in the sense related to the matter itself, then a war cannot be just in relation to both parties, in the way that a legal dispute cannot be just in relation to both parties involved. It is possible, though, that none of the parties involved acts unjustly: even if one has no right to wage war, one may not be faulted for this if one could not have known that no corresponding right existed. In this case the legal status of a justified party is to be applied in relation to both parties. For our purpose it is legitimate to turn this statement into its opposite: if one has a right, but does not know or does not believe that one has it, one may not exercise it. Therefore, even if a party is justified in waging a war, but does not know it and wages the war out of an unjust motivation, then this party is to be regarded unjustified. Thus, there is indeed a subjective re-

---

61 Cf. F. H. Russell, *The Just War in the Middle Ages* (1975), 65 et seq.
62 Cf. Grotius, *De Iure Belli ac Pacis*, II.XXIII.ii.
63 Cf. Grotius, *De Iure Belli ac Pacis*, II.XXIII.xiii.

quirement for a just war in the sense that the party engaging in a war has to do so with the right intention.

3.2 Law in War

While Grotius seeks to offer a comprehensive presentation of the contemporary law in war in *De Iure Belli ac Pacis*, this is only one aim in Grotius' agenda. A second dominating feature of Grotius' comments on the law in war is a – sometimes quite harsh – critique of the predominant contemporary practice as regards war in the light of the overarching categories of natural law and arbitrary divine law. Thus Grotius here attempts to present the law in war as it is, but also, and probably more importantly, as it should be.

3.2.1 General Rules of the Law in War

According to Grotius, there are three basic principles regarding the means that may be employed in a war. First, virtually anything which serves the pursuit of the aims set for the war is deemed permissible.[64] This presupposes the principle that the moral judgement on any means is dependent upon the purpose for which it is used. If a just war is waged by the right authority, because of just causes, in the right intention, and if the war presents an appropriate means to reach a legitimate aim, in particular the restoration of justice, then in principle any measure may be used which is conducive to successfully end the war. If the war is inherently just, then the measures employed in the course of the war are justified, too. This statement might seem to present a contradiction to Grotius' above-mentioned demand to moderate warfare. Yet this is not the case: while Grotius certainly is in favour of employing only legitimate measures in warfare which are in proportion to the aim pursued, he nevertheless contends that a justified war has to be undertaken effectively. Hence, there is no general requirement to fight a war in an open or so-called honest way; the justified party may deceive the other party, or it may use hidden tactics to overcome the opponent as long as the war is covered by the justified aim. Consequently, a justified war may be undertaken with the help of ambushes or other tricks.[65] Grotius here follows the traditional approach to the use of cunning and trickery.[66]

---

64 Cf. Grotius, *De Iure Belli ac Pacis*, III.I.ii.
65 Cf. Grotius, *De Iure Belli ac Pacis*, III.I.vi et seq.

However, this is not to say that natural law is suspended as regards measures taken in a war. The war-faring parties still have to adhere to natural law in all their actions. Thus, if a promise has been given to the enemy, this promise has to be honoured[67], as this is required by expletive justice. The principles of natural law apply to situations of war as much as they apply to situations of peace. The aforementioned general principles of the law in war apply to Christians and non-Christians alike: there are no specific Christian principles of a law in war. Likewise, there are no different aims for warfare for Christians than there are for non-Christians. Thus, there are also the same means to be employed by Christians and non-Christians alike. Consequently, Christians may take recourse to ambushes as well as may non-Christians. However, the measures that may legitimately be taken by all under natural law are still subject to an additional check under arbitrary divine law, and therefore Christians may face further restrictions in the acts they may engage in during a war.

According to the second principle, the right one has against one's enemy is not to be judged from the reason for the war only, but also under other aspects that may arise in the course of the war as well.[68] This is to say that changes in the legal situation after the war has been started have to be taken into account to measure the respective legitimacy of warfare. Thus, if former allies form a new alliance with the enemy, these former allies may be treated as enemies as well.

The third principle regarding the law in war concerns collateral effects of wars: certain consequences which might not legitimately be intended in themselves, may in proportion be treated as an acceptable price to pay for pursuing hostilities. For example, women or little children may not normally be attacked in war; a direct attack on women or children will hardly ever be covered by the aim of the war, and thus is prohibited in general. However, if women and little children are on a ship which is a legitimate target of military action, then their killing may be acceptable.[69] In such a case, the primary aim, the destruction of a military ship of the enemy, is truly legitimate. The legitimacy of this measure is not affected by circumstantial events which entail side-effects or "collateral damages" according to the modern terminology that are not intended and could

---

66 Cf. F. H. Russell, *The Just War in the Middle Ages*, 23 et seq.; cf. C. A. Stumpf, "Vom Heiligen Krieg zum gerechten Krieg", *ZRG kan. Abt.* 87 (2001): 29 et seq.

67 Cf. Grotius, *De Iure Belli ac Pacis*, III.XIX.

68 Cf. Grotius, *De Iure Belli ac Pacis*, III.I.iii.

69 Cf. Grotius, *De Iure Belli ac Pacis*, III.I.iv.

not even be justifiably intended. In such cases it is rather the duty of the opponent to exclude the occurrence of such effects, but there is no duty of the justified party to avoid them. Still, Grotius qualifies his position by pointing out that negative side-effects may not be acceptable under any circumstance. One may not always fully exercise one's own rights, regardless of the circumstances and regardless of the effects that such actions entail. In particular, the commandment to love our neighbours requires a qualification. Thus, the law of the Gospel may require Christians rather not to insist on one's legal position if this cannot be done without bringing harm upon innocent people.

3.2.2 Critique of Practice

When discussing particular issues of the law in war in *De Iure Belli ac Pacis*, Grotius on the one hand presents the respective legal situation as he sees it devised in international law.[70] On the other hand, however, Grotius focuses keenly on the assessment of which limitations in the sense of a moderation of the international law are necessary under the overarching principles of natural law and arbitrary divine law.[71]

At the core of Grotius' discussion of the law in war is the term "licence". Grotius here uses the "licence" in the sense of an absence of punishment, not in the sense of justification or permission of the relevant conduct. He thus first presents which licenses the international law grants for the conduct of war-faring parties. By this he presents the contemporary legal practice in relation to war, which he himself finds rather abhorrent.

However, Grotius then moves on to discuss the law in war as provided for by natural law and arbitrary divine law. Here the true character of the rules of the international law in relation to war becomes apparent: much of what is granted as licence is simply morally and therefore also legally unacceptable.

Thus after having asserted relatively far-reaching rights of the war-faring party under the international law to kill enemies or to enslave them[72], Grotius limits these rights severely under natural law and arbitrary divine law.[73] Likewise, while far-reaching rights regarding the destruction and re-

---

70 Cf. P. Haggenmacher, *Grotius et la doctrine de la guerre juste*, 597 et seq.
71 Cf. Grotius, *De Iure Belli ac Pacis*, III.X.
72 Cf. Grotius, *De Iure Belli ac Pacis*, III.IV.
73 Cf. Grotius, *De Iure Belli ac Pacis*, III.XI.

moval of things are granted under international law[74], most of these rights appear to be taken away again under divine law.[75] The same applies respectively to the acquisition of property[76], to the right over prisoners of war[77], to the principles of the state power of the defeated party[78], and to the return of goods.[79]

4 Conclusion

The above should have shown that Grotius does indeed not intend to separate law in general or natural law in particular from theology, that he does intend to establish certain subjective obligations, rather than individual rights, and that he expects certain, higher, standards of conduct from Christians, but a minimum standard from anyone.

Seeing that Grotius is not an author to turn to if one really seeks for a secular understanding of law, it remains to be asked how Grotius still can be relevant for just war tradition today. Two suggestions may be given here: First, one of the much lamented defects of the "classic modern" international legal system is its exclusive focus on states as the only responsible and entitled agents on the international level. Grotius here helps to identify the moral and legal rôle of the individual as reference point for rights and responsibilities even in a transnational context.

Secondly, it may be humbly suggested here that the very relevance of Grotius for modern public law does not stem from an alleged secularism, but rather from his acknowledgement that there are indeed moral values at the core of anyone's conduct in the international arena: Even in the light of varying moral concepts on the international level, it should prove more worthwhile to identify potential common moral grounds in order to build on them an international legal framework, than to ignore morality altogether in favour of legal positivism as had been attempted in the past decades.

---

74 Cf. Grotius, *De Iure Belli ac Pacis*, III.V.
75 Cf. Grotius, *De Iure Belli ac Pacis*, III.XII.
76 Cf. Grotius, *De Iure Belli ac Pacis*, III.VI.; III.XIII.
77 Cf. Grotius, *De Iure Belli ac Pacis*, III.VII.; III.XIV.
78 Cf. Grotius, *De Iure Belli ac Pacis*, III.VIII.; III.XV.
79 Cf. Grotius, *De Iure Belli ac Pacis*, III.IX.; III.XVI.

Kant's Cosmopolitanism:
Resource for Shaping a "Just Peace"

Philip J. Rossi, SJ

1.

In Part I of *The Metaphysics of Morals*, the *Rechtslehre,* Kant presents the most extensive systematic treatment of issues of justice, law, and public order that he published during his lifetime. His discussion of a number of matters that lie within the scope of classical just war theory is included under the more general heading of "The Right of Nations" (*das Völkerrecht*), a relatively brief section of nine pages *in toto* (AA 6: 343–351 [§§53–61])[1]; this is followed by a section on "Cosmopolitan Right" (*das Weltbürgerrecht*) (AA 6: 352–353 [§ 62]) and a "Conclusion" (AA 6: 354–355) that pertains to "the entire final end of the doctrine of right within the limits of mere reason." His account of war, peace, and international order was articulated within a context of a late eighteenth century European political order that reverberated with the aftershocks of the French Revolution. Even though more than two centuries separate us from Kant and his context, there are, as I will argue in this essay, at least three features of his account that continue to have import for discussions about the legitimacy and the limitations of war in the context of a contemporary global international order in which pressure for change comes from a variety of new configurations of political, economic, technological, and social forces. The relevant features of Kant's account are:

---

1 Citations of Kant's work give the volume and page references to the appropriate volume of *Kants Gesammelte Schriften* (Ausgabe der Königlichen Preußichen Akademie der Wissenschaften, Berlin 1902-) [hereafter AA] in the form AA 6: 343–351. The English translations used are from the Cambridge Edition of the Works of Immanuel Kant, eds. Paul Guyer and Allen W. Wood (Cambridge: Cambridge University Press, 1997).

1. His treatment of what we would now most likely call "international order"[2] as a topic that is fully co-extensive with questions of war and peace.
2. His treatment of this topic in the form of a tripartite division that includes not only matters that in classical just war theory fall under the headings of *ad bellum* and *in bello* considerations, but also matters that pertain to what have come to be termed *post bellum* considerations.
3. His treatment of the full ensemble of just war considerations (*ad bellum*, *in bello*, and *post bellum*) as functions of the larger claim that he makes in the "Conclusion," viz. that the attainment of perpetual peace is be understood as the *highest political good* (AA 6: 355).

Kant does offer, as part of the second feature of his account, a number of specific considerations–e. g., "a defeated state or its subjects do not lose their civil freedom through the conquest of their country" or "the concept of a peace treaty already contains the provision that an *amnesty* goes along with it" (AA 6: 349)–that deserve attention in view of the development that contemporary just war thinking has given to the articulation of *post bellum* conditions. These, however, may not be the features of his discussion with most extensive import for the project of re-casting of just war theory for the twenty-first century. It is the first and third features of his account that this essay will highlight as more pertinent to efforts to re-shape just war theory so that it can address more adequately and appropriately the circumstances, both old and new, that draw states, as well as non-state actors, into armed conflict.

This is so, I will argue, in view of the broader framework in which Kant sets his thinking about matters of peace and war, namely, his placement of the question of war and peace as the controlling moral and political issue of international order: in the absence of an enduring order for peace, international relations stand as a field devoid of any law for interaction among states other than that of "might makes right." In the earlier essay, "Toward Perpetual Peace," Kant had already suggested that, to the extent that we take the right of nations to go to war as the defining framework for international order, our thinking borders upon the unintelligi-

---

2   Although the heading for the sections that deal with the relations among nations is *Das Völkerrecht*, Kant remarks (AA 6: 343) that a more appropriate designation would be *das Staatenrecht* ["the right of states"] as a counterpart to the Latin terminology *jus publicum civitatem*.

ble.[3] In that text, as well as in the discussion of international order in the *Rechtslehre*, he then proposes that the appropriate way to counter such unintelligibility is through a proper exercise of practical reason, i.e., though an acknowledgement that with respect to international order our reason issues a imperative that is morally binding upon our humanity. This imperative is to work toward the construction of a "cosmopolitan" world order in which the relations among nations provide a set of moral and political conditions that, instead of constantly offering a setting for war, open possibilities for securing lasting peace. What constitutes such a world order as "cosmopolitan" is the orientation it provides to members of a political community so that they can envision ways for ordering the dynamics of the relations among nations in ways that best serve human good, rather than bowing to the rule of might. Fundamental to this orientation, on Kant's account, is recognition that human reason places upon the political dynamics that arise from human social interdependence a compelling moral demand for the establishment of conditions for enduring peace; this imperative thus places responsibility upon political communities to find effective ways to respond to such a demand. The chief among such ways, Kant believes, is the establishment of an effective international adjudicatory order that will make it possible for nations to settle conflicts without resort to armed combat.

The general aim of this essay will thus be to explore the extent to which Kant's articulation of peace in terms of a moral demand provides a basis, first, for enlarging the framework for just war theory into a moral framework for a world order that takes the establishment of conditions for securing "just peace" as a primary goal and, second, for then reconfiguring some of the specific elements of just war theory in accord with such an enlarged framework. I will argue that Kant's discussion provides a basis for doing both. At the basis of my argument is the interpretive claim that in designating perpetual peace as "the highest political good" Kant takes the attainment of peace to function as a *regulative* principle with respect to our understanding of–and the overall scope we accord

---

3   "The concept of the right of nations as that of the right to go to war is, strictly speaking, unintelligible" (AA 8:357). The unintelligibility here is the moral [practical] unintelligibility of self-defeating action; I believe that a case can be made for taking the moral unintelligibility of the "right to war" to be, with respect to the moral responsibility incumbent upon humanity as a species, on a par with the moral unintelligibility that, in *Religion within the Boundaries of Mere Reason*, Kant attributes to "radical evil" with respect to the moral responsibility of individual agents.

to–what he terms "the right of states." What is required for the attainment of peace to function as a regulative principle is that it be recognized
as a condition of international order that "ought to be"–a recognition
that, in Kant's understanding of the practical use of reason (most starkly
posed as "ought implies can"), carries with it the consequence that this
condition of peace *can be made actual by what human moral agents do.*
As a regulative principle, peace is neither an empty velleity nor a form
of political wishful thinking; it is a demand for action placed upon our
humanity.

The attainment of peace, in Kant's view, thus provides *the* fundamental framework for giving moral direction to the interaction among nations
in the functioning of the international order.[4] These relations will accord
with this regulative principle to the extent we construe and construct "the
right of states" *as ordered in its exercise to the social finality to which our
human practical reason orients us* as members of the world-wide community of humanity. While Kant most expansively–and most abstractly– characterizes this social finality as "a kingdom of ends," it is, as I shall set forth
below, his more specific characterization of it as "a cosmopolitan point of
view" that is most pertinent to the functioning of the ideal of "perpetual
peace" as a concrete regulative principle for the refashioning of just war
theory.

I am using "regulative" here in the sense that Susan Neiman sets forth
in her reading of Kant in *The Unity of Reason* and *Evil in Modern
Thought.* As I understand her characterization, a (morally) regulative
principle sets forth the horizon of possibilities that enable us to act in
ways that serve to transform the "the world as it is" to "the world as it
ought to be."[5] Action enabled by that horizon of possibilities concretely
exhibits the finality of the practical use of reason, a finality that Kant has
most notably characterized in expressions such as "a kingdom of ends,"
"the ethical commonwealth," and "a cosmopolitan society" (*weltbürgerli-*

---

4   Kant's account of international order does not initially seem to provide concep-
     tual space for the functioning of non-state agents on a moral par with nations as
     the primary *loci* for the functioning of the international order.
5   "… it is an unshakable demand that the world come to meet the claims that rea-
     son advances, permitting the hope that sustains all efforts to make it so" (*The
     Unity of Reason*, Oxford: Oxford University Press, 1994, 181). "It is not an
     idea that we derive from the world, but one that we bring to it… [it is] a
     drive essential to reason itself" (*Evil in Modern Thought: An Alternative History
     of Philosophy*, Princeton: Princeton University Press, 2002, 320).

che Gesellschaft).[6] It is important to note that, as a regulative principle, the "perpetual peace" that Kant envisions thus does not function conceptually in his thinking about war and peace in the same way that specific *post bellum* considerations function in contemporary just war thinking. It is not simply an additional *criterion* for judging the moral adequacy of particular policies or conduct upon the cessation of armed hostilities; nor is it directly a prescription for the rebuilding of civil societies crippled by war, though it may, in fact, entail that steps must be taken to do so. It is rather a principle for *a practical re-orientation of our thinking* about the capacity human beings have, as agent participants in the history of the human species, for enacting peace in the face of the dynamics of war that issue from our human "unsociable sociability."[7] While such a practical re-orientation does not by itself immediately prescribe particular courses of conduct, it alters the space of possibilities for the articulation and the use of specific practical principles (such as those that have been formulated within just war theory) by framing those possibilities by explicit reference to "perpetual peace" as the highest social good that Kant considers humans capable of aiming for and effecting in the concrete circumstances of human socio-political history.[8]

If this is a proper way to read Kant's thinking about the role that "perpetual peace" should play in our dealing with questions about peace and war, it then suggests there may be greater significance to the current interest in articulating *post bellum* considerations beyond the

---

6   The last expression is found in the second part of *The Conflict of the Faculties*; AA 7: 92; see the parallel expressions *weltbürgerliche Verfassung* in *Theory and Practice*, AA 8: 310; *weltbürgerlich Zustand*, in "Idea for a Universal History" AA 8: 26.

7   Kant describes "unsociable sociability" as "the propensity [of human beings] to enter into society, which, however, is combined with a thoroughgoing resistance that constantly threatens to break up this society" ("Idea for a Universal History" AA 8: 20).

8   The concluding two paragraphs of the *Theory and Practice* essay (AA 8: 312–313) provide a particularly clear articulation of perpetual peace functioning according to Neiman's construal of a "regulative principle," i.e., an envisioning of possibilities for action by reference to "what ought to be." See, in particular, the beginning of the last paragraph: "For my own part, I nevertheless put my trust in theory, which proceeds from the principle of right, as to what relation between among human beings and states *ought to be*, and which commends to earthly gods the maxim always to behave in their conflicts that such a universal state of nations will thereby be ushered in and so to assume that it is possible (*in praxi*) and that it *can be*."

most evident one of the usefulness of specifying a further set of criteria pertinent to contemporary circumstances in which the thoroughgoing destructiveness of modern warfare has given greater urgency to devising ways of dealing with its aftermath. At the very least, attention to the role Kant gives to "perpetual peace" sets a horizon of possibilities for re-framing some of the central issues that fall within the scope of the *ad bellum* and *in bello* considerations, i.e., for reframing them precisely in terms of a larger vision of international order that would make possible taking concrete steps toward the enactment of conditions for enduring peace. Kant's account thus indicates how we might begin to place at least some of the judgments made in accord with *ad bellum* and *in bello* considerations into an larger integral vision of the form and the manner of peace that nations are obligated to put in place, not merely upon the conclusion of armed combat, but also to narrow and to forestall, particularly through the establishment of robust adjudicatory procedures, the possibilities for armed hostilities taking place.

More significantly, however, Kant's account also urges us to place the full scope and structure of just war theory into an overarching vision of how an order of international peace might be shaped so as to diminish, with an increasing degree of effectiveness, the conditions and circumstances that bring states (and non-state actors) into armed combat. This vision is one that would encompass more than the cessation of particular armed hostilities, more than a settlement regarding the specific conditions that brought about the conflict, matters that, of necessity, often are framed retrospectively in terms of rectifying the *ante-bellum* dynamics that led to conflict. The understanding of Kant's account that I am proposing thus does not simply provide a way for re-framing some individual elements of just war theory within the context of an account of an international order for just peace. It requires as well that the theory as a whole be indexed to such an account in a way that would enable states to make effective practical commitments to work for the attainment of such an order, such as working for the establishment of effective adjudicatory bodies and procedures to resolve disputes between nations.

Kant's articulation of perpetual peace as a regulative principle within a cosmopolitan world order thus provides two related "coordinates" from which to effect a re-orientation of just war thinking. One of these coordinates is the ideal of "perpetual peace" itself as a regulative principle that functions explicitly as the shaping moral imperative for just war theory. Re-orienting just war theory along this coordinate would enable us to reconfigure at least some of the classical just war criteria by attending to them in the light of a larger dynamic of international peace making and peace building. Placing these criteria within such a larger orienting framework for bringing about peace as a moral imperative might then result in a reconfiguration along lines such as the following:

1. Making part of the employment of the "last resort" criterion a more thorough and more careful consideration of a full set of modalities for conflict resolution – including possibilities of establishing new regional or international procedures and *fora* for doing so – *prior to* the making of an *ad bellum* judgment;

2. Taking into account the impact upon *post-bellum* outcomes that is likely to follow from the authorization, in accordance with *in bello* criteria of discrimination and proportionality, of particular means of engaging in combat; and,

3. Establishing means – e.g. concrete practices and institutional procedures – by which the satisfaction of *post bellum* criteria provides a settlement effecting more than just a reduction of possibilities for future combat between the particular parties who have been at war. Satisfaction of these criteria in this way would serve to create conditions for putting more firmly in place the mechanisms and the dynamisms of an international order that could be more effective than the current ones for reducing the possibilities for subsequent armed combat within the larger regional or international community, not merely between those who have most recently been at war.

Fundamental to Kant's articulation of perpetual peace as a regulative principle, moreover is its placement in relation to the "cosmopolitan" world order that he envisions arising from human efforts to heed the moral demand of reason to establish conditions for perpetual peace. This suggests that a cosmopolitan world order, envisioned precisely as conditional upon human effort, provides a second coordinate upon which to base a reorientation of just war thinking. Basic to a reorientation along this coordinate would be a repositioning of just war theory so that it functions as a part of a larger account of an international order of peace. With regard to this second coordinate, it is of importance to note that Kant places his own account of just war thinking within the ambit of what he calls the "preliminary articles" for perpetual peace.[9] These "preliminary articles" pertain to an international order that, with respect to the relationships among nations, *is not yet* "cosmopolitan,"

---

9   AA 8: 343–349.

and thereby in ever present danger of slipping into the moral unintelligibility of war. It is, rather, an order that exhibits a "state of nature"–a condition of inevitable conflict that, in Kant's view, nations stand under a
moral imperative to exit. The import of this may be that a reorientation
of just war thinking along this coordinate requires one to construe the
finality of just war theory as ordered to establishing conditions that
will ultimately render its use unnecessary: Just war theory may then be
most appropriately understood as primarily oriented to the establishment
of international order that functions to provide an effective locus in
which issues that have hitherto led to war may now be settled without
resort to armed combat. Kant himself envisions such an order as one
that allows for "deciding disputes [between states] in a civil way, as if
by a lawsuit, rather than in a barbaric way (the way of savages), namely
by war" (AA 6: 351).[10]

2.

Up to this point I have presented the possibilities that Kant's account
opens up for revising just war theory in rather broad and overarching
terms. In this section, I would like to provide at least a few details
drawn from Kant's texts that I hope will indicate how his identification
of perpetual peace as the highest political good positions these two coor-

---

10 Kant's construal of "perpetual peace" as a regulative principle for just war think-
    ing might serve as helpful resource for an alternate way to conceptualize a point
    made by those who, from the framework of Catholic teachings on war and peace,
    argue that just war thinking appropriately starts from a basis it shares with paci-
    fism, i.e., a presumption against war. Construing this "presumption" as a "reg-
    ulative" principle may better highlight its robustly normative function. For
    brief discussions of the issues that have been raised within Catholic discussion
    with respect to the presumption against war see Kenneth Himes, O.F.M., "Paci-
    fism and the Just War Tradition in Roman Catholic Social Teaching." In *One
    Hundred Years of Roman Catholic Social Thought*, ed. John A. Coleman, S.J.,
    (Orbis: Maryknoll, NY, 1991) 329–344, Lisa Sowle Cahill, *Love Your Enemies:
    Discipleship, Pacifism, and Just War Theory* (Fortress: Minneapolis 1994), 205–
    213. Some of these issues were in dispute in exchanges that took place in
    2003 among a number of Catholic theologians regarding the applicability of
    the *ad bellum* just war criteria to the US-Iraq war; see Drew Christiansen,
    "Whither the Just War." *America*, March 24 (2003): 7–11; John Langan,
    "Bush's Iraq Project: Can War Be Justified?" *Commonweal*, March 14 (2003):
    15–19; George Weigel, "The Just War Case for War." *America*, March 31
    (2003): 7–10.

dinates so that they offer important possibilities for reorienting just war theory. To do so, it will be necessary, first, to examine the context from which he enunciates "the right of states" as concretely ordered to the prosecution of war and, then, to set forth the relationship between that context, which he characterizes as a "state of nature," and "the highest political good" of "perpetual peace" that he proposes in following section on "cosmopolitan right." I will then take, as the conclusion of my discussion, some of the unresolved issues that attend the way Kant envisions the establishment of the international adjudicatory order that he proposes as an institutional instrument for the attainment of "perpetual peace." Since this feature of his account may prove to be particularly helpful in efforts to revise just war thinking for contemporary contexts it will helpful to be aware of the exploratory nature of Kant's own presentation of this order. Kant provides only a sketchy outline of the structure and the dynamics of such an adjudicatory order, a shortcoming that has given rise to a long-standing dispute among commentators over the extent to which his analyses and arguments constitute a brief for a unitary "world state."[11] This shortcoming, however, should not obscure the importance that Kant's proposal of such an adjudicatory order has as a marker of the re-orientation of our thinking about the issues of power and sovereignty that Kant sees ensuing once "perpetual peace" serves as prime coordinate/regulative principle for the shaping of international order.

The "right of states" consists of a tripartite set: a "right *to go to war*," a "right *in* war," and a "right *after* war" (AA 6: 343). He characterizes the context in which this right functions as "a state of nature" in which states stand to one another as "lawless savages"; this context thus constitutes a "nonrightful condition" that is a "condition of war (of the right of the stronger)" (AA 6: 344). Kant's mention of "the right of the stronger" suggests the definition of justice offered by Thrasymachus in Plato's *Republic:* "the just is nothing else than the advantage of the stronger" (Book I, 338c). Kant's depiction of this state of nature as the setting for his discussion of the tripartite components of the right of states also has a Hobbesian resonance to it: "Here a state, as a moral person, is considered as liv-

---

11 Pauline Kleingeld provides an overview of the competing interpretations that have been given to the role that Kant envisions for individual sovereign states in an international order framed by the ideal of "perpetual peace" in "Approaching Perpetual Peace: Kant's Defense of a League of States and his Ideal of a League of States." *European Journal of Philosophy* 12 (2004): 304–325 and "Kant's Theory of Peace." In *The Cambridge Companion to Kant and Modern Philosophy,* ed. Paul Guyer (Cambridge: Cambridge University Press 2006) 477–504.

ing in relation to another state in the condition of natural freedom and therefore in a condition of constant war" (AA 6: 343). There is an ironic tonality to Kant's treatment of these matters. This is of some pertinence to the conclusion he eventually draws regarding moral status of war. War evokes nothing less than a robust, "irresistible veto" on the part of practical reason: "*there is to be no war*, neither war between you and me in the state of nature nor between us as states …for war is not the way in which everyone should seek his rights" (AA 6:354).

These texts in *The Metaphysics of Morals* in which Kant treats a "state of nature" as the context in which states function as moral agents may be usefully read, I believe, in the light of his discussion, in Book Three of *Religion*, of the distinction between the "juridical" and the "ethical" states of nature (6: 93–100). In that earlier text, Kant articulates dimensions of the relationship between the "juridical state of nature" – which forms the context from which individual agents are called to public mutual moral responsibility in their external relations of right to one another as members of a "juridico-civil (political) state" – to the "ethical state of nature" – which forms a counterpart context from which individuals then move to a more encompassing form of mutual moral responsibility in pursuit of virtue as members of an "ethical commonwealth." It is of import to note that this second, "ethical" state of nature is one in which human beings find themselves functioning even when, by virtue of their presence and participation in a political state, they are no longer in the "juridical" state of nature.

Kant discusses the first form of the state of nature in earlier sections of *The Metaphysics of Morals* (AA 6: 311–312 [§§ 43–44]) in a way that is consonant its treatment in *Religion*. The second form of "state of nature" that provides the context for his discussion of war and peace in *The Metaphysics of Morals*, however, is not identical with the second form of the state nature that he treats of in *Religion*. They are similar in that both are conditions that obtain for human beings who, by virtue of their presence and participation in a political state, no longer stand individually to one another in a "juridical" state of nature. But a fundamental difference between these two treatments lies in the fact that the ethical state of nature depicted in *Religion*–and the obligation to leave it–pertains to individual moral agents, while the second "state of nature" as depicted in *The Metaphysics of Morals* holds not among individuals but among nations. It is a state that pertains not primarily to individual moral agents (even though their lives may very well be affected by it) but to states as "moral persons." This difference coordinates with the outcomes that

Kant then envisions as the result of leaving each form of this second "state of nature." In leaving the ethical state of nature individuals move in the direction of an "invisible" moral bond that unites them in an "ethical commonwealth" (Kant's counterpart to "the church universal"). Establishing this bond unites them, no matter which civil state they may live in, as members of a "community according to the laws of virtue" (AA 6: 124), a community that Kant identifies as "the church." Kant indicates that such a supranational and ecumenical community, even though it will have external and public dimensions to it, would yet have "nothing in its principles that resembles a political constitution" (AA 6: 102). Though such a community would have a form of governance that is public, the manner in which such governance would be exercised is ethical, not juridical, i.e., it would not rely upon the coercive means that are legitimate for the enforcement of juridical right. Though Kant is much clearer about what such manner of governance is not–"Its constitution is neither *monarchical* (under a pope or a patriarch), nor *aristocratic* (under bishops or prelates), nor *democratic* (as of sectarian *illuminati*)" (AA 6: 102)–than what it might be, he provides some clue to its form in his various discussions of the "public use of reason" in other writings.[12]

In contrast to the movement out of the ethical state of nature by individuals, when nations leave the "international" state of nature Kant conceives of them moving in the direction of a cosmopolitan world order in which there would be a public bond that takes form as what he variously calls, in this text and in the essays on perpetual peace and on theory and practice, "a permanent congress of states" (AA 6: 350), "a republicanism of all states, together and separately" (6: 354), "a federalism of free states,"(AA 8: 354), "a pacific league (*foedus pacificum*)" (AA 8: 356), or a "cosmopolitan constitution" (AA 8: 310). Establishing this public bond provides conditions that Kant suggests make possible an international adjudicatory order for "deciding disputes [between states] in a civil way, as if by a lawsuit, rather than in a barbaric way (the way of savages), namely by war" (AA 6: 351). Kant offers one tantalizing reference to a parallelism in the dynamics involved in the constitution of an ethical

---

12 For a further discussion of this point see Onora O'Neill, "The Public Use of Reason." In *Constructions of Reason: Explorations of Kant's Practical Philosophy* (Cambridge: Cambridge University Press, 1989) 28–50; Philip J. Rossi, SJ, *The Social Authority of Reason: Kant's Critique, Radical Evil, and the Destiny of Humankind* (Albany: State University of New York Press, 2005) 99–107.

commonwealth and the establishment of a cosmopolitan world order in an extensive footnote in *Religion*, but does not subsequently provide any further elaboration of it:

> ...the idea [of the objective unity of the religion of reason] is one of reason which is impossible for us to display in an intuition adequate to it but which, as a practical regulative principle, has nonetheless the objective reality required to work toward this end of unity of the pure religion of reason. It is the same here as with the political idea of the right of a state [*Staatsrecht*], insofar as this right ought at the same time to be brought in line with an international law [*Völkerrecht*] which is universal and *endowed with power* [*machthabendes*]. Experience refuses to allow us any hope in this direction. There seems to be a propensity in human nature (perhaps put there on purpose) that makes each and every state strive, when things go its way, to subjugate all others to itself and achieve a universal monarchy but, whenever it has reached a certain size, to split up from within into smaller states. So too each and every church entertains the proud pretension of becoming a universal one; as soon as it has propagated and acquires ascendency, however, a principle of dissolution and schism into various sects makes its appearance (AA 6: 123).[13]

In the various texts in which Kant makes a cosmopolitan world order serve as a fundamental marker of the form of international relations that effects progress toward perpetual peace, he leaves unsettled a number of important specifics about the structure and working of that order. I have already noted the dispute over the extent to which he affirms that a cosmopolitan world order would eventually take the form of a unitary world state. An ambiguity of greater significance for discussions of just war thinking pervades his treatments of the means and the motivations by which states are moved to enter into the cosmopolitan world order. The ambiguity arises in part because the issues at stake are embedded within a persistent concern that plays a fundamental role in shaping Kant's entire critical project, viz., the relationship between the causal workings of nature and the exercise of human freedom. Within the context of that larger concern, Kant frequently frames the relationship between the workings of nature and human freedom in his writings on politics, culture and history in terms of questions about the respective roles

---

13 Even more tantalizing may be the addition Kant made to this footnote in the second edition of *Religion:* "If we are allowed to assume a design of providence here, the premature and hence dangerous (because it would come before human beings have become morally better) fusion of states into one is averted chiefly through two mightily effective causes, namely, the difference of languages and the difference of religion" (6: 123).

of nature and providence, on the one hand, and human freedom, on the other, in effecting the final destiny of the human species. In those discussions, Kant considers it important to affirm an effective role for human freedom in the attainment of that destiny, even as he recognizes that movement toward that destiny also lies in forces that stand beyond human capacity to alter.[14]

With respect to the attainment of "perpetual peace," one specific role that Kant gives to human freedom lies in the manner in which the international order providing conditions for peace comes about as a *voluntary* federation of states. Unlike the coerced movement that brings individuals out of the "juridical" state of nature, movement out of the international state of nature is, in an important measure, uncoerced. It is a movement that ensues in consequence of the exercise of human moral freedom, with national states as agents of such freedom. In this it is parallel to the movement out of the "ethical state of nature," which Kant also affirms to take place in virtue of an uncoerced exercise of human freedom on the part individual moral agents. Kant does not himself address the undoubtedly important questions about the adequacy and coherence of his at least implicit affirmation of the moral agency of states in terms of his own account of individual human moral freedom.[15] One reason Kant does not address this issue may very well lie in the fact that he takes the locus of such an exercise of freedom to be most appropriately embodied in the person of a monarch who holds the sovereign power of the state.[16] At the same time, he does see the citizenry playing a role in the dynamics that lead to perpetual peace, most notably in terms of (self-interested) resistance to bearing of the increasing economic burdens of war (AA 8: 331).[17] Kant's account here stands in need of recasting into a framework

---

14 Although Kant does not formally articulate his discussion of these matters as an "antinomy" generated by not attending to the distinction between the theoretical and the practical uses of reason, the dynamism at work clearly resonates with this argumentative strategy, one that is central to his discussions in the 1st and 2nd *Critiques* of the human finite freedom that is located within context of the causal nexus of nature.

15 Cf. the passage noted above (p. 226) "Here a state, as a moral person, is considered as living in relation to another state in the condition of natural freedom and therefore in a condition of constant war" (AA 6: 343). Also unresolved in Kant's account is an appropriate way to characterized moral agency and responsibility with respect to non-state actors in the international order.

16 Cf. AA 6: 311–323; 338–339 for Kant's account of sovereign authority.

17 The economic side of this mechanism is stressed in passage from the *Theory and Practice* essay just noted; there also is be a political side, based on the principle of

for understanding political sovereignty in terms of the successes and failures in the emergence of forms of representative government in a postcolonial, post Cold War international environment. Such a recasting would be of import for rethinking questions about the proper locus, within the structures of a democratically governed state, of the moral and political responsibility for making decisions in accord with the *ad bellum* criteria of just war theory.

Finally, it may be important to pay explicit attention to the fact that a primary focus of Kant's proposal for a cosmopolitan international order is on the establishment of an *adjudicatory* order for the settlement of disputes that would otherwise lead to war. As noted earlier, there has a been longstanding issue about the nature of the "federalism of free states" that Kant proposes: Is this a proposal for some form of unitary world government or for a standing international body of the kind that was unsuccessfully instantiated in first part of the twentieth century by the League of Nations or so far only imperfectly in the successor United Nations? My suggestion here is that it may be more important with respect to the project of rethinking just war theory that Kant takes such a body to function primarily in the arena of adjudication rather than that of either sovereign legislation or executive governance. Kant's vision of a cosmopolitan world order that provides conditions for perpetual peace involves, first and foremost, the constitution of an effective internationally recognized body for the resolution of disputes between states. It may be thus most properly be taken be a proposal urging us to explore, as an important new field for the extended *application* of renewed theory of just war for the twenty-first century, proposals for the development of effective *fora* and means (including the establishment of adjudicatory bodies) for regional and international conflict resolution. Such exploration may help to exhibit concretely ways in which the finality of just war theory serves the establishment of an enduring order of just peace.

---

the co-legislative power of the citizenry that Kant notes with respect to the sovereign's power to enlist citizens in the waging of war (AA 6: 344–46).

Kant and the Just War Tradition

Thomas Mertens*

1 Introduction: the 'triumph' of Just War Theory

In 2004, the just war theorist Michael Walzer published a collection of his essays entitled 'Arguing about War'.[1] In the opening chapter, he claims that the vocabulary of the just war tradition now dominates philosophical discussions about war: as he puts it, 'the triumph of just war theory is clear enough'. According to Walzer, when we discuss war, we no longer do so in the categories of the doctrine of realism, according to which international relations should not be measured by considerations of justice, but by those of national interest and force alone. Instead, we use other categories inspired by an old doctrine according to which 'war's occasions and its conduct' should be measured by considerations of justice: the justice or injustice of the outbreak of war and the justice or the injustice of the conduct of it – known in homage to their Middle Age origins as the doctrines of 'jus ad bellum' and the 'jus in bello'. The years since the publication of Walzer's collection appear to confirm his claim. In contemporary consideration of war, recourse to the moral discourse of the just war tradition seems inevitable. No politician can afford to argue in favour of or against military action solely in terms of national interest and without reference to considerations of justice. These considerations are embedded in international law. The field of law with regard to the use of military force, as is frequently noted, is strongly indebted to the tradition of just war. Norms regarding the commencement of a war can be found primarily in the Charter of the United Nations, and those regarding the conduct of war, primarily within the Geneva Conventions. President Obama, in his Nobel Peace Prize acceptance speech, explicitly endorsed the just

* This paper is based on a reflection on Kant's juridico-political views during several years. I benefitted from comments by audiences at the Hermeneutics of Just War Thinking conference in Hamburg and at the European University Institute, both in 2009, and as always from Morag Goodwin.

1 Michael Walzer, *Arguing about War* (New Haven and London, 2004).

war tradition. In endorsing 'the concept of a 'just war'', he suggested that 'war is justified only when it meets certain preconditions: if it is waged as a last resort or in self-defense; if the force used is proportional, and if, whenever possible, civilians are spared from violence'. He further noted that 'there will be times when nations – acting individually or in concert – will find the use of force not only necessary but morally justified'.[2]

The pervasiveness of the just war tradition is such that some Kant scholars[3] increasingly feel the need to interpret Kant's theory of peace and international law within the lines of this tradition. Kant may have been fiercely critical of the just war tradition in his 'towards perpetual peace' – its representatives, Hugo Grotius, Pufendorf, Vattel and the rest are described as 'sorry comforters' who are dutifully quoted in justifying military aggression but whose arguments have never prevented states from resorting to war (ZeF, 350; Reiss 103)[4] -, but these remarks, according to this new 'school' of interpretation, should not be taken at face value. Instead, emphasis is put on the most mature formulation of his 'doctrine of right', in which Kant clearly embraces the perspective of the just war doctrine. Of course, this interpretation is not uncontest-

---

2   Barack Obama, Nobel Lecture, 2009, available at: http://nobelprize.org/nobel_prizes/peace/laureates/2009/obama-lecture_en.html.

3   I mention: Brian Orend, *War and International Justice. A Kantian Perspective* (Waterloo, 2000), 41–64; Susan Meld Shell, "Kant on Just War and 'Unjust Enemies'." In *Kantian Review* 10/1 (2005): 83–111; Sharon B. Byrd and Joachim Hruschka, "Kant, das Recht zum Kriege und der rechtliche Zustand im Verhältnis der Staaten zueinander." *Archiv für Rechts- und Sozialphilosophie* 94/1 (2008): 70–85.

4   References and abbreviations: references to Kant's writings are given in brackets. The first page number refers to the Prussian Academy Edition (Berlin: De Gruyter 1968), the second page number to the English translation in Hans S. Reiss, *Kant's Political Writings* (Cambridge University Press, 1970) (Ed. with introd. and notes H. Reiss. trans. by H. B. Nisbet = Reiss); or to the English translation in: Mary J. Gregor, trans and ed. (= Gregor), *Immanuel Kant, Practical Philosophy. Cambridge Edition of the Works of Immanuel Kant*, (Cambridge: Cambridge University Press, 1996). The following abbreviations are used: Idee = *Idee zu einer allgemeinen Geschichte in weltbürgerlicher Absicht* (AE, VIII); TuP= *Über den Gemeinspruch: Das mag in der Theorie richtig sein, taugt aber nicht für die Praxis* (AE, VIII); ZeF = *Zum ewigen Frieden* (AE, VIII); Rel = *Die Religion innerhalb der Grenzen der bloßen Vernunft* (AE, VI); MdSR = *Die Metaphysik der Sitten, Rechtslehre* (AE, VI); SdF = *Die Streit der Fakultäten* (AE, VII); Refl = *Reflexionen zur Rechtphilosophie* (AE, XIX) .

ed.[5] Traditionally Kant's writings are read as emphasizing the need to establish international institutions in order to create a lasting peace and that the just war tradition, as primarily a moral (and not a legal) doctrine, lacks this outlook. Kant's theory of law is thus understood primarily as a theory of global peace in which any legal ground to start military hostilities is explicitly excluded.[6]

How, then, should we understand Kant's thinking on war and peace? Is it necessary to shoe-horn his work into the popular mode of thought in order for it to have relevance for our times? Our starting point should be the texts themselves, and the acknowledgement that Kant indeed rejected the 'realist' position, but that he at the same time also rejected the kind of 'immediate' pacifism according to which the abolition of war is possible without the establishment of cosmopolitan legal rules and institutions.

2 Kant's rejection of both pacifism and realism

There can be little doubt that Kant was a pacifist in the sense in which 'pacifism' denotes the view that war necessarily entails immoral human behaviour and should therefore be condemned. According to Kant, practical reason pronounces the irresistible veto: 'there shall be no war' (MdSR 354; Reiss 174). For Kant, this implies at least two things. The first is a reflection on the institutional conditions under which war can be abolished and a lasting peace upheld. Kant argues here, as is well known, that it is both the internal structure of the so-called republican state as well as the international legal order between states that are important. What this means in more detail is the object of a wide range of interpretations. Some have argued that a republican way of governing is reconcilable with different constitutional orders, while others have contended that Kant clearly favours a liberal democratic constitution. In terms of international relations, again it has been argued that Kant advocated or intended to advocate a form of world government; others instead

---

5   Georg Cavallar, "Commentary on S. Meld Shell's 'Kant on Just War' and 'Unjust Enemies': Reflections on a 'Pleonasm'." In *Kantian Review* 11/1 (2006): 117–124. Thomas Mertens, "Warring to End War (Review of B. Orend, War and International Justice)." In *The Review of Politics* 64/3 (2002): 558–560.
6   Gerhard Beestermöller, *Die Völkerbundsidee* (Stuttgart, 1995), 19–93; Georg Geismann, "Kants Rechtslehre vom Weltfrieden." In *Zeitschrift für philosophische Forschung* 37/3 (1983): 362–388, esp. 372.

emphasize the federal character of Kant's peace-proposal.[7] The second
issue is what follows from practical reason's prohibition of war under
non-ideal circumstances, to borrow Rawls's terminology. Should we simply stop engaging in war and expect that peace will follow? Yet Kant does
not believe that we can simply rely on the peace loving nature of mankind. Kant's view of human nature is rather grim. War itself, writes
Kant, 'does not require any particular kind of motivation, for it seems
to be ingrained in human nature'. (ZeF 365; Reiss 111) Elsewhere, he
emphasizes the importance of war in the development of mankind.

   Yet, this does not mean for Kant as it does for the 'realist' that we simply have to learn to live with war. For Kant, the importance of war in the
history of mankind does not exclude the possibility of peace and his rejection of realism is not built on moral considerations alone. For Kant,
'realism' is nonsensical as a political theory. He saw it as constituting
an impossible basis upon which to develop guidelines for decision making
and acting in the international sphere. Given this, politicians that rely
upon the doctrine of realism inevitably make use of the concept of
right. (ZeF 355, 380; Reiss, 103, 125) Man's 'warlike' nature does not
make 'realism' inevitable, but rather demands moral and legal considerations. This does not solve the question as to how we should act in ordinary situations in which lasting peace has not been realised. If morality is
relevant in the international realm at the same time as the war prone nature of mankind is true, would not the tradition of just war thinking be
the most likely position? Does Kant's moral condemnation of war under
non-ideal circumstances apply solely to unjust wars or to wars in general,
only to the unjustified means of waging war or to all means? Can a war
ever be justified according to Kant? The most relevant texts with regard
to what Kant calls '*status iustitia vacuus*' (in the preliminary articles of *Towards Perpetual Peace* and in several paragraphs in the *Rechtslehre*) seem to
point in different directions. This confusion is all the greater when we
place Kant into his historical context.

   The 17th and 18th century saw a number of authors advocate peace,
notably Crusé, Sully and the Abbé of St. Pierre, but their proposals
were rarely met with approval. Therefore Kant's sympathy for the

---

7   See e.g. Sidney Axinn, "Kant on world government." In *Proceedings*, eds. Ger-
     hard Funke and Thomas Seebohm, Sixth International Kant Congress (Washing-
     ton, 1989), 243–251; Otfried Höffe, "Die Republik frei verbündeter Völker." In
     Kategorische Rechtsprinzipien. Ein Kontrapunkt der Moderne, ed. O. Höffe (Frank-
     furt, 1990) 249–279.

Abbé's *Projet pour rendre la paix perpétuelle en Europe* (1712 – 3) was a rare exception (Idee, 24; TuP, 313; Reiss, 47, 92). Voltaire ridiculed the Abbé's proposal as a chimera and Leibniz was reminded 'of a device in a cemetery, with the words: *Pax Perpetua*; for the dead do not fight any longer: but the living are of another humour; and the most powerful do not respect tribunals at all'.[8] Kant's position was therefore odd in its own day in constituting a combination of supporting the prospect of peace at the same time as seemingly accepting the realist position of war as an intrinsic feature of human nature. The latter places Kant closer to Hobbes, often considered the intellectual father of 'realism' and therefore Kant's 'natural' counterpart, than is frequently admitted by Kantians.[9] To Hobbes' dictum of war as the '*status hominum naturalis*', Kant merely adds that it is not necessarily a '*bellum omnium in omnes*', but a '*status belli omnium in omnes*'. (Rel, 97n.) According to Kant, war is not limited to man's public life, but also plays a dominant role in his private realm, as marriage, so Kant felt, proves. Marriage, Kant writes, is often depicted in terms of love. Yet, the relationship between husband and wife is seldom without conflict and therefore requires legal regulation. Without such regulation, even those bound by the most intimate relations would treat each other solely as objects instead of as ends in themselves. It is Kant's insistence on the warlike nature of man – his realism – that makes his pacifism so confusing. Is it possible to reconcile them?

We need to go back to Kant's interpretation of the realist position and his view that the position of the 'practical politician' is an impossible one. For Kant, although this 'practical politician' despises the theoretical, i.e. moral, politician and holds that one should act on the basis of experience and not of moral ideas, he is unable to formulate valid guidelines for viable policies. Kant's argument runs as follows: imagine that it is in the state's interest to pursue peace. Is the realist able to conceive of ways of upholding such 'peace'? In studying the chaotic and unceasing series of clashes between nations he would develop a poor theory for action, namely that of pursuing peace through an equilibrium between nations. Yet, such an equilibrium is necessarily unstable and fragile, according to

---

8   It is likely that the opening of Kant's ZeF (343, Reiss, 93) is a reference to this. See Gottfried Wilhelm Leibniz, *The Political Writings of Leibniz*, ed. Patrick Riley (Cambridge, 1979), 183, 166.

9   As in Robert Kagan's *Of Paradise and Power: America and Europe in the New World Order* (New York, 2003).

Kant, because it depends on international actors' assessment of each other's (changing) economic and military power. A state of balance could
only come into being where these actors believe it to already exist and
it is therefore dependent on subjective estimations and thus fragile and
temporary. The objective of 'peace' by realistic means fails, and hostilities
are likely to break out at any moment. (Rel, 97n.; TuP, 312; Reiss, 92)
Realism produces similar results for the state whose interest lies in war.
Again, the realist wants to derive a plan for action from experience.
Yet, the results of his analysis are again unhelpful, as opportunistic guidelines such as 'act first and justify your acts later', 'deny everything' and
'divide and conquer' will not be of much help. No-one can overtly subscribe to such 'maxims' because they are self-refuting. All that is left to the
'realist' is the concept of right. The fact that statesmen make use of moral
concepts such as those formulated in the just war tradition is thus in a
sense inevitable and does not necessarily constitute respect for considerations of justice.

While this argument shows that 'realism' is inconsistent and reference
to morality inevitable, Kant adds a second element namely that war
though immoral is instrumental in bringing about peace. Here we
touch upon Kant's teleological understanding of human history, according to which history itself, with all its instances of 'realism', is nonetheless
oriented toward creating the conditions for a lasting peace. Kant's understanding of the possibility of peace is thus based on a combination of
pragmatic considerations, moral imperatives and historical progress. In
the post-metaphysical era in which we now live, the optimism Kant displays with regard to the development of history cannot easily be shared.
Fortunately, this optimism is not relevant for the discussion of whether
Kant admits of the possibility of a just war, i.e. the legitimacy of the
use of military force under non-ideal circumstances. Before I address
that question straightforwardly, we need to consider Kant's proposal for
peace.

3 Kant's theory of peace

Kant holds that lasting peace consists of three basic elements: republican
constitution, federation of states and cosmopolitanism. These elements
must be realised through moral actions within a historical process. This
historical process is determined by what Kant calls: 'man's unsocial sociability' (Idee, 20; Reiss, 44), according to which man's social life is

marked both by cooperation and conflict. Thus in the establishment of a republican constitution and a federation of free states, this 'social unsociability' must be taken into account. A situation of lasting peace does not result from spontaneous harmony between men but by regulating their unsociability through law. A republican constitution will thus follow from a process of gradual and constant reform in which the violence on which any state was originally based will gradually give way to a political system in which the laws are made in accordance with the general will of all who obey them. (ZeF, 350–1; Reiss, 99–100) The most important constitutional element of the Kantian republic is that it puts the decision of whether or not to declare war into the hands of its citizens. This provision would, according to Kant, make the decision to go to war very unlikely as war contradicts the self interest of those selfsame citizens.

Yet, the republican constitution is not in itself sufficient for a lasting peace. Although self interest will inhibit citizens from embarking on war, a federal association of free states is still a necessity. In the absence of international rules, a state of nature would exist between the 'free' states. Even benevolent and law-abiding states would be confronted with what Kant calls the 'a priori' idea of a non-lawful condition as well as with the 'a posteriori' experience of conflicts even among the benevolent. Both individual men and states cannot be secured against acts of violence until a legal situation is established (MdSR, 312; Reiss, 137) and that requires an international federation of free states. (ZeF, 354; Reiss, 102) The fact that Kant opts for a federation and rejects the idea of a world state has been discussed widely. Kant seems to hold that a federation is able to establish a system of checks and balances –necessary in the light of man's 'unsociability' – whereas the creation of a global centre of international power would result in the tyranny of what Kant calls a 'universal monarchy'. A federation of free states is therefore suitably sufficient from a legal point of view as well as realistic from an anthropological point of view, given the linguistic and religious differences among the peoples of the world. (Rel, 34n; ZeF, 367; Reiss, 113–4) Kant adds as the third condition for a lasting peace cosmopolitanism in the sense of a universal hospitality, which enables individuals and nations to seek peaceful, commercial contacts with one another. This third rule prescribes that foreigners and foreign communities treat each other with hostility. (ZeF, 358; Reiss, 106)

4 The conditions for peace and the use of force

Summarizing our course so far: on moral grounds, Kant rejects war and
advocates world peace. His peace proposal is not based on a rosy view of
human nature, nor does he think that peace is an immediate possibility.
Instead, the establishment of peace is a historical process in which the
conditions for peace will eventually be realised. War should be taken seriously as an essential element of human nature and thus of human history; yet lasting peace is possible, both on prudential and moral grounds.
But the question as to what this means for the present day, in which the
three conditions of republicanism, federalism and cosmopolitanism have
not been established, remains. Should Kant's theory be given a pacific
hue? Or should it rather be understood in line with the tradition of
the just war? This question can be answered by further developing
Kant's argument, but there are various options for doing so and with different outcomes.

   One could focus on Kant's proposal for a 'federation of free states'
and continue the line of argumentation developed so far – what we
shall call the first option. This would require answers to questions such
as the nature of coercive force that should be attributed to such a federation; and whether it would have the right to impose its judgements on
non-cooperative member states by force or to coerce non-member states
to join, given that such a federation is required for a lasting peace. Kant
argues that it is a moral duty to leave the state of nature, both for individuals and for states (MdSR 350; Gregor 487). He also argues that individuals have the right to use force against each other in order to bring
about a 'status juridicus': 'one is authorised to use coercion against someone who already by his nature, threatens him with coercion'. (MdSR,
307; Gregor 452) In more general terms, Kant argues that there is connected with right by the principle of contradiction an authorisation to coerce someone who infringes upon it'. (MdSR, 231; Gregor 388) It therefore is likely, if one follows Kant's argument through, that what is true for
individuals is true for states as well, authorising them to use force to bring
each other out of the state of nature. And if this is the case, is it not an
example of a 'just war'?

But does Kant indeed grant such permission? Is the analogy between individuals and states as straightforward as some commentators suggest?[10] Kant is ambiguous here. On the one hand, he indeed stresses the analogy between the situation of individuals living in the state of nature and that of the states in the absence of international law. Both have the same obligation to leave the state of nature. On that basis, states are obliged to enter into a federation of states, in which each of them derives its security from a 'united power' and its 'law-governed decisions'. Elsewhere he writes: international law must be based upon public laws, which can be enforced and to which each state must submit. (Idee, 24, 26; Reiss, 47, 49; TuP, 312; Reiss, 92)

However, Kant stresses time and again that the analogy is limited. Individual states run a risk by accepting the strong ties represented by international law. A federation that resembles a 'state' might – because of its centralized power – develop into a hegemonic despotic regime and so destroy the realm of freedom already obtained by and within individual states. Whereas natural right indeed obliges individual men to abandon the lawless state of nature, the same is not equally true for states because 'they already have a lawful internal constitution'. Therefore 'the coercive right of others to subject them to a wider legal constitution in accordance with their conception of right' is not applicable to them. (ZeF, 355; Reiss, 104) And even in the 'Doctrine of Right' Kant holds that the international alliance that is to replace the state of nature among states 'involves no sovereign authority' and 'can be renounced at any time' (MdSR, 344; Gregor, 483). Apparently, Kant conceptualises the legal relations between individuals differently than those between states. This is the basis for his rejection of the positive idea of a world republic in place of a negative substitute of a gradually expanding federation necessary in order to prevent war. (ZeF, 357; Reiss, 105) According to his final words on the subject, in the Doctrine of Right, the idea of international law merely demands a voluntary federation of peoples, which is to be renewed periodically. (MdSR, 344; Gregor, 483) This suggests that the moral obligation to opt-in does not preclude the possibility of opting-out. The idea of a public right of states requires a 'congress', an 'association' of states which all states are 'free' to join. (MdS R, 350 – 1; Gregor, 488) Despite the state of nature among them, states must join this 'congress' out

---

10   Sharon B. Byrd and Joachim Hruschka build their case on this analogy in: "Kant, das Recht zum Kriege und der rechtliche Zustand im Verhältnis der Staaten zueinander." In *Archiv für Rechts- und Sozialphilosophie* 94/1 (2008): esp. 79–80.

of their own will and not because of external coercion. It is indeed note-worthy that this remark on the liberty of the states to join and to leave the international congress is made in the context of the *Rechtslehre*, indeed Kant's last formulation on this subject, on which the proponents of Kant as a just war theorist rest their claim. His statements concerning the need for stronger ties between states are generally made in his earlier texts, in the context of his philosophy of history. For this first option, then, it is far from certain whether Kant's 'league' or 'congress' of nations could justifiably resort to war on the basis of a 'jus ad bellum'.

The second option reflects on the situation in which there is not yet such a federation. Does a 'jus ad bellum' exist in the absence of interna-tional law and international institutions? It is inevitable here that we turn to *Towards Perpetual Peace*, in which Kant not only formulates the con-ditions under which a lasting peace is possible, but also the rules on how to act when these conditions are not fulfilled. These rules are formu-lated as prohibitions in the so-called preliminary articles. These prohib-itions are either of the strictest sort (enumerated in preliminary articles 1, 5 and 6) or of a more permissive kind (in articles 2, 3 and 4). The per-missive articles are relevant only indirectly: they stipulate the conception of a political community as a self-governing body; they prohibit states from having standing armies and of creating debts with an eye to prepar-ing for war. While the emphasis on political autonomy is obviously im-portant, the articles 'of the strictest sort' are directly relevant. They pro-hibit, respectively, the search for new grounds for war after the establish-ment of a peace agreement, the intervention of one state in the affairs of another out of respect for the integrity of a political community, and breaches of the *jus in bello*.[11]

Of these three prohibitions, Article 5 regarding intervention is espe-cially important: 'no state shall forcibly interfere in the constitution and government of another state'. This can only mean that the integrity of all states, republican and non-republican alike, must be respected. Kant gives a number of reasons for why this is so. The first is that every state is a society of human beings and therefore cannot be disposed of by others without their consent. The concept of political community entails the right of a people to determine for itself a civil constitution. As such, im-posing on foreign communities a republican form of government would therefore be self-contradictory. The second reason for respecting the in-

---

11   The fact that Kant prohibits certain conduct during war obviously not make of
      him a just war theorist.

tegrity of all states, regardless of their internal arrangement, is that intervention also constitutes a violation of the 'harm principle'. Just as an individual person cannot be punished as long as he does not harm others, a political society cannot be sanctioned if it does not violate the rights of other communities; internal violent turmoil is a bad example for other states, but it does not harm them. Hence, the mere fact of a non-republic constitution does not provide a *casus belli* and thus there is no right of interference.

For Kant, self-defence is the only legitimate ground for using force against another state. Kant's preliminary article 3 prohibits standing armies, both as a threat to peace itself and as a violation of the rights of a man in his own person. Citizens are only to be required 'to undertake voluntary military training from time to time' in order that they can defend 'themselves and their fatherland against attacks from outside' should the need arise. Of course, where they act in self-defence, states must respect unconditionally certain rules of what we now call humanitarian law. (ZeF 345–6; Reiss, 95–6)[12] The second option – in the absence of a federation of states – therefore points in a similar direction as the first: that of an explicit rejection of the just war tradition, and the only justification for war is self-defence.[13]

The third option, however, builds upon certain passages in the Doctrine of Right in which Kant appears to take the opposite position, i. e. to subscribe fully to the just war tradition. This third option describes the quasi legal regime that Kant attributes to states in the (international) state of nature. While the first and the second option consider the legal infrastructure both after and before the establishment of the federation, i. e. with and without positive international law, the third option suggests something entirely different, namely that states have certain 'rights'. This is not to deny that the Doctrine of Right also emphasises the need to establish a federation but Kant presents us here nonetheless

---

12 It is remarkable to notice that Kant's prohibition of these acts is based not only on their inherent evil character ('intrinsically despicable'), but also on their effect for a future peace. This is a consequentionalist argument, that Kant fully accepts.

13 Kant adds that their argumentations as laid down in carefully drafted 'philosophically and diplomatically codes' are ever dutifully quoted, but solely in the justification of military aggression. Never has a state given up its desire to make war on the basis of their arguments. (ZeF, 355; Reiss, 103) In the state of nature, politicians and states do indeed refer to the concept of right, including the concept of just war, but not to refrain from resorting to war. The tradition of just war gives them ample opportunity for abuse.

(MdSR, 346–350; Reiss, 167–170) – in a rather straightforward manner – with the central tenets of the just war tradition. In the state of nature, he writes, the right to engage in war is the 'permitted means' by which a state 'prosecutes its rights against another state'; yet because of the obligation to leave the state of nature, war should be conducted in such a manner that it leaves the possibility of a future federation intact. It is for this latter reason that certain means of warfare are forbidden: soldiers should not become unfit as future citizens, nor should warfare destroy the mutual confidence that is needed for a future peace. In addition to these well known issues of *jus ad bellum* and *jus in bello*, Kant considers *jus post bellum*. Under this heading, Kant determines that while a victorious state may set the conditions of the peace treaty, it cannot claim compensation or bring the vanquished state under its rule. He also discusses the rights of peace, namely the right of neutrality when neighbouring states are at war; the right of guarantee, which is the right to secure existing peace; and the right to form alliances for common defence. Finally, Kant discusses the concept of an 'unjust enemy'. On the basis of these passages, Kant clearly belongs to the just war tradition, including a right to resort to war on moral grounds.

5 Kant and the 'jus ad bellum'?

Any acknowledgment of a 'right to war' introduces the distinction between just and unjust wars; and it is on the supposed attribution to Kant of such an acknowledgment that some scholars have defended recent wars as justified on Kantian grounds.[14] But is it really the case that Kant makes this distinction? A careful consideration of these passages in the *Rechtslehre* is necessary.

It is certainly true that Kant introduces the right to war as the 'permitted means' by which a state can claim its rights against another and he gives this right a very broad understanding.[15] The right to war can

---

14 See e. g.: Volker Gerhardt, "Die Macht im Recht. Ideologie und Politik nach dem 11. September 2001." In *Merkur* no. 651 (2003): 557–569; Roger Scruton, "Immanuel Kant and the Iraq war" (2003) In *OpenDemocracy*, available at: http://www.opendemocracy.net/faith-iraqwarphiloshophy/article_1749.jsp.

15 Kant is defended as a just war theorist by: S. Meld Shell, *Kant on Just War and 'Unjust Enemies'*, 90, on the basis of a distinction between an 'international state of nature' and outright anarchy. I doubt whether this distinction is warranted by Kant's texts.

be invoked on the basis of both actively inflicted injuries and on the basis of threats. Moreover, whenever a state believes itself to be injured by another, by 'an alarming increase of its power' or even because it is simply 'more powerful', it has the right to war, including a preventive war. (MdSR, 346; Reiss, 167)[16] In addition, Kant introduces the concept of an 'unjust enemy' and holds that the rights of a state against such enemy are unlimited, i. e. that any state can make use of all permissible means to assert its rights against such an enemy. This concept of 'unjust enemy' also has a broad meaning. 'In accordance with international law', it is defined as a state that displays a 'maxim' expressed either in word or deed that would make peace among nations impossible, i. e. it would lead to a perpetual state of nature if it were made into a general rule (MdSR, 312; Reiss, 137). Such a maxim is displayed, for example, when a state violates public contracts such as those assumed to be in the interest of all nations. These nations have then the right to unite against such an enemy and prevent such breaches of the common order. Kant adds that that these allied states do not have the right to destroy this unjust enemy, but they are nonetheless allowed to enforce on that state a constitution of a less warlike nature. (MdSR, 349; Reiss, 170) To the astonishment of devotees of *Towards Perpetual Peace*, Kant appears to argue here in favour of justified wars on the basis of a state's own estimation of the violation of its rights.[17] Not only does the right to war include preventive wars but it allows for what nowadays would be called 'regime change', possibly by a coalition of the willing.

It would seem that accepting such a right would be the best guarantee for perpetual war, since it makes every state judge in its own case. This 'right to war' contradicts Kant's earlier remark, in *Towards Perpetual Peace*, that such a right is problematic, if not plainly contradictory, for it would indeed determine what is lawful not by universally valid laws, but by one-sided physical force. 'Right' cannot be decided by military force. (ZeF, 356–7; 355; Reiss, 105, 104) Could Kant have so radically altered his views in so short a period of time that he accepted a conditional right to use force as a last resort or to enforce the judgment of a coa-

---

16 This is even more astonishing while Kant explicitly denies a right to such a preventive war under the circumstances of a 'potentia tremenda' in *Towards Perpetual Peace* (ZeF, 384; Reiss, 128).

17 This is S. Meld Shell's starting point in *Kant on Just War and 'Unjust Enemies'*, 83–111; for a similar view, see: B. Orend, *War and International Justice. A Kantian Perspective* (Waterloo, 2000), esp. 51–56; Critically is: G. Cavallar, *Commentary on S. Meld Shell's Kant on Just War and 'Unjust Enemies'*, 117–124.

lition of states on an unwilling state? Obviously, such a right to war would give states ample room to define what counts as justified *casus belli*, and thus open up the possibility of arbitrariness. How can one independently decide on what counts as violations of what needs to become international law and on violations that would destroy the possibility of a league of republican states? (Refl, 598)

These inconsistencies suggest that the first impression of Kant's texts must be wrong. His consideration of the 'right to war' and the 'justified enemy' fits only with the description of the international realm before the establishment of positive international law. In the 'state of nature' each state has the 'right' to further its interests in any way it sees fit, including by use of the 'right to war'. Analogously, individuals in the state of nature are 'authorised' to enforce their natural rights. As these rights cannot be made secure in the state of nature, Kant calls them 'provisional'; individuals have the moral duty to enter into a civil constitution, under which these rights lose their provisional character and become 'peremptory'.

This is the way to understand Kant's concepts of 'right to war' and 'unjust enemy', namely as provisional rights, as the means by which states must secure their rights within the state of nature. The particular estimation of each state is the only thing that matters. This explains why the 'right to war' includes not only the right to self-defence in the case of 'active injuries', but also a preventive war against an alarming increase of the power of another state. What counts as self-defence is fully up to the state that feels its security under attack. In the state of nature, as Hobbes explains in *Leviathan*'s famous chapter 13, even a trifle is sufficient to start a quarrel. Along similar lines, Kant writes that nothing more than an affront, an insult, would be enough to trigger the 'right of war'. (MdSR 346, Reiss, 167)

On this basis, it seems likely that when discussing the 'right to war', Kant does no more than describe the provisional 'right' of each state in the international state of nature, in which states indeed define their 'rights' solely on the basis of their own interpretations and estimations. Consequently, it is a situation in which war can indeed break out at any moment. It could even be said that such a broadly understood 'right to war' defines the state of nature among states. This then sheds light on Kant's use of the concept of 'unjust enemy': introducing the 'right to war' implies the concept of unjust enemy. Imagine a situation in which state A has been, by its own estimation, injured by state B and is seeking recompense. Whether the injury actually took place and whether the request for compensation is reasonable is entirely dependent on the interpretation of the states involved. In the state of nature, there is no procedure by which such a conflict can be settled impartially. If no agreement is reached, state A has no other option but to pursue its claim by forceful means, although the injury may consist of nothing more than the increasing military power of state B, which state A sees as a threat. Rather than limiting the reasons for which a resort to war is justified by the introduction of the criteria of the 'jus ad bellum', as the just war tradition in theory does, Kant argues that the 'right to war' knows no such limitations. It includes active and passive injuries, and it includes the right to self defence and to prevention. Inevitably, then, every state is able to claim that the resort to war is justified. It is 'easy' for a state to 'pay homage' to the concept of 'right'. By declaring its cause 'justified', it simultaneously makes the claim that its opponent is an unjust enemy. Affirming the opposite, namely fighting against a just enemy, would be a contradiction. Indeed, Kant writes: 'the expression 'an unjust enemy' is a pleonasm in the state of nature, for this state is itself one of injustice. A just enemy would be one whom I could not resist without injustice. But if this were so, he would not be my enemy in any case'. (MdSR, 346; Reiss, 170)

The *Rechtslehre* gives two indications of why this line of argumentation is sound. The first is the case in which states claim justifications. Kant rejects these claims. The European nations have justified their colonial wars of conquest by claiming the right to establish settlements abroad by either violence or by fraudulent purchase. It would be in the best interest of the world as a whole and the territories were in any case unoccupied. Kant rejects these justifications. Even were one to suppose good intentions on the part of the colonizing Europeans, such intentions cannot wash away the 'stain of injustice', as Kant puts it. (MdSR, 266, 353; Reiss, 172–3). Colonial wars cannot be seen as 'just wars'. In *Towards Perpetual Peace*, Kant condemns the wars between 'civilised peoples' categorically; in place of urging European states to restrict themselves to just wars only, he demands that they subject themselves to an 'external legal constraint' prohibiting war. (ZeF, 354, Reiss, 103)

The second indication builds on what Kant writes about the conduct of war and its conclusion. Imagine again the situation of conflict between states A and B in which each of them claims to fight a justified war. Why would the justice of the war itself not justify the overruling of the restrictions of the conduct of war, as some theorists of the just war tradition admit in the case of a supreme emergency?[18] Why would the justice of the war not justify the seeking of compensation or the punishing of the enemy after victory? It is not evident within the tradition of the just war that considerations of 'jus ad bellum', 'jus in bello' or 'jus post bellum' are valid independently. Why can the justice of the cause of the war not set aside the limitations of the *jus in bello* and justify the rectification of the wrong after the war? Kant clearly states that this is not permitted. Regarding the 'jus in bello', he stresses that no war between independent states can be a punitive one as it would presuppose 'a relation between a superior and a subject which is not the relationship that exists between states'. For the same reason, Kant condemns wars of extermination and subjugation. (MdSR, 347; Reiss, 168) In the context of the right applicable after war, Kant writes that the victor may set the conditions for the peace treaty but that it may not claim compensation for the costs of the war because that would imply that the vanquished state had fought an unjust war. Although the victor may 'hold' that this is the case and that his opponent has committed a wrong against him, he cannot make use of that argument for therewith he would declare the war to be a punitive one. In the state of nature, the concept of a punitive war is 'self-contradictory'. (MdSR, 348; Reiss, 168) Would Kant indeed have accepted the concept of a 'just war', this would not be so evident. In the context of criminal law Kant holds that crimes ought to be punished categorically. In other words: although every state when engaging in war must think that it wages a just war because otherwise it would fight a 'just enemy', this is irrelevant with regard to the conduct of war and to its conclusion. For Kant, the rules of the 'jus in bello' have categorical validity; they cannot be set aside in the name of some supreme emergency derived from the 'jus ad bellum'.[19] Nor does a 'just war' affect the outcome of the war. The 'right' of the victor to set the conditions of peace is based solely on power not on 'the pretended right which he possesses over his opponent because of an alleged injury the latter has done him'. (MdSR, 349; Reiss, 169) The conclusion must be, I think, that for Kant the statement that a state has the right to war is an analytical judgement in the state of nature. He does not support the theory of the just war.

---

18   This is argued in M. Walzer, *Just and Unjust Wars* (Basic New York, 1977), esp. Chapter 16.

19   See: Th. Mertens, "Kant's Cosmopolitan Values and Supreme Emergencies." In *Journal of Social Philosophy* 38/2 (2007): 222–241.

6 Conclusion

The main topic of this paper was a consideration of Kant's prohibition of war under non-ideal circumstances, and whether it needed to be understood as distinguishing between just and unjust wars. The first two interpretive options clearly reasoned against the acceptance of a right to war. Here Kant only accepts a limited right to self-defence by citizens who undertake a 'voluntary military training'. (ZeF, 345; Reiss, 95) The third line of argumentation followed Kant's apparent endorsement of the elements of the just war tradition in the Doctrine of Right. Yet, by introducing concepts such as 'right to war' and 'unjust enemy' Kant merely describes the implications of the international state of nature. Indeed, the moral imperative urges us to leave this situation, including the supposed 'right to war', behind. Until that moment 'all international rights, as well as the external property such as can be acquired or preserved by war, are purely provisional'. (MdSR, 350; Reiss, 171) Kant may be ambiguous on how the international state of nature should be overcome institutionally in mentioning both a 'universal union of states' and a 'permanent congress of states', but he is not ambiguous about his rejection of the just war tradition.

For as long as states remain in the state of nature, the quasi legal regime Kant describes consist of the main elements of the just war tradition. States have the provisional right to defend their own interests, and they have to do so within the boundaries of the *jus in bello*. However, Kant does not accept this tradition because he does not believe that its central elements – just authority, just cause, just intention, ultimate resort and reasonable chance for success – deal adequately with the immorality of war. The just war tradition is not able to constrain the 'wicked frenzy' of war. (ZeF, 357; Reiss, 105) Only international law can do so. According to Kant, the hope that international relations can be regulated by means of such a moral 'right to war' is a vain one. Thus what is needed is the transition from a lawless world of provisional rights to a world governed by peremptory rights by means of the preliminary and definitive articles for a perpetual peace. Such a peace is for Kant the supreme political good. (MdSR, 355, Reiss, 175) With all the benefit of hindsight, we know that Kant was too optimistic about the pace with which these articles could be achieved. Yet, the important lesson that Kant teaches us is that the just war tradition is not a genuine alternative. In place of limiting the occurrence of wars, the prime function of just war theory is to justify the resort to war. Its representatives are merely 'sorry comforters'.

The Holy See as International Person and Sovereign and Participant in International Law

Robert Araujo, SJ

At the foundation of this discussion are the mutual quest for peace, order, and the rule of law shared by the Holy See and the international community. As with any legal relationship in the international order, that between the international law and the Holy See has important historical and legal roots. This essay concentrates on the Holy See and its participation in the legal institutions of the international order.

In the context of this examination of the Holy See's relation with international law and legal organizations, the issue of Holy See's legal status and personality are of central importance because its impact and effectiveness in the efforts to achieve the mutual objectives just mentioned are formed in large part by the personality it enjoys under international law. While a variety of perspectives concerning its sovereignty and personality has surfaced over time,[1] the Holy See is a unique entity vis-à-vis public international law.

---

1   See generally, Jacques Maritain, *The Things That Are Not Caesar's,* trans. J.F. Scanlan, French ed. (1930); Carl Conrad Eckhardt, *The Papacy and World Affairs* (1937); Joseph Bernhart, *The Vatican As A World Power,* trans. George N. Shuster (1939); Charles Pichon, *The Vatican and Its Role in World Affairs,* trans. Jean Misrahi, (1950); Robert A. Graham, S.J., *Vatican Diplomacy: A Study of Church and State on the International Plane* (1959); Hyginus Eugene Cardinale, *The Holy See and the International Order* (1976); J. Derek Holmes, *The Papacy in the Modern World* (1981); Eric O. Hanson, *The Catholic Church in World Politics* (1987); see also *Church and State Through the Centuries: A Collection of Historic Documents With Commentaries,* trans. and eds. Z. Ehler, LL.D. and John B. Morrall, M.A., PH.D (Sidney, 1954), hereinafter Church and State (containing an anthology of documents and commentary on the general themes of this essay). A work not yet published in English that contains significant insight on the general topic is: Richard Arès, S.J., *L'Eglise Catholique Et L'Organisation de la Société Internationale Contemporaine* (1949).

When studying the Holy See, it is essential to understand and appreciated its historical role in world affairs.[2] History reveals that the Holy See commenced its earliest participation in international affairs and relations when Jesus commissioned his apostles—the predecessors of the college of bishops—to continue His work in the world by bringing the Good News to those whom they met. Special emphasis must be placed on Jesus's commission of Peter as His principal follower and successor. Peter received the keys of the Kingdom of Heaven [a symbol of the papacy] and primacy among the college of apostles.

These origins of the apostolic mission of the Holy See and the Roman Pontiff continue to the present day. Early in the Church's history, the Holy See and the Papacy actively participated in international relations.[3] Although the Christian Church received little recognition from the Roman Empire or local authorities, that trend began to change with the conversion of the Emperor Constantine in the fourth century.[4] The Church's international role then began to manifest itself through the convocation of a series of important councils.[5] These councils were not restricted to spiritual, theological, or ecclesiastical issues because they also considered the Church's relationship with the temporal sovereign powers. In this context, Pope Leo the Great sent emissaries to both Church councils and to the courts of temporal sovereigns[6] and included discussions on temporal matters.[7]

---

2   See Waldemar Gurian and M.A. Fitzsimons, eds., *The Catholic Church in World Affairs* (1954) (providing an overview of essays focusing on the twentieth century).

3   See generally Philip Hughes, "The International Action of the Papacy." In *The Tablet* (November 2 1940): 345–346; November 9 (1940): 365–366; November 16 (1940): 386–387; and November 23 (1940): 405–407.

4   See Francis X. Murphy, "Vatican Politics: The Metapolitique of the Papacy." *19 Case W. Res. J. Int'l L.* (1987): 375 (reviewing the Church's history in the realm of international politics and relations); see also Joseph Lecler, S.J., *The Two Sovereignties: A Study of the Relationship Between Church and State* (1952) (providing a more detailed, historical perspective about the transformation of the Christian church).

5   See generally *The Catholic Encyclopedia, General Councils,* vol. IV. (1908), 423–435.

6   See J.N.D. Kelly, *Oxford Dictionary of Popes* 44 (1986). Pope Leo the Great sent an emissary to the Council of Calcedon in 453. See id. He also sent Julian of Cos as his legate to the Emperor in Constantinople to serve as the pope's representative at court.

7   See Cardinale, supra note 1, at 34–35. To this day, the Holy See continues to be in, but not of, the political world. It does so principally through Papal diplomacy,

The Reforms of Pope Gregory VII transformed the exercise of papal power and the authority of the Holy See beginning in the eleventh century.[8] While the position of temporal sovereigns, including the Holy Roman Emperor, waxed and waned during this period, the authority of the pope generally grew and stabilized.[9] At the origin of the Second Millennium, Europe essentially functioned as a Christian realm united in faith under the Papacy. As a result, the Holy See wielded considerable influence throughout this period because Western Europe remained largely a Catholic world under the spiritual and temporal authority of the popes until the end of the Fifteenth Century.[10]

It is crucial to remember that the Holy See demonstrated that its international mission, regardless of territorial holdings, was not a mere duplication of those held by temporal leaders. Rather, its mission, even at this early stage, was to establish a moral voice in the realm of international relations. In course, the papacy developed a role as a mediator and assisted other sovereigns in resolving conflicts. This activity enabled the Holy See to prevail over potential belligerents to avoid war or at least delay it in some instances.[11] One illustration is provided by Pope Alexander VI's Line of Demarcation which separated the zones of colonial exploration between the then great world powers, Portugal and Spain.[12]

---

serving as an arbitrator or mediator in disputes between other sovereigns; entering into treaties, concordats, or other international agreements; and, participating in International Organizations. See id.

8   See generally Ehler, *supra* note 1, at 23–37; see also Walter Ullmann, *The Growth of Papal Government in the Middle Ages: A Study in the Ideological Relation of Clerical to Lay Power*, (1955); R. F. Wright, *Medieval Internationalism: The Contribution of the Medieval Church to International Law and Peace* (1930).

9   See I. S. Robinson, *The Papacy 1073–1198: Continuity and Innovation* (1990) (providing a detailed introduction to this growth of the Papacy's influence in the western world during this era).

10 Philip Hughes, "The International Action of the Papacy—Introductory: Before the Reformation." In *The Tablet*, (November 2 1940): 346. For a useful understanding of the relationship between the exercise of Papal and temporal authority during the Medieval era, see Walter Ullmann, "The Development of the Medieval Idea of Sovereignty." In *Eng. Hist. Rev.* 1 January (1949): no. CCL.

11 See John Keating Cartwright, "Contributions of the Papacy to International Peace." In *8 Cath. Hist. Rev.* (1928): 155, 160; F. Matthews-Giba, O.F.M., "Religious Dimensions of Mediation." In *27 Fordham Urb. L.J.* (2000): 1695.

12 See Edward G. Bourne, "The Demarcation Line of Alexander VI: An Episode of the Period of Discoveries." In *1 Yale Review* (1892): 35, 55. The text of the Bull

The end of the medieval period and the rise of European global exploration and colonization introduced a new role for the Holy See in international affairs. As global exploration strengthened national monarchs and their temporal sovereignty, national challenges arose against the Holy Roman Emperor and the papacy. Indeed, the Holy See participated in the quest of strong monarchs for new empires by bringing the message of Christ to those who had not yet heard of Him. Some may believe that the Church either participated or served as a silent bystander in the brutal exploitation of native peoples. However, the voice of Francisco de Vitoria, a Spanish Dominican priest, paved the way for the Holy See to advocate for the rights and protection of native peoples.[13] This development set the stage for Pope Paul III to issue the papal brief *Sublimus Dei*, which urged that native peoples be recognized by European colonialists not as objects for enslavement but as fellow human beings.[14]

By the end of the Sixteenth Century, permanent diplomatic representatives of the Holy See replaced the earlier temporary legations and were stationed in capitals and in the courts of several temporal sovereigns.[15] Unmistakably, this early and stable diplomatic presence evolved in the

---

Inter Caetem Divinae promulgated on May 4, 1493, *reprinted in* Ehler and Morall, *supra* note 1, 155–59.

13 See generally James Brown Scott, *The Spanish Origin of International Law* (1928), 22–59; James Brown Scott, *The Catholic Conception of International Law* (1934); James Brown Scott, *The Spanish Origin of International Law: Francisco De Vitoria and His Law of Nations* (1934).

14 Pope Paul III, *Sublimus Dei*, promulgated May 29, 1537, John Eppstein, *The Catholic Tradition of the Law of Nations* (1935), 420. While noting that Jesus encouraged Christians to go and teach all nations, Pope Paul III stated that in any missionary activities, Christians must acknowledge that "the Indians, who are true men, not only are capable of the faith, but, as we are informed, earnestly desire to embrace it." He added that the "Indians or any other people, who may be hereafter discovered by Catholics, although they be not Christians, must in no way be deprived of their liberty or their possessions, and that on the contrary they may and must be allowed to enjoy freely and lawfully the said liberty and possessions; that they must not be in any manner enslaved; and that, if they be so enslaved, their slavery must be considered as null and void." Other Popes reiterated the Paul III's concerns during their pontificates. More specifically, in 1435, Eugene IV condemned the Canary Islands' slave trade. Subsequent popes, such as Urban VIII's Bull of April 22, 1639, Benedict XIV's Bull of December 20, 1741, and Gregory XVI's Constitution Against the Slave Trade of November 3, 1839, did the same. See Eppstein, 418–26.

15 Joseph J. Murphy, "The Pontifical Diplomatic Service." In *The Ecclesiastical Rev.* 1 (1909): 41.

age of the new nation-state temporal sovereigns that still acknowledged the Holy See's personality and continuing role in the world of diplomatic relations despite the dissolution of the European Catholic World. In essence, the Holy See did not disappear as a subject of international law nor did it lose its international personality.[16]

In 1870 even without its former territorial possessions—sometimes viewed as essential to international status—the Holy See maintained its standing as an international person and increased the number of States with which it exchanged legations.[17] New papal diplomatic missions surfaced during this era.[18] As one observer of this period noted, "Governments which had no relations have established them. Governments which had broken off relations have restored them. Governments which had second-class relations have raised them to first class."[19] Moreover, this growth in diplomatic relations was not only with Catholic sovereigns but with democratic states of parliaments and prime ministers as well.[20]

---

16 See generally S. William Halperin, *Italy and the Vatican at War: A Study of their Relations From the Outbreak of the Franco-Prussian War to the Death of Pius IX* (1939); see also Lillian Parker Wallace, *The Papacy and European Diplomacy— 1869–1878* (1948).

17 See Robert A. Graham, S.J., *The Rise of the Double Diplomatic Corps in Rome: A Study in International Practice (1870–1875)* 1 (1952). As the author notes: "In the following decades [after 1870] the growing European rivalries inevitably had their repercussions in the Vatican and made this diplomatic post more important than it had ever been when the Pontiffs were in peaceful possession of the Temporal Power. The outbreak of the first World War only confirmed this trend." Id. at 101.

18 See, e.g., Josef Kunz, "The Status of the Holy See in International Law." In *46 Am. J. Int'l L.* (1952): 308, 311. See also Luke Lee, M.A., LL.B., Ph.D., *Vienna Convention on Consular Relations* 176 n.18 (1966). Lee points out that: "It should be emphasized that, between 1870 and 1929, the diplomatic corps accredited at the Vatican was not only not dissolved, but also increased through the years, except for a period just before World War I. Thus, there were 18 permanent diplomatic missions at the Vatican in 1890. The number was dropped to 14 on the eve of World War I, but rose to 24 in 1921. At the time of the Lateran Treaty in 1929, there were 27 permanent diplomatic missions at the Vatican."- Lee, supra, at 176 n.18.

19 L. J. S. Wood, "Vatican Politics and Policies." In *128 Atlantic Monthly* 1921): 398, 404.

20 Id. at 405. Interestingly, this same commentator speculated about a rapprochement between the Holy See and Italy. Id. at 403–404. This reconciliation came about eight years later with the Lateran Treaty of February 11, 1929.

States called upon the Holy See as an influential sovereign for assistance in the temporal matters of the international order. For example, in 1885 Germany and Spain engaged the Holy See in one of the better known dispute resolutions of the time. The parties requested that the Holy See mediate their competing claims for the Caroline Islands.[21] European, Latin American, and other States followed suit and requested the Holy See to arbitrate or mediate their disputes.[22] Some of the countries that requested the Holy See's assistance were not traditionally Catholic countries, e.g., Great Britain, the United States, and Germany.[23] Indisputably, the Holy See reinvigorated its role as an international instrument of peace through these efforts.

States also relied upon the neutrality and unique moral voice of the Holy See to assist in the amicable resolution of their international disputes.[24] For example, the United States turned to the Holy See for assistance in settling land disputes in the Philippine Islands over claims involving ecclesiastical property, which arose from the Spanish-American war. Governor Taft traveled to Rome during the summer of 1901 to further this effort. Although one commentator has suggested that the Taft mission essentially constituted negotiations with a private owner of property rather than a sovereign with international personality,[25] other commentators strongly disagreed with this contention by noting that the Governor was dealing with an ancient, international sovereign.[26]

---

21 James Brown Scott, Sovereign States and Suits Before Arbitral Tribunals and Courts of Justice (1925), 95. Scott stated that the "case of the Carolines [between Spain and Germany] is very famous, and shows that the role of the Papacy in the settlement of disputes is not ended, if it be desired, as it was frequently and to good effect in times past." Id. Scott further details that the Pope "gladly complied with their request to mediate between them, and in 1885 proposed a method of adjustment which, accepted by both and incorporated in a treaty, ended the difficulty." Id. at 96.

22 See Eppstein, supra note 14, at 470–474 (cataloguing 30 instances in which the Holy See either mediated or arbitrated disputes between rival States).

23 See Cardinale, supra note 1, at 89.

24 See id. at 88–89.

25 See Simon E. Baldwin, "The Mission of Gov. Taft to the Vatican." In *12 Yale L.J.* 1 (1902).

26 For a different perspective on the significance of the Taft Mission and the extremely delicate issue of the presence of Spanish clergy in the Philippines, see Edward F. Gross, S.J., "The Taft Commission to the Vatican, 1902." In *45 Rec. Amer. Cath. Hist. Soc'y* 184 (1935); see also John T. Farrell, "Background of the 1902 Taft Mission to Rome." In *36 Cath. Hist. Rev.* 1 (1950). Chile and Argentina, in the early 1980's, made one of the most recent requests for the Holy

Pope Leo XIII, without the benefit of a territorial sovereignty, explained the Holy See's international personality and its status as a subject of international law. As he stated,

> "It cannot be called in question that in the making of treaties, in the transaction of business matters, in the sending and receiving ambassadors, and in the interchange of other kinds of official dealings [temporal rulers] have been wont to treat the Church as with a supreme and legitimate power. And assuredly, all ought to hold that it was not without a singular disposition of God's providence that this power of the Church was provided with a civil sovereignty as the surest safeguard of her independence."[27]

Thus, popes of the modern age have understood that peace in the world must be established upon justice on both domestic and international levels. Leo XIII reiterated this principle in his encyclical *Rerum Novarum*.[28] Without criticizing or condemning any particular form of temporal government,[29] he made the moral argument that the mutual goal of every political structure is to foster the common good.[30]

While it was not concerned about purely temporal matters,[31] the Holy See has continued to view itself as an essential participant in inter-

---

See to resolve a boundary dispute between them. I will discuss this situation in greater detail during the discussion on treaties.

27 *Imortale Dei*, at N. 12.

28 See *Rerum Novarum* [On the Condition of Workers], promulgated on May 15, 1891. Succeeding popes, such as Pius XI recalled and renewed this encyclical in *Quadragesimo Anno* [On Social Reconstruction], promulgated on May 15, 1931; Paul VI in his Apostolic Letter *Octogesima Adveniens*, promulgated on May 14, 1971; and John Paul II in his encyclical *Centesimus Annus* promulgated on May 1, 1991. Each statement called attention to the domestic and international consequences of failing to respond to the needs of people and to advance the common good.

29 See *Immortale Dei*, promulgated on November 1, 1885, at N. 36.

30 See id. at N. 18. Philip Hughes notes that Leo "understood that, to save the world, the Church must consent to remain in the world, to make all possible contacts with the world, and to explain itself to the world in the only language that the world now understood." Hughes, "The International Action of the Papacy: The New Papacy—1878–1940." In *The Tablet* (November 23, 1940): 406. The social teachings of the Church and in the pronouncements of the Holy See frequently confront the theme of common good. See generally Jacques Maritain, *The Person and the Common Good* (1948).

31 See also Robert A. Graham, S.J., "The Vatican in World Diplomacy: France." In *America* (November 10, 1951): 149 (discussing the "unique blend" of the temporal sovereignty and religious and moral authority of the Holy See in the context of restoring diplomatic relations with France).

national discussions and actions concerning peace in the world.[32] This became evident during the rising tensions in Europe in the early twentieth century that were the harbingers of World War I. Pius X sent a letter concerning world peace to the Holy See's Apostolic Delegate in the United States, which quickly came to the attention of both the secular and the religious worlds. His letter received a most favorable review in an editorial comment that appeared in the reputed American Journal of International Law.[33] In his message, the Pope expressed his concern about growing global tensions, and he did not restrict himself to the emerging conflict within Europe. Following in the footsteps of his remote predecessor, Paul III of the sixteenth century, Pius X issued an encyclical exhorting Latin Americans to act more justly in the social and economic spheres, especially with regard to native peoples.[34] He also addressed the outrageous practice of trafficking women and children for pecuniary benefit.[35] He further noted that Christian charity required Catholics to "hold all men, without distinction of nation or color, as true brethren ... [T]his charity must be made manifest not so much by words as by deeds."[36]

The papacy of Benedict XV was immersed in the events of World War I and its aftermath. Prior to the outbreak of the armed conflict, he eloquently and indefatigably counseled the parties against going to

---

32 See, e.g., Editorial Comments, "The British Mission to the Vatican." In *9 Am. J. Intl. L.* (1915): 206, 208. The author states: "In a material world we are over inclined to underestimate the force of spiritual power and of spiritual agencies . . . . [T]he spiritual power of the Pope stands out in broad relief untrammeled and unspotted by temporal connections, and there is reason to believe that the Pope as the spiritual head of the Church can exercise a greater and a more beneficent influence in the world at large in the future than in the past." Id. at 208.

33 See Editorial Comment, "The Pontifical Letter of June 11, 1911, on International Peace." In *5 Am. J. Int'l. L.* (1911): 707, 708.

34 See *Lacrimabili Statu* [On the Indians of South America], promulgated on June 7, 1912.

35 See id. at N. 2. The Second Vatican Council reiterated this concern among with many others. See *Pastoral Constitution on the Church in the Modern World* In *The Documents of Vatican II*, 199, 226 (*Gaudium et Spes*) (stating in pertinent part, "whatever insults human dignity, such as . . . the selling of women and children"). Interestingly, many years later the drafters of the Statute for the International Criminal Court, acknowledged these concerns as crimes against humanity. *See* Statute of the International Criminal Court, Article 7.1(c) (noting that Article 7.2(c), which deals with crime against humanity specifically addresses enslavement, trafficking in persons, particularly women and children).

36 *Gaudium et Spes,* at N. 5.

war.[37] At the conclusion of the First World War, Pope Benedict initiated concrete actions to bring relief to the victims of the war's devastation especially highlighting the plight of children.[38] Moreover, he sought means for esstablishing permanent peace and devised measures necessary to implement this peace. In this effort, he issued two encyclicals on these issues. The first exhorted the worldwide community to participate in an international conference that would guarantee peace.[39] The second called all individuals to practice forgiveness and reconciliation.[40] It also urged all States to put aside mutual suspicion and unite in one league or a family of peoples "calculated both to maintain their own independence and safeguard the order of human society."[41] States, through the establishment of an "association of nations," could:

> abolish or reduce the enormous burden of the military expenditure which [they] can no longer bear, in order to prevent these disastrous wars or at least to remove the danger of them as far as possible. So would each nation be assured not only of its independence but also of the integrity of its territory within its just frontiers.[42]

He thus demonstrated his interest in a universal international organization dedicated to establishing and maintaining world peace. Benedict also encouraged other world leaders to join the Holy See in providing humanitarian aid to the many innocents victimized by the war.[43] His understanding of the importance of diplomatic relations and its contribution toward world peace enabled him to increase the number of diplomatic exchanges by the Holy See from fourteen to twenty-six during his Pontificate.[44]

At the League of Nations Conference, states such as Germany wanted the Holy See to be present to assist in resolving some of their disputes. Italy, however, objected—most likely on the grounds that papal participa-

---

37 See, e. g., *Ad Beatissimi Apostolorum* [Appealing for Peace], promulgated on November 1, 1914.

38 See, e. g., *Paterno Iam Diu* [On the Children of Central Europe], promulgated on November 24, 1919.

39 See *Quod Iam Diu* [On the Future Peace Conference], promulgated on December 1, 1918.

40 See *Pacem, Dei Munus Pulcherrimum* [Peace, the Beautiful Gift of God], promulgated on May 23, 1920, NN. 8 and 14.

41 Id. at N. 17.

42 Id.

43 See Eckhardt, supra note 1, at 260–261.

44 See 2 *New Catholic Encyclopedia* 280 (1967).

tion would create an international status for the Holy See, which the Italian government was not yet prepared to confer.[45] However, Italian efforts to ignore the Holy See's international personality and important role in peacemaking did not interfere with its contributions to the causes of international and domestic peace and justice.

Some of the most important aspects of the Holy See's international peace efforts during the twentieth century involved the intense undertakings of Pius XI and Pius XII to avoid the Second World War and the Holocaust.[46] Shortly after he was installed as Pope in 1922, Pius XI noted in his encyclical *Ubi Arcano Dei Consilio* that individuals, classes of societies, and the nations of the world had not found "true peace" since the close of World War I.[47] This encyclical elaborated on and warned about continuing tensions that endangered global and regional stability and a just peace. This exercise of sovereignty allowed Pius XI to encourage nations to avoid the type of ardent nationalism that insulates one group of people from others.[48] This encyclical also presented Pius XI's unswayable goals of avoiding war and maintaining peace. As time passed, Pius XI recognized that not all temporal leaders—particularly the German and Italian leaders—had accepted the wisdom of his moral teaching, which contained essential elements for global justice and peace.[49]

In two extraordinary measures, this pope addressed two subsequent encyclicals to Italy and Germany because he perceived correctly that their actions threatened peace in the world and violated the rule of law. In *Non Abbiamo Bisogno*, Pius spoke out against two matters: (1) the restrictions that Fascist Italy had imposed on Italy's flourishing Christian political and social movements, and (2) the attacks on the Church,

---

45 See Cardinale, supra note 1, at 88.
46 See Anthony Rhodes, *The Vatican in the Age of Dictators: 1922–1945* (1973) (investigating how the Holy See dealt with the totalitarian States during the first half of the Twentieth Century).
47 See *Ubi Arcano Dei Consilio*, promulgated on December 23, 1922, at N. 7.
48 See id. at N. 25.
49 See Christopher Dawson, "Religion and the Totalitarian State." In *14 Criterion* 1, (1934). The author concludes with the reflection: "The Church exists to be the light of the world . . . A secularist culture can only exist . . . in the dark. It is a prison in which the human spirit confines itself when it is shut out of the wider world of reality." Id. at 16; see also Douglas L. Reed, "The German Church Conflict." In 13 *Foreign Aff.* 483 (1935).

clergy, and faithful.[50] As the Pope publicly raised his concerns, he also judiciously noted that his voice and the moral and sovereign authority for which it spoke transcend "all party politics."[51]

Several years later, the emerging and horrifying developments in Germany compelled Pius XI to promulgate his encyclical *Mit Brennender Sorge*.[52] The publication of this encyclical in Germany proved to be difficult and entailed great risk that produced devastating consequences, which the National Socialists realized countered their immediate interests.[53] This encyclical catalogued the general abuses of the Third Reich,[54] the threats to religious freedom,[55] and the persecution of certain groups of people such as the members of the Jewish faith.[56] The pope's simple, but unmistakable references to the Old Testament and the "so-called myth of race and blood" called attention to the plight of the Jewish people.[57]

On the eve of the Second World War, Pope Pius XII inherited the challenges of global and regional unrest that faced his immediate predecessor.[58] Within several months of his papal election of March 2, 1939, he issued his first encyclical letter, *Summi Pontificatus*. In it he acknowledged the need to address the growing military tension that was beginning to consume Europe and much of the rest of the world.[59] The pope considered the mounting hostilities between Germany and Poland,[60] and noted that the underlying cause of evil in the world, and in Europe, included "the denial and rejection of a universal norm of morality as well for individuals as for international relations."[61] He pointed out

---

50 See *Non Abbiamo Bisogno*, promulgated on June 29, 1931. Professor Binchy offers one of the most detailed studies of the relationship between Fascism and the Holy See. See generally D. A. Binchy, *Church and State in Fascist Italy* (1941).

51 *Non Abbiano Bisogno*, promulgated on June 29, 1931, N. 22.

52 See *Mit Brennender Sorge* [On the Church and the German Reich], promulgated on March 14, 1937.

53 See *Church and State*, supra note 1, at 518–519.

54 See *Mit Brennender Sorge*, Nos. 5–6. For background on this point, see Charles Pichon, *The Vatican in World Affairs* (Dutton: 1950), 145.

55 See id.

56 See id. at NN. 8, 10, 23.

57 See id. at NN. 15, 16, 17, 23.

58 See generally Gwynn.

59 *On the Unity of Human Society*, promulgated on October 20, 1939.

60 See *Summi Pontificatus*, at N. 22.

61 Id. at N. 28. The Pope spoke diplomatically when he addressed the evils of National Socialism as "signs of a corrupt and corrupting paganism." Id. at N. 30.

two "pernicious errors" that played a part in corrupting Germany. The first was the betrayal of the "law of human solidarity and charity which is dictated and imposed by our common origin and by the equality or rational nature in all men."[62] The second error that surfaced in Germany incorporated "those ideas which do not hesitate to divorce civil authority from every kind of dependence upon the Supreme Being ... and from every restraint of a Higher Law derived from God."[63] The Pope cautiously but distinctly highlighted the grave dangers posed by National Socialism which elevated the state as "the last end of life."[64] He further noted that states must "control, aid and direct the private and individual activities of national life [so] that they converge harmoniously towards the common good."[65] The pope further argued that German policies that considered "the State as something ultimate to which everything else should be subordinated and directed" threatened the international prosperity of all persons, especially those in Europe.[66] If one state were to control others, the mutual independence of all peoples who are "bound together by reciprocal ties ... into a great commonwealth directed to the good of all nations" would decay.[67]

Further, the Pope lamented over the number of people abandoning the teachings of Christ and "being led astray by a mirage of glittering phrases" who failed to foresee the consequences of "bartering the truth that sets free, for error which enslaves." Id. at N. 31.

62 Id. at N. 35. The Pope elaborated on the meaning of our "common origin" when he quoted from St. Paul's letter to the Colossians, which asserted that, "there is neither Gentile nor Jew, circumcision nor uncircumcision, barbarian nor Scythian, bond nor free." Id. at N. 48; Colossians 3:10–11.

63 *Summi Pontificatus*, at N. 52 (describing how a State may attribute to itself the power that belongs to God and how this practice grates the Christian conscience).

64 Id. at N. 53.

65 Id. at N. 59. He also suggested that the common good "can neither be defined according to arbitrary ideas nor can it accept for its standard primarily the material prosperity of society, but rather it should be defined according to the harmonious development and the natural perfection of man." Id.

66 Id. at N. 60.

67 Id. at N. 72. As one trained in the law, Pope Pius XII understood the principles of international natural law as those that "regulate [peoples'] normal development and activity" and "demand respect for corresponding rights to independence, to life and to the possibility of continuous development in the paths of civilization." Id. at N. 74. In fact, they require "fidelity to compacts agreed upon and sanctioned in conformity with the principles of the law of nations." Id. at N. 74. Pius envisioned the Church's role in this struggle as one that would inform consciences so: "that the truth which she preaches, the charity which she teaches

Throughout his pontificate, Pius XII issued the annual Christmas messages on the state of the world and the presence or absence of the spirit of the Prince of Peace. He issued one of his most significant Christmas messages in 1941, in which he called attention to Europe's plight and spoke against "oppression of minorities"—a carefully worded and discrete, but still obvious reference to the Jewish people.[68] At the time, the Western press saluted this bold initiative and Pius XII for placing "himself squarely against Hitlerism."[69] In subsequent Christmas messages, Pope Pius delivered equally blunt words about those responsible for the suffering of millions of the Second World War's innocent victims.[70] He prudently maintained neutrality once hostilities commenced, but his prudence did not signify that the Holy See would be neutral on the moral issues surrounding this conflict that was to unsettle the world for many years.[71] The influential press repeatedly acknowledged

---

    and practices, will be the indispensable counselors and aids to men of good will in the reconstruction of a new world based on justice and love, when mankind, weary from its course along the way of error, has tasted the bitter fruits of hate and violence." Id. at N. 108.

68 See "Pope Broadcasts Five Peace Points: Condemns Aggression, Curbs on Minorities, Total War and Persecutions." In *N.Y. Times* (Dec. 25, 1941): 1 [hereinafter *Pope Broadcasts Five Peace Points*]. The publishers, in that same edition, stated that, "[t]he voice of Pius XII is a lonely voice in the silence and darkness enveloping Europe this Christmas." Id. at 24. Further, this editorial acknowledged that the Pope's words "sound[ed] strange and bold in . . . Europe . . ., and we comprehend the complete submergence and enslavement of great nations, the very sources of our civilization, as we realize that *he is about the only ruler left on the Continent of Europe* who dares to raise his voice at all." Id. (emphasis added).

69 See "Pope Broadcasts Five Peace Points." supra note 68, at 24. This editorial concluded by noting that the Pope "left no doubt that the Nazi aims are also irreconcilable with his own conception of a Christian peace. 'The new order which must arise out of this war,' [the Pope] asserted, 'must be based on moral principles,' and that implies only one end to the war." Id.

70 See, e. g., Pius XII, "Christmas Message (1942)." In *Papal Pronouncements on the Political Order* 209 (Francis J. Powers, C.S.V. ed. 1952). The Pope declared that while the Church did not intend to take sides during the conflict, it "cannot renounce her right to proclaim to her sons and to the whole world the unchanging basic laws, saving them from every perversion, frustration, corruption, false interpretation and error." Id.

71 See id. On Christmas Day 1942, the Pope said that the Church "does not intend to take sides for any of the particular forms in which the several peoples and States strive to solve the gigantic problems of domestic order or international collaborations, as long as these forms conform to the law of God." Id.

the Pope's public efforts to assist the victims of the atrocities of National Socialism, including the Jewish people.[72] Shortly after the conclusion of hostilities, the Pope wasted no time to muster the world's attention to the plight of destitute children victimized by the war.[73] He reminded all people of good will that "these children will be pillars of the next generation and … it is essential that they grow up healthy in mind and body if we are to avoid a race infected with sickness and vice."[74]

Pope John XXIII, was no stranger to the world of international affairs since he served as a papal diplomat for many years.[75] He dealt with the Cold War among the nuclear powers, and pleaded for peace and international security of the human family in his 1963 encyclical *Pacem in Terris*.[76] This important declaration about the common good for all humanity drew attention to the interrelated rights and responsibilities of individuals and nations.[77] He noted, as his immediate predecessor, Pius XII, did

---

72 See, e.g., "Pope Is Said to Plead for Jews Listed for Removal from France." In *N.Y. Times* (Aug. 6, 1942): 1; "Vichy Seizes Jews; Pope Pius Ignored." In *N.Y. Times* (Aug. 27, 1942): 1, 3; "Pope Said to Help In Ransoming Jews." In *N.Y Times* (Oct. 17, 1943): 1; "Vatican Scores Germans: Denounces Decision to Intern and Strip All Jews in Italy." In *N.Y. Times* (Dec. 5, 1943): 3. Some 55 years later, however, *The New York Times* printed an editorial, which commented: "John Paul, however, has resisted a critical look at the Catholic response to the Holocaust and has defended the silence of Pope Pius XII during the Third Reich . . . . The document does not even mention Pope Pius's failure to speak out against Nazi atrocities . . . . It now falls to John Paul and his successors to take the next step toward full acceptance of the Vatican's failure to stand squarely against the evil that swept across Europe." "Editorial, The Vatican's Holocaust Report." In *N.Y. Times* (March 18, 1998): A20. Perhaps those responsible for drafting this editorial lacked familiarity with the newspaper's earlier editorials, which reported Pope Pius XII neither remained silent nor failed to stand against Nazi atrocities. For detailed discussions of Pope Pius XII's role during the Holocaust, see Pierre Blet, S.J., Pius XII and the Second World War (Lawrence J. Johnson trans., 1999); Saul Friedländer, Pius XII and the Third Reich: A Documentation (Charles Fullman trans., 1966), which relies principally upon German sources of the era; Pinchas Lapide, *Three Popes and the Jews* (1967); and Ronald J. Rychlak, *Hitler, the War and the Pope* (2000).
73 See *Quemadmodum*, promulgated on January 6, 1946.
74 Id. at N. 6.
75 See Kelly, supra note 6, at 320–321.
76 See *Pacem in Terris*, promulgated on April 11, 1963.
77 In his earlier encyclical *Mater et Magistra* [Mother and Teacher], the Pope stated that: "As regards the common good of human society as a whole, the following conditions should be fulfilled: that the competitive striving of peoples to increase output be free of bad faith; that harmony in economic affairs and a friendly and

on many occasions, the need for a "public authority"[78] that could address the need for and achieve those policies and attitudes essential to securing the universal common good.[79] It is clear that John XXIII acknowledged the existence of the United Nations, but he did not equate the organization with the public authority of which he spoke and for which he hoped. As he said,

> this general authority equipped with world-wide power and adequate means for achieving the universal common good cannot be imposed by force. It must be set up with the consent of all nations. If its work is to be effective, it must operate with fairness, absolute impartiality, and with dedication to the common good of all peoples. The forcible imposition by the more powerful nations of a universal authority of this kind would inevitably arouse fears of its being used as an instrument to serve the interests of the few or to take the side of a single nation, and thus the influence and effectiveness of its activity would be undermined. For even though nations may differ widely in material progress and military strength, they are very sensitive as regards their juridical equality and the excellence of their own way of life. They are right, therefore, in their reluctance to submit to an authority imposed by force, established without their co-operation, or not accepted of their own accord.[80]

Thus, John XXIII acknowledged the United Nations, while an important institution offering promise to the world, was not the general or public authority that he had in mind. This does not, of course, preclude the possibility that reform of this important institution could take stock of the essential criteria spelled out by the pope so that it could become the public authority he envisioned.

Nevertheless, other important elements of *Pacem in Terris* acknowledged the role of the United Nations in achieving the common good for all peoples.[81] The Holy See's particular role "safeguarded the principles of ethics and religion, but also ... intervene[d] authoritatively with Her children in the temporal sphere, when there is a question of judging the application of [principles of the natural law] to concrete cases."[82] This

---

beneficial cooperation be fostered; and, finally, that effective aid be given in developing the economically underdeveloped nations." Pope John, *Mater et Magistra* [Mother and Teacher], promulgated on May 15, 1961, at N. 80.

78 See, e.g., *Christmas Message of 1944*, NN. 55–56, 62–64.

79 *Pacem in Terris*, N. 137.

80 Id., N. 138.

81 Id, NN. 142–145.

82 Id. at 160. Pope John called attention to the encyclicals of his predecessors Leo XIII [*Immortale Dei*] and Pius XI [*Ubi Arcano*], which were discussed earlier.

declaration restrictively interpreted Article 24 of the Lateran Treaty, which suggested that the Holy See would not involve itself in the affairs of the temporal world.[83] Legal commentary, however, has noted that this article of the Lateran Treaty has not prevented the Holy See from speaking out on right and wrong in the realm of international affairs—especially in times of armed conflict.[84] This was evident when Paul VI spoke out about the horrors of the Viet Nam conflict and John Paul II addressed the pressing need for peace in the Balkans and the Gulf.

Pope John's immediate successor, Pope Paul VI, left the Vatican, in October 1965, to proclaim this message before the United Nations. In the first papal address made before the General Assembly, he commented on his role and the presence of the Holy See in the world community. The Pope humbly chose to use the third person singular at one point when he declared before the General Assembly,

> He is your brother, and even one of the least among you, representing as you do sovereign States, for he is vested—if it please you so to think of Us—with only a mute and quasi-symbolic temporal sovereignty, only so much as is needed to leave him free to exercise his spiritual mission and to assure all those who treat with him that he is independent of every worldly sovereignty. He has no temporal power, no ambition to compete with you. In point of fact, We have nothing to ask for, no question to raise; at most a wish to express and a permission to request: to serve you, within Our competence, disinterestedly, humbly and in love ... Whatever your opinion of the Roman Pontiff, you know Our mission: We are the bearer of a message for all mankind.[85]

---

83 Article 24 of the Lateran Treaty states: "The Holy See in relation to the sovereignty it possesses also in the international sphere, declares that it wishes to remain and will remain extraneous to all temporal disputes between States and to international congresses held for such objects, unless the contending parties make concordant appeal to its mission of peace; at the same time reserving the right to exercise its moral and spiritual power. In consequence of this declaration, Vatican City will always and in every case be considered neutral and inviolable territory."

84 See Marjorie M. Whiteman, *1 Digest of International Law* 591 (1963).

85 *Address of Pope Paul VI to the United Nations*, Oct. 4, 1965. The Pope continued by saying that: "We have been carrying in Our heart for nearly twenty centuries [a wish]. We have been on the way for a long time and We bear with Us a long history; here We celebrate the end of a laborious pilgrimage in search of a colloquy with the whole world, a pilgrimage which began when We were given the command: 'Go and bring the good news to all nations.' And it is you who represent all nations." Id. Pope Paul noted that the Holy See's position as an "expert in humanity" provided the foundation for the "moral and solemn ratification" of the UN. Id. The Pope's UN address reflected the Pastoral Constitution on the

In essence, Pope Paul's address delivered a message of peace to the whole world and spoke on the obvious issues as well as the subtle.[86] His message also offered hope to a world filled with human-generated misery. One year earlier in 1964, Pope Paul sent an Observer of the Holy See to the United Nations. The Holy See's "supra-national" voice finally became a formal part of the global dialogue in the UN deliberations affecting peace and the common good.[87]Almost four years after his UN address, Paul VI detailed the Holy See's role in the international order. He did so when he promulgated his apostolic letter on the duties of papal representatives sent into the world of diplomacy to secure peace amongst the nations.[88] The major purpose for continuing the practice of active and passive diplomatic exchange embraced an open dialogue on the "good of the individual and of the community of peoples."[89]

Church in the Modern World [*Gaudium et Spes*], which was to be promulgated at the end of the Second Vatican Council on December 7, 1965. While noting that Christ did not give the Church a "proper mission in the political, economic or social order," the Pastoral Constitution also acknowledged that the Church functioned as "a light and energy which can serve to structure and consolidate the human community. As a matter of fact, when circumstances of time and place create the need, she can and indeed should initiate activities on behalf of all men." *Gaudium et Spes*, at N. 42.

86 For example, Pope Paul eloquently pronounced the need to end armed conflict once and for all when he declared: "never again one against another, never, never again! Is it not to this end above all that the United Nations was born: against war and for peace? . . . . Never again war, war never again! Peace, it is peace, which must guard the destiny of the peoples and of all mankind." The Times [London], in another editorial, remarked that the Pope's "noble address . . . has brought the United Nations face to face with its charter, and so, collectively and individually, with its conscience." "Editorial, To the World." In *The Times* (Oct. 5, 1965).

87 See Cardinale, supra note 1, at 93–94.

88 See *Sollicitudo Omnium Ecclesiarum*, promulgated on June 24, 1969, reprinted in Cardinale, supra note 1, at 309–318.

89 Id. at 312. Pope Paul also observed that: "[W]hile this dialogue aims at guaranteeing for the Church free exercise of its activity so that it may be able to fulfill the mission entrusted to it by God, it ensures the civil authority of the always peaceful and beneficial aims pursued by the Church, and offers the precious aid of its spiritual energies and of its organisation for the achievement of the common good of society. *The trusting colloquy which thus begins when there exists between the two societies and official relationship sanctioned by the body of habits and customs collected and codified in international law makes it possible to establish a fruitful understanding and to organise an activity truly salutary for all.*" Id. (emphasis added)

A month-long papacy failed to give Paul VI's immediate successor, John Paul I, much time to define or to implement the Holy See's sovereignty or to exercise its international personality. Still, in an address to the diplomatic corps accredited to the Holy See, he provided some insight on the Holy See's role in world affairs. The pope commented on the uniqueness of the Holy See's mission and its competence as an international person.[90] He also identified two services that the exchange of legations with the Holy See could accomplish. First of all, diplomatic exchanges provided a standing mechanism for seeking better solutions to contemporary world issues including détente, disarmament, peace, justice, humanitarian measures and aid, and development.[91] He stated that the second service helps develop the consciences of people "regarding the fundamental principles that guarantee authentic civilization and real brotherhood between peoples. These principles ... help peoples and the international community to ensure more effectively the conditions for the common good."[92]

John Paul II was no stranger to exercising sovereignty and the Holy See's international personality in the world. He first visited the United Nations on October 2, 1979, when he addressed the General Assembly as his predecessor, Paul VI, had done. On June 7, 1982 he sent a message to the General Assembly stressing the immediate need to concentrate on the interrelation of peace and disarmament.[93] His second personal appearance before the General Assembly occurred on the thirtieth anniversary of Paul VI's October 4, 1965 visit to the UN. The 1995 address fo-

---

90 See *Pope John Paul: Purposes of Vatican Diplomacy*, Origins (Sept. 14, 1978): 198. The Holy Father elaborated: "Obviously we have no temporal goods to exchange, no economic interests to discuss, such as your States have. Our possibilities for diplomatic interventions are limited and of a special character. They do not interfere with purely temporal, technical and political affairs, which are matters for your governments. In this way, our diplomatic missions to your highest civil authorities, far from being a survival from the past, are a witness to our deep-seated respect for lawful temporal power, and to our lively interest in the humane causes that the temporal power is intended to advance . . . . On both sides there is presence, respect, exchange and collaboration, without confusing competences." Id.

91 See id. at 198.

92 See id. at 199.

93 See John Paul II, *Message to the General Assembly of the United Nations* (June 7, 1982), reprinted in *Origins* (June 24, 1982): 81. The Pope used moral arguments when he noted that the production and possession of both nuclear and conventional arms reflected "an ethical crisis gnawing into society in all directions, political, social and economic. Peace . . . is the result of respect for ethical principles." Id. at 86.

cused on universal human rights, the rights of nations, and the search for freedom and moral truth.[94] John Paul II followed his predecessors lead when he noted that he spoke "not as one who exercises temporal power ... nor as a religious leader seeking special privileges ... [but] as a witness ... to human dignity, a witness to hope, a witness to the conviction that the destiny of all nations lies in the hands of a merciful Providence."[95]

John Paul II frequently participated in international dialogue and diplomatic conversation across the globe. Throughout his pontificate, he followed the practice initiated by Pope Paul VI and has issued a World Day of Peace Message on the first of the New Year. Shortly after New Year's Day every year, he would convene the Diplomatic Corps accredited to the Holy See for discussions on contemporary issues of international concern. In his May, 2000 address to the ambassador from New Zealand, the Pope commented that the Holy See's position enables it to share with other sovereigns its unique perspective on international issues such as the dignity of the human person, the notion of a freedom that is linked to truth, and the pursuit of the common good.[96] The Pope greeted the ambassador from Kuwait by expressing his hope for peace in the Middle East and stressing the need for dialogue between Muslims and Christians to encourage harmony and a lasting peace.[97] John Paul II commented to the ambassador from Greece that the supra-national interests of the Holy See enable it to focus on the "loving concern for the common good of all peoples and nations." The Holy See's diplomatic efforts seek to help others embrace the dignity and inalienable

---

94 See John Paul II, "Address of His Holiness Pope John Paul II to the Fiftieth General Assembly of the United Nations Organization." (Oct. 5, 1995), reprinted in *Origins* (Oct. 19, 1995): 293.

95 See "The Fabric of Relations Among Peoples.", reprinted in 25 *Origins* (Oct. 19, 1995):1, 299; see also *Lateran Treaty*, art. 24, supra note 83 (demonstrating that Popes did not consider themselves prohibited from participating in discussions regarding important international issues).

96 See John Paul II, "Address of the Holy Father to the New Ambassador of New Zealand to the Holy See." (May 25, 2000), reprinted in *L'Osservatore Romano* (May 31, 2000): 5.

97 See John Paul II, "Address of the Holy Father to the New Ambassador of Kuwait to the Holy See." (May 25, 2000); see also Alessandra Stanley, "Pope Arrives in Israel and Gets Taste of Mideast." In *N.Y Times* (March 22, 2000): at A8 (detailing the Pope's trip to the Middle East, which focused on reconciling Israel-Palestinian relations).

rights of every individual, "especially the weakest and most vulnerable."[98] With these numerous and frequent diplomatic encounters, it is understandable why the number of the Holy See's diplomatic exchanges has grown from 86 in 1979 (the first full year of John Paul II's pontificate) to one hundred and seventy-seven in 2010.[99] In this outreach to the nations of the world, many of the newer diplomatic exchanges involve states that are neither traditionally Catholic nor Christian.[100]

Here one must consider the address given by Pope Benedict XVI to the General Assembly of the United Nations on April 18, 2008, in which he dwelt at length on the "responsibility to protect"—the primary duty of every state to protect its own population.[101] The responsibility to protect is a new idea that is finding its way into international legal discussions. If a state is incapable or unwilling to respond in the affirmative to this duty, then the obligation is transferred to the international community via juridical means, as the pope noted.[102] But the question remains, what happens if the international community is also incapable of responding in a timely manner to some humanitarian crisis? What then? These situations generate the need to pause and consider whether the use of force may be required to contend with a human agent that threatens the security and peace of innocents. As His Holiness suggested, it is indifference or failure to intervene that can compromise their safety, and this is where "real damage" follows.[103] What is needed in these circumstances is a deeper search for ways of pre-empting and managing conflicts by exploring

---

98 John Paul II, "Address of the Holy Father to the New Ambassador of the Hellenic Republic to the Holy See." (May 6, 2000), reprinted in *L'Osservatore Romano* (May 31, 2000): 6.

99 See *Annuario Pontificio 1110–1150* (1979); see also http://www.vatican.va/roman_curia/...0010123_holy-see-relations_en.html. The Holy See has diplomatic relations with the European Union and the Sovereign Order of Malta; it also has relations of a special nature with the Russian Federation and with the Palestine Liberation Organization. Id.

100 *Annuario Pontificio 1398–1457* (2000). These States include most of the traditionally non-Catholic and non-Christian States of the world. In addition, States with traditional ties to Islam or connections with various types of Eastern religions also participated in these diplomatic exchanges. See generally George Huntston Williams, "John Paul II's Relations with Non-Catholic States and Current Political Movements." In *25 J. Church & State* 13 (1983).

101 Address of Benedict XVI to the General Assembly of the United Nations (April 18, 2008).

102 Id.

103 Id.

every possible diplomatic avenue, and giving attention and encourage-
ment to even the faintest sign of dialogue or desire for reconciliation.[104]

104 In his intervention during the General Debate of the General Assembly on Sep-
     tember 29, 2008, Archbishop Celestino Migliore, the Permanent Observer of the
     Holy See to the United Nations, had these further thoughts on the matter of the
     "responsibility to protect": 'For his part, Pope Benedict XVI, in his address to the
     General Assembly of the United Nations last April, also recognized that from the
     very ancient philosophical discourses on governance to the more modern devel-
     opment of the nation-state, the responsibility to protect has served and must con-
     tinue to serve as the principle shared by all nations to govern their populations
     and regulate relations between peoples. These statements highlight the historical
     and moral basis for States to govern. Likewise, they reassert that good governance
     should no longer be measured simply within the context of "state's rights" or
     "sovereignty" but rather, by its ability to care for those who entrust leaders
     with the grave moral responsibility to lead. Despite the growing consensus be-
     hind the responsibility to protect as a means for greater cooperation, this princi-
     ple is still being invoked as a pretext for the arbitrary use of military might. This
     distortion is a continuation of past failed methods and ideas. The use of violence
     to resolve disagreements is always a failure of vision and a failure of humanity.
     The responsibility to protect should not be viewed merely in terms of military
     intervention but primarily as the need for the international community to
     come together in the face of crises to find means for fair and open negotiations,
     support the moral force of law and search for the common good. Failure to col-
     lectively come together to protect populations at risk and to prevent arbitrary
     military interventions would undermine the moral and practical authority of
     this Organization. The "we the peoples" who formed the United Nations con-
     ceived the responsibility to protect to serve as the core basis for the United Na-
     tions. The founding leaders believed that the responsibility to protect would con-
     sist not primarily in the use of force to restore peace and human rights, but above
     all, in States coming together to detect and denounce the early symptoms of every
     kind of crises and mobilize the attention of governments, civil society and public
     opinion to find the causes and offer solutions. The various agencies and bodies of
     the United Nations also reaffirm the importance of the responsibility to protect
     in their ability to work in close proximity and solidarity with affected populations
     and to put into place mechanisms of detection, implementation and monitor-
     ing." In his October 14, 2008 intervention at the 63rd Session of the UN General
     Assembly on "The Rule of Law at the National and International Levels," Arch-
     bishop Migliore further addressed the "responsibility to protect" in the context of
     the "rule of law" and had this to say: "The rule of law is a vital component for
     assisting States in their responsibility to protect. While this responsibility entails
     the States' primary and legal obligation to protect their populations from geno-
     cide, war crimes, ethnic cleansing and crimes against humanity, it also provides
     for the international community to intervene when a State is unable or unwilling
     to exercise this fundamental responsibility. This capacity to intervene should not
     be seen, however, only in the form of actions taken by the Security Council or use
     of force. It is also the cooperation of the international community to help States

Logic necessitates consideration of the use of force particularly in those instances where an aggressive agent relies on the slowness of diplomacy and negotiation to attack innocents. Indeed, there exist in the world today powerful entities for which diplomacy and juridical mechanisms mean little or nothing. Pope Benedict acknowledged that "natural reason [can be] abandoned" by those for whom peaceful resolution of disputes means little or nothing and, as a consequence, "freedom and human dignity [are] grossly violated."[105] In such cases, sovereign states with the international community must not stand by and allow the aggressor who abides not by the instruments of peace erase from the face of this earth the aggressors' victims.

In 2009, Pope Benedict continued his discussion of the role and need of international organizations. In his encyclical letter *Caritas in Veritate*,[106] the pope found it necessary to comment on the growing need of interdependency prompted by the global economic crisis for reform of the United Nations.[107] As the pope suggested considering the plight of the global community today, the concept of the family of nations needs "real teeth."[108] Another comment he made regarding the reform of the United Nations was in the context of a major theme of his April 2008 address to the General Assembly: the responsibility to protect. In this regard, the pope suggested that the kind of reform for the institution that he has in mind would facilitate the deliberations of the political, juridical, and economic order that would benefit "international coopera-

---

with the necessary capacity and legal expertise in the field of protection. The building up of national legal structures will help States to avert atrocities by establishing mechanisms that promote justice and peace, ensure accountability and recourse under the law, provide for the foundation of a stable economy and protect the dignity of every person... One area in which the United Nations serves as a forum for enhancing the rule of law is in the making of international treaties and conventions. Indeed, it has been the ability of the United Nations to bring people together and give greater attention to international norms. Hence, it is of great importance that when implementing and enforcing these norms, the United Nations' agencies and monitoring bodies respect the intent and desire of States. A treaty body system which moves away from the original intent of the parties and expands its mandates beyond the power given by States, risks undermining its own credibility and legitimacy and can discourage States from joining conventions."

105 Address of Benedict XVI to the General Assembly of the United Nations (April 18, 2008).
106 June 29, 2009.
107 *Caritas in Veritate*, N. 67.
108 Id.

tion for the development of all peoples in solidarity."[109] In relying on the Pastoral Constitution of the Church in the Modern World,[110] Pope Benedict exhorted that the reform he had in mind could facilitate the achievement of an international authority that could be universally recognized and vested with the effective power to ensure security for all, regard for justice, and respect for rights. Noting the importance of solidarity and the cooperation that entails by all, the pope cautioned that another important principle of Catholic social doctrine, i.e., subsidiarity, must not be forgotten.[111]

It should be apparent to the reader that the Holy See's traditional exercise of sovereignty, while diversified, frequently emphasizes matters concerning international peace, human dignity, human rights, the common good, and the rule of law—the law being the moral natural law and the law of nations (i.e., public international law). The Holy See actively participates with other sovereigns in negotiating and formulating international legal instruments that are the principal means for achieving specific goals relating to global affairs. The Holy See participates in the formation of bilateral and multilateral treaties and concordats, which amply demonstrate its involvement in peace, human dignity, and the common good into international affairs.

In the exercise of its international personality, the Holy See identifies itself as possessing an "exceptional nature within the community of nations; as a sovereign subject of international law, it has a mission of an essentially religious and moral order, universal in scope, which is based on minimal territorial dimensions guaranteeing a basis of autonomy for the pastoral ministry of the Sovereign Pontiff."[112] Yet, it would be mistak-

---

109 Id.
110 *Gaudium et Spes*, N. 82.
111 *Caritas in Veritate*, N. 67.
112 Malcolm Shaw, International Law 172 (Cambridge: 4th 1997), 172 (quoting the Joint 11th and 12th Reports to the United Nations Committee on the Elimination of Racial Discrimination, U.N. Doc. CERD/C/226/Add.6,(1993)); *accord* Summary Record of the 991st Meeting of the Committee on the Elimination of Racial Discrimination, U.N. Doc. CERD/C/SR.991 (1993). The Summary Record of the Committee states in part: "As the supreme governing body of the Catholic Church, the Holy See was recognized as a sovereign subject of international law. Its territory, the Vatican City State, was very small, its only function being to guarantee its independence and the free exercise of its religious, moral and pastoral mission. Its participation in international organizations, most notably the United Nations, and its accession to international conventions such as the Convention on the Elimination of All Forms of Racial Discrimination differed

en to conclude that the Holy See does not view itself having a role in the world of international order concerned with issues of peace, the common good, and the general welfare of all men, women, and children.[113] As the Second Vatican Council noted in the Pastoral Constitution on the Church in the Modern World, the Holy See "does not lodge its hope in privileges conferred by civil authority. Indeed, it stands ready to renounce the exercise of certain legitimately acquired rights if it becomes clear that their use raises doubt about the sincerity of its witness ..."[114] Nonetheless, the Council hastened to add that due to its teaching authority and moral vision for all people throughout the world, it is always and everywhere legitimate for her to preach the faith with true freedom, to teach her social doctrine, and to discharge her duty among men without hindrance. She also has the right

> "to pass moral judgments, *even on matters touching the political order*, whenever basic personal rights or the salvation of souls make such judgments necessary ... [h]olding faithfully to the gospel and exercising her mission in the world, the Church consolidates peace among men, to God's glory. For it is her task to uncover, cherish, and ennoble all that is true, good, and beautiful in the human community."[115]

The consequence of these diplomatic practices and the participation in international law and international organziations, which have spanned many centuries, is this: notwithstanding its status as a unique person

---

    profoundly from those of States which were communities in the political and temporal sense." Id. at N. 2.

113 See Kunz, "The Status of the Holy See in International Law.", supra note 18, at 310, where Mr. Kunz noted that, "The Holy See is . . . a *permanent* subject of *general* customary international law *vis-à-vis* all states, Catholic or not. That does not mean that the Holy See has the same international status as a sovereign state. But the Holy see has, under general international law, the capacity to conclude agreements with states . . . [be they concordats or general international treaties]." Id. (citations omitted).

114 *Gaudium et Spes*, supra note 35, at N. 76.

115 Id. (emphasis added). Toward the conclusion of the Pastoral Constitution, the Council stated that, "In pursuit of her divine mission, the Church preaches the gospel to all men and dispenses the treasures of grace. Thus, by imparting knowledge of the divine and natural law, she everywhere contributes to strengthening peace and to placing brotherly relations between individuals and peoples on solid ground. Therefore, to encourage and stimulate cooperation among men, *the Church must be thoroughly present in the midst of the community of nations.* She must achieve such a presence both through her public institutions and through the full and sincere collaboration of all Christians . . ." Id. at N. 89 (emphasis added).

in international law, the Holy See deals with virtually all other sovereign states in the world as a co-equal. The Holy See is respected by the international community of sovereign states and is treated as a subject of international law having the capacity to engage in diplomatic relations and to enter into binding agreements with one, several, or many states under international law. It is unequivocal that the sovereign states of the world have acknowledged that there is no impediment in the Holy See's unique status that would deprive it of the ability to exercise fully its membership in the community of sovereigns who are subjects of the law of nations. Its voice in this realm speaks not just for some, but for all of humanity in its quest for peace, justice, charity, freedom, and truth under the rule of law.

From an Ethics of War to an Ethics of Peacebuilding

Gerard F. Powers

Catholicism boasts a rich tradition of reflection on war and peace that is situated within an equally rich tradition of social teaching. But there is an underdeveloped aspect of this tradition: peacebuilding. This peacebuilding lacunae in Catholic teaching manifests itself in two ways. First, the connections between the Church's just war ethic and a peacebuilding ethic are often left unexamined. On the one hand, those who embrace a permissive interpretation of just war, such as George Weigel and Michael Novak, make the connection insofar as they view just war as an integral element of statecraft and building a just order. Yet they do not explore the connection in depth and they give scant attention to an ethics of peacebuilding. On the other hand, those who focus on an ethic of peacebuilding often reject the just war tradition altogether or, at least, want to "move beyond it." In this chapter, I make the case that the Church has embraced a restrictive, or strict, interpretation of just war which is incomprehensible apart from a peacebuilding ethic. A restrictive just war ethic and an ethic of peacebuilding are inherently complementary approaches that incorporate and depend upon each other. In fact, a restrictive just war analysis should be considered an important element of peacebuilding, a critical tool in conflict prevention, conflict management, and post-conflict reconstruction and reconciliation. Yet, without a broader peacebuilding ethic, even a restrictive just war analysis risks becoming a sort of procedural check-list unmoored from its deeper foundations in social ethics. Moreover, even properly grounded, the just war tradition simply does not address some of the most pressing issues of war and peace in the contemporary world.

The second dimension of the lacunae in Catholic teaching is that a peacebuilding ethic is relatively underdeveloped. Just as just war norms are often racing to keep pace with new technology and strategies of warfare, a peacebuilding ethic needs to catch up to the practice of peacebuilding. Since the end of the Cold War, peacebuilding has become a cottage industry among secular actors at all levels, from the UN Peacebuilding Commission to countless grassroots peacebuilding initiatives by non-governmental organizations (NGOs). Within the Catholic Church, as within other religious entities, there has been a proliferation of programs that consciously seek to nurture the kinds of peacebuilding activities in which the Church has long been involved. Sant'Egidio's peacebuilding work in Mozambique and elsewhere is a notable example. Less well known are the peacebuilding activities of Catholic Relief Services and other Caritas agencies which have developed well-funded, long-term peacebuilding programs.[1] While there is a growing literature on the spirituality, theology and ethics of peace and reconciliation, this literature is not nearly as well developed as the literature on the ethics of war and peace.[2] Moreover, this literature could benefit from a deeper dialogue with those involved in the praxis of peacebuilding.

---

1   For an overview of CRS peacebuilding, see William R. Headley and Reina C. Neufeldt, "Catholic Relief Services: Catholic Peacebuilding in Practice." In *Peacebuilding: Catholic Theology, Ethics and Praxis*, Robert Schreiter, Scott Appleby and G. Powers, eds. (New York: Orbis, 2010): 125–154; for case studies of CRS peacebuilding, see Mark M. Rogers, Tom Bamat and Julie Ideh, eds., *Pursuing Just Peace* (Baltimore: CRS, 2008); for an example of peacebuilding by Caritas Internationalis, see *Peacebuilding: A Caritas Training Manual* (The Vatican: Caritas Internationalis, 2002, 2006).

2   See, e. g., R. Scott Appleby, *The Ambivalence of the Sacred: Religion, Violence, and Reconciliation* (Lanham, MD: Rowman & Littlefield Publishers, 2000); Andrea Bartoli, "Christianity and Peacebuilding." In *Religion and Peacebuilding*, Harold Coward and Gordon Smith, eds. (Albany: State University of New York Press, 2004); Gregory Baum and Harold Wells, *The Reconciliation of Peoples: Challenge to the Churches* (Maryknoll: Orbis Books, 1997); William Bole, Drew Christiansen and Robert T. Hennemeyer, *Forgiveness in International Politics: An Alternative Road to Peace* (Washington, D.C.: United States Conference of Catholic Bishops, 2004); Daniel L. Buttry, *Christian Peacemaking* (Valley Forge: Judson Press, 1994); Mary Ann Cejka and Thomas Bamat, eds. *Artisans of Peace: Grassroots Peacemaking among Christian Communities* (Maryknoll, N.Y.: Orbis, 2003); Drew Christiansen, S.J., "Catholic Peacemaking, 1991–2005: The Legacy of Pope John Paul II." In *The Review of Faith and International Affairs* 4:2 (Fall 2006): 21–28; Mary Elsbernd, *A Theology of Peacemaking: A Vision, a Road, a Task* (Lanham, MD: University Press of America, 1989); German Bishops' Conference, *A Just Peace* (Bonn: Sekretariat der Deutschen Bischofskonferenz, 2000); Joseph Grassi, "Peace on Earth: Roots and Practices from Luke's Gospel." In *Catholic-Biblical-Quarterly* 67:1 (Jan. 2005): 147–148; James Heft, *Beyond Violence: Religious Sources of Social Transformation in Judaism, Christianity, and Islam* (New York: Fordham University Press, 2004); Raymond Helmick & Rodney Petersen, eds., *Forgiveness and Reconciliation: Religion, Public Policy, and Conflict Transformation*, (Radnor, Pennsylvania: Templeton Foundation Press, 2001); Maximiano Ngabirano, *Conflict and Peace Building: Theological and Ethical Foundations for a Political Reconstruction of the Great Lakes Region of Africa* (Kampala, Uganda: Uganda Martyrs University Book Series, 2010);

This article is divided into two main parts. The first and major part makes the case for the interdependence or complementarity of a restrictive just war and a peacebuilding ethic. Both share foundational principles of which I consider five: a cosmopolitan ethic, a positive conception of peace, solidarity, the importance of non-violence, and the role of the virtues. While permissive approaches to just war are rightly criticized for legitimizing war, a strict just war analysis is more appropriately seen as an essential aspect of peacebuilding insofar as it contributes to preventing war, limiting violence during war, and creating the conditions for post-war reconstruction and reconciliation. I conclude this section by showing how humanitarian intervention and the return of holy war illustrate the need for an ethic and praxis of peacebuilding to complement a restrictive just war ethic. In the second major part of this article, I suggest, by way of illustration, two "gaps" in Catholic teaching that should be filled by the further development of an ethic of peacebuilding. An ethic of self-determination is needed to prevent and/or resolve the many contemporary conflicts over secession and related issues. And further reflection is needed on what can be learned about conflict resolution and reconciliation from the Church's engagement with armed actors in places like Colombia.

This article is decidedly U.S.-centric. I was a senior advisor on war and peace to the U.S. Conference of Catholic Bishops (USCCB) for seventeen years, so it is what I know best. More important, the USCCB's statements on war and peace have been particularly influential over the past thirty years, not least because they have addressed military policies of the U.S. government that have had enormous consequences for the rest of the world.

Theodore Runyon, ed., *Theology, Politics, and Peace* (Maryknoll, NY: Orbis Books, 1989); Robert Schreiter, *The Ministry of Reconciliation: Spiritualities and Strategies* (Maryknoll, NY: Orbis Books, 1998); Donald Shriver, *An Ethic for Enemies: Forgiveness in Politics* (New York: Oxford University Press, 1995); Glen Stassen, *Just Peacemaking* (Westminister: John Knox Press, 1992); Charles Thomas Strauss, *Waging Peace in Sacred Space : a Comparative Study of Catholic Peacebuilding in South Africa, Zimbabwe and Mozambique, 1963–2003. Dissertation manuscript* 2004; Susan Thistlethwaite, ed., *A Just Peace Church* (New York: United Church Press, 1986).

1 The Complementarity of Just War and Peacebuilding

There is no single just war tradition or common understanding of what constitutes a just war. This paper uses what could be called the restrictive, or strict, interpretation of just war that is found in contemporary official Catholic teaching.[3] As with just war, there is no common understanding of what is meant by peacebuilding.[4] The UN, governments, and many scholars tend to define it as post-war efforts to institutionalize peace, especially after internal conflicts, with a primary focus on governments and public policies.[5] I use a broader definition of peacebuilding that covers the entire conflict cycle – before, during, and after war; that includes all kinds of armed conflicts, whether inter-state or intra-state; and that is concerned not just with avoiding the relapse into war in the "post-conflict" phase but also preventing the initial outbreak of war and mitigating violence and preventing its escalation during war. This broader understanding of peacebuilding focuses not just on the public policies, political

---

3   I rely especially on the U.S. bishops' 1983 pastoral, *The Challenge of Peace: God's Promise and Our Response*, their 1993 pastoral statement, *The Harvest of Justice Is Sown in Peace*, and recent papal teaching. For excellent assessments of recent papal teaching on war and peace that support this restrictive interpretation of just war, see Heinz-Gerhard Justenhoven, "The Peace Ethics of Pope John Paul II." In *University of St. Thomas Law Journal* 3:1 (Summer 2005): 110–138, and Drew Christiansen, S.J., "Catholic Peacemaking, 1991–2005: The Legacy of Pope John Paul II." In *The Review of Faith and International Affairs* 4:2 (Fall 2006): 21–28. The tension between papal teaching and neo-conservative support for a more permissive approach to just war is examined in Daniel McCarthy, "Bush vs. Benedict: Catholic neoconservatives grapple with their church's Just War tradition." In *The American Conservative* (August 29, 2005). Available at http://theamericanconservative.com/article/2005/aug/29/00011/.

4   For example, peacebuilding is used in a wide variety of ways by inter-governmental and governmental agencies, but is "generically understood as external interventions that are intended to reduce the risk that a state will erupt into or return to war." Michael Barnett, Hunjoon Kim, Madalene O'Donnell and Laura Sitea, "Peacebuilding: What Is in a Name?" In *Global Governance* 13 (2007): 37. In a widely-used typology of engagement in the conflict cycle, peacebuilding refers only to *post-conflict* rapprochement, reconstruction and reconciliation. See Michael S. Lund, "Conflict Prevention: Theory in Pursuit of Policy and Practice." In *The Sage Handbook of Conflict Resolution*, eds. J. Bercovitch, V. Kremenyuk, & I. W. Zartman (Los Angeles: Sage Publications, 2009): 290.

5   "Report of the Secretary-General on the work of the Organization." Supplement to an *Agenda for Peace:* Position Paper of the Secretary-General on the occasion of the fiftieth anniversary of the United Nations," A/50/60-S/1995/1, 3 January 1995.

institutions, and laws that are a major concern of some narrow approaches to peacebuilding (and much of Catholic social ethics), but also on a range of other actors, factors, and practices at all levels that are integral to healing broken societies and building and sustaining a just peace. Peacebuilding, therefore, involves a broad spectrum of tools, from mediation, demobilization and infrastructure development to constitutional reform, truth and reconciliation processes, trauma healing, and human rights advocacy.[6]

This definition of peacebuilding can be criticized as overbroad, essentially coterminous with Catholic social teaching writ large. For purposes of this article, it is not necessary to resolve such definitional issues. My principal argument is that there is an integral relationship between just war and the kinds of peace-promoting activities described variously as "peacebuilding," "peacemaking," "crisis diplomacy," "conflict prevention," and "reconciliation," and that there are gaps in Catholic social teaching that suggest the need for further development of an ethic to address these issues.

1.1 Foundational Ties that Bind

The starting point for discussing the relationship between just war and peacebuilding is to understand how they are situated within a wider Catholic social ethic. At a foundational level, what ties together a just war and a peacebuilding ethic is the fact that they are rooted in common theological and moral principles. Five aspects of Catholic social teaching are especially important: a cosmopolitan ethic, a positive conception of peace, solidarity, the importance of non-violence, and the role of virtues.

A Catholic ethic of just war and peacebuilding can only be understood in the context of a broader *cosmopolitan ethic* defined by the twin goals of protecting human dignity and promoting the common good. Several elements of this ethic are especially relevant. First, it is human-centric, not state-centric; states remain important, but the human person and the global human family are the ultimate objects of concern. Catholic social teaching is more compatible with conceptions of just war and

---

6   John Paul Lederach and R. Scott Appleby, "Strategic Peacebuilding: An Overview." In *Strategies of Peace*, eds D. Philpott and G. Powers (New York: Oxford, 2010): 19–44; Michael S. Lund, "A Toolbox for Responding to Conflicts and Building Peace." In *Peacebuilding: A Field Guide*, eds. L. Reychler and T. Paffenholz (Boulder: Lynne Rienner, 2001): 16–20.

peacebuilding aimed at protecting "human security" and the global common good than with narrower conceptions concerned mainly with "national security" and a nation's common good. Second, contra some realists, in Catholic social teaching, the "international community" is not an
oxymoron. Catholic social teaching is quite realistic about sin in the
world and the challenges involved in building up the international community. But it insists that it can and must be done. Development of a
cooperative security regime based in strengthened international norms
and institutions will reduce and eventually eliminate the occasions
when nations feel compelled to resort to force. It will also improve
their capacity to address global problems that even the most powerful nations cannot expect to solve on their own. Third, since greater power entails greater moral responsibility, nations like the United States have an
especially heavy moral responsibility for the global common good. Powerful nations must not misuse their power (sins of commission), nor must
they avoid failing to use their power to be peacebuilders (sins of omis-
sion). The U.S. bishops have repeatedly appealed to the just war tradition
to prevent the misuse of U.S. military power. They have also appealed to
a positive duty to be a peacebuilder, to use its influence to help resolve
conflicts, even where vital U.S. national interests are not at stake, and
to work with others to strengthen international norms and institutions.
Finally, the cosmopolitan perspective explains why, in certain circumstances, the Church believes international norms of state sovereignty and non-
intervention have to be reconsidered in light of claims of self-determination and duties of humanitarian intervention, even though those whose
moral prism is restricted to national interests can deride such claims as
dangerous and such duties as mere "social work."

A second element of Catholic social teaching – *a positive conception of
peace* – is obviously central to an understanding of just war and peacebuilding. Kenneth Himes describes three ways of talking of positive
peace in Catholic social teaching. The Shalom of Isaiah, where the
wolf and lamb lie down together (Isa. 11:6), is the eschatological meaning
of peace. The spiritual meaning of peace is the interior peace that comes
through communion with, and by being part of, the Body of Christ.
Tranquilitas ordinis is the political meaning of peace, the peace of a rightly
ordered political community, with people living in truth, charity, free-

dom, and justice directed toward the common good.[7] More specifically, political, peace consists of four primary components: (1) promotion and protection of human rights, (2) advancing integral human development, (3) supporting international law and international organizations, and (4) building solidarity between peoples and nations.[8] Drew Christiansen suggests that these somewhat disparate components are related "like a series of ships in a convoy" (a "convoy concept" of peace).[9]

This political peace is not merely a utopian ideal but something that is achievable in human history. The just war, therefore, is an interim ethic. As Pope Paul VI noted, moving beyond a state of affairs where war is a sad necessity is a moral obligation akin to abolishing slavery and eradicating diseases.[10] And like the efforts to eliminate slavery and diseases, political peace is not a static, once-and-for-all achievement. It will be the fruit of constantly changing, innovative, and necessarily particularistic and contingent efforts to achieve communities of right relations in many different places and at many different levels of society.[11]

Himes maintains that the three conceptions of positive peace complement each other. An "anticipatory eschatology" – the Kingdom is here but not yet – means that shalom "influences the present by inspiring and requiring human beings to build a more adequate political order now"; we cannot remain satisfied with a realpolitik "peace of a sort" based on balance of power or dominance.[12] An interior spiritual peace constantly reminds us that the challenge of peace is not just to get things

---

7   Kenneth Himes, "Peacebuilding and Catholic Social Teaching." In *Peacebuilding: Catholic Theology, Ethics and Praxis*, eds. R. Schreiter, S. Appleby and G. Powers (New York: Orbis, 2010): 268–269.

8   *Called Together to be Peacemakers*, Report of the International Dialogue between the Catholic Church and Mennonite World Conference, 1998–2003, para. 153. In analyzing John Paul II's ethic of peace, Justenhoven emphasizes the centrality of a human rights perspective, rooted in a distinctive Catholic anthropology and Christology, and the need to further develop credible international law and institutions. See Heinz-Gerhard Justenhoven, "The Peace Ethics of Pope John Paul II." In *University of St. Thomas Law Journal* 3:1 (Summer 2005): 110–138.

9   Drew Christiansen, S.J., "Catholic Peacemaking, 1991–2005: The Legacy of Pope John Paul II." In *The Review of Faith and International Affairs* 4:2 (Fall 2006): 22.

10 Paul VI, "Homily on the World Day of Peace" (January 1, 1970), cited in Himes, "Peacebuilding and Catholic Social Teaching," 280.

11 Himes, "Peacebuilding and Catholic Social Teaching", 269.

12 Ibid, 270.

political in right order, but also requires a radical transformation of our hearts and souls.

Obviously, there is considerable debate within the Church on the relationship between a negative peace and a positive peace, how the three dimensions of positive peace are related to each other, the precise nature of the political peace that is achievable short of the eschaton, and the means for achieving that peace. A similar debate rages, albeit in much different terms, among various secular approaches to war and peace. Where there is wide agreement, however, is that a major function of both just war and peacebuilding is to hold the United States (and other nations) morally accountable for maintaining a negative peace – i.e., avoiding war and helping to prevent and manage conflicts around the world. That is no small moral feat.

The much more difficult, long-term challenge is building a positive peace, the obvious challenge for an ethic of peacebuilding. The just war's contribution to a positive peace might not be so obvious. A look at three just war criteria is illustrative. Right intention not only rules out hatred and dehumanization of the enemy, but also calls for all acts in war to be considered in relation to their impact on a post-war political peace. This interpretation of right intention is particularly relevant to peacebuilding after humanitarian interventions (e.g., East Timor and Kosovo) and after wars that lead to occupation (e.g., Iraq and Afghanistan). The positive conception of peace is also evident in how the Church has evaluated claims of just cause and legitimate authority. The Holy See, for example, has vigorously opposed expansive interpretations of just cause that go beyond defense against on-going aggression or violate a narrow interpretation of Article 51 of the UN Charter, which restricts force to defense against "armed attack." It has also increasingly defined legitimate authority as requiring a role for the UN Security Council in authorizing uses of force in accord with the Charter, even though that might not be strictly required by this criterion.[13] Such applications of the criteria re-

---

13 According to Heinz-Gerhard Justenhoven, Pope John Paul II was explicit on legitimate authority: "it is for the UN to decide on the use of force, not a national government." "The Peace Ethics of Pope John Paul II." In *University of St. Thomas Law Journal* 3:1 (Summer 2005): 134–135. It is not clear whether the Holy See would consider the requirements under international law as coterminous with just war's understanding of legitimate authority. The Holy See did emphasize that the interventions in Kosovo in 1999 and Iraq in 2003 were illegal because they lacked UN Security Council approval. Interestingly, the U.S. bishops have supported a strong role for the UN but have focused less on the legal re-

flect the Church's long-term goals of strengthening international law, international institutions, and means of conflict transformation to the point that war will become obsolete.

Solidarity is a third element of Catholic social teaching that connects a just war and a peacebuilding ethic. Grounded in the unity of the human family, the unity of the Body of Christ, and the love of neighbor, solidarity is a glue that is necessary for any social order based in right relations. It reminds us that a moral calculus of what is just, whether in war or in politics, is cold and sterile if separated from Jesus' Love Command. Solidarity is the virtue that transforms the fact of interdependence into a genuine commitment to achieve the good of the other.

Solidarity is a term that is largely foreign to the foreign policy lexicon. Lisa Cahill claims that it is also one of the hardest concepts in Catholic social teaching to embrace in practice because it is so antithetical to the conventional wisdom that nations are in the business of protecting their national security, not collaborating to build the structures of cooperative security that are called for in Catholic social teaching.[14] Solidarity is antithetical to the exceptionalism (the United States need not abide by the same rules as other nations) and muscular unilateralism that have characterized much of U.S. military policy, and the corresponding national security doctrines premised on maintaining U.S. economic, political and military hegemony.[15]

---

quirements under the Charter. In Somalia, Haiti, Bosnia-Herzegovina and Rwanda, the bishops assumed U.N. approval was important, and, in *The Harvest of Justice Is Sown in Peace*, they said multilateral interventions, under the auspices of the UN, are "preferable because they enhance the legitimacy of these actions and can protect against abuse" (para. 40). Since, in Kosovo, the U.N. Security Council was incapacitated by the Russian veto, the U.S. bishops were less willing than the Holy See to insist on U.N. approval, especially given that the intervention was multilateral and had widespread international support. In the floor debate on the bishops' November 2002 statement opposing war in Iraq, the major question at issue was whether legitimate authority required U.N. Security Council approval as a matter of principle or only as a matter of prudence in that case. They concluded it was the latter. See Gerard Powers, "The U.S. Bishops and War since the Peace Pastoral." In *U.S. Catholic Historian* 27:2 (Winter 2009): 86.

14 Lisa Sowle Cahill, "Goods for Whom? Defining Goods and Expanding Solidarity in Catholic Approaches to Violence." In *Journal of Religious Ethics* 25:3 (1997): 198, cited in Himes, "Peacebuilding and Catholic Social Teaching," 273.

15 S. Brooks & W. Wohlforth, "American Primacy in Perspective," Foreign Affairs (July/ August 2002): 20; See, e.g., *National Security Strategy of the United States, 2002*, especially the treatment of so-called "preemptive force" on 9–10.

Solidarity influences how we interpret the just war tradition insofar as it reinforces the duty of care owed civilians, giving it a deeper sense of a special option for the victims in war that is akin to the option for the poor. In considering the morality of humanitarian interventions, solidarity is the norm that counters any temptation of the great powers to use humanitarian interventions as a cloak for new forms of imperialism. It is also the norm that compels the Church around the world to overcome, through its own peacebuilding and accompaniment efforts, the chasm that divides the world's zones of peace and prosperity from the zones of war and deprivation.

A fourth concept that shapes how both just war and peacebuilding are understood is the new prominence of *nonviolence* in Catholic social teaching since Vatican II. In recognizing the legitimacy of principled non-violence, Vatican II limited it to an option for individuals not states. Since then, papal teaching and statements by episcopal conferences have not discarded the just war tradition, as even some Vatican voices have urged, but have given much more weight to nonviolence.[16] The report of the international Catholic-Mennonite dialogue summed up the Catholic view that nonviolence

> is both a Christian and a human virtue. For Christians, nonviolence takes on special meaning in the suffering of Christ who was "led as a sheep to the slaughter" (*Is* 53:7; *Acts* 8:32). "Making up the sufferings lacking in Christ" (*Col* 1:34), the nonviolent witness of Christians contributes to the building up of peace in a way that force cannot, discerning the difference "between the cowardice which gives into evil and the violence which under the illusion of fighting evil, only makes it worse." In the Catholic view, nonviolence ought to be implemented in public policies and through public institutions as well as in personal and church practice.[17]

This is just one of many statements that reflect a growing appreciation of the normative power of nonviolence as well as its practical efficacy. On the one hand, the experience of total war in the 20th century, the threat

---

16 In their 1993 statement, the U.S. bishops emphasized the interdependence of the two traditions: "One must ask, in light of recent history, whether nonviolence should be restricted to personal commitments or whether it also should have a place in the public order with the tradition of justified and limited war." National Conference of Catholic Bishops, *The Harvest of Justice Is Sown in Peace* (Washington, D.C.: USCC Office of Publishing, 1993), 12.

17 *Called Together to be Peacemakers*, Report of the International Dialogue between the Catholic Church and Mennonite World Conference, 1998–2003, para 152; http://www.bridgefolk.net/wp-content/uploads/2009/04/ctp_english.pdf.

of a nuclear holocaust, and the fact that civilians have increasingly been the main victims of war have led the Church to be skeptical of the ability of modern war to meet just war criteria. On the other hand, from the demise of Marcos in the Philippines to the demise of the Soviet bloc, recent history has demonstrated the power of nonviolence.[18] "A cornerstone of John Paul II's thinking," according to Heinz-Gerhard Justenhoven, "was his belief that the Cold War ended as a result of three factors: non-militaristic diplomacy that centered on ethical and legal positions, the nonviolent commitment of the population for political changes, and, particularly, the inclusion of the human rights catalogue in the Helsinki Final Act."[19] Given these developments, Drew Christiansen concludes that contemporary Catholic teaching on conflict "has evolved into a doctrine of resistance to evil with a priority on nonviolent means —a doctrine that must be applied in the context of a wider vision of peace, including forgiveness between antagonists."[20]

Some consider just war and peacebuilding as inherently incompatible. They are convinced that the Catholic Church can become an effective peacebuilder and an effective advocate for peacebuilding only when it takes a page out of the Mennonite hymnal, discards the just war tradition and embraces pacifism. I would make a very different argument. A theology, ethics and praxis of peacebuilding must learn from the tradition of principled non-violence but an ethic of peacebuilding is not an alternative to the just war tradition but a necessary complement to it. The new emphasis on peacebuilding is a logical consequence of the Church's increasingly restrictive just war ethic, as well as an acknowledgement of the importance of non-violent means in resolving conflict. It is no accident that Mennonites, notably John Paul Lederach, have been the lynchpin in training Catholic bishops in many countries in peacebuilding strategies. But abandoning the just war tradition is not a precondition for improving the Church's capacity to be a peacebuilder. Rather, the challenge is for both adherents of just war (restrictive and permissive) and pacifism to enlarge the conversation by reflecting much more seriously and systemati-

---

18 John Paul II, *Centesimus Annus* (1991), no. 23.
19 Heinz-Gerhard Justenhoven, "The Peace Ethics of Pope John Paul II." In *University of St. Thomas Law Journal* 3:1 (Summer 2005): 120. Justenhoven provides an excellent analysis of John Paul II's teaching on non-violence and just war; see especially 118–121, 131–137.
20 Drew Christiansen, S.J., "Catholic Peacemaking, 1991–2005: The Legacy of Pope John Paul II." In *The Review of Faith and International Affairs* 4:2 (Fall 2006): 24.

cally than either have done to date on peacebuilding, an area where they should be able to find common ground. A further development of a theology, ethics and practice of peacebuilding, not further refinement of the old debate on just war versus pacifism, will enable the Catholic community to achieve its full potential in becoming a "peace Church" in an authentically Catholic way.

Virtues are a final aspect of Catholic social teaching that grounds both the just war and peacebuilding. Both the professional military and professional peacebuilders, religious and secular, talk of peace as their vocation, their way of life, their calling. As the U.S. bishops said in *The Harvest of Justice is Sown in Peace*, peacebuilding requires that individuals and communities cultivate peaceable virtues:

> True peacemaking can be a matter of policy only if it is first a matter of the heart.... Amid the violence of contemporary culture and in response to the growing contempt for human life, the Church must seek to foster communities where peaceable virtues can take root and be nourished. We need to nurture among ourselves *faith and hope* to strengthen our spirits by placing our trust in God, rather than in ourselves; *courage and compassion* that move us to action; *humility and kindness* so that we can put the needs and interests of others ahead of our own; *patience and perseverance* to endure the long struggle for justice; and *civility and charity* so that we can treat others with respect and love.[21]

Some consider an emphasis on the virtues and character as the decisive difference between a just war ethic that is rule-centered – a "checklist of criteria" to guide policymakers – and a just war ethic that is virtue-centered – substantive principles animated by the witness of a community of Christian disciples.[22] One need not resolve the church-world theological issues involved in that distinction to agree with the conclusion that a Christian just war ethic entails "becoming people of a certain kind of character who are, among other things, habitually disposed to love and seek justice for their neighbors as if such a disposition were a second nature."[23] The same can be said of a Christian peacebuilding ethic. The extent to which the same human and theological virtues are required for both, and whether and how they can and should be translated into the

---

21 *The Harvest of Justice Is Sown in Peace*, 6–7; cf. *Called Together to be Peacemakers*, para. 158.

22 Daniel M. Bell, *Just War as Christian Discipleship: Recentering the Tradition in the Church rather than the State* (Grand Rapids, MI: Brazos Press, 2009).

23 Ibid, 83.

political and social order, is an ongoing issue that deserves further examination.

A cosmopolitan ethic, a positive conception of peace, solidarity, the importance of non-violence, and the role of virtues are some of the principal foundational concepts underlying both a just war and peacebuilding ethic. I now consider how a strict just war ethic is properly considered one important element of peacebuilding.

1.2 Restrictive Just War as an Element of Peacebuilding

In their 1983 peace pastoral, the U.S. bishops suggested that the presumption "in favor of peace and against war" was the common starting point for the just war and non-violent traditions, making them "distinct but interdependent methods of evaluating warfare." This strong presumption may be overridden only for "extraordinarily strong reasons."[24] The same factors that have led to the growing emphasis on non-violence in Catholic teaching and practice have reinforced this presumption: the negative experience of total war in the 20th century and the risk of global nuclear annihilation, on the one hand, and the positive experience of the dramatic and unforeseen success of non-violence in the Philippines, the Soviet bloc, and elsewhere, on the other. Moreover, since Vietnam, the U.S. bishops, like many other religious leaders in the United States, have adopted a healthy – and well-justified! – skepticism about the morality of U.S. military interventions, a skepticism evident in their just war arguments against the contra war in Nicaragua, the interventions in Grenada and Panama, and the two Iraq wars. This skepticism corresponded with official teaching and the Holy See's pronouncements on these conflicts. Interestingly, while the U.S. bishops' statements have explicitly relied on just war arguments, the Holy See's have only occasionally appealed to just war criteria, instead emphasizing international law, the power of dialogue, the negative consequences of war, and hortatory appeals, such as "war never again" and "war is not the answer."

The just war starting point of Catholic neo-conservatives such as George Weigel and Michael Novak is very different. They appeal to a robust, traditional conception of just war as an expression of the "moral realism" of Augustine, Aquinas, the Scholastics and others. For neo-conser-

---

24 National Conference of Catholic Bishops, *The Challenge of Peace: God's Promise and Our Response* (Washington, D.C.: USCC Office of Publishing, 1983): 51.

vatives, the just war is a "theory of statecraft" that "begins by defining the moral responsibilities of governments [to defend the common good], continues with the definition of morally appropriate political ends and then takes up the question of means."[25] Weigel finds common ground with Clausewitz on one central point: "unless war is an extension of politics, it is simply wickedness."[26] He argues that the presumption underlying the just war tradition is for justice, not against war. War is sometimes necessary to achieve the minimum conditions of a just peace in a quasi-anarchic international system, not something to be equated with illegitimate violence or decried as a threat to peace and order.

Unlike Weigel, the bishops' presumption draws a sharp line between war and politics. War is the failure of politics, not its extension. Moreover, the bishops' presumption gives war much less pride of place in ensuring international order than in the neo-conservatives' permissive interpretation. The resort to military force is sometimes necessary, to be sure, but it is not a primary means of achieving even a negative peace.

The presumption against military force cannot simply be subsumed under the last resort criterion, nor can its significance be relativized as merely a restatement of the general truth that peace is the fruit of justice. Rather, the presumption creates a hermeneutic that governs how the just war criteria are used. This hermeneutic is the difference between just war criteria that readily justify war and just war criteria that severely limit it. It operates in two ways that are relevant to the relationship between just war and peacebuilding: First, it reinforces the notion that just war criteria are strict restraints on when, why and how to use force, and it creates a heavy obligation to find and pursue non-violent means of resolving conflict – i.e., to develop an ethic and praxis of peacebuilding. Second, it suggests that each of the just war criteria should be interpreted in light of a realistic assessment of the end of restoring or establishing, not just a negative peace, but also a more just and sustainable positive peace than what prevailed before the war. Since military force often does not even achieve a negative peace, this restrictive approach is extremely wary of the common tendency to fashion pre-war worst-case scenarios about the enormity of

25 George Weigel, "The development of just war thinking in the post-Cold War world: An American Perspective." In *The Price of Peace: Just War in the Twenty-First Century*, eds. Charles Reed and David Ryall (Cambridge: Cambridge University Press, 2007): 24.

26 Ibid, 23. See also George Weigel, *Against the Grain: Christianity and Democracy, War and Peace* (New York: Crossroad, 2008) and *Faith, Reason, and the War Against Jihadism: A Call to Action* (New York: Doubleday, 2007).

threats faced (prior to Iraq 2003 mushroom clouds in Manhattan), as well as ideal-case speculation about the "good" to be achieved by war (freedom for Iraq and a transformed Middle East). This hermeneutic reminds us that Christian realism is realistic about the consequences of not acting in cases like Iraq, but is equally realistic about the consequences of doing so; it compels us to act with extreme caution, keeping in the forefront the fact that wars rarely bring the freedom, justice or lasting peace envisioned when they are begun.

1.2.1 Just war as war prevention

Given this restrictive approach, the role of just war in war prevention becomes more obvious. Permissive approaches are rightly criticized for legitimizing war and for being more susceptible to misappropriation by those seeking to bless wars fought for unholy and immoral purposes. A strict just war analysis is much less susceptible to such critiques. In fact, it should be considered an essential aspect of peacebuilding insofar as it contributes to preventing war, limiting violence during war, and creating the conditions for post-war reconstruction and reconciliation. The claim here is not that just war norms are decisive or even prominent in policy debates and decision-making; they rarely are.[27] My claim is more modest: that just war norms are integral to Catholic approaches to peacebuilding, and to many other peacebuilding approaches that rely, at least implicitly, on just war arguments.

As already mentioned, just war arguments have played a prominent role in the U.S. bishops' opposition to most U.S. military interventions

---

27 More than any other single document, the peace pastoral revived the just war tradition's place in the public policy debate. While realism retains its dominant place in national security debates, it is now more possible to raise moral issues about nuclear weapons and other security issues in polite company without being accused of being "soft-headed." Morality is no longer an uninvited guest at an exclusive party. That said, one need not be a cynic to question whether the use of variations on the just war tradition by successive U.S. presidents to justify such military interventions as Panama, Iraq I and II, and Kosovo reflects a tendency to (mis)use morality to justify decisions made on other grounds. Ensuring that morality has its proper place in decision-making on national security issues remains perhaps the most fundamental challenge 25 years after the pastoral.

since Vietnam.[28] (Catholic pacifists have also relied on just war arguments to rally public opposition to war.) The bishops' vigorous opposition to the Iraq intervention in 2003 is illustrative. They developed
their position against U.S. intervention in Iraq in late 2001. Despite
being preoccupied with the sex abuse crisis, they launched a vigorous effort to convince the Catholic community, the Bush administration, and
the wider public that military intervention in Iraq raised grave moral concerns. The bishops were clear that the international community had a
moral duty to address the threat the Iraqi regime posed to its neighbors
and its own people. But, with the Holy See and Catholic leaders around
the world, they rejected the Bush administration's preventive war argument as a dramatic expansion of traditional interpretations of just war
norms. They also argued that war could have unpredictable negative consequences not only for Iraq but for peace and stability elsewhere in the
Middle East. Like other opponents of the war, the bishops proposed alternatives to the use of force, including targeted sanctions, inspections
and other efforts by the U.N. to ensure compliance with U.N. resolutions
and contain and deter threats posed by Iraq.[29]

A second example of the role of just war in violence prevention is its
role in delegitimizing holy war. Today, the problem of religious violence
lies principally with extremist forms of Islam and extremist forms of religious nationalism. While they would consider themselves bitter enemies, contemporary holy warriors, such as al Qaeda's Islamic terrorists
and Christian religious-nationalists in Bosnia-Herzegovina, would be
united in rejecting the restraints imposed by the just war tradition. Fortunately, today, there are no significant voices within Catholicism or, for
that matter, within mainline Christianity as a whole, seeking to justify
holy war.

One response to religious violence is to try to break the link between
religion and violence by rejecting the just war tradition and embracing
principled non-violence. Perhaps paradoxically, however, religiously-mo-
tivated violence has been and is being delegitimized, not mainly by pacifists but by those religious traditions holding to some version of a restric-

---

28 For a detailed analysis of the bishops' actions, see Gerard Powers, "The U.S.
    Bishops and War since the Peace Pastoral." In *U.S. Catholic Historian* 27:2 (Win-
    ter 2009): 73–96.

29 Ibid., 87–91. The two most important USCCB statements were by the full body
    of bishops on November 13, 2002, and a statement by Bishop Wilton Gregory,
    president of the USCCB, on February 26, 2003. These and other statements are
    available at the USCCB website: www.usccb.org/sdwp/international.

tive interpretation of just war. The Christian tradition has a long and less-than-proud record of holy war. It was the refinement and narrowing of the just war tradition, not the embrace of pacifism, which ultimately delegitimized holy war within mainstream Christianity. To cite two contemporary examples, in Northern Ireland, one of the most important contributions of Catholic and Protestant leaders was to condemn IRA and loyalist paramilitary violence as a violation of just war norms.[30] Similarly, the misappropriation of "jihad" by Islamic terrorists is being countered most effectively not by Islamic pacifists but by those who are demonstrating by careful exegesis that Islamic teaching on "jihad" does not justify al Qaeda's notions of holy war.[31]

1.2.2 Just war as violence management

The most obvious contribution of the just war to violence management is the role of the *jus in bello* criteria of noncombatant immunity and proportionality in limiting violence. These criteria provide the basis for condemning genocidal and terrorist violence, and the self-reinforcing cycle of violence that makes these types of conflict so difficult to resolve. They also provided the basis for the concerns the bishops raised about the U.S. military's doctrine of overwhelming force and emphasis, until Afghanistan, on fighting "zero-casualty" wars. These policies led to targeting basic infrastructure, bombing from 15,000 feet, and other tactics that effectively reversed the duty of care soldiers owed civilians. It is widely acknowledged that the U.S. military has taken important steps since Vietnam to improve its compliance with *jus in bello* criteria, as embodied in the laws of war. That is significant moral progress. But the laws of war are more permissive than the restrictive interpretation of *jus in bello* used by the bishops. In their statements on Iraq, Kosovo and other U.S. military

---

30 See, e.g., Berkley Center for Religion, Peace, & World Affairs Case Study Series, "Northern Ireland: Religion in War and Peace" (2009): http://repository.berkley-center.georgetown.edu/NorthernIrelandConflictCaseStudy.pdf.

31 On the just war debate within Islam, see, e.g., Sohail Hashmi, "War," in *Key Themes for the Study of Islam*, ed. Jamal J. Elias (Oxford: Oneworld, 2010): 336–55; Abdulaziz Sachedina, "From Defensive to Offensive Warfare: the Use and Abuse of Jihad in the Muslim World." In *Religion, Law and the Use of Force: Their Influence on Conflict and Conflict Resolution*, eds. Joseph I. Coffey and Charles Mathewes (Ardsley, N.Y.:Transnational 2002): 23–37; John Kelsay, *Arguing the Just War in Islam* (Cambridge: Harvard University Press, 2007).

interventions, the bishops have insisted that Americans must value "the lives and livelihood of Iraqi and Afghani civilians as we would the lives and livelihood of our own families and our own citizens."[32] In raising these concerns, the bishops emphasized that this approach was intended not only to limit the physical and human toll of war, but also to make post-war reconstruction and reconciliation more feasible and likely. The *jus in bello* norms have also provided a primary rationale for the bishops' long-standing campaigns urging the United States to join the global ban on landmines and to take a leadership role in nuclear arms control and disarmament.

1.3 Restrictive Just War Requires an Ethic of Peacebuilding

I have made the case that a restrictive interpretation of just war should be considered an integral element of peacebuilding insofar as it can provide and has provided a moral rationale for opposing resort to military force, limiting the use of force during war in ways that both make the conflict more manageable and improve chances for a sustainable peace. I now turn to two examples of how a restrictive just war ethic presumes the further development of an ethic and praxis of peacebuilding: humanitarian intervention and the return of holy war.

1.3.1 Humanitarian intervention

Without elaborating on the nuances of the position or how it has been applied in recent cases,[33] suffice it to say that in the face of the Somalias, Bosnias, and Rwandas, the Church had a clear answer to Cain's question: "Yes, we are our brother's keeper." Unlike most foreign policy elites who argued that it was not in the U.S. interest to get involved in such intractable conflicts involving "ancient hatreds," Pope John Paul II said in 1993 that the international community had not only a right but a duty to intervene "where the survival of populations and entire ethnic groups is seriously compromised."[34] More recently, Pope Benedict XVI has offered

---

32 Bishop Wilton Gregory, president of the USCCB, Statement on Iraq, February 26, 2003.
33 Gerard Powers, "The U.S. Bishops and War since the Peace Pastoral." In *U.S. Catholic Historian* 27:2 (Winter 2009): 82–86.
34 John Paul II, "Address to the International Conference on Nutrition." In *Origins* 22:28 (December 24, 1992): 475.

strong support for the nascent concept in international law of a "respon-sibility to protect."[35] The most cogent treatment of humanitarian inter-vention by the U.S. bishops is in *The Harvest of Justice is Sown in Peace.*[36]

A composite analysis of these and other statements leads to several observations about the relationship between humanitarian intervention and peacebuilding. First, humanitarian intervention has raised an inter-esting debate about whether it is best understood as a form of interna-tional policing, as an application of the just war, or as a hybrid of the two.[37] However that debate is resolved, the legitimate fear that humani-tarian intervention could be a cloak for "new forms of imperialism or endless wars of altruism"[38] suggests that the strong moral preference is for interventions short of war-fighting. The responsibility to protect was developed precisely to refocus the debate from forceful military inter-ventions to developing the capacities of states to protect their own citi-

---

35 Benedict XVI, "Address to the General Assembly" United Nations (April 18, 2008).

36 *The Harvest of Justice Is Sown in Peace*, 38–41.

37 See Gerald Schlabach's effort to elaborate a theory of just policing as an alterna-tive to the just war assumption that military force is an international equivalent to policing. Gerald W. Schlabach, "Warfare vs. Policing: In Search of Moral Clarity." In *Just Policing, Not War: An Alternative Response to World Violence,* ed. G. Schlabach (Collegeville, MN: Order of St. Benedict, 2007): 69–110. His effort to delineate the differences between war and policing is consistent with the UN's approach to peace operations, which can be distinguished from collective self-defense and collective security. It is also consistent with the diver-sity of types of humanitarian interventions, whether undertaken by the UN and regional bodies or by individual nations. If the focus is on objectives and means, it is easy to see the similarities between humanitarian intervention and policing. For example, ensuring the delivery of aid in Somalia or Sudan by deploying mili-tary forces with highly restrictive rules of engagement has more in common with policing than warfare. Using the military, in cooperation with local security forces, to detain war criminals in Bosnia is a police function. Enforcing economic sanctions against Iraq and no-fly-zones in Bosnia and preventive deployments of lightly-armed UN forces in Macedonia to deter an outbreak of violence fall somewhere between policing and war, but, in most cases, are closer to the former. See Gerard Powers, "The Meaning of War: An Ethical Analysis of Sanctions and Humanitarian Intervention." In *The Meaning of Armed Conflict in International Law*, eds. Mary Ellen O'Connell (Martinus Nijhof, 2012) and D. Christiansen, S.J., and G. Powers, "The Duty to Intervene: Ethics and the Varieties of Human-itarian Intervention." In *Close Calls: Intervention, Terrorism, Missile Defense, and "Just War" Today*, ed. Elliott Abrams (Washington, D.C.: Ethics and Public Policy Center, 1998), 183–208.

38 *The Harvest of Justice Is Sown in Peace*, 41.

zens. Even when states fail to do so, a variety of nonmilitary interventions are available, including diplomatic measures, political pressure, targeted sanctions, various kinds of non-forceful UN peace operations, indictments and prosecutions by international tribunals, and other forms of conflict prevention and conflict management. Military interventions that rise to the level of war-fighting should be strictly limited to cases of genocide, mass starvation, or similar mass suffering where survival of a significant segment of the population is at risk.

Second, an ethic of humanitarian intervention must be tied to a much broader ethic that can address the root, as well as proximate, causes of these internal conflicts. Many recent genocidal conflicts have been over religious, ethnic, tribal, or national identity. That has generated a robust literature on the religious and ethical dimensions of identity conflicts. Interestingly, these conflicts have not generated a comparable literature on self-determination, which is at issue in so many of the world's most deadly identity conflicts. Unfortunately, while the Vatican and local episcopal conferences have taken positions, sometimes quite controversial ones, on issues of self-determination, there is little in official Catholic social teaching on the topic.[39] A peacebuilding ethic would benefit from the further development of an ethic of self-determination, and its relationship to an understanding of nationalism, state legitimacy, and an ethic of the use of force.

Third, if humanitarian intervention is legitimate, much more reflection is needed on the host of post-intervention issues that arise in such cases. While they do not exhaust the issues raised by an expansive post-intervention agenda, two sets of issues illustrate the nature of the moral challenge. In recent years, a growing number of ethicists have begun to develop a theory of *jus post bellum* but this remains at an

---

39   The term "self-determination" is not widely used in official church documents. For example, the *Compendium of the Social Doctrine of the Church* mentions, without elaboration, "a right to self-determination and independence" in the context of a discussion of economic globalization (para. 365). It also begins a brief discussion of minority rights with an acknowledgment, again without elaboration, of the fact that "[F]or every people there is in general a corresponding nation, but for various reasons national boundaries do not always coincide with ethnic boundaries." (para. 387). Pontifical Council for Justice and Peace, *Compendium of the Social Doctrine of the Church* (Washington, D.C.: U.S. Conference of Catholic Bishops, 2005). For related references, see, e.g., Paul VI, *Populorum Progressio*, para. 65; 1971 Synod of Bishops, *Justice in the World*, paras 17, 71.

early stage of development. This discussion is complemented by a more wide-ranging, and generally more developed, discourse on a theology and ethics of reconciliation. While the *jus post bellum* is more closely tethered to just war analysis than reconciliation, both would benefit from a deeper exploration of the dynamic relationship between their analyses and various approaches to just war. How does one reconcile, for example, the limited humanitarian ends of military interventions and the unlimited needs of societies that are trying to recover from genocidal-type conflicts? Can an unjust war lead to a just peace if norms governing the *jus post bellum* are met? Do violations of *jus ad bellum* or *jus in bello* create heavier post-war moral obligations that might entail longer and more robust military engagement? Can notions of restorative justice that are increasingly being used for ordinary crime be extended to genocidal conflicts?[40]

In short, a just war analysis that permits limited, mostly non-military, forms of multi-lateral humanitarian intervention depends on finding more effective ways of conflict prevention, conflict management, and

---

40 Several chapters in *Peacebuilding* provide an excellent overview of the current state of the Catholic debate on post-intervention issues: Kenneth Himes, "Peacebuilding and Catholic Social Teaching"; Daniel Philpott, "Reconciliation: A Catholic Ethic for Peacebuilding in the Political Order"; Maryann Cusimano Love, "What Kind of Peace Do We Seek? Emerging Norms of Peacebuilding in Key Political Institutions"; Peter-John Pearson, "Pursuing Truth, Reconciliation, and Human Dignity in South Africa: Lessons for Catholic Peacebuilding"; and Robert Schreiter, "A Practical Theology of Healing, Forgiveness, and Reconciliation"; in *Peacebuilding: Catholic Theology, Ethics, and Praxis*, Robert Schreiter, R. Scott Appleby, & Gerard F. Powers, eds (Maryknoll, N.Y.: Orbis 2010). For analyses not rooted specifically in Catholic social teaching, see Brian Orend, "Justice after War." In *Ethics and International Affairs 16:1* (April 2002)): 43–56; Gary Bass, "Jus Post Bellum." In *Philosophy & Public Affairs*: 384–412; T. Govier, "War's Aftermath: The Challenge of Reconciliation." In Larry May, *War: Essays in Political Philosophy* (New York: Cambridge University Press, (2008): 229–248; Mark Evans, "Moral Responsibilities and the Conflicting Demands of Jus Post Bellum." In *Ethics and International Affairs* 23:2 (Summer 2009): 147; William Bole, Drew Christiansen, S.J., and Robert Hennemeyer, *Forgiveness in International Politics: An Alternative Road to Peace* (Washington, D.C.: U.S. Conference of Catholic Bishops, 2004); Raymond Helmick and Rodney Petersen, eds, *Forgiveness and Reconciliation: Religion, Public Policy, and Conflict Transformation* (Philadelphia: Templeton Foundation Press, 2001); Donald Shriver, *An Ethic for Enemies: Forgiveness in Politics* (Oxford: Oxford University Press, 1998). On the ethics of exit from Iraq, see Noah Feldman, *What We Owe Iraq: War and the Ethics of Nation Building* (Princeton: Princeton Unicersity Press, 2004) and Gerard Powers, "Our Moral Duty in Iraq." In *America* (Feb. 18, 2008): 13–16.

post-conflict reconciliation, and addressing the ethical issues that arise in doing so.

1.3.2 The return of holy war

In the previous section, I argued that the just war tradition, far more than pacifism, plays a key role in delegitimizing contemporary forms of holy war. The just war's rejection of the holy war claim that war and unconstrained violence are justified by the "holy" ends at stake addresses only one dimension of the problem. Two other dimensions of holy war require going beyond the well-trod pacifism-just war-holy war debate. First, addressing the identity conflicts in which religion is a major factor is less about marshalling just war arguments against religious violence and more about further developing a political ethic capacious enough to deal with religious nationalism. The link between religion and nationalism may seem less terrifying but it is arguably a much greater source of injustice and violence than religious militants preaching holy war. To counter religious nationalism, more work needs to be done on the distinction made in Church documents between inclusive forms of civic nationalism and legitimate expressions of patriotism, on the one hand, and the "idolatry" of chauvinist and exclusivist forms of religious nationalism, on the other.[41] As already mentioned, this moral analysis of nationalisms has to be tied to an ethic of self-determination.

A second challenge arising from the new holy wars that cannot be addressed by the just war tradition alone is more subtle, and therefore more insidious. It comes, not from the advocates of holy war, but from the response of foreign policy elites in Washington, Berlin, London, Tokyo, Paris, and elsewhere. According to the conventional wisdom, which can be called the secularist paradigm: religion is and should be an increasingly waning force in world affairs, but to the extent that is not the case, religion remains mostly a problem, a source of conflict in international affairs. The secularist challenge to the just war tradition is different from other challenges. Religious militants justifying violence and religious nationalists seek to dramatically reshape the tradition in ways that would emasculate it. The secularist paradigm assumes that the tradition, itself, is as anachronistic as the religious institutions that still promote it. The secularist solution to the new holy wars is not to promote a more restrictive interpretation of the just war tradition or to promote a positive role

---

41   See, e. g., Daniel Philpott, "Explaining the Political Ambivalence of Religion." In *American Political Science Review* 101:3 (August 2007): 505–525.

for religion in international affairs, but rather to take religion and morality out of the public square (and the foreign ministry) and marginalize and privatize it.

Without getting into a detailed argument about why the secularist paradigm is descriptively and normatively flawed, it should be obvious that one antidote to the secularist paradigm, as well as to holy warriors of both kinds, is to develop further an ethic and practice of peacebuilding. On the one hand, the secularist paradigm loses much of its ideological appeal if religion is, and is seen to be, a force for peace and liberation, not a source of conflict and injustice. Religious violence and religious-nationalist conflicts are hardly ever as "religious" as many holy warriors hope and secularists fear. Nevertheless, when there is a religious dimension to a conflict, however much it is just a marker of identity or a convenient means of manipulation by cynical political leaders, the Church, at all levels, has a special obligation, not only to have a clear peacebuilding ethic, but to be a peacebuilder in practice.

On the other hand, if secularism prevails and religion is marginalized and privatized, its ability to influence peace will obviously be attenuated. The issue here is similar to the question of the political relevance of the just war tradition. Many of the same foreign policy elites who want to marginalize and privatize religion also dismiss the just war tradition, and the religious voices who seek to sustain it, as anachronistic or of use mainly to justify decisions made on other grounds. Both the just war ethic and a peacebuilding ethic are grounded in a political theology that is fundamentally at odds with the secularist paradigm. Moreover, just as military strategies must be informed by norms if war is not to become any more hellish than it is, peacebuilding strategies will be significantly impoverished if they preclude a public role for ethics and religion. Many of the concepts that make religion a powerful force for peace and that are essential for building a culture of peace in conflict-torn societies are deeply spiritual. Forgiveness, reconciliation, solidarity, and healing, for example, are generally not found in conventional political discourse or lose much of their power when separated from their religious and moral meaning. The "soft underbelly of security" in failing and divided states, according to Amitai Etzioni, is the challenge of developing a "moral culture," which, he argues, is often dependent upon religion.[42]

---

42 Amitai Etzioni, *Security First: For a Muscular, Moral Foreign Policy* (New Haven: Yale University Press, 2007), 152. A growing literature demonstrates how the secularist paradigm fails to adequately account for the peacebuilding role of religion.

Humanitarian intervention and the new holy wars are just two examples of how a just war ethic requires further development of a peacebuilding ethic.[43] Whether it is making the case that there are alternatives to
preventive war in Iraq in 2003 or Iran in 2012, defining the post-intervention responsibilities for nation-building in Iraq and Afghanistan,
charting a morally-appropriate approach to secessionist self-determination and nationalism in Bosnia and Sudan, balancing competing imperatives of peace processes in Colombia and Northern Uganda, developing
more effective and appropriate UN peace operations in Congo, or promoting post-genocide reconciliation in Rwanda, the common challenge
is peacebuilding. This is a challenge not only for governments, the
UN, and NGOs but also for pacifists and all variety of just war proponents.

2 Toward a Catholic Ethic of Peacebuilding

In the U.S. bishops' 1983 peace pastoral, *The Challenge of Peace*, they
called for further development of a theology of peace, rooted in "biblical
studies, systematic and moral theology, ecclesiology, and the experience
and insights of members of the Church who have struggled in various
ways to make and keep the peace in this often violent age."[44] To be
sure, many have responded to this invitation, but much more needs to
be done to develop what Scott Appleby calls, "a conceptually coherent,
theologically sophisticated and spiritually enlivening" approach to Cath-

---

See, e. g., Monica Toft, Daniel Philpott and Timothy Shah, *God's Century: Re-
surgent Religion and Global Politics* (New York: W.W. Norton, 2011); Gerard
Powers, "Religion and Peacebuilding." In *Strategies of Peace*, eds. Daniel Philpott
and Gerard Powers (Oxford: Oxford University Press, 2010): 317–352; Chicago
Council on Global Affairs, "Engaging Religious Communities Abroad: A New
Imperative for U.S. Foreign Policy" (2010); http://www.thechicagocouncil.org/
taskforce_details.php?taskforce_id=10.

43 The same is true of other issues. A strict interpretation of just war that calls for a
global ban on nuclear weapons presumes the need to develop a political ethic of
cooperative security that offers effective alternatives to existing nuclear deterrents
and to preventive war as a way of halting nuclear proliferation. In post-intervention Iraq and Afghanistan, it is essential to distinguish between the ethics of preventive war and the ethics of exit, an issue mostly not addressed by the just war
tradition.

44 *The Challenge of Peace*, 12.

olic peacebuilding that can begin to match the sophistication of Catholic thinking on the ethics of war and peace.[45]

As the bishops acknowledged in 1983, the characteristics of a theology of peace are very much present in Catholic social teaching; the Catholic peacebuilding slate is hardly blank. What David Little says about religious peacebuilders generally runs deep in official Catholic social teaching and Catholic practices around the world: a "hermeneutics of peace, namely, an interpretive framework that begins with the conviction that the pursuit of justice and peace by peaceful means is a sacred priority."[46] In the first section of this article, I outlined some of the conceptual building blocks for peacebuilding found in the social encyclicals, the annual World Day of Peace statements, and countless statements of national and regional episcopal conferences. This teaching has been lived out through the Church's role in peacebuilding from El Salvador and East Timor to Colombia and Northern Uganda.

Catholic social teaching and practice provide a rich foundation on which to build, but a spirituality, theology and ethic of peacebuilding cannot simply be coterminous with Catholic social teaching writ large. Distinguishing between the two raises numerous questions. I will focus on two. First, does Catholic peacebuilding practice offer any insights about gaps in Catholic social teaching that could benefit from deeper theological and ethical reflection? Second, how would Catholic teaching and practice in such areas as human rights, development, inter-religious dialogue, and sacramental theology lead to new insights if seen through a peacebuilding lens?[47] Both of these questions suggest that an inductive approach must be an integral component of the process of further devel-

---

45 Scott Appleby, "Catholic Peacebuilding." In *America* (September 8, 2003): 12.
46 David Little, "Religion, Violent Conflict, and Peacemaking." In D. Little, *Peacemakers in Action: Profiles of Religion in Conflict Resolution* (New York: Cambridge University Press, 2007): 438.
47 These questions are adapted from a larger set that were the focus of five international conferences and an associated research project sponsored by the Catholic Peacebuilding Network from 2004 to 2009: 1) What peacebuilding practices could inform and benefit from deeper theological and ethical reflection? 2) What characteristics of Catholic theology and ethics inform the praxis of peacebuilding, and to what extent are they distinctively Catholic? 3) How would the life and mission of the Catholic community be different if it were defined more explicitly in terms of a vocation of peacebuilding? 4) What is the significance of a theology and ethics of peacebuilding for the wider search for peace? 5) What lessons can be learned about "best practices" from the Church's peacebuilding experience in a diverse range of conflict situations?

oping a theology and ethic of peacebuilding. Reading the peacebuilding "signs of the times" involves understanding the nature of contemporary conflicts, mapping and analyzing the mostly unheralded peacebuilding work of the Catholic community amidst these conflicts, and identifying ways in which existing teaching can be enriched by insights from practice and practice can be enriched by developments in teaching. What is needed, in other words, is a practical theology of peacebuilding, "an ongoing practice of reflection and action that keeps theory and informed practice in constant conversation with each other."[48]

The Catholic Peacebuilding Network (CPN), a network of two dozen Catholic academic institutes, development agencies, lay organizations, and episcopal conferences has begun to examine these and related questions through five major international conferences since 2004 and by working with the Church in areas of conflict on new capacity-building initiatives.[49] These initiatives were tied to an intensive research project that included 20 leading scholars and scholar-practitioners working together over a 4-year period to produce a compilation of original articles entitled, *Peacebuilding: Catholic Theology, Ethics, and Praxis.*[50] With articles on Catholic peacebuilding in Colombia, the Philippines, the Great Lakes Region of Africa, Indonesia, and South Africa, as well as on the relationship between peacebuilding and official social teaching, interreligious dialogue, Christology, pastoral theology, ritual, and ecclesiology, this volume is indicative of the breadth of topics to be explored in further developing a peacebuilding theology and ethics.

---

48 Robert Schreiter, "A Practical Theology of Healing, Forgiveness, and Reconciliation" In *Peacebuiding*, 366.
49 In an effort to to enhance the study and practice of Catholic peacebuilding, the Catholic Peacebuilding Network (CPN) was founded in 2004, spearheaded by the University of Notre Dame's Kroc Institute and Catholic Relief Services. Starting with 7 affiliated institutions, the CPN now numbers some two dozen universities, episcopal conferences, development agencies, and other Catholic organizations. The first phase focused on deepening engagement and understanding best practices through a series of five major international conferences – at Notre Dame in 2004, in the Philippines in 2005, in Burundi in 2006, in Colombia in 2007, and at Notre Dame in 2008 (papers and video at cpn.nd.edu). Each of these conferences brought together between 100 and 300 scholars, leaders, and peacebuilding specialists from about two dozen countries, mostly ones torn by conflict.
50 Robert Schreiter, R. Scott Appleby and Gerard F. Powers, eds. *Peacebuilding: Catholic Theology, Ethics, and Praxis* (Maryknoll, N.Y.: Orbis 2010).

Efforts like these to enhance the study and practice of Catholic peace-building complement the just war tradition by providing an antidote to the secularists who would marginalize and privatize religion, as well as to the holy warriors who foment religious violence and/or religious nation-alism. Engagement with the lived reality of Catholic peacebuilding also highlights issues that a restrictive just war ethic is not designed to address. Earlier I noted some of the host of post-intervention issues raised by re-cent military interventions, whether justified on humanitarian (Kosovo), defense against terrorism (Afghanistan), or preventive war (Iraq) grounds. Here, I will elaborate on two gaps in teaching: an ethic of self-determi-nation, and the Church's role in dialogue and negotiation with armed ac-tors. These two issues have received less scholarly attention than the post-intervention issues and they illustrate nicely the wide range of theological and ethical issues that are part of a theology and ethic of peacebuilding.

2.1 The underdeveloped ethic of self-determination

The religious-ethnic-nationalist conflicts that have been at the heart of so many conflicts since the end of the Cold War have generated a substantial literature on religion and violence, and on religion and national or ethnic identity. But the issue that is at the heart of so many of these conflicts[51]–disputes over self-determination and secession – has not been addressed to the same extent. As mentioned earlier, the Church has been deeply en-gaged in debates over secession in individual cases, but there is little in official Catholic teaching on the topic.[52]

Preventing and managing the identity and secessionist conflicts which have necessitated so many humanitarian interventions, and designing the complex operations involved in promoting reconstruction and reconcili-ation after these interventions, requires a more systematic, multifaceted ethical analysis. A political ethic must address questions about the evolv-ing understanding of self-determination and sovereignty, new ways of in-stitutionalizing these principles, and the relationship between these prin-

---

51 From 1989 to 2009, 64 of 130 conflicts were intrastate conflicts over territorial issues related to self-determination (e. g., efforts to gain greater autonomy or full independence). *Uppsala Conflict Database*, September 16, 2010. Compiled by Rachel Miller for Peter Wallensteen, *Understanding Conflict Resolution* (London: Sage, 3rd ed., 2011).

52 See footnote 39.

ciples and institutions and various conceptions of national identity and democracy. A political ethic must also address the relationship between an ethic of self-determination and the nascent concept of a responsibility to protect; and the role of the United Nations, regional organizations, and other external actors in intervening in internal conflicts to safeguard peace. A political ethic cannot be developed in isolation from an economic ethic that can address the central role of economics in preventing (or fueling) secessionist conflicts, and in building a sustainable peace that respects the rights of and promotes solidarity among conflicting parties. Both a political and economic ethic must be complemented by an ethic of institutions that can translate moral norms into fair and effective structures and processes that are essential to building a positive peace. This multifaceted, building block approach to peace recognizes both the complexity of the tasks as well as the richness that must be part of any moral framework used to address the complexities of today's internal conflicts over self-determination.

The underdeveloped state of Catholic reflection on these issues of self-determination parallels, in some respects, the state of the legal debate.[53] In practice, the Church has responded in different ways to different secessionist claims, but common threads suggest that the Church's position is similar to what some call a "remedial rights" approach to secession.[54] The cases of Northern Ireland and the break up of Yugoslavia are exemplary.

In the case of Northern Ireland, the Church long supported the long-term aspiration of a united Ireland, but the principal focus of its approach to the conflict was to insist on constitutional and political efforts to re-

---

53 At the end of the Cold War, international law recognized a right to self-determination, but full independence or secession was limited to mutually-agreed separations (e.g., the break up of Czechoslovakia and the USSR) and liberation movements seeking to escape colonial rule; even then, the existing colonial boundaries had to be maintained under the doctrine of uti posseditis. Since the end of the Cold War, the break up of Yugoslovia and East Timor's successful independence bid, in particular, have left the state of customary international law on secession in doubt. For a summary of recent cases and current law, see Christine Gray, *International Law and the Use of Force*, 3rd ed. (Oxford: Oxford Press, 2008), 55–66.

54 See, e.g., Alan Buchanan, "Secession, state breakdown, and humanitarian intervention." In *Ethics and Foreign Intervention*, eds. Deen Chatterjee and Donald Scheid (Cambridge: Cambridge University Press, 2003) 189–211; Tom Farer, "The Ethics of Intervention in Self-determination Struggles." In *Human Rights Quarterly* 25:2 (May 2003): 382.

solve conflicting claims of self-determination, while rejecting out of hand the IRA's permissive use of just war criteria to legitimize its terrorist violence. The Church supported self-determination measures short of a united Ireland, such as the cross-border institutions, power-sharing within Northern Ireland, and protection of minority and human rights that were incorporated into the Good Friday Agreement. The Church also insisted on the ultimate importance of overcoming sectarianism and promoting reconciliation between Catholics and Protestants, nationalists and loyalists.

I would argue that the Church's approach to the Northern Ireland conflict represents the paradigmatic moral case. Its approach to the dissolution of Yugoslavia illustrates how this moral approach does not exclude, in extraordinary cases, unilateral, or nonconsensual, secession.

As in Ireland, Croatian cultural and national identity is closely identified with Catholicism in Croatia and Bosnia-Herzegovina.[55] The Catholic Church exhibited at least three forms of nationalism: the integrative strand sought union between Croatian, Serbian and other nationalist groups; the strong ethno-nationalist strand equated Catholic identity with exclusivist and chauvinistic forms of Croatian nationalism and the more dominant strand reflected a weak form of ethno-religious nationalism. The latter version supported independence for ethnically- and religiously-diverse states of Slovenia, Croatia, and Bosnia-Herzegovina as a way to nurture and protect religious freedom and democracy in the face of communism and Serbian dominance, and Western cultural identity at the fault lines of the Ottoman and Orthodox East.[56]

The Vatican led the way in recognizing Slovenia and Croatia, and later Bosnia-Herzegovina and Macedonia, largely as a defensive measure in the face of a failed Yugoslavia and a destructive war in Croatia. Even after Croatia and Slovenia declared independence in 1991, the Catholic bishops of Yugoslavia and the Vatican presumed that newly independent republics could, through negotiation, remain integrated into a reconstituted confederal Yugoslavia. When an aggressive and unjust war against Croatia made negotiation of a confederal solution impossible, the Vatican

---

55   For a fuller account of the Church's approach to self-determination in response to the dissolution of Yugoslavia, see Gerard Powers, "Religion, Conflict and Prospects for Reconciliation in Bosnia, Croatia, and Yugoslavia." In *Journal of International Affairs* 50:1 (Summer 1996): 221–252.

56   Pedro Ramet, "Religion and Nationalism in Yugoslavia." In *Religion and Nationalism in Soviet and East European Politics*, ed. P. Ramet (Durham, N.C.: Duke University Press, 1989): 319, 322.

supported full independence, conditioned on maintaining the existing boundaries of Yugoslavia's republics, and respecting minority and human rights. The Church consistently opposed the Croatian extremists' efforts to create an ethnically "pure" Greater Croatia and partition Bosnia along ethnic-religious lines.

Given the Church's support for an independent Bosnia, Croatia, and Slovenia, it reiterated traditional Catholic teaching about the right and duty of these new states to defend themselves against aggression in accord with the just war tradition and the laws of war.[57] While some Catholic leaders spoke of a sacred duty to defend the nation, Church support for the use of force in self-defense was relatively restrained. Even during the worst of the ethnic cleansing in Bosnia-Herzegovina, the bishops did not embrace lifting the arms embargo imposed by the UN for fear of widening and escalating the conflict. Rather, with Pope John Paul II, they appealed for (mostly non-military forms of) "humanitarian intervention" by the international community "to disarm the aggressor" and begin a process of demilitarizing the region.[58] Other secessionist cases, notably East Timor in 1999 and southern Sudan in 2011, reflect an approach similar to that followed in the Balkans.[59]

One of the few efforts in a Church document to define universally-applicable criteria for self-determination is found in the U.S. bishops' 1993 statement, *The Harvest of Justice Is Sown in Peace*. The bishops concluded:

> Self-determination, understood as full political independence, should neither be dismissed as always harmful or unworkable nor embraced as an absolute right or a panacea in the face of injustice. Rather, efforts to find more crea-

57 See, e.g. Croatian Catholic Bishops, "Urgent Appeal from the Bishops of Croatia" (Zagreb: July 30, 1991).

58 John Paul II, "Address to the International Conference on Nutrition." *Origins* 22:28 (December 24, 1992): 475; "Address to the Diplomatic Corps." January 16, 1993, *Origins* 22:34 (February 4, 1993): 587. Cardinal Vinko Puljic, Archbishop of Sarajevo, "Address at the Center for Strategic and International Studies." March 30, 1995, *Catholic News Service*, (April 3 1995): 7.

59 For the Church's role in East Timor's struggle for independence, see Arnold S. Kohen, "The Catholic Church and the Independence of East Timor." In *Bulletin of Concerned Asian Scholars* (Jan-Jun 2000): 19; and Patrick A. Smythe, *"The Heaviest Blow": The Catholic Church and the East Timor Issue* (Munster: Lit Verlag, 2004). For a local church's position on a more recent case, the referendum in southern Sudan, see Sudan Catholic Bishops' Conference, "A Future Full of Hope," July 22, 2010. Available at http://cpn.nd.edu/conflicts-and-the-role-of-the-church/other-conflicts/sudan/.

tive ways to uphold the fundamental values embodied in self-determination claims are called for; peoples have a right to participate in shaping their cultural, religious, economic and political identities. Self-determination does not necessarily entail secession or full political independence; it can be realized through effective protection of basic human rights, especially minority rights, a degree of political and cultural autonomy and other arrangements, such as a federal or confederal system of government. While full political independence may be morally right and politically appropriate in some cases, it is essential that any new state meet the fundamental purpose of sovereignty: the commitment and capacity to create a just and stable political order and to contribute to the international common good.[60]

Given the Church's response to self-determination since the end of the Cold War, I would argue that what is emerging in Catholic practice and statements such as that cited above is something like the "remedial rights" approach to secession. This approach can be summarized as follows. The initial presumption is to respect the sovereignty and territorial integrity of the existing state. Aggrieved peoples within this state have a responsibility to make all reasonable efforts to realize the moral right of self-determination through less-than-sovereign alternatives – ranging from securing protection of basic human rights, including minority rights, to various forms of political autonomy. If these efforts have been exhausted, the people must prove that they are willing and capable of establishing a legitimate state, and therefore, represent a self which can qualify for secession. Even then, secession is a remedy (not a right) only if (1) the people in question have just cause – an historic territorial grievance, unjust discrimination, or self-defense; (2) the benefits of secession outweigh the foreseeable harms; (3) political dialogue and nonviolence are the strongly preferred means to secure secession; and (4) military force is permitted only as a last resort in conformity with a restrictive just war analysis, with the strong preference that it be authorized by the UN Security Council.[61]

---

60 *The Harvest of Justice Is Sown in Peace*, 28–29.
61 Gerard Powers, "Testing the Moral Limits of Self-Determination: Northern Ireland and Croatia." *The Fletcher Forum of World Affairs* 16:2 (1992): 29–50.

2.2 Engaging armed actors

Himes argues that the presumption against war and the positive conception of peace (and, I would add, the strict just war analysis) found in
Catholic teaching is not matched by "a comparable set of theological
and ethical principles to guide conflict resolution."[62] He elaborates:

> The Catholic bias toward communitarianism has tended toward avoidance
> when confronted by social conflicts and the need to develop strategies for
> resolving them. A weakness of Catholic social teaching stemming from its
> communitarian vision is that conflict is viewed as more apparent than
> real; the organic metaphor of society, so prevalent in Catholic social teach-
> ing, induces a belief that harmony and cooperation are easier to achieve than
> is the case. Popes often appeal to parties in conflict to use reason to recognize
> mutual duties in support of the common good. ... The failure to acknowl-
> edge the deeply conflictual nature of human reality has permitted Catholic
> social teaching to remain underdeveloped in strategies of conflict resolution,
> even though, in practice, the church is deeply engaged in such efforts around
> the world.[63]

Evidence of Himes' point is the fact that in virtually every major war in
the past two decades, Church leaders have insisted that dialogue and negotiation were viable alternatives to military force. In the case of the two
Iraq wars, for example, U.S. bishops' statements questioned whether
enough had been done to find a diplomatic solution to meet the requirements of last resort. In other cases, the U.S. bishops have shown how far
removed they are from realist theories of international relations by insisting that the United States has a heavy moral responsibility to use its enormous power and influence, in collaboration with others, to be an honest
broker in peace negotiations. The success of U.S. mediation in two of the
world's truly intractable conflicts, Northern Ireland and Sudan, would
seem to support the realism of the bishops' idealism. The Clinton administration risked considerable political capital in taking a leading role in
negotiating the Good Friday Agreement, ending decades of violence
and putting Northern Ireland on a road, albeit full of potholes and road-
blocks, to a relatively stable political peace. Similarly, the Bush administration risked considerable political capital in taking the lead in helping to
negotiate the 2005 accords in Sudan.

These cases notwithstanding, Himes' overall thesis remains valid.
Catholic social teaching has much to learn from the now well-developed

---

62 Himes, *Peacebuilding and Catholic Social Teaching*, 282.
63 Ibid.

field of conflict transformation and resolution in developing more substantive norms for what is called "Track I", or government-to-govern-
ment, diplomacy.

The Church can also learn much from deeper reflection on its own
experience in what is called "Track II" diplomacy. The case of the Sant'E-
gidio Community's role in negotiating the end of the Mozambique conflict is perhaps the most well known and celebrated.[64] Catholic engagement with armed actors in Colombia offers another example. In Colombia, as in Uganda and the Philippines, to cite two other cases, the Church
has acknowledged the right of the government to use military force, within the constraints of a restrictive approach to just war, to combat a variety
of terrorist, rebel and paramilitary groups. Yet this position on force must
be understood in the context of the Church's broader spectrum of peacebuilding activities at all levels.

John Paul Lederach, a renowned Mennonite peacebuilding specialist
who has worked closely with Catholic leaders and groups in Colombia
and elsewhere, recounts an off-the-record meeting convened by the Colombia bishops' social pastoral office and the CPN in 2007. In this meeting, Colombian bishops described one aspect of their peacebuilding activities: engaging armed groups in various ways, from negotiating hostage
releases to observing the demobilization of paramilitaries, from formal
engagement in the national peace process to innovative use of Catholic
rituals and symbols in dealing with rebel commanders. Lederach left
this meeting with two observations: "How extensive and widespread
this particular church leadership's experiences of dealing with armed actors really was, and how little has been documented in any formal way
of the bishops' extraordinary activity."[65] Lederach describes "the boiling

---

64 See Andrea Bartoli, "NGOs and Conflict Resolution." In *The Sage Handbook of
    Conflict Resolution,* eds. J. Bercovitch, V. Kremenyuk and I. W. Zartman (Los
    Angeles: Sage, 2009): 392–412; Andrea Bartoli, "Mediating Peace in Mozambi-
    que: The Role of the Community of Sant'Egidio." In *Herding Cats,* eds. Pamela
    Aall, Chester Crocker and Fen Hampson (Washington, D.C.: U.S. Institute of
    Peace Press, 1999): 245–273; Thania Paffenholz, "Thirteen Characteristics of
    Successful Mediation in Mozambique." In *Peacebuilding: A Field Guide,* eds.
    Luc Reychler and Thania Paffenholz (Boulder, CO: Lynne Rienner, 2001):
    121–127; Dínis Sengulane and Jaime Pedro Gonçalves, "A calling for peace:
    Christian leaders and the quest for reconciliation in Mozambique." *Conciliation
    Resources* (1998): http://www.c-r.org/our-work/accord/mozambique/calling-for-
    peace.php.
65 John Paul Lederach, "The Long Journey Back to Humanity: Catholic Peace-
    building with Armed Actors." In *Peacebuilding:* 23–24.

cauldron of the core dilemma" arising from such engagement, especially in protracted conflicts where the Church's presence is "ubiquitous": "How to address the need for deep social, economic, and political changes that protect and improve the plight of the most vulnerable while being in *inevitable* relationship with leaders and groups, whether inside or outside of law, who justify the use of violence to achieve their competing vision of those same goals?"[66]

In dealing with this dilemma, Lederach finds that Church actors consistently use metaphors for journey – e.g., dialogue is a "bridge," "trail to truth," "pathway to justice." They also place a primary emphasis on the Church's role of accompaniment, "the quality of being present with, being alongside people as they make a journey." According to Lederach, "[s]ociologically, the church is, literally, present in and with the communities most affected by violence. Theologically, leaders consider their active presence, their engagement with both victims and perpetrators, as an expression of their pastoral vocation." Consequently, they rarely use secular terms, such as mediation or negotiation, to describe their engagement with armed actors, but prefer terms such as "pastoral dialogue." Lederach points out that, as pastoral imperatives, these dialogues trump the political tactic of isolation of "terrorists" and "insurgents" often imposed by governments. They also involve a delicate balance between the pastor, who engages and accompanies, and the prophet, who denounces and calls for accountability (often using just war categories) for the violence and abuses of armed actors. Lederach concludes:

> While the formal literature of peacebuilding and the political delineation of conflict-resolution roles describes the actions of church leadership as mediator, facilitator, guarantor, observer, advocate, or human rights activist, the *emic*, and perhaps more accurate, understanding of church leadership finds itself embracing the space that lies between the spiritual and ecclesiological roles of pastor and prophet, with the difficulties, weaknesses, and potential such a space affords.[67]

The delicate nature of this dual role of pastor and prophet is especially apparent in dealing with the neuralgic issue of justice versus peace (of a sort) which arises in most peace processes. In Colombia, the Church has faced a divisive debate over the justice and peace law. Those emphasizing the pastoral approach of dialogue and engagement with armed actors tend to support amnesty as a necessary ingredient of the formal peace

---

66   Ibid, 29.
67   Ibid., 52.

process and reconciliation as a necessary ingredient of reintegrating para-militaries into society. Those taking a more prophetic approach tend to insist on the need to hold the perpetrators of violence accountable through war crimes trials and to provide reparations for victims so as to end a culture of impunity and break the cycles of violence that so often characterize these intractable conflicts. Still others see these issues as inherently political and beyond the Church's competence to address.[68] To a certain extent, these dilemmas are matters of prudential judgment that can only be resolved on a case-by-case basis. But they also reflect a largely unexamined dimension of Catholic social teaching that warrants at least as much reflection as these issues are given in the secular literature.

The concern about the "political" implications of pastoral engagement with armed actors and peace processes raises an ecclesiological issue that follows from but is not addressed in Lederach's article. International relations and peace studies scholars consider the Church's engagement in formal and informal peace processes in Colombia as an example of Track II diplomacy and the role of civic society in promoting peace. For theologians and the Church, however, this engagement also raises the ecclesiological issue of the relationship between clerical and lay roles. Because engagement in peace processes and in peacebuilding writ large is so tied up with policy and politics, there is an inherent reluctance of institutional Church leaders, whether the president of a bishops' conference or a local pastor, to become too involved in peacebuilding. They often feel incompetent to do so, both in the ecclesiological and the ordinary sense of the term. When they do get involved, they tend to want to stay at a very general level that they consider appropriate for their role as pastors and teachers. In some countries, especially where the Church has traditionally played a leading role in society and the laity is largely uneducated, pastoral accompaniment by bishops and priests often involves a substitute political role, accepting formal roles in offcial negotiations, or in electoral commissions, constitutional reform processes, and truth commissions that are tied to peace accords. This kind of political engagement by the Church can be highly effective in the short-term, but a stronger, more engaged laity in these roles might be more effective over the long-term.[69]

---

68 Ibid., 52–53.
69 See, e.g., David O'Brien, "Stories of Solidarity: The Challenges of Catholic Peacebuilding." In *Peacebuilding*, 404–410.

Apart from the issue of effectiveness, a theology and ethics of peace-building should help better define the different ways different parts of the Church should engage in peacebuilding, with much greater emphasis given the Second Vatican Council's admonition that the laity has the principal role in transforming the social order in light of the Gospel. What is the ecclesiological basis for the substitute political role in peacebuilding that the institutional Church sometimes plays, especially in Catholic-majority countries? Is more reflection needed on delineating the different peacebuilding roles within the Catholic community? How would a practical theology of the lay vocation be different if it were defined more explicitly in terms of the Church's vocation of peacebuilding?

Lederach's evaluation of the Church's engagement with armed actors points to another issue that deserves further examination: Is there anything distinctive about Catholic peacebuilding? From his perspective as a prominent specialist in conflict transformation, he believes there is. He points, first, to the Church's "ubiquitous presence," a sociological fact in some countries that arises out of a particular ecclesiology. This presence gives the Church a "unique if not unprecedented presence in the landscape of the conflict." At least in majority Catholic countries like Colombia, the Church has relationships with every level and nearly every area of conflict, creating a depth and breadth of access that few religious or secular institutions enjoy. He concludes, "there are few places where the infrastructure and ecclesiology of church structure so neatly aligns with the multilevel and multifaceted demands of peacebuilding."[70]

A second distinctive aspect of Catholic peacebuilding is the role of the sacraments, especially the centrality of the Eucharist:

> While for the common person it may remain a ritual of habit, in settings of protracted conflict, time and again, the Eucharist creates moments pregnant with potential to mobilize both the sacramental and the moral imagination in reference to reconciliation, restoring the broken community, and taking personal and corporate responsibility for the suffering of others. It provides a basis for reparation robustly understood and an ethic of respect and forgiveness. This stands as an important, perhaps unique, contribution of the Catholic tradition and how the sacramental act, symbolic and real, connects, heals, and challenges people affected by, and who can affect, the wider conflict.[71]

---

70 John Paul Lederach, "The Long Journey Back to Humanity: Catholic Peace-building with Armed Actors," 50–51.

71 Ibid., 51.

Lederach's description of the power of the sacraments in Catholic peace-building in Colombia offers a glimpse into the larger question of the role of the Catholic social imaginary – ritual, sacrament and spirituality – in Catholic peacebuilding. Schreiter argues that ritual can play an important role in conflict prevention, negotiations, and post-conflict reconciliation. He attributes the dearth of research on this topic to a secular bias in peacebuilding. The Eucharist can create a safe place of hope amidst violence and despair, can form a bridge of communication between warring parties who share the same faith, and, of course, is the central Christian sign of the unity, reconciliation and peace for which peacebuilders strive. Spiritualities of nonviolence and reconciliation offer ways to integrate peacebuilding into the faith life of Christian communities in ways that sustain them during the often long, arduous struggle against violence and injustice.[72]

This brief foray into the Church's pastoral engagement with armed actors in Colombia nicely illustrates how Catholic peacebuilders can enter the "political" realm of dialogue and negotiation with warring parties without primarily relying on classic secular conflict resolution techniques. Instead, the Church relies on a "distinctive set of teachings, practices, sensibilities, and institutional resources" that might not be "exclusive" to Catholicism but come together in a special way in Catholic peacebuilding.[73] The implications for Catholic teaching that dialogue and negotiation are genuine alternatives to war, from Iraq and Iran to Colombia and Congo, need further exploration.

3 Conclusion

The Church's teaching on war and peace is at a crossroads. The new holy wars – religious terrorism and religious-nationalist conflicts – and the responses to them – preventive war, humanitarian intervention, and secularist efforts to marginalize religion – pose serious challenges for the Church's restrictive interpretation of the just war tradition. These challenges have also created an especially propitious moment for the Church's

---

72 See Robert Schreiter, "The Catholic Social Imaginary and Peacebuilding: Ritual, Sacrament, and Spirituality." In *Peacebuilding*, 221–239.

73 Scott Appleby, "Peacebuilding and Catholicism: Affinities, Convergences, Possibilities." In *Peacebuilding*, 12; see also Robert Schreiter, "Future Directions in Catholic Peacebuilding." In *Peacebuilding*, 422–425.

teaching on war and peace to develop in new directions. The credibility of the strict just war approach will depend, of course, on whether it prevails against the permissive interpretations promulgated by neo-conservative ethicists and realist policymakers. But its credibility will depend even moreso on whether it is married to a comprehensive theology, ethics, and praxis of peacebuilding that remains in a relatively early stage of development. The two depend upon each other. A strict just war is an important form of peacebuilding, but it is radically incomplete apart from an ethic of peacebuilding that can deal with secession, engagement with armed actors, and other issues not addressed by the just war tradition. Peacebuilding is the missing dimension of a Catholic ethic of war and peace.

The Peace Ethics of Pope John Paul II*

Heinz-Gerhard Justenhoven

Though Pope John Paul II did not leave a peace encyclical, he did leave a comprehensive peace agenda that he developed over the course of his more than twenty-six-year pontificate. The agenda is a milestone because of its firm commitment to human rights, particularly the right to freedom of religion and conscience. His idea that human rights are the cornerstone of a well-ordered, peaceful society is a sort of leitmotif in many of his public statements, and it moved him to oppose the communist system in the early years of his pontificate. In later years, John Paul's commitment to freedom of religion and conscience became the linchpin of his dialogue with other religions as he attempted to move them toward a united commitment for peace and away from a "clash of cultures or religions." He believed there was little use of holding human rights if the basic foundations for their realizations were not laid. John Paul often denounced the lack of these basic foundations in speeches he gave during his more than one hundred papal pilgrimages across the world, identifying their absence as a root cause of violence and injustice and discord, particularly between the first and third worlds. Globalization made the world smaller, he believed, but the need for rules and regulations between states increased substantially; protecting human rights should be the standard by which international law regulates relations between peoples and states. John Paul II believed that the United Nations (UN) provided the institutional framework by which the modern state community should solve its problems.

In the following, the systematic framework of John Paul II's peace teachings shall be reconstructed from his writings and speeches,[1] including his series of encyclicals, his twenty-six messages for the World Day of

* First published in: University of St. Thomas Law Journal 3:1 (Minneapolis 2005): 110–138.
1 Based on the texts of Pope John Paul II, 1978–2004, published in L'Osservatore Romano. The author used the German edition of the L'Osservatore Romano; quotations are translated into English.

Peace,[2] his speeches to the diplomatic corps[3] and before the UN and its suborganizations, as well as his speeches from over one hundred journeys abroad, from thematic initiatives like the Dialogue of Religions,[4] and from his interventions on contemporary crises[5] of his pontificate.

1 The Foundation of the Pope's Peace Agenda

1.1 The Basis: Human Dignity

The basis for John Paul II's peace doctrine is anthropology. The human being in all his ambivalence is the center of theological-ethical thinking:[6] On the one hand, John Paul saw the human being as "the only creature wanted by God for his own sake."[7] On the other hand, the "inner ambivalence" of human beings[8] has been the recurrent theme of uncountable texts: the sinful human being does not take advantage of his possibilities, and it is only through "the redemption that resulted from the cross [that] man is given back his dignity and the meaning for his being in the world."[9] Thus, "human beings have gained in Christ and through Christ complete knowledge of their dignity, ... of the transcendental value of

---

2   Pope John Paul II's messages for World Peace Day, 1979–2000, are edited with commentaries in two volumes: Donate Squicciarini ed., *Die Weltfriedensbotschaften Papst Johannes Pauls II: 1993–2000* (Berlin: Duncker & Humblot, 2001); Donato Squicciarini, ed., *Die Weltfriedensbotschaften Papst Johannes Pauls II* (Berlin: Duncker & Humblot 2005).

3   Pope John Paul II's speeches to the diplomatic corps, 1978–2002, are published in *John Paul II and the Family of Peoples: The Holy Father to the Diplomatic Corps (1978–2002)* (Pontifical Council for Justice and Peace, 2002).

4   Byron L. Sherwin and Harold Kasimow, eds., *John Paul II and Interreligious Dialogue* (New York: Orbis Books, 1999).

5   A text collection discussing the Gulf War was produced on the basis of texts published in L'Osservatore Romano: Mario Agnes, ed., *Per la Pace nel Golfo* (Vatican, 1991).

6   A collection of early texts from Pope John Paul II on the issue of human dignity and rights is found in Juliusz Stroynowski ed., Karol Wojtyla, *Von der Königswürde des Menschen* (Stuttgart: Seewald, 1980).

7   Pope John Paul II, *Redemptor Hominis,* No. 13 (Mar. 4, 1979) (available at http://www.vatican.va/edocs/ENG0218/_INDEX.HTM).

8   Id. at No. 14.

9   Id. at No. 10.

their own being human and of the meaning of their existence."[10] This Christologically interpreted anthropology can help explain an oft-quoted statement in which the Pope's high appreciation for humankind is expressed: "How precious must man be in the eyes of the Creator," John Paul II wonders, "if he 'gained so great a Redeemer.'"[11] Human dignity is based on this integral view of the human being as "God's creation, created in His image, as a being that is capable of recognizing the invisible; that reaches for the absolute, for God; that is made to love and that is destined to an eternal calling."[12] From this theological reasoning of human dignity, John Paul concluded that which is elsewhere inferred philosophically, namely that "the human being in his dignity must never be reduced to a means that one can regard and manipulate as an instrument."[13] On his uncountable papal pilgrimages, John Paul II bore with him the idea of the dignity of every individual human being, and he never tired of addressing its violation. He believed the Church must perceive the human being "with the eyes of Christ Himself" in order to discover "what is deeply human: the search for truth, the insatiable thirst for the Good, the hunger for freedom, the longing for beauty, the voice of the conscience."[14] Looking at the human being in today's world with the eyes of Christ reveals what pertains to the human being as a human being. In this way, "the entire concept of human rights is based on the idea of the dignity of the human person, i.e., on one fundamental value, the source of inalienable rights."[15] In contrast to his predecessors, who argued from the perspective of natural law, John Paul II's "Christocentric human-

---

10 Id. at No. 11; Joachim Giers proves that Pope John Paul II followed the argumentation of section 22 of the pastoral constitution, *Gaudium et Spes*. Joachim Giers, "Der Weg der Kirche ist der Mensch. Sozialtheologische Aspekte der Enzyklika 'Redemptor Hominis' Papst Johannes Pauls II." *Münchener Theologische Zeitschrift* 30 (1979): 278–92, 283.

11 Pope John Paul II, *Redemptor Hominis, supra* n. 7, at No. 10.

12 Pope John Paul II, "Forschung nicht von der Ethik lösen: Ansprache Johannes Pauls II. an die Teilnehmer des Kolloqiums der internationalen Stiftung 'Nova Spes'." *L'Osservatore Romano* 1 (Nov. 9, 1987): 18 (Supp.).

13 Id.

14 Pope John Paul II, *Redemptor Hominis, supra* n. 7, at No. 18.

15 Pope John Paul II, "Chemische Waffen vernichten: Rede von Erzbischof Sodano bei der internationalen Konferenz in Paris zur Achtung chemischer Waffen." *L'Osservatore Romano* 10 (Mar. 10, 1989): 19 (Supp. IX).

ism"[16] permitted him to perceive human rights as part of his theological anthropology.[17]

1.2 Defending Human Rights as Part of the Christian Joyous Message

The Church has evolved from being a church that, under John Paul II's predecessors, struggled with human rights to being a church that is permeated by Christologically based human rights and that defends them as an integral part of its joyous message.[18] When human beings are perceived as being endowed with these rights, "human beings [become] the path of the Church …, the path of her daily life and experience," and the Church must learn to see them with Christ's eyes. Human existence is kept open by the eschatological tension in Christ's message concerning a possible step towards the realization of the *humanum*. It is hardly surprising that on his more than one hundred journeys abroad John Paul II sought personal meetings with commoners to discuss with them their lives; by doing this, he hoped to make "the Church of our times always realize anew the situation of the human being."[19] He understood that, in order to advance to a time when "all areas of this life correspond to the true dignity of human beings,"[20] an integral part of his papacy would be to speak repeatedly about human rights and about their violation. John Paul II's significance in motivating support for human rights groups within the former Soviet Union's reach of power and in the revolutionary upheavals at the end of the 1980s is often cited. His political effect was rooted in his theological anthropology, which he knew the public would embrace.[21]

---

16 Hermann J. Pottmeyer, "Christliche Anthropologic als kirchliches Programm: Die Rezeption von 'Gaudium et Spes' in 'Redemptor Hominis'." *Trierer Theologische Zeitschrift* 94 (1995): 173–87, 17.

17 Ernst-Wolfgang Böckenförde, "Das neue politischen Engagement der Kirche. Zur 'politischen Theologie' Johannes Pauls II." *Stimmen der Zeit* 198 (Apr. 1980): 219–34, 221.

18 Helmut J. Patt, "Das Menschenbild von Papst Johannes Paul II. nach 'Redemptor Hominis'." *Renovatio* 36 (1980): 137–43, 140. For a collection of texts on the issue of "human rights" according to the teaching of recent popes, see Giorgio Filibeck, ed., *Human Rights in the Teaching of the Church: From John XXIII to John Paul II* (Vatican Press, 1994).

19 Pope John Paul II, *Redemptor Hominis,* supra n. 7, at No. 14.

20 Id.

21 Cf. Jan Roß, *Der Papst: Johannes Paul II – Drama und Geheimnis* (Fest, 2000), 160.

In his first speech before the UN General Assembly in 1979, John Paul II praised the General Declaration on Human Rights as a "milestone in the long and stony road of humankind,"[22] as human rights denote "the substance of the dignity of the human being, understood in his entirety, not as reduced to one dimension only." The union of people and states, as envisioned by the UN, "is through each human being, through the definition and recognition of and respect for the inalienable rights of individuals."[23] Inasmuch as every policy has to serve the human being, human rights should be the motivating force in an individual state's policies, just as they are for the UN's policies.

In his speech to the General Assembly of the UN, John Paul II endorsed individual freedom rights, rights of political self-determination, and social rights:

> "The right to life and liberty and to personal safety; the right to food, clothes, and a shelter, to health, relaxation and recreation; the right to free speech, to education and culture, the right to freedom of thought, of conscience, of religion as well as the right to confess one's religion in private and in public, by oneself and in a community; the right to choose one's lifestyle, to have a family and to have all necessary conditions for a family life; the right to property and work, to adequate working conditions and fair pay; the right to hold meetings and join in associations; the right to freedom of movement in one's own country and foreign countries; the right to citizenship and to a place of residence; the right to political co-determination and the right to participation in free elections of the political system of the people to whom one belongs.[24] Not to satisfy these rights means very simply to scorn the dignity of the human being."[25]

John Paul II acknowledged that some human rights are a human construct in that they represent a positive-law response to some of the sorrowful experiences of human history. But he also pointed to the "world-encompassing character" of the human rights movement as "a first and basic 'chiffre' that affirms that there are truly general human rights that

---

22 Pope John Paul II, Speech, *To the General Assembly of the United Nations* (N.Y., Oct. 2, 1979) (available at http://www.vatican.va/holy_father/john_paul_ii/speeches/1979/october/documents/hf_jp_spe_19791002_general-assembly-onu_ge.html) [hereinafter *Address to the UN General Assembly*].

23 Id.

24 Id.

25 Pope John Paul II, Speech, *Address of the Holy Father at the Exchange of Greetings with the Diplomatic Corps* (Vatican City, Jan. 10, 2000) (available at http://www.vatican.va/holy_father/john_paul_ii/speeches/documents/hfjp-ii_spe_20000110_diplomatic-corps_en.html) [hereinafter *Address of the Holy Father*].

are rooted in the nature of each person which reflect the objective and undeniable demands for a universal moral law."[26] This consideration allowed the Pope to make the connection to traditional natural law reasoning:[27]

> "It appears to me that what the Church's teachings knows as the "natural
> order" of living together, "the God-given order," partly finds its expression
> in the culture of human rights, if one can characterize a culture that is
> based on the respect for the transcendental value of a person like this."[28]

John Paul II believed that the relation between the law of nature and positive law is comparable to the relation between fundamental human rights
and single legal norms:

> "Natural law does not provide the law-maker with a single norm; these re-
> main to be complemented continually. It does not claim to establish a social
> code of conduct by itself, for all times, and detached from history. It does
> demand, however, that human dignity is ensured in the different areas of ex-
> istence."[29]

The Pope referred to the human rights movement as empirical evidence
that what befits human beings as human beings is universally acknowledged as self-evident. Derived from the "common good of humankind,"
these evident rights correlate with the consciousness that every human
being has the capacity to reach and which directs what one feels one
ought to do: "Human rights ... go into everybody's conscience."[30]
From this point of view, human rights can be seen as the "general, in

---

26 Pope John Paul II, *Speech, Address of His Holiness Pope John Paul II to the Fiftieth
    General Assembly of the United Nations Organization* (N.Y., Oct. 5, 1995) (available
    at   http://www.vatican.va/holy_father/john_paul_ii/speeches/1995/october/docu-
    ments/hfjp-ii_spe_05101995_address-to-uno_en.html) [hereinafter *Address to the
    UN*].

27 On the term of natural law according to Pope John Paul II, cf. Helmut Weber, "Zur
    Enzyklika 'Veritatis Splendor'." *Trierer Theologische Zeitschrift* 103 (1994): 161–87,
    169. Zur Auseinandersetzung mit der Enzyklika. Cf. Dietmar Mieth, ed., *Moral-
    theologie im Abseits? Antwort auf die Enzyklika "Veritatis Splendor"* (Freiburg: Herder,
    1994).

28 Pope John Paul II, Speech, *Address at the New Year's Reception of the Diplomatic Corps*
    (Vatican City, Jan. 9, 1988) (available at http://www.vatican.va/holy_father/
    john_paul_ii/speeches/1988/january/documents/hfjp-ii_spe_ 19880109_corpo-dip-
    lomatico_sp .html).

29 Pope John Paul II, "To the Participants of the International Colloquium on 'Natur-
    recht und Menschenrechte vor Beginn des 21. Jahrhunderts'." *L'Osservatore Roma-
    no* 5 (Feb. 1, 1991): 21 (Supp. V)

30 Id.

the heart of human beings' engraved moral law," as "a kind of 'grammar' that serves the world to deal with this discussion about its own future."[31] Introducing this ethical grammar into the (world) political discourse is, according to John Paul II, the task of the Church; in this, "[the Church] offers a reflection on the principles that should guide the lives of people and nations."[32]

The Pope highlighted two central threats to human rights at the beginning of his pontificate and made them a subject of discussion in subsequent years: the threat resulting from the worldwide justice deficit between rich and poor (the "terrible inequalities between human beings and groups in excessive wealth on the one side and the demographic majority of the poor on the other"), and the threat resulting from "forms of injustices in the spiritual sphere," which harm the human being "in his inner relationship to truth."[33] As Christian philosophy believes that the freedom of a human being is fully realized through his or her relationship to truth,[34] John Paul II classified violations of the right to freedom of belief and conscience as among the most serious human rights violations.

As human freedom "is realized in the search and action for truth,"[35] the need to freely search for truth justifies the freedom of belief and conscience; it is "the core of human rights."[36] With respect to the right to freedom of belief and conscience, John Paul II offered the following insights: First, as he expressed in his famous talk with Mikhail Gorbachev in 1989 in the Vatican, John Paul II believed the introduction of religious freedom[37] is an integral part of the attainment of political freedom.[38] Se-

---

31 See Pope John Paul II, *Address to the UN, supra* n. 26.
32 Memorandum from Vatican Secretary of State "Wie weiter mit KSZE? Aide-Memoire des Staatssekretariats." *L'Osservatore Romano* 36 (Sept. 4, 1992): 22 (Supp. XXXII).
33 See Pope John Paul II, *Address to the UN General Assembly, supra* n. 22.
34 Cf. Jörg Splett, *Der Mensch ist Person* 62 (Freiburg: Knecht 1978).
35 See Pope John Paul II, *Address to the UN, supra* n. 26.
36 Pope John Paul II, *Message on the Occasion of the World Day of Peace* (Jan. 1, 1999) (available at http://www.vatican.va/holy_father/john_paul_ii/messages/peace/documents/hfJp- ii_mes_l 4121998_xxxii-world-day-for-peace_en.html).
37 A collection of documents with texts of John Paul II on religious freedom: cf. Alessandro Colombo ed., *La libertà religiosa negli insegnamenti di Giovanni Paolo II (1978–1998)* (Vita e pensiero, 2000).
38 Cf. Pope John Paul II, Speech, *To the President of the USSR, Michail Gorbachev* (Vatican City, Dec. 1, 1989) (available at http://www.vatican.va/holy_father/john_paul_ii/speeches/ 1989/december/documents/hfJp-ii_spe_19891201_president-gorbaciov_it.html).

cond, he criticized democratic societies that attempted to block out religion from public discourse: "Should those citizens whose judgment concerning ethics is influenced by their belief be less free to voice their deep-felt persuasions than others?"[39] Third, he believed that religious freedom includes the freedom to change religions: it constitutes human nature to follow the conscience in a search for truth, and thus nobody should be forced to act against his conscience.[40] John Paul II emphasized this third point in his discussions with Islamic persons.[41]

1.3 The Protection of Human Rights as a Responsibility of Every Legal System

John Paul II believed that it is, above all, the responsibility of the state authority to protect human rights. If the fundamental rights of the individual are protected, the community is well-ordered: "The common good that authority in the State serves is brought to full realization only when all the citizens are sure of their rights."[42] Engrained in the dignity of the person, human rights are "no concession of the state"; instead, by securing human rights, the state is acknowledging that which had "been a priori given to his own legal system."[43] In the dispute with communist totalitarianism in the 1980s, the Polish Pope referred again and again in support of the notion that the negation of indisposable human rights is only possible at the cost of repression:

> "The Brothers have shown in the countries, in which a party has for years dictated the truth one had to believe and the meaning one had to give to history, that it is not possible to suffocate elementary freedoms that give meaning to the life of a human being: the freedom of thought, of conscience, of religion, of expressing your opinion, of political and cultural pluralism."[44]

---

39 Pope John Paul II, Message to the Congress "Säkularismus und Religionsfreiheit." *L'Osservatore Romano* 5 (Feb. 2, 1996): 26.

40 Pope John Paul II, *Message of John Paul II on the Occasion of the World Day of Peace,* supra n. 36, at No. 5.

41 Pope John Paul II, "Dialog schließt Zusammenleben in Frieden ein." *L'Osservatore Romano* 38 (Sept. 21, 1990): 20 (Supp. XXXV).

42 Pope John Paul II, *Redemptor Hominis,* supra n. 7, at No. 27.

43 Pope John Paul II, "Leiden der Völker beenden." *L'Osservatore Romano* 11 (Mar. 17, 1989): 19 (Supp. X).

44 Pope John Paul II, "Einheit der menschlichen Familie festigen und vervollständigen." *L'Osservatore Romano* 5 (Feb. 2, 1990): 20 (Supp. V).

Accordingly, John Paul II saw the development of the human rights movement as inevitable, as the movement gave "concrete political expression to one of the great dynamics of contemporary history."[45]

The human rights movement in Europe of the 1980's systematically laid out what would have political consequences twenty years later. With the Conference on Security and Cooperation in Europe's (CSCE) Final Document (the "Helsinki Accords"), human rights became recognized as a limit to the sovereignty of a state: "Governments that respect the rule of law indeed recognize the limits of their power and of their spheres of interest. For these governments concede that they are themselves subject to law and not the rulers of law."[46] At the end of the 1980s, the people of Eastern Europe demanded that their governments comply with the human rights and political freedoms encompassed in the Helsinki Accords. Only years later did the question arise as to whether the international community had to help oppressed peoples – victims of massive violations of human rights – when their respective government is not able or not willing to do so.[47]

1.4 Humanity as the Constitutive Community

From the fundamental notion that every human being is endowed with inalienable rights because of his dignity, John Paul II believed that it followed, in principle, that every human being has the duty to help whenever a person's rights are endangered. In support of this principle, John Paul II referred to the biblical demand for universal love of one's neighbor: "Sacred Scripture … demands of us a shared responsibility for all of humanity. This duty … extends progressively to all mankind, since no

---

45 Pope John Paul II, *Pacem in terris: A Permanent Commitment,* No. 4 (Jan. 1, 2003) (available at http://www.vatican.va/holy_father/john_paul_ii/messages/peace/documents/hfjp- ii_mes_20021217_xxxvi-world-day-for-peace_en.html).

46 Pope John Paul II, "Die Menschenrechte sind ein gemeinsamer Besitz." *L'Osservatore Romano* 46 (Nov. 11, 1988): 18 (Supp. XL); cf. also Agostino Casaroli, "Vorlesung des Kardinalstaatssekretärs Agostino Casaroli bei der Verleihung der Ehrendoktorwürde der juristischen Fakultät der Universitat Parma" *L'Osservatore Romano* 20 (Apr. 13, 1990): 15–16.

47 Cf. Heinz-Gehard Justenhoven, "Die friedensethische Debatte im deutschen Katholizismus seit dem Ende des II. Weltkrieges." In *Festschrift 50 Jahre Katholische Militärseelsorge* (Cordier, 2006) 285–317; the respective sources are published in Ortwin Buchbender and Gerhard Arnold, eds., *Kämpfen für die Menschenrechte: Der Kosovo-Konflikt im Spiegel der Friedensethik* (Nomos, 2002).

one can consider himself extraneous or indifferent to the lot of another member of the human family."[48] Humanity, "beyond its ethnic, national, cultural and religious differences, should form a community"[49] from which universal solidarity claims are derived. John Paul II developed these claims in his 1991 social encyclical *Centesimus Annus.*

2 The Pope's Peace Agenda in Specific Circumstances

2.1 Option for Non-Violence

Time and again, John Paul II forcefully and publicly opposed recourse to violence in international relations. As a result, some criticize him as being a pacifist who ignored the reality of international politics. Other wellmeaning critics believe his passionate appeals against war and violence were rooted in his decisive stance for human life. I believe that neither critique goes far enough. I would first like to document the decisiveness with which John Paul II opposed violence, using a few quotes from his speeches:

> "Violence only generates further violence,[50] [because] violence destroys and never builds up,[51] [for] no type of violence brings about a settlement to conflicts between persons or nations.[52] [T]he wounds [war] causes remain long unhealed, and … as a result of conflicts the already grim condition of the poor deteriorates still further, and new forms of poverty appear.[53] [R]ecourse to violence [fails] as a means for resolving political and social problems. War destroys, it does not build up; it weakens the moral foundations of society and creates further divisions and long-lasting tensions.[54]

---

48 Pope John Paul II, *Centesimus Annus,* No. 51 (May 1, 1991) (available at http://www.vatican.va/edocs/ENG0214/_INDEX.HTM).

49 Pope John Paul II, *To Build Peace, Respect Minorities,* No. 3 (Jan. 1, 1989) (available at http://www.vatican.va/holy_father/john_paul_ii/messages/peace/documents/hfjp-ii_mes_19881208_xxii-world-day-for-peace_en.html).

50 Pope John Paul II, "Auf alle Formen von Gewalt und Haß verzichten." *L'Osservatore Romano* 42 (Oct. 14, 1988): 18 (Supp. XXXV).

51 Pope John Paul II, *If You Want Peace, Reach Out to the Poor,* No. 4 (Jan. 1, 1993) (available at http://www.vatican.va/holy_father/john_paul_ii/messages/peace/documents/hfjp- ii_mes_08121992_xxvi-world-day-for-peace_en.html).

52 Pope John Paul II, "Dialogbereitschaft ist Grundverhalten für Friedensforderung." *L'Osservatore Romano* 27 (July 7, 1995): 25 (Supp. XXVI).

53 Pope John Paul II, *If You Want Peace, Reach Out to the Poor,* supra n. 51, at No. 4.

54 Pope John Paul II, *Message of John Paul II on the Occasion of the World Day of Peace,* supra n. 36, at No. 11.

[The] increase of violence in the world [can] . … not be brought to a halt by responding with more [violence].[55] [The use of violence leads to hate on both sides; this] hate shuts us away from others by making communication and reconciliation impossible.[56]

[V]iolence always needs to justify itself through deceit, and to appear, however falsely, to be defending a right or responding to a threat posed by others.[57]

Violence is only a way of death and destruction, and it dishonours the holiness of God and the dignity of man.[58] War cannot be an adequate means … to solve completely existing problems between nations. It never was and it never will be!"[59]

In *Centesimus Annus,* in response to political realists who argued that violence is a natural interstate condition, John Paul II cited the contrasting experience and worldwide political significance of non-violence: "It seemed that the European order resulting from the Second World War and sanctioned by the *Yalta Agreements* could only be overturned by another war. Instead, it has been overcome by the non-violent commitment."[60] The Pope attributed this success to the "commitment of people who … [had always refused] to yield to the force of power." Against the dictatorship of the powerful, the protesting demonstrators bore "witness to the truth."[61] "This disarmed the adversary."[62] John Paul II saw the overthrow of the Eastern European totalitarian regime as a "warning" to those figures in world politics "who, in the name of political realism, wish to banish law and morality from the political arena."[63] The overthrow represents a warning because it was driven by morality, by a dedication to truth and freedom; the demonstrators fought a non-violent battle with the "weapons of truth and justice."[64]

---

55 Pope John Paul II, *If You Want Peace, Reach Out to the Poor,* supra n. 51.
56 Id.
57 Pope John Paul II, *Centesimus Annus,* supra n. 48, at No. 23.
58 Pope John Paul II, *Angelus Prayer,* No. 1 (Oct. 21, 2001) (available at http:// www. Vatican. va/holy_father/j ohn_paul_ii/angelus/2001 /documents/hfjp-ii_ang_20011021 _en.html).
59 Pope John Paul II, "Frieden erfordert den vollen Einsatz der internationalen Gemeinschaft." *L'Osservatore Romano* 25 (Jan. 25, 1991): 4.
60 Pope John Paul II, *Centesimus Annus,* supra n. 48, at No. 23.
61 Id.
62 Id.
63 Id. at No. 25.
64 Id, at No. 23.

John Paul II knew all too well that many people paid a high personal price for this non-violent commitment, including paying with their lives. He interpreted this suffering for political change Christologically as a sacrifice for others: "[B]y uniting his own sufferings for the sake of truth and freedom to the sufferings of Christ on the Cross ... man is able to accomplish the miracle of peace."[65] To stoically tolerate violence is not to emulate Christ; following Christ's example entails opposing violence and consciously accepting the consequences of this political commitment. If one does so, one would then be able to "discern the often narrow path between the cowardice which gives in to evil and the violence which, under the illusion of fighting evil, only makes it worse."[66] Citing the positive experiences of the year 1989, John Paul II wished that "people [would] learn to fight for justice without violence, renouncing class struggles in internal disputes and war in their international ones."[67]

John Paul II believed nonviolence in international relations was possible, and supported his belief by citing the continuous negotiation marathons of the CSCE (or Helsinki) process, a process by which countries overcame differences during the Cold War. Agostino Cardinal Casaroli, the then Cardinal Secretary of State, summed up the position of the Holy See after 1989's bloodless revolution: "The patient efforts of the 'process of Helsinki' [had] ... a significant part in the almost revolutionary development of European security these last few years."[68] In 1990, Cardinal Casaroli emphasized that such a process takes time: "Since 1975 we can observe a quiet, discreet – often even frustrating – preparation ... of those events that have led to the current changes in Middle and Eastern Europe."[69]

A cornerstone of John Paul II's thinking was his belief that the Cold War ended as a result of three factors: non-militaristic diplomacy that centered on ethical and legal positions, the non-violent commitment of the population for political changes, and, particularly, the inclusion of the human rights catalogue in the Helsinki Final Act. As church leader and Polish patriot, he supported and assisted these processes in his home country to a considerable extent. Drawing upon the experience

---

65 Id. at No. 25.
66 Id.
67 Id. at No. 23.
68 Agostino Casaroli, Die Konferenz über Sicherheit und Zusammenarbeit in Europa, supra n. 46.
69 Id.

of the first ten years of his pontificate, John Paul II would advise the conflicting parties to engage in dialogue and to have patience when he believed (often justifiably) that the use of military force would not be the
parties' last but rather first resort. In response to the "realist" view that
denied that viability of non-violence in international relations, he articulated his position this way:

> "As you all know, the Holy See has reminded [us] of the ethical imperative
> that must predominate under all circumstances: of the inviolability of the
> human person, on whichever side he or she is, the legal force, the importance
> of dialogues and negotiations, the respect for international agreements.
> These are the only "weapons" that confer honour to the human being as
> God wanted him."[70]

It was apparent to the Pope that the protection of life requires a political
order. He believed that although, generally speaking, the democratic constitutional state has prevailed over anarchical, violent conflict settlement,
the international community still resides in the state of anarchy, as conflicts are too often settled by violent means. His regular and passionate
calls against violence in international relations were rooted in his belief
that violence does not lead to a more peaceful world. According to
John Paul II, to overcome violence, we must actively search for and address the roots of violence, and upon this idea he identified two different
areas of responsibility: the international community is responsible for addressing the world's existing injustices, and the believers of all confessions
and religions are responsible for addressing the imminent threat of a
"clash of civilizations." While the Pope actively campaigned for non-violent solutions, he did not deny the necessity of the use of force as a last
resort, as we shall see later.

2.2 Reconciliation and Dialogue between Confessions and Religions as a Peace Program

Certain groups, such as al-Qaeda and those groups involved in the war in
former Yugoslavia, search for historical and religious justifications for
their politically motivated eruptions of violence. The Pope saw a necessity
to take countermeasures against these groups. "In the depths of our
faith," he said in 1988, "the decision for dialogue and friendship with

---

70 Pope John Paul II, "Das Vaterland braucht Schweiß, kein Blut." *L'Osservatore Romano*
    4 (Jan. 24, 1992): 22 (Supp. III).

the followers of other religions is rooted in order ... to cooperate ... in the pursuit of promoting the unity of the human family."[71] This belief is not a political calculation, but a religious conviction in the light of the peace message, a conviction upon which John Paul II often acted: for example, beginning in 1986, in an effort to establish a visible testimony against the instrumentalization of beliefs, he repeatedly invited representatives of all religions to Assisi to engage in common prayer. Given the multiple historical burdens, John Paul II believed that an honest dialogue was only possible when the past had been dealt with. As a result, he did not confront other religions with their offenses against Christians, but confronted his own church, us, with our offenses against believers of other confessions and religions. The history of the Church, the Pope wrote in preparation of the Holy Year 2000, records many events "which constitute a counter-testimony to Christianity."[72] Moreover, John Paul II was concerned with more than just the offenses of past generations: "Yet we too, sons and daughters of the Church, have sinned ... As the Successor of Peter, I ask that in this year of mercy the Church ... should kneel before God and implore forgiveness for the past and present sins of her sons and daughters."[73]

This confession of guilt and the diverse requests for forgiveness have prompted approval but also critique. Konrad Repgen asks critically whether events of past epochs can be judged adequately from today's perspective.[74] According to Olaf Blaschke, assigning the blame to the "Sons and Daughters of the Church" is an obscure attempt to absolve the Church itself of its guilt.[75] While agreeing to this assertion, Pierre Gervais asks how it might change the understanding of the Church as a mystery.[76]

After asking God for forgiveness for the sins, John Paul II demanded, as the necessary second step, that the Church approach the other confes-

---

71 Pope John Paul II, "Die Verpflichtung von Assisi vertiefen." *L'Osservatore Romano* 53 (Dec. 22, 1988): 52–53 (Supp. XL VI).

72 Pope John Paul II, *Incarnationis mysterium: Bull of Indiction of the Great Jubilee of the Year 2000,* No. 11 (Nov. 29, 1998) (available at http://www.vatican.va/jubilee_2000/docs/documents/hf_jp-ii_doc_30111998_bolla-jubilee_en.html).

73 Id.

74 Konrad Repgen, "Kirche und Vergangenheit." *Internationale Katholische Zeitschrift Communio* 29 (2000): 396–405, 403.

75 Olaf Blaschke, "Nicht die Kirche als Solche? Anfragen eines Historikers an die vatikanische 'Reflexion über die Shoa'." *Blätter für deutsche und internationale Politik* 43 (1998): 862–74, 864.

76 Pierre Gervais SJ, "La demande de pardon de Jean-Paul II et ses implications theologiques." *Nouvelle Revue Theologique* 123 (2001): 4–18, 16.

sions and religions and ask them for forgiveness for the injustice they endured at the hands of the Catholics. The remembrance of the events entailed by this task "should ensure that evil will never again win the upper hand."[77] The request the Pope made of the Greek Orthodox Church during the meeting with its leader in Greece, Archbishop Christodoulos of Athens, in the year 2001 illustrates the importance and graveness John Paul II placed on requesting forgiveness:

> "For the occasions past and present, when sons and daughters of the Catholic Church have sinned by action or omission against their Orthodox brothers and sisters, may the Lord grant us the forgiveness we beg of Him. ... I am thinking of the disastrous sack of the imperial city of Constantinople, which was for so long the bastion of Christianity in the East ... The fact that they [the aggressors] were Latin Christians fills Catholics with deep regret ... Division between Christians is a sin before God and a scandal before the world. It is a hindrance to the spread of the Gospel, because it makes our proclamation less credible."[78]

The Holy Father initiated a huge program within the Church in view of the Jubilee Year 2000, which he primarily understood as a year of asking for forgiveness, so that the jubilee had a *fundamentum in re*. He wanted to take the first step of confessing one's own guilt towards all other confessions and religions himself. At the memorial Yad Vashem he confirmed, as

> "Bishop of Rome and Successor of the Apostle Peter, ... that the Catholic Church ... is deeply saddened by the hatred, acts of persecution and displays of anti-Semitism directed against the Jews by Christians at any time and in any place. The Church rejects racism in any form as a denial of the image of the Creator inherent in every human being."[79]

A bit later, he prayed at the Wailing Wall in Jerusalem: "God of our fathers, ... we are deeply saddened by the behavior of those who in the course of history, have caused these children of yours to suffer and[,] asking for forgiveness[,] we wish to commit ourselves to genuine brother-

---

77 Pope John Paul II, "Trauer um die Tragödien – Weg zu neuer Beziehung zwischen Christen und Juden." *L'Osservatore Romano* 13 (Mar. 31, 2000): 30.

78 Pope John Paul II, *Address of John Paul II to His Beatitude Christodoulos, Archbishop of Athens and Primate of Greece* (May 4, 2001) (available at http://212.77.L245/holy_father/john_paul_ii/speeches/2001/documents/hf Jp-ii_spe_20010504_archbishop-athens_en.html).

79 Pope John Paul II, Trauer um die Tragödien – Weg zu neuer Beziehung zwischen Christen und Juden, supra n. 77.

hood with the people of the Covenant."[80] Israeli Prime Minister Ehud Barak, whose parents had died in the concentration camp Treblinka, recognized the visit of the Pope as a historical moment for Israel: "The atmosphere tilted in Israel on this day ... The majority of Jews accepted the apology of Catholic Christians through the Pope."[81]

In the context of the five hundred-year celebrations, John Paul II spoke of the injustices connected to the conquest of America in 1492 and the subsequent missionary work: he directed his request for forgiveness "[primarily] to the indigenous people of the New World, to the Indios – and then also to all who have been dragged from Africa as slaves for forced labour."[82] In this context, John Paul II emphasized the "scream of conscience" by "Pedro de Montesinos, Bartholome Las Casas,[83] and Cordoba, Fray Juan del Valle," who had stood up for the rights of Indios and whose protests manifested at the "University of Salamanca and the School of Vitoria."[84] Francisco de Vitoria had proven "that Indios and Spanish people are essentially equal as humans ... for the rights are based on their personhood and in their human nature."[85]

More than twenty years before the attacks of September 11, 2001, in the first years of his papacy, John Paul II intensified the dialogue with Islam which the Second Vatican Council had initiated with the Declaration on Religious Freedom *Nostra Aetate*. Unlike any pope before him, he not only visited Islamic countries but also sought dialogue with Muslims. He spoke with Muslim youth in Morocco, with the Egyptian Grand Mufti Mohamed Sayed Tantawi in the al-Azhar University in Cairo,

---

80 Pope John Paul II, "Vergebungsbitte an der Klagemauer." *L'Osservatore Romano* 13 (Mar. 31, 2000): 30.

81 Andreas Englisch, *Johannes Paul II. Das Geheimnis des Karol Wojtyla* (Berlin: Ullstein 2003), 289.

82 Pope John Paul II, "Bitte um Vergebung an die Indios und Afroamerikaner." *L'Osservatore Romano* 44 (Oct. 30, 1992): 22.

83 Cf. Matthias Gillner, *Bartholome de Las Casas und die Eroberung des indianischen Kontinents: das friedensethische Profil eines weltgeschichtlichen Umbruchs aus der Perspektive eines Anwalts der Unterdrückten* 1 Reihe Theologie und Frieden 12 (1997).

84 Pope John Paul II, "Jesus Christus gestern, heute und in Ewigkeit." *L'Osservatore Romano* 43 (Oct. 23, 1992): 22.

85 Pope John Paul II, "Dokumente belegen den Einsatz der Kirche für die Indios." *L'Osservatore Romano* 35 (July 2, 1992): 22; to Vitoria cf. Heinz-Gerhard Justenhoven, *Francisco de Vitoria zu Krieg und Frieden*, 5 Reihe Theologie und Frieden 57 (1991); on Vitoria's text sources see Ulrich Horst, Heinz-Gerhard Justenhoven and Joachim Stüben, eds., *Francisco de Vitoria, Vorlesungen II (Relectiones): Völkerrecht-Politik-Kirche,* 8 Reihe Theologie und Frieden 1 (1997).

and with Islamic dignitaries in the Omaijade Mosques in Damascus. In these meetings, he emphasized the commonalities of Abrahamitic religions and advocated respectful dialogue between Christians and Muslims. Since the history of conquests and crusades burdened the relationship between Christians and Muslims, the Pope called upon both to forgive: "Whenever Muslims and Christians have offended each other, we must ask the Almighty for forgiveness for that and offer forgiveness to one another."[86] Based on the dialogue that he cultivated for more than twenty years, the Holy See and the al-Azhar University in Cairo were able to condemn the terrorist attacks of September 11 in a joint declaration just one day later: "Such acts of violence do not lead to peace in the world."[87] With regard to a consensus with the Islamic authorities, the Pope could pass judgment when it was urgently needed: "The use of force in the name of one's own confession is a distortion of what the great religions teach. As different religious leaders have often emphasized, I would thus also like to emphasize that the use of force can never find a valid religious justification nor can it promote the development of true religiousness."[88] "Nobody is allowed to kill in the name of God."[89]

The confession of guilt is for John Paul II the first step of a real dialogue between religions and confessions. John Paul II also took this step with respect to the churches of the Reformation on the occasion of the canonization of Jan Sarkander in the Czech Republic:

> "Today I, the Pope of Rome, ask in the name of all Catholics for forgiveness for the injustices committed against non-Catholics in the course of the turbulent history of these people; and, at the same time, I assure you of the forgiveness of the Catholic Church for all the wrongs that her children have suffered."[90]

Given the multitude of Christian churches and confessions, the Pope's main concern was to reestablish the lost unity of God's people in hopes

---

86 Pope John Paul II, Speech, *Meeting with the Muslim leaders – Omayyad Great Mosque, Damascus: Address of the Holy Father* (May 6, 2001) (available at http://www.vatican.va/holy_father/john_paul_ii/speeches/2001/documents/hf_Jp-ii_spe_20010506_omayyadi_en.html).

87 Matthias Kopp ed., Pope John Paul II, *Versöhnung mit der Welt: Im Gespräch mit den Religionen,* 109, 111 (May 2004).

88 Pope John Paul II, "In der Achtung der Menschenrechte liegt das Geheimnis des wahren Friedens." *L'Osservatore Romano* 1 (Jan. 1, 1999).

89 Pope John Paul II, "Begegnung mit den Muslimen muß mehr sein als geteilter Lebensalltag." *L'Osservatore Romano* 17 (Apr. 26, 1996).

90 Pope John Paul II, "Das Zeugnis der Heiligen – Licht des Reiches Gottes." *L'Osservatore Romano* 21 (May 26, 1995): 25.

of offering the restored communion as a testament to peace. Pope John Paul II was well aware that for many of the other Christian churches it is precisely his office that constituted the main obstacle to the unity he sought. Indeed, his offer of communication with other Christian religions reflected this understanding, implicitly at least: "[i]f certain forms of unity from the past no longer meet with the impulses for unity that the Holy Ghost stimulates in Christians nowadays everywhere, then all of us have to follow more openly and attentively what the Ghost tells the Church now."[91]

The Pope's objective in approaching the other Christian confessions, on one hand, was a united authentic testimony for the belief in a God who overcomes hate and violence. God's people, the Pope argued, should "shine [again as] a sign and means for the closest union with God, for the unity of the entirety of humankind in the world."[92] On the other hand, the aim of the Pope's dialogue between other religions was to promote the joint work of religions to secure world peace while, at the same time, respecting the differences in their theologies.[93] The Pope argued that the theological explanation for this relationship between the Catholic Church and non-Christian religions was a recognition of the "truth" that can be found in other religions:

"While the Catholic Church clearly applies its identity, its teachings and its missionary creed to all people, she does not renounce any part of all what is true and sacred in other religions. With sincere severity, she looks at the deeds and way of life, those principles and doctrines that deviate in some respects from what she herself believes and teaches but all the same not seldom hold a stream of that truth that enlightens all human-beings."[94]

The Pope believed that through mutual understanding and respectful dialogue, religions would be able to ward off becoming a political instrument, as well as religious fanaticism or terrorism.[95]

---

91 Pope John Paul II, "Im Geiste brüderlicher Nächstenliebe die Spannungen der Vergangenheit überwinden." *L'Osservatore Romano* 31 (May 11, 2001).
92 Id.
93 Pope John Paul II, "Päpstlicher Rat für den Interreligiosen Dialog, Dialog und Verkündigung. Überlegungen und Orientierungen zum Interreligiösen Dialog und zur Verkündigung des Evangeliums Christi." *L'Osservatore Romano* 21 (Aug. 2, 1991): 31–32.
94 Pope John Paul II, "Die Gläubigen vereint im Aufbau des Friedens." *L'Osservatore Romano* 51 (Dec. 20, 1991): 52.
95 Cf. Pope John Paul II, Speech, *Address at the New Year's Reception of the Diplomatic Corps* (Vatican City, Jan. 13, 2003) (available at http://www.vatican.va/holy_father/john_paul_ii/speeches/2003/january/documents/hfjp-ii_spe_20030113_diplomatic-corps_en.html).

Overcoming violence, as I have said before, for John Paul II meant to look actively for the root causes of violence and address them if possible. The Pope saw it as the responsibility of Christians, through authentic testimony, to commit to the Christian peace message: together with the believers of the other religions, we are called to install an international order that is rooted in the dignity of and respects the rights of all human beings, to lobby for the continuous development of international law and UN institutions, and to advocate for nonviolent conflict resolution.[96] Part of this effort is also a commitment to ensure justice among the world's peoples and states. John Paul II developed his vision for this in the social encyclics *Sollicitudo Rei Socialis* (1987) and *Centesimus Annus* (1991): "God has given the earth to the human race so that she could nourish all her members." "Here," John Paul II concludes, "is rooted the universal purpose of the earth's goods."[97] Given the situation of many people – even whole peoples – the "stronger nations (must) offer ... the weaker the opportunity to integrate into the international life."[98] This is, the Pope summarized, the demand of justice: we must protect the world's most vulnerable, "whom the state and the market have to serve."[99]

For John Paul II a justice that ends at the borders of one's own state and subjects other human beings and nations solely to the calculus of power and the interests of political realism is nothing more than the behaviour of a band of gangsters who divide their bounty among themselves according to principles of equality. John Paul II made such global justice deficits a subject of discussion time and again – while not neglecting intrastate justice deficits, such as corruption in developing countries, for example.[100] Simply put, the Pope thought that an international law that was ethically committed to, and thus oriented by, human rights, is an essential step towards accomplishing justice for all. But how can existing international law gain importance?

---

96 Cf. Sekretariat der deutschen Bischofskonferenz, ed., *Christen und Buddisten: Miteinander in der Hoffnung*. In *Der Apostolische Stuhl 1998* (Cologne 2001): 1226.

97 Pope John Paul II, *Centesimus Annus,* supra n. 48, at No. 31.

98 Id. at No. 35.

99 Id. at No. 49.

100 Cf. Pope John Paul II, Speech, *Address to the XXVIII Session of the Conference of FAO* (Vatican City, Nov. 23, 1995) (available at http://www.vatican.va/holy_father/john_paul_ii/speeches/1996/documents/hf Jp-ii_spe_23111995_xxviii-session-fao-conference_en.html).

3 The Pope's Teaching on International Law

3.1 Creating Trust by Respecting International Law

Referring to the experiences in the CSCE, John Paul II made clear that peace does not primarily depend on military security but, above all, on developing a trust between nations.[101] Given an international legal system in which the global-public authority is (still) missing, trust in the legal system – or legal security – only develops if subjects of international law (nation states) themselves submit to the basic norms of the law. Consequently, international law can "not be the right of the stronger and not even the right of a minority of states nor the right of an international organization."[102] Given a world consisting of "unequal states,"[103] then, genuine trust in international law can only develop if "those states that carry more weight and thus have greater responsibility do their utmost [to ensure] that the principles of international law are respected faithfully."[104] Only the example of leading powers submitting to international law can bring about a certain degree of legal security, which is essential to creating and maintaining world peace.

While there had been some hope a secure and just international legal order would emerge immediately after the end of the Cold War – the Charter of Paris, for example, proclaimed just such hope – the years that followed were disappointing. This was reflected in John Paul II's assessment of the NATO-led intervention, without a UN mandate, in Kosovo: "Never before had the actors of the international community had a comprehensive work of such precise and complete norms and conventions at their disposal as today. What is lacking is the will to respect and apply them."[105] Thus, international law, the Pope recognized, has no chance of really being recognized if the relevant actors on the interna-

---

101 Cf. Pope John Paul II, *Einheit der menschlichen Familie festigen und vervollständigen*, supra n. 44.

102 Pope John Paul II, Speech, *Address at the New Year's Reception of the Diplomatic Corps* (Vatican City, Jan. 11, 1999) (available at http://www.vatican.va/holy_father/john_paul_ii/speeches/1999/documents/hfjp-ii_spe_l 1011999_diplomatic-corps_en.html) (hereinafter *Address to the Diplomatic Corps*).

103 Cf. Pope John Paul II, *Address of the Holy Father*, supra n. 25.

104 See Pope John Paul II, *Einheit der menschlichen Familie festigen und vervollständigen*, supra n. 44, at 30.

105 See Pope John Paul II, *Address to the Diplomatic Corps*, supra n. 102.

tional stage do not consider it indispensable – or, at the very least, in their own interests – to abide by law.

Here, in John Paul II's view, seemed to be the central problem of the international order: "the political will to apply the existing (legal texts or legal instruments) indiscriminately"[106] was still largely absent. Because the law as such is not abided by, and there is no global-public authority with the necessary law enforcement authority, "it is up to the international community to take effective action in accordance with the [UN] Charter."[107] Even so, as the Pope recognized, since the states that are members of the UN "have so far not been [able] to work out effective [political] instruments instead of war to resolve international conflicts,"[108] conflicts were still resolved by violent means.

3.2 The United Nations as a Sub-Goal toward a Global Public Authority

Pius XII and John XXIII had already argued globalisation imposed on the international community the responsibility to submit to an order. Relying on these ideas, John Paul II built upon the idea of the "interdependence of humanity" to argue that the "welfare [of] humanity" requires an "attitude of worldwide solidarity."[109] Just like John XXIII before him, John Paul II considered international welfare as analogous to public welfare. If the "welfare that serves the authority of the state can only be fully realized if all citizens are secure [in] their rights,"[110] the Pope observed, this was also analogically true on the global level. Thus, human rights form the basis for the intrastate legal order as well as for the international legal order. The Pope recognized that this had not always been the case; instead, he thought, international law had gone through a transformative process from "a kind of extension of unlimited sovereignty" to "a code of conduct for the human family[,] … by putting … universally

106 See Pope John Paul II, *Address of the Holy Father,* supra n. 25.
107 Pope John Paul II, "Den Rüstungswettlauf beendigen." *L'Osservatore Romano* 36 (Sept. 2, 1988): 18 (Supp. XXXI).
108 Pope John Paul II, *Centesimus Annus,* supra n. 48, at No. 21.
109 Pope John Paul II, "Greeting of the Pope to the President of the United States, George Bush." *L'Osservatore Romano* 19 (July 28, 1989): 30–31 (Supp. XXVII).
110 Pope John Paul II, *Centesimus Annus,* supra n. 48, at No. 47.

valid principles before the internal law of the states."[111] It appears, then, that John Paul II – like the theological ethic developed since the Spanish Scholastic[112] – did not recognize a terminological difference between intra-state and international law. Thus, John Paul II thought that "[t]he func-tion of law is to give each person his due, to give him what is owed to him in justice. Law therefore has a strong moral implication. And *international law itself is founded on values.*"[113] These values are codified as the charter of human rights. Therefore, in order for a just international order to emerge, human rights must be observed as the basis of international law.

The Pope thought that human rights were, as pre-state law, part of international law and, thus, a limit on state sovereignty.[114] Despite the ad-vancement achieved by international law in the twentieth century, the Pope believed the international community, at least as it seemed to regard the validity of international law, to be closer to the "law of the jungle"[115] than to a system of law and order: "[j]ust as the time has finally come when in individual States a system of private vendetta and reprisal has given way to the rule of law, so too a similar step forward is now urgently needed in the international community."[116] The Pope's main concern was not that international legal norms were lacking, but rather that states must learn to rely "on common legal structures of [a] supranational character on [a] continental or even [a] worldwide level" when interacting with one an-

---

111 Pope John Paul II, "Der Friede ist noch möglich." *L'Osservatore Romano* 4 (Jan. 18, 1991): 21 (Supp. III).

112 The Spanish Scholastic, being connected with names like Francisco de Vitoria (1483–1546) and Francisco Suarez (1548–1617), introduced Thomas Aquinas' *Summa Theologia* as a fundamental textbook of theological studies and thus re-formed Catholic theology in 16ᵗʰ century Spain, the site of the Council of Trent (1546). Cf. Kirstin Bunge, Anselm Spindler and Andreas Wagner, eds., *Die Normativität des Rechts bei Francisco de Vitoria*, Politische Philosophie und Rechtstheorie des Mittelalters und der Neuzeit vol. II, 2 (Fromann-Holzboog, 2011).

113 Pope John Paul II, Speech, *Address of His Holiness Pope John Paul II in Response to the New Year Greetings of the Diplomatic Corps Accredited to the Holy See,* No. 4 (Vatican, Jan. 13, 1997) (available at http://www.vatican.va/holy_father/john_paul_ii/speeches/1997/documents/hfjp-ii_spe_13011997_diplomatic-corps_en.html).

114 Paul Kirchhoff, "Aus der Gerechtigkeit für den Einzelnen erwächst der Friede für alle." In *Die Weltfriedensbotschaften Papst Johannes Pauls II,* ed. Donato Squicciar-ini (2001) 175–93, 176.

115 Pope John Paul II, *Centesimus Annus,* supra n. 48, at No. 52.

116 Id.

other.[117] As the Pope saw it, world security through law, which was sustainable only if states had the necessary confidence in the law, would only be achieved when there are "universally valid rules for [states] living together [that are] … respected under all circumstances."[118]

The reasons for the Pope's harsh critique of the Bush administration, when it was obvious that Bush may enter a war against Saddam Hussein in utter disregard of international law and the UN, can be found in the already indicated importance that John Paul II attributed to international law.[119] Ultimately, the institutional union of the international community was a result of the catastrophe of World War II, as well as from the demands of globalisation.[120] "The Holy See," so the Pope said before the UN General Assembly, "has supported the ideals and goals of the UN Organization from the very beginning."[121] With these ideas, and in the context of the United States' imminent threat against the regime of Saddam Hussein at the beginning of 2003, Pope John Paul II used the fortieth anniversary of John XXIII's encyclical *Pacem in terris* to convey his response to the United States government's decision: forty years ago John XXIII had put forth the demand "for *a public authority, on the international* level, with effective capacity to advance the universal common good."[122] The United States' decision to bypass the UN, in the Pope's view, violated this basic requirement of international peace, security, and justice.

While this visionary political demand goes far beyond what can realistically be achieved with the UN today, John Paul II was in agreement with the Fathers of the Second Vatican Council who "championed a world authority that is based on the consent of the people and [that] is equipped with effective means to warrant the respect of justice and truth."[123] Hence, the concrete institutional architecture of the "world au-

---

117 Pope John Paul II, "Europa hat die Pflicht, Greueltaten anzuprangern." *L'Osservatore Romano* 1–2 (Jan. 10, 1992): 22.

118 Pope John Paul II, *Der Friede ist noch möglich,* supra n. 111.

119 Cf. Pope John Paul II, *Address of His Holiness Pope John Paul II to the Diplomatic Corps,* supra n. 95.

120 Cf. Pope John Paul II, *Address to the UN General Assembly,* supra n. 22.

121 Pope John Paul II, Speech, *Address of His Holiness Pope John Paul II to the Fiftieth General Assembly of the United Nations Organization,* No. 1 (N.Y., Oct. 5, 1995) (available at http://www.vatican.va/holy_father/john_paul_ii/speeches/1995/october/documents/hf Jp-ii_spe_05101995_address-to-uno_en.html).

122 Pope John Paul II, *Pacem in terris: A Permanent Commitment,* supra n. 45, at No. 5 (emphasis in original).

123 Pope John Paul II, "Seid Kirche in eurer Welt." *L'Osservatore Romano* 18 (May 5, 1989): 19 (Supp. XV).

thority" is not further developed in John Paul II's teaching, besides his support for the existing UN. The Pope realized that the UN as an institution was still not capable of doing what she was supposed to do for achieving her declared goals – and for fulfilling the role John Paul II assigned to her. And, indeed, shortly before his death, John Paul II had renewed his demand for UN reform with the goal of achieving "a greater degree of international ordering."[124]

John Paul II regretted that this "vision of an effective international public authority at the service of human rights, freedom and peace has not been entirely realized."[125] At the same time, he made clear that the main concern should not be about creating a "global super-state."[126] While we do not find any further-developed ideas within papal messages, one could presume that the principle of subsidiary, which is well established in Catholic political ethics, would require that only those tasks to be handed over to the global authority would be the tasks states were not able to deal with. A global federal system could be the answer from this perspective. And, it appears that John Paul II regarded the already-started processes of developing the UN into a public authority as the adequate means to comply with this goal.

John Paul II was clear on the mechanism that should establish the global public authority, even though he was less clear on the shape the authority would eventually take. "It means continuing and deepening processes already even in place to meet the almost universal demand for participatory ways of exercising political authority, international authority, and for transparency and accountability at every level of public life."[127] The global public authority "could not... be established by coercion but only by the consent of nations."[128] John Paul II did not, however, elaborate on how the question of global power division should be addressed in practice. This is not the responsibility of the church as she

---

124 Pope John Paul II, *An Ever Timely Commitment: Teaching Peace,* No. 7 (Jan. 1, 2004) (available at http://www.vatican.va/holy_father/john_paul_ii/messages/peace/ documents/hfJp-ii_mes_20031216_xxxvii-world-day-for-peace_en.html).
125 Pope John Paul II, *Pacem in terris: A Permanent Commitment,* supra n. 45, at No. 5.
126 Id. at No. 6.
127 Id.
128 Id. at No. 5.

"does not propose economic and political systems or programs,"[129] but demands from them respect for human dignity.

Notwithstanding his wish for progress toward this goal, John Paul II was realistic enough to observe that the international community has not only not developed in the direction that she should have as a consequence of the peace teachings of the twentieth-century popes, but that she is also not yet on the path toward global peace at the beginning of the third millennium. John Paul II recognized that the UN, which had been viewed by the twentieth-century popes as the nucleus of a global public authority, tended to struggle against political insignificance or was simply circumvented. "Is this not the time for all to work together for a new constitutional organization of the human family, truly capable of ensuring peace and harmony between peoples, as well as their integral development?"[130] John Paul II asked, barely hiding the critical undertone.

Just like his predecessors, John Paul II announced the sketched ethical ideal of the UN as a global public authority. All the same, he was realistic enough to recognize that the UN was not going to become the global public authority anytime soon; even so, he continually demanded that the status quo move toward that goal. This meant for John Paul II that the UN's existing institutions were respected and strengthened if possible. He expected that existing international law, as well as corresponding international institutions, were to be respected by states as the relevant actors, especially since there was not yet an effective international authority that could enforce states' adherence to the law if necessary.

3.3 Right and Responsibility of Defense

Unfortunately, war remains ever present in the international community, not only as a means to settle disputes among states, but also in the form of military interventions, or even the war against international terrorism. Given his decisive stance advocating for the recognition of the dignity of every human being and ensuring inviolable respect for God-created life, John Paul II voted for overcoming violence by supporting nonviolent action. Governments go to war much too often and far too quickly, accord-

---

129 Pope John Paul II, *Sollicitudo Rei Socialis,* No. 41 (Dec. 30, 1987) (available at http://www.vatican.va/edocs/ENG0223/_P7.HTM).

130 Pope John Paul II, *Pacem in terris: A Permanent Commitment,* supra n. 45, at No. 6.

ing to the Pope's assessment, without really having been forced to use violence as a last resort; he clearly denounced this practice and thus brought
himself under the suspicion as a potential pacifist.

At the same time, John Paul II argued in line with Catholic tradition
and faced the problem of conflicting norms. In the encyclical *Evangelium
Vitae,* John Paul II briefly discusses the problem of *minus malum:*

> "There are in fact situations in which values proposed by God's Law seem to
> involve a genuine paradox. This happens for example in the case of legiti-
> mate defence, in which the right to protect one's own life and the duty
> not to harm someone else's life are difficult to reconcile in practice. Certain-
> ly, the intrinsic value of life and the duty to love oneself no less than others
> are the basis of a true right to self-defence ... no one can renounce the right
> to self-defence out of lack of love for life or for self. This can only be done in
> virtue of a heroic love which deepens and transfigures the love of self into a
> radical self-offering, according to the spirit of the Gospel Beatitudes (cf. Mt
> 5:38–40) ... Moreover, "legitimate defence can be not only a right but a
> grave duty for someone responsible for another's life, the common good of
> the family or of the State" (Catechism of the Catholic Church No. 2265).
> Unfortunately it happens that the need to render the aggressor incapable
> of causing harm sometimes involves taking his life. In this case, the fatal out-
> come is attributable to the aggressor whose action brought it about, even
> though he may not be morally responsible because of a lack of the use of rea-
> son."[131]

This conflict of norms is reflected in John Paul II's views on several world
events. For example, despite his strong emphasis on peaceful resolution of
conflict, John Paul II regarded western states' long – maybe too long –
process of trying to come to an answer to the question of whether they
should intervene militarily in the Bosnia and Herzegovina war as a case
in point of these conflicting norms. "The European States and the UN
have the duty and the right to intervene to disarm somebody who
wants to kill. This does not mean to fuel the war but to stop it."[132]

While John Paul II viewed the situation in the former Yugoslavia as a
"fratricidal war" – one that required the use of military force, as a last resort, in order to end "unbearable sufferings for countless innocents"[133] – he

---

131 Pope John Paul II, *Evangelium Vitae,* No. 55 (Mar. 25, 1995) (available at http://
      www.vatican.va/edocs/ENG0141/_P.P.HTM).

132 Angelo Sodano, "Den zu entwaffnen, der töten will, ist rechtens. Kardinalstaatssek-
      retär Sodano sprach mit dem Papst über Bosnien-Herzegowina." *L'Osservatore Ro-
      mano* 34 (Aug. 14, 1992): 32.

133 Pope John Paul II, "Wo Sind wir vom Evangelium abgewichen? Eine Gewissenser-
      forschung für die Welt an der Schwelle zum Jahr 2000." *L'Osservatore Romano* 45
      (Nov. 12, 1993): 23.

characterized the Gulf War, which aimed for the expulsion of Iraq from Kuwait in 1991, completely differently: "In its second phase, this was, in my opinion, not so much a defensive war, but rather likened to a war for punishment. Further, the general atmosphere in that region is very tense. The intention was to turn this war into a religious war."[134]

The Pope thus draws a very fine distinction between defending against aggression and a situation in which the principle of legitimate defense is invoked by the supposed defender, but the "defender" has another objective for acting. Even if he assumed that there was, in principle, a right of defense – possibly a duty to defend – John Paul II, who witnessed World War II in his home country of Poland with his own eyes, was well aware of the consequences: the Pope was quoted in a semiofficial article as saying "[a] defensive war is bad, but if somebody attacks and tramples on the right to life, the right to be, there is a right to defense." But, "[w]e feel in a special way connected to all those who suffer, regardless on which side they may stand."[135] It is the immeasurable suffering of the civilian population in every war that makes it obviously so difficult for John Paul II to advocate for the just war theory. Moreover, he was well aware that every use of force is itself a seed of new violence. And, thus, he thought that "war will never be a real solution for the problems of peoples! The more respectable way for mankind is negotiations."[136]

With the establishment of the UN, member states made an international agreement that the use of force in international relations was forbidden. As the Pope understood the Charter's prohibition on the use of force, "[it] makes provision only for two exceptions."[137] These two exceptions are "the natural right to legitimate self-defence"[138] and the use of force in the framework of the collective security system, in which the UN Security Council is allotted the decision making power, in accordance with Chapter VII, to keep world peace. It is significant that John Paul II explicitly conditioned states' right to self-defence on that it is "to be exercised in specific ways and in the context of the UN."[139] In this statement, John Paul II alluded to Article 51 of the UN Charter in which the right to self-defense is subordinated to the Security Council's primary responsibility to keep world

---

134 Id.
135 *Recht auf Verteidigung,* 31 L'Osservatore Romano 25 (July 28, 1995).
136 Id.
137 Pope John Paul II, *An Ever Timely Commitment: Teaching Peace,* supra n. 124, at No. 6.
138 Id.
139 Id.

peace and is consequently only valid "until the Security Council has taken appropriate measures to keep world peace and international security."[140]

For the Pope, then, the UN was the competent authority, in the just war tradition, that held the responsibility for keeping world peace. As mentioned above, the UN is, however, only a first step toward a global-public authority. John Paul II was, like his predecessors, well aware that the decisions of the Security Council tended to serve more the confined interests of its members – especially its permanent members – than the peace and security of the international community. Nevertheless, the UN was a step in the right direction towards strengthening and building the institutions in which all nations' interests can be balanced against each other in order to strive for universal welfare. As a result, the UN is, according to John Paul II, "the right forum for the international community to take on the responsibility toward its various members that are not in the position to resolve their own problems by themselves."[141]

3.4 The United Nations as a Competent Authority

The "authority of law" and the "moral power of the highest international" authorities form the basis on which the right to intervene is founded – the purpose of saving "the ethnic groups that have become the victims of the deadly madness of the war-drivers."[142] Thus, international law's competence consists of "making the international community take effective action in harmony with the Charter … so that such measures are taken that are appropriate to ward off potential aggressors."[143] Accordingly, the Pope demanded, after the United States had snubbed the UN in its attack on Iraq in 2003, that "[i]t [was] more urgent than ever to return to effective collective security that confers on the organizations of the UN the place and the role that it deserves."[144] Simply put, resolving international

---

140 Albrecht Randelzhofer, ed., *Artikel 51 der Charta der Vereinten Nationen,* 7 Völkerrechtliche Verträge 14 (Nördlingen: 1995) .

141 Pope John Paul II, "Den Mut zum Frieden haben." *L'Osservatore Romano* 11 (Mar. 19, 1993): 23.

142 Id.

143 Pope John Paul II, *Den Rüstungswettlauf beendigen,* supra n. 107; cf. also Heinz-Joachim Fischer, "Die differenzierte Position des Vatikans." *Frankfurter Allgemeine Zeitung* (Feb. 28, 2003).

144 Pope John Paul II, "Die Kirche schlägt eine Pädagogik des Friedens vor." *L'Osservatore Romano* 3 (Jan. 16, 2004): 34.

conflicts, especially if the solution's ultima ratio involves a military intervention, must take place within the UN.

It is evident that John Paul II's teaching on the use of military force
was developed within the framework of traditional just war teaching. It
should be noted that the Pope was explicit on the question of authority:
it is for the UN to decide on the use of force, not a national government.
With this position, the Pope did not articulate a new position, but stuck
to the position of the Second Vatican Council.[145]

3.5 The Use of Military Force as the Last Resort

Faced with his decisive stance on the defense of life, it was out of the
question for John Paul II that the use of military force could ever be considered as anything other than the ultima ratio.[146] At the same time, the
Pope had seen that during the war in former Yugoslavia, the European
states and the UN took too long before taking effective action and, as
a consequence, innocent civilians suffered needlessly. The Pope noted
publicly that the "the worst [thing] to happen to today's Europe would
be to accept war, which cruelly torments millions of men and women,
in particular in the Balkan states and in the Caucasus."[147]

Because he approached the conflict from the perspective of human
rights, it became a question of justice and solidarity to come to the rescue
of those suffering. "It is possible," John Paul II remarked concerning the
suffering of the civil population in the Balkans, "to put an end to this if
one takes up measures that enforce the rules of law"[148]; elsewhere, he
called this the "principle of non-indifference."[149] These statements
might still be interpreted to support the claim that John Paul II relied
solely on nonmilitary means – even in 1993 at the height of the Balkan

---

145 Cf. Pope Paul VI, *Pastoral Constitution on the Church in the Modern World: Gaudium
et Spes,* No. 79 (Dec. 7, 1965) (available at http://www.vatican.va/archive/hist_coun-
cils/ii_vatican_council/documents/vat-ii_cons_19651207_gaudium-et-spe-
s_en.html).

146 Cf. *Recht auf Verteidigung,* supra n. 135.

147 Pope John Paul II, "Gemeinschaft der Nationen – Ziel politischer Zusammenarbeit
in Europa." *L'Osservatore Romano* 50 (Dec. 17, 1993): 23 (Supp. XL VI).

148 Id.

149 Pope John Paul II, "Streitkräfte im Dienst der Verteidigung von Freiheit und Sicherheit." *L'Osservatore Romano* 15 (Apr. 15, 1994): 24.

wars – like negotiations and sanctions.[150] A bit later, however, he made clear that

> "the dialogue and the negotiations can under no circumstances release one from the duty to disarm the aggressors that have taken entire ethnic groups hostage. One has to support the international organizations to collect and distribute the humanitarian aid supplies; if necessary, one has to use force in the process so that the aid supplies can access the needy population as it is a case of justified "humanitarian intervention.""[151]

After September 11, 2001, the question that demanded an answer was whether the al-Qaeda attacks against the USA legitimized, as an act of pre-emptive defense, an attack on Afghanistan, since the Taliban regime had offered its country as a base for the terror organization. In answering this question, John Paul II pointed out that there is "a right to defense against terrorism," because "these terror organizations have used their own followers as weapons to send them out against unarmed, unsuspecting people." Thus, terrorism is based "on the neglect scorn of human life" and commits "unbearable crimes against humanity."[152] Defense against terrorism, the Pope said, is "a right that must abide like any other right by moral and ethical rules in the choice of both the aims and the means."[153] Here, the Pope was arguing that regardless of the reprehensibility of terrorism, combating terrorism cannot unhinge existing international law, as the case of preemptive self-defense at least threatens to do.[154] Simply put, any use of military force that goes beyond immediate self-defense can, according to the Pope, only be used to enforce elementary legal norms, like efforts to stop the most severe human rights violations. The decision of whether this use of force is warranted belongs to the institution that is above particularistic interests, the UN.

In his last peace message, the Pope admitted freely that there were no persuasive legal answers to the new questions raised by the "plague of terrorism," because international law has so far been based on interstate conflicts. The Pope recognized that "[a] legal order of norms that has been

---

150 Cf. Gino Concetti, *Il diritto di intervento umanitario* 197 (Vigodarzere 1994).
151 Ernesto Gallina, "Botschafter der Vergangenheit – Gestalter der Zukunft." *L'Osservatore Romano* 46 (Nov. 17, 1995): 25 (Supp. XLIV) cf. "Hilfe auch mit Gewalt durchsetzen." *L'Osservatore Romano* 6 (Feb. 12, 1993).
152 Pope John Paul II, "Kein Friede ohne Gerechtigkeit – keine Gerechtigkeit ohne Vergebung." *L'Osservatore Romano* 31 (Dec. 21, 2001): 51–52.
153 Id.
154 Cf. "Friedensappelle von Papst Johannes Paul II. angesichts der tragischen Ereignisse in den vergangenen Monaten." *L'Osservatore Romano* 31 (Dec. 21, 2001): 51–52.

worked out over the course of centuries to organize relations between sovereign states is hard pressed to face conflicts in which groups become active that cannot be captured by conventional definitions of statehood."[155]

That being said, the UN does not have plenary authority to wage war; it must be a last resort. The Pope thought that when the UN – though it would be more precise to say the Security Council of the UN – begins debating whether using force is an appropriate response against international human rights violators that there are still important limitations within which it must make its decision. "[W]ar is ... a means like [no] other that can be used to settle disputes between nations," the Pope recalled at the beginning of 2003, at the beginning of the Iraq war. "The Charter of the UN and international law reminds us that even if the security of common welfare is concerned, war is only to be chosen in the worst case and under very strict conditions."[156]

The Pope had thus grappled with the question of *ius ad bellum,* competent authority, just cause, and the ultima ratio and, though starting from a traditional just war posture, has developed some textual adaptations insofar as he put ultima ratio at the core of his admonitions regarding the use of force. That being said, concerning the ethical limits of using force, the Pope hardly deviated from what is already known.

When John Paul II spoke to these questions, his emphasis was on the suffering of the civilian population. He had experienced the effects of war as a young man in Poland. And, thus, cautioned that whoever decides to resort to military means must not forget "the effects [on] the civilian population during and after the fighting."[157] The discriminatory principle was, thus, at the core of his thoughts. And, with the entire weight of his papal authority, with "the authority given to Peter and his successors by Christ," and "in community with the bishops of the Catholic Church," John Paul II taught, in the encyclical *Evangelium Vitae,* the tradition that "the direct and voluntary killing of an innocent human being is always gravely immoral."[158] This prohibition concerns, of course, the "deliberate decision to deprive an innocent human being of his life ... as a means to a good end."[159]

155 Pope John Paul II, "Eine stets aktuelle Aufgabe: Zum Frieden zu erziehen." *L'Osservatore Romano* 33 (Dec. 19, 2003): 51–52.

156 Pope John Paul II, "Nein zum Tod! Nein zum Egoismus! Nein zum Krieg! Ja zum Leben! – Ja zum Frieden!" *L'Osservatore Romano* 4 (Jan. 24, 2003): 33.

157 Id.

158 Pope John Paul II *Evangelium Vitae,* supra n. 131, No. 57.

159 Pope John Paul II, *Evangelium Vitae,* supra n. 131.

Conclusion

Sadly, even if killing the civilian population is not intended in a war, the so-called "new wars" confront soldiers, politicians, and international leaders with problems unknown so far. Asymmetric warfare has replaced interstate war – the opponents of conventional armies are now irregular armies, which, because they are militarily inferior, evade open battle. This type of warfare could be the military campaigns of rebel armies against unpopular regimes, insurgencies of ethnic minorities against majority regimes, or the activities of criminal gangs, terrorist attacks, or, last but not least, regular armies fighting against these types of threats. In his last peace message, John Paul II admitted freely that there are no persuasive solutions to these problems so far: "A legal order of norms that has been worked out in the course of centuries to organize relations between sovereign states is hard pressed to face conflicts in which groups become active that cannot be captured by conventional definitions of statehood."[160]

---

160 Pope John Paul II, *Eine stets aktuelle Aufgabe: Zum Frieden zu erziehen,* supra n. 155.

List of Authors

Robert J. Araujo S.J. is John Courtney Murray, S.J. University Professor at Loyola University of Chicago, School of Law, IL, USA

William A. Barbieri, Jr. is Associate Professor of Theology and Religious Studies at the Catholic University of America, Washington, DC, USA

Gerhard Beestermöller is Deputy Director of the Institute for Theology and Peace, Hamburg, Germany and Adjunct Professor at the Fachhochschule Vechta, Germany

Johannes Brachtendorf is Professor at the department of Catholic Theology at Eberhard Karls University of Tübingen, Germany

Heinz-Gerhard Justenhoven, is Director of the Institute for Theology and Peace, Hamburg, Germany and Adjunct Professor at the Faculty of Theology at the University of Freiburg/Breisgau, Germany

Roland Kany is Professor at the department of Catholic Theology at Ludwig-Maximilians University of Munich, Germany

Andrea Keller, Dr., is Lecturer in Adult Education at the Catholic Academy "St. Jakobushaus" in Goslar, Germany

Markus Kremer, Dr., is Secondary School Teacher (College level) for Religious Education in Baden-Württemberg, Germany

Thomas J. M. Mertens is Professor of Philosophy of Law at the Faculty of Law, Radboud University Nijmegen

James Muldoon is Invited Research Scholar, The John Carter Brown Library and Professor of History (Emeritus) of Rutgers University –Camden/NJ, USA

James Bernard Murphy is Professor of Government at Dartmouth College, Hanover, NH, USA

Gerard F. Powers is Professor of the Practice of Catholic Peacebuilding Studies at the Joan Kroc Institute for International Peace Studies, University of Notre Dame/IN, USA

Philip J. Rossi S.J. is Professor of Theology, Marquette University Milwaukee/WI, USA

Volker Stümke is Lecturer for Social Ethics at the Führungsakademie der Bundeswehr, Hamburg, Germany and Adjunct Professor at the Kirchliche Hochschule Wuppertal/Bethel

Christoph Stumpf is lawyer and Adjunct Professor at the Department of Law and Economics, Martin-Luther University of Halle-Wittenberg, Germany

Index of Names